JOURNAL FOR THE STUDY OF THE OLD TESTAMENT SUPPLEMENT SERIES
176

JSOT Press
Sheffield

Studies in Biblical Law

From the Hebrew Bible to the Dead Sea Scrolls

Gershon Brin

Translated from the Hebrew
by Jonathan Chipman

Journal for the Study of the Old Testament
Supplement Series 176

Copyright © 1994 Sheffield Academic Press

Published by JSOT Press
JSOT Press is an imprint of
Sheffield Academic Press Ltd
343 Fulwood Road
Sheffield S10 3BP
England

Typeset by Sheffield Academic Press
and
Printed on acid-free paper in Great Britain
by Bookcraft
Midsomer Norton, Somerset

British Library Cataloguing in Publication Data

A catalogue record for this book is available
from the British Library

ISBN 1-85075-484-5

CONTENTS

PREFACE

Although the material for this book was composed over the course of many years, the impulse for its final completion took place during the course of my stay as a Visiting Fellow at Princeton University during 1990–91.

The book deals with various aspects of biblical law, and is divided into two parts: (1) general problems in biblical law; (2) the problem of the first-born in biblical law. Theological and social aspects of the birthright are dealt with in the first part of my new book in Hebrew, *Issues in the Bible and the Dead Sea Scrolls* (Tel Aviv: Ha-Kibbutz ha-Meuhad and Tel-Aviv University Press, 1994).

I wish to express my thanks to the Dean of the Faculty of Humanities of Tel-Aviv University, Professor Anita Shapira, for providing a grant from the Faculty of the Humanities which helped defray the costs involved in translating the manuscript from Hebrew to English. An additional part of the expenses was defrayed by the Yaniv Fund for the Study of Jewish History and Jewish Philosophy, which granted me an award for this work.

I wish to thank Rabbi Jonathan Chipman of Jerusalem for his excellent translation of the manuscript, and for calling my attention to various matters during the course of the work of translation.

Special thanks are due to Professor David J.A. Clines of Sheffield Academic Press, for accepting this book for publication in the JSOT Supplement Series. Dr J. Webb Mealy of Sheffield Academic Press deserves many thanks for his efforts in editing and preparing the manuscript for publication.

Gershon Brin
Tel-Aviv University
May 1994

PREVIOUSLY PUBLISHED MATERIAL

Certain chapters of this book or portions thereof have been previously published in various forums. The author wishes to thank the editors and publishers concerned for their gracious permission to republish the above chapters in the present book. In each case, the material has been re-edited and in some cases specially translated for the present volume.

Part of Chapter 1 was published as 'The Development of some Laws in the Book of the Covenant', in H. Graf Reventlow and Y. Hoffman (eds.), *Justice and Righteousness: Biblical Themes and their Influence* (FS B. Uffenheimer; JSOTSup, 137; Sheffield: JSOT Press, 1992), pp. 60-70.

Chapter 2 is due to appear in D.N. Freedman, D.P. Wright and A. Hurvitz (eds.), *Studies in Biblical, Jewish, and Near Eastern Ritual: Law, and Literature in Honor of Jacob Milgrom* (Winona Lake, IN: Eisenbrauns).

Chapter 4 has been published as 'שימושי "או" בטקסטים משפטיים במקרא', *Shenaton le-Ḥeqer ha-Miqra veha-Mizraḥ ha-Qadum* 5 (1983), pp. 19-26.

Chapter 5 §4 is due to appear as 'The Laws of the Prophets in the Sect of the Judaean Desert—Studies in 4Q375' in *JSP* 10 (1994).

Chapter 6 was published as 'דיני בכורות במקרא', *Tarbiz* 46 (1977), pp. 1-7.

Chapter 8 was published in *JQR* 68 (1977), pp. 1-15.

Parts of Chapter 10 were published as שתי סוגיות בדיני ירושה של התקופה המקראית in *Dinei Yisra'el* 6 (1975), pp. 231-49.

ABBREVIATIONS

For abbreviations relating to the Mesopotamian texts cited in Chapters 10 and 11, see the list of abbreviations in *CAD*.

AfO	*Archiv für Orientforschung*
AJSL	*American Journal of Semitic Languages and Literatures*
ANET	J.B. Pritchard (ed.), *Ancient Near Eastern Texts Relating to the Old Testament*
AO	*Der Alte Orient*
AOAT	*Alter Orient und Altes Testament*
ARM	Archives royales de Mari
ArOr	*Archiv Orientálni*
ATD	Das Alte Testament Deutsch
BASOR	*Bulletin of the American Schools of Oriental Research*
Bib	*Biblica*
BZAW	Beihefte zur *Zeitschrift fur die alttestamentliche Wissenschaft*
CAD	*The Chicago Assyrian Dictionary*
CAH	Cambridge Ancient History
CB	Cambridge Bible
CBQ	*Catholic Biblical Quarterly*
DJD	Discoveries in the Judaean Desert
DOB	H.H. Rowley (ed.), *Dictionary of the Bible*
EncBib	*Encyclopaedia Biblica* (Hebrew)
EncHeb	*Encyclopaedia Hebraica* (Hebrew)
ERE	*Encyclopaedia of Religion and Ethics*
GHAT	Handkommentar zum Alten Testament, Göttingen
GKC	*Gesenius' Hebrew Grammar*, ed. E. Kautzsch, trans. A.E. Cowley
HAT	Handbuch zum Alten Testament
HKAT	see GHAT
HSS	Harvard Semitic Series
HUCA	*Hebrew Union College Annual*
ICC	International Critical Commentary
IDB	*Interpreter's Dictionary of the Bible*
JBL	*Journal of Biblical Literature*
JCS	*Journal of Cuneiform Studies*

JJS	*Journal of Jewish Studies*
JNES	*Journal of Near Eastern Studies*
JPS	The Jewish Publication Society of America
JQR	*Jewish Quarterly Review*
JSP	*Journal for the Study of the Pseudepigrapha*
JSOT	*Journal for the Study of the Old Testament*
JSS	*Journal of Semitic Studies*
KAT	Kommentar zum Alten Testament
KHAT	Kurzer Hand-Commentar zum Alten Testament
NCB	The Cambridge Bible Commentary on the New English Bible
NCBC	The New Century Bible Commentary
OTL	Old Testament Library
OTS	*Oudtestamentische Studien*
PRU	Palais royal d'Ugarit
PW	Pauly–Wissowa, *Realenzyklopaedie der klassischen* *Altertumswissenschaft*
RA	*Revue d'assyrologie et d'archéologie orientale*
RB	*Revue biblique*
RHD	*Revue historique de droit Français et étranger*
RQ	*Revue de Qumran*
SBT	Studies in Biblical Theology
TBü	Theologische Bücherei
ThWNT	*Theologisches Wörterbuch zum Neuen Testament*
VT	*Vetus Testamentum*
WC	Westminster Commentaries
WO	*Die Welt des Orients*
ZA	*Zeitschrift für Assyriologie*
ZAW	*Zeitschrift für die alttestamentliche Wissenschaft*
ZDMG	*Zeitschrift der deutschen morgenländischen Gesellschaft*

INTRODUCTION: ISSUES IN BIBLICAL LAW

The present work consists of a series of studies of two different types. The first part includes studies of various legal issues as these are expressed in the totality of legal collections preserved in the Torah, while the second part is comprised of a group of studies concerning the laws of firstlings and the first-born, an issue with which I have been involved since the early 1970's.

The totality of these two groups of studies will provide the reader with some conception of my approach to biblical law, an approach based not upon a total or comprehensive view but rather one that is shaped cumulatively through the issues upon which I have seen fit to concentrate, following the spirit of the rabbinic dictum, 'A person does not learn Torah save in that place which his heart wishes' (*b. 'Abod. Zar.* 19a).

The opening chapter, on 'double' laws in the Bible, is concerned with a certain structural-textual phenomenon that reflects the process of development within biblical law. The same phenomenon may also be defined in terms of textual study: just as there are scriptural passages containing glosses and other later additions intended to alter or clarify the text, so are there passages of a legal nature that contain glosses of this nature. My concern here is to focus upon a particular example of this phenomenon—namely, that of a passage that is in effect a proposal for a new stage or option within an existing law or laws. In other words, these laws, at least *prima facie*, contain more than one option for executing their demands.

But this definition is an inadequate characterization, both of the double law as a type and of the consequences that result from these laws. For example, there are certain laws in which both alternative options presented are original—that is, both were already included in the original formulation of the law—while there are others, which are evidently the majority, in which the second stage was added after the formulation of the original law. In other cases, the original option was effectively abandoned following the formulation of the second, later stage. There are yet other laws in which the two stages carry different consequences, as we shall discuss presently, as well in the final section of Chapter 1.

The reason for the creation of double laws differed from one case to another. At times, the addition was introduced so as to mitigate the severity of the law, while in others cases it served the opposite tendency—namely, to strengthen the sanction inherent in the original law. In one group of double laws, the second option is no more than a sanction, added by the legislator to frighten potential transgressors who might fail to fulfil the original law. We thus find that the term 'double laws' is a kind of overall rubric covering a variety of different phenomena, unified only in terms of external and superficial appearances.

Chapter 2 presents the clause, used in a number of laws, which opens with the phrase, 'if he shall not (do)'. This clause is used in various biblical laws to denote the possibility of non-compliance with the basic law. At times this may relate to refusal to carry out the law, while at others the non-fulfilment of the law stems from some other reason. All those laws which utilize this wording are discussed in this chapter. The material is classified according to types of law: those laws that reflect an automatic obligation, and those laws in which the obligation is the result of a commitment the person has made. In both uses, one effectively receives the same picture, whether it applies to the entire community or whether it applies to those in a particular situation in which they are required to execute a certain obligation. In either event, the legislator describes, through the use of this formula, a situation in which the obligation imposed by the basic law is not fulfilled.

The inclusion, within the laws belonging to both groups, of the clause pertaining to refusal to fulfil the obligation bears a clear and immediate result: the explicit stipulation of the punishment applying to the one who refuses. One should note that, as a general rule, the biblical laws do not detail punishments in this sort of way.[1] We therefore find a certain correspondence between the 'if not' clause and the mention of sanctions.

In this chapter, I also present the question as to why this formula

---

1.   A distinction should be drawn between the fixed punishment stipulated in the law for certain transgressions, such as 'When men quarrel and one strikes the other...he that struck him shall be clear; only he shall pay for the loss of his time, and shall have him thoroughly healed' (Exod. 21.18-19), and that given in the laws discussed in this chapter.

(including the sanction) only appears in this particular type of law. Is there some common denominator of the group of laws in which these sanctions appear? Further on in the discussion, I shall note a number of common characteristics of these laws, which are taken from various different areas of life.

This chapter also includes another kind of 'if not' wording, included in these laws for a totally different reason: namely, economic barriers to the fulfilment of the law. I refer to those laws in which the clause 'if he does not' (or a variant thereof) refers to a state in which a person is unable to fulfil an obligation because of poverty. It is clear that in such a case the clause 'if not' is not used to introduce the punishment meted out to one who is unable to fulfil an obligation, whether the obligation is automatic (Type A) or one that the person has taken upon him- or herself (Type B).

The use of the phrase 'if he does not' in explicitly non-legal texts may be explained by the fact that legal phrases were widely known during the biblical period, and influenced the public.

Another central issue discussed in this chapter concerns the period during which the 'if not' clause was incorporated within the law. There are two possibilities: first, that the clause is original, namely, that it goes back to the date of composition of the law as a whole; second, that the clause emerged over the course of time in order to deal with those who refused to fulfil the law, or out of the desire to respond to the needs of those whose obligations or commitments outstripped their wherewithal. It seems to me that the greater number of those laws discussed in this chapter reflect the second option, namely, that the clause in question is later than the basic core of the law, the specific reason for its emergence varying from law to law, depending upon the circumstances mentioned here.

In Chapter 3, I discuss a number of passages dealing with the poor. I begin with an extensive discussion of those laws enabling the poor to behave in a less expensive, alternative manner, one that is more suited to their economic capabilities. In the second part of this chapter, I deal with the sprinkling of cases in which the poor are given additional, alternative options for fulfilling the obligation or commitment stated in the law. The difference between these two groups of laws is that, whereas in the former case a special clause controlling the alternative execution of the laws by the economically weaker sector of society was added over the course of time, in the latter case the original law proposed additional ways of fulfilling the law, alongside of (but not instead of) the primary means.

In the third section of this chapter, I discuss a number of passages located on the borderline of this type of law, in that they include statements and exhortations, which are not actually to be considered as laws per se. These include appeals to the public at large to grant the poor certain different legal rights, such as the returning at sundown of the poor person's pledge, because it serves as a covering at night.

In Chapter 4, I discuss the meaning of the word אֹו ('or') in biblical legal texts. In some cases, אֹו is used as an alternative introductory formula to a secondary clause of the law, alongside אִם ('if', in the sense of 'in the event that...'). It is likewise used to expand or clarify the applicability of the basic law. Tracing the various uses of אֹו helps us to reconstruct various aspects of the development of the laws including this phrase, similar to the material in Chapter 1 of the book.

Chapter 5 is concerned with legal material from Qumran. The first two parts of the chapter are concerned with laws from the *Temple Scroll*: the laws of Passover and the list of prohibited marriages. The other, more comprehensive sections deal with new documents from Cave 4 (4Q251 relating to prohibited sex issues, and 4Q375) relating to issues concerning prophets.

In all four sections of this chapter, the formulation of the law in the scrolls is compared with parallel biblical material. In this way, it is possible to trace the development of a particular law within the literature of the sect. Thus, in the list of prohibited marriages at the end of the *Temple Scroll*, we find a combination of different kinds of material: its beginning is based upon the text in the Book of Deuteronomy, which serves as the main text in this part of the *Temple Scroll*, while further on the author goes on to gather relevant material on the same subject from other parts of the Torah. In the particular list in question, the reconstruction is based upon the list of prohibited consanguinities in Lev. 18.6-20. The author also utilizes other sources characteristic of various circles during the Second Temple period, but absent in the Bible, such as those prohibiting marriage with one's sister's daughter.

The document discussed in the fourth section of this chapter—4Q375—may indicate the manner in which the Qumran authors utilized legal material in order to arrive at the desired image of the laws. Their method of reworking legal material seems similar, in the final analysis, to their method of reworking other kinds of biblical material. They attempt with all their might to write in a biblical language and style so as to lend their words authority and primary sanctity, as if this scroll were simply a copy of material found in the ancient texts of the Torah laws. But in practice they are constantly and carefully changing, and even creating new legal material (such as the right of the tribe to appeal the death sentence against a prophet who has led others astray), in contradiction to Deuteronomy 13, which the author of the document himself quotes.

The second part of this work revolves around the subject of firstlings and the first-born. I discuss this topic here in an overall and comprehensive manner, addressing myself to a series of issues. While this discussion does not in itself constitute a complete monograph on the subject, it nevertheless constitutes a broad and comprehensive overview of the subject as a whole and of its various components, particularly regarding the legal aspects of the first-born. Our involvement here with the laws of the first-born and firstling complements the studies incorporated in my new book, *Issues in the Bible and the Dead Sea Scrolls* [Hebrew], the first section of which, 'On the First-Born', contains seven chapters exploring various social and theological aspects of the subject of the first-born. This matter is discussed at greater length below, in the introduction to the second part of this work.

The subject of the first-born has legal, social and religious ramifications. In Chapters 6–9, I discuss the laws concerning the sanctity of the first-born as a type, illustrating the manner of their growth. The section opens with a chapter discussing the development of the laws of the first-born in principle. I identify the earliest core of these laws, the sentence containing the 'general law', which over the course of time was transformed into the introductory element of these laws as they appear in the present text. Further on in this section, there appear discussions of the development of the laws of the firstlings of clean animals (Chapter 7) and of unclean animals (Chapter 8).

In the chapter on the first-born of human beings (Chapter 9), I elucidate the concept of the sanctity of the first-born and the manner in which this sanctity is removed. In this context, I also discuss the question of the substitution of the Levites for the first-born Israelites.

In Chapters 10–11, I elaborate upon the civil aspect of the first-born: namely, the first-born's preferential rights of inheritance. Chapter 10 concludes with a discussion of various problems involving departures from the system of inheritance by the first-born, resulting from the application of the father's authority. I clarify here the extent to which the father was free to behave as he wished regarding these questions. Finally (Chapter 11), I examine the question of the special status enjoyed by the first-born of the king and his portion in the inheritance of his father's monarchy.

The method I have chosen to follow in the first part of this work has caused me to mention certain laws more than once in the course of the discussion. Thus, for example, if a certain rule included the formula 'if he does not (do)', it is discussed extensively in the second chapter; equally, if it also belonged to the category of double laws, it may also have been mentioned in the first chapter. In any event, a full discussion of any given law appears only once, in the relevant chapter. Another example: the law of the firstling ass is discussed at length in the second part of the work, in the chapter on firstlings of unclean animals, but it is also alluded to in the chapter on double laws, while a less comprehensive reference also appears in the chapter on the formula, 'if he does not'.

The issues discussed in the present work can teach us about the manner of formulation of biblical law, the comparative development of the laws in the various collections in the Torah, and the development of the law as such, whether through the discussion of the question of double laws or by tracing the use of the term אז, which appears in many laws.

The question of the mention made of punishment in some of these laws is discussed in particular in relation to the formula, 'if he does not (do)'. The appearance of biblical laws in the Dead Sea Scrolls literature is treated in a separate unit. The latter discussion revolves around three groups of laws: laws of passover, laws of incest and laws of prophecy. Study of these subjects can shed light both upon the biblical laws as such and on the manner of their reworking by the Judaean Desert sect. I also discuss here questions relating to the style, ideas, and historical and ideological background underlying the reworking of these laws in Qumran.

The second part of the book presents quite a comprehensive picture of the issues involved in the laws of the first-born, presenting the development of the laws and questions pertaining to the relationship between the first-born of human beings and the firstlings of animals. A special place is occupied by discussion of the sanctity of the first-born and his inheritance rights.

Part I

SELECTED PROBLEMS IN BIBLICAL LAW

Chapter 1

'DOUBLE' LAWS IN THE BIBLE:
THE DEVELOPMENT OF SOME BIBLICAL LAWS

An entire group of biblical laws reflects more than one stage of execution. By this, I refer specifically to those cases in which there are two different means of executing the law pertaining to the same situation; otherwise, one would be speaking of two distinct laws or two principal parts of the same law. An example of the latter is the case of the law concerning a pregnant woman who was pushed by a group of people fighting with one another, there are two principal clauses: '...so that there is a miscarriage, and yet no harm follows' (Exod. 21.22); whereas the second clause begins: 'if any harm follows...' (v. 23). This is not to be seen as a double law, since we have here two different degrees of damage caused to the pregnant woman, and the varying punishments meted out are a consequence of the nature of the incident and do not, for example, reflect a change in the form or degree of punishment for the same trangression itself.

I shall enumerate below those biblical laws in which one may find the phenomenon of 'double laws'.[1] Because of the relatively infrequency of the phenomenon, one must examine all those cases in which there is a double law, and thereby derive conclusions regarding both the history of its development until it reached its final version, and the meaning of the law in its earliest stage and in the later stage reflected in the text.[2] The term 'double' laws is problematic; further on, I shall attempt to elucidate it in greater detail. We shall also examine, in the final section of this chapter, the various practical consequences of these laws. At this point, I shall merely observe the fact that there are indeed double laws which, under suitable conditions, present two alternatives for the required

1. I use below the phrases '"double" laws' or 'double laws' (without quotation marks) with the identical intention.
2. But see below, n. 44.

execution of the laws. On the other hand, there are some cases in which the later stage does not provide a further alternative option, but presents the law anew, so that the previous stage is in effect negated and remains a 'dead letter'. There are yet other cases in which the relationship of the two stages is different from that described here (but see below in this chapter).

Classification of the double laws reveals that they include different types. I have arranged these laws according to the relationship between the stages of the law. Our discussion shall accordingly be structured around the following types of laws: 1. alternative methods of execution: (a) original doubling in the law; (b) doubling as reflecting a development in the law; 2. alternative laws directed towards the poor; 3. laws doubled thanks to the addition of sanctions as a threat for non-compliance with the basic law; 4. doubling in the laws of sacred things—Leviticus 27.

I shall begin with the first group of laws having a double nature, in which the relationship between the two parts of the law is between two alternative means of execution. We shall need to examine the history of this alternative relationship in each particular case. The discussion is divided into two parts: we shall begin with those laws in which the doubling is part of the original law, while in the second group those laws will be treated in which the doubling is a result of later development.

1. *Alternative Methods of Execution Traceable to an Original Duplication within the Law*

i. *The Law of the Slave: Leviticus 25.47-54*
In the law of the slave in Lev. 25.47-54, Scripture speaks about the form of his servitude and the means of his liberation. The passage explicitly mentions several different means of redemption: 'Then after he is sold he may be redeemed; one of his brothers may redeem him...or if he grows rich he may redeem himself' (vv. 48-49). The formulation of this law may be seen as imposing an obligation upon the members of the family to redeem their relative, or upon the slave to redeem himself, since the verse explicitly states that 'after he is sold he may be redeemed' (v. 48). If, however, an attempt to redeem him is unfeasible (for economic reasons), the slave still has the opportunity for automatic liberation in the jubilee year: 'And if he is not redeemed by these means, then he shall be released in the year of jubilee, he and his children with him' (v. 54).

Examination of the formulation of this law reveals that the legislator wished to make it clear that slaves' lack of sucess does not prejudice their right to be freed in the general redemption of the jubilee year.

It seems to me that the present law is not an example of later development—that is, the alternative stage was not added to the law later because of one or another development. This is shown by the fact that the possibility of redemption in the jubilee year is formulated here *ab initio*, whereas the possibilities of earlier redemption of the slave by relatives or himself are treated as preferable by the legislator. It is only their non-performance that restores the initial possibility of automatic liberation in the jubilee.

ii. *Redemption of the Inheritance of the Poor: Leviticus 25.25-28*
Lev. 25.25-28 contains the law of the person who has sold a homestead because of economic reverses. This law likewise mentions the obligation of the relatives to come to the assistance of their poor relative,[3] as well as raising the possibility of redemption on the part of indigent persons, should they become capable of doing so from an economic viewpoint. Verse 28 states, 'But if he has not sufficient means to get it back for himself, then what he sold shall remain in the hand of him who bought it until the year of jubilee; in the jubilee it shall be released, and he shall return to his property'.

The phrase 'if he has not sufficient means' or its like appears in various laws portraying the inability of the poor to function in the same manner as the rest of the population.[4] As in the previous law, various possibilities for the redemption of an inheritance, including the right of automatic liberation during the jubilee, are part of the basic law, rather than the result of any gradual emergence of the law.

iii. *The Law of One who Sells a House in a Walled City: Leviticus 25.29-30*
The law of an individual who sells a residential house in a walled city

---

3. Some have noted that the circle of close relatives called upon to help the poor person who has fallen into slavery is wider than that of the present law concerning one who lost an inheritance, because in the case of saving a person from slavery one is required to make a greater effort—that is, to enlist a wider circle of relatives to come to the help of their relative who has fallen into slavery. Compare J.R. Porter, *Leviticus*, p. 206.

4. I discuss these formulae in Chapter 3, 'Caring for the Poor in Biblical Law'.

states that the redemption of the house must be 'within a whole year after its sale' (Lev. 25.29). The legislator did not rely upon the inferences that might be drawn from the law, but concluded with the explicit statement that 'If it is not redeemed within a full year, then the house that is in the walled city shall be made sure in perpetuity to him who bought it, throughout his generations; it shall not be released in the jubilee' (v. 30). It follows that the legislator gave the seller the option to retract the sale by means of redemption, because the rule of general release of property in the jubilee year does not apply to properties of the type mentioned. Thus, the phrase 'if it is not redeemed...' continues the basic thrust of the law, indicating the effective significance of the one-year limitation imposed by Scripture. We therefore infer that we have here a law that was originally double, and that by the second option, 'and if it is not redeemed', the legislator explains what will happen to the sale of the house in such a case. It states here explicitly what one might have guessed from this formula, namely, that such property does not return to its original owners in the jubilee year. However, a substitute is provided for the automatic redemption in the jubilee by the possibility of redemption during the first year following the sale.

iv. *The Law of the Slave: Exodus 21.2-6*
The law in Exod. 21.2-6 deals with the case of a slave, from the manner of indenture through the process of liberation, specifying in secondary clauses the conditions of one's life during the period of servitude. The law stipulates that the slave must serve for six years and go free in the seventh. Further along in the discussion, after dealing with the family situation and its relation to the manner of liberation, it returns to the subject of the slave's liberation: 'But if the slave plainly says, "I love my master"...his master shall bore his ear through... and he shall serve him for life' (v. 6). It would therefore seem that the law initially presents two forms relating to the subject of liberation: liberation in the seventh year, or renunciation of the right of liberation by dint of family ties.

On the other hand, the structure of the presentation here arouses the suspicion that this may reflect a secondary, later stage in the law, one allowing the keeping of the slave beyond the period of six years stipulated in the law. The revolution wrought by the legislator by restricting the length of time a slave could be held to six years led to a request on the part of the masters, but perhaps no less so by the slaves themselves, to permit the continuation of servitude beyond that limit. The legislator's

new answer was therefore given in a later clause, in vv. 5-6, at the end
of the law.[5] After the law touched upon three other issues relating to
family situation, it again returned to the subject of liberation and
introduced a new option—namely, the possibility that slavery might
continue beyond the basic stipulation of the law[6] (v. 2).[7]

2. *Doubling as an Expression of Development in the Law*

i. *The Law of Kidnapping: Exodus 21.16*

Exod. 21.16 reads: 'Whoever steals a man, whether he sells him or
[literally: "and"] is found in possession of him, shall be put to death'.
This law is worded in the *participle* form (an intermediate form between
the casuistic and apodictic forms).[8] It is worth noting that several other
laws in the same chapter are worded in similar manner: 'Whoever
strikes a man so that he dies' (21.12); 'Whoever strikes his father or his
mother' (21.15); 'Whoever curses his father or his mother' (21.17).

The law states that it is forbidden to kidnap and sell a person, and that
one who does so will be put to death. However, the phrase ונמצא בידו
('and is found in possession of him') creates a difficulty in this simple
explanation, namely, how are we to understand the situation according
to the wording of the law? The victim cannot be simultaneously sold by
the kidnapper and found in his possession. On the other hand, it could
be that the form ונמצא בידו only refers to procedures of proof, as in

---

5.   As stated by Daube with regard to the placing of the additions in these laws;
see D. Daube, *Studies in Biblical Law*, pp. 85-86, 88, 97.

6.   A. Phillips, 'Laws of Slavery', p. 51, in fact sees vv. 5-6 as a change and
correction of the law of liberation given in vv. 2-4, so that it is an expression of the
fixed holding of the slaves. See p. 62, on the fact that the law of freeing the slave was
not carried out in actuality, and that this was the background to the prophets' rebuke
concerning this subject.

7.   Another question to be considered is whether the law of the altar (Exod.
20.24-26) may not also be considered a double law, as defined here. This assertion is
based upon the statement in this law: 'an altar of earth you shall make for me' (v. 24),
which would seem to imply that this is the only cultic form known by to this law. Yet
in v. 25 we read, 'And if you make me an altar of stone...', implying that, according
to this verse, an altar of stone is also legitimate. It may be that this law 'grew' in two
stages, where according to the later option an altar of stones was also legitimate, a
point not intended by the author of the earlier law. See H. Holzinger, *Exodus*, pp. 80-
81.

8.   See A. Alt's well-known study, 'Die Ursprunge des israelitischen Rechts',
esp. pp. 308, 311ff.

Rashi's explanation: 'That the witnesses saw him [i.e. the kidnapped person]...[in his (the kidnapper's) possession] prior to the act of selling' (Rashi *ad loc.*, following the rabbis, as in *Mek. SbY., Mishpatim* sect. 5, to Exod. 21.16). Compare also Ibn Ezra: '...in the market before being sold'. That is, even though the kidnapped person is now in a third place, there is evidence connecting him or her with the kidnapper prior to the selling. However, this explanation deviates sharply from the usual manner of the law, which generally does not include procedural elements of this type. Ordinarily, laws deal with the case itself, without delving into procedural issues, such as the definition of the judge, the nature of proof, witnesses, and the like.

Hence, ונמצא בידו must mean: 'and he (the kidnapped person) is found in his hands'.[9] Thus, the law deals with two separate cases: one, that of a person who kidnaps and sells the victim; two, that of one who kidnaps someone, but continues to hold the person (continued possession). In either case, the penalty is death.[10]

One may adduce the following proofs in support of this explanation:

1. The sequence of actions seems strange, because the act of selling is mentioned prior to that of holding the victim in the kidnapper's possession (which would be the immediate result of the kidnapping).

2. In the Bible, the form ו (= 'and') is sometimes used in the sense of או (= 'or'), especially in judicial texts, as in 'one who strikes his father and his mother (ואמו)', meaning '*or* his mother'.[11]

On this basis, as well as that of the parallel law in Deut. 24.7 (see below), it is clear that the present wording of Exod. 21.16 is intended to define the kidnapping of a person as an absolute transgression, punishable by death, regardless of the victim's fate—that is, whether the victim is sold to a third party or held as a slave in the kidnapper's house.

But this is not the entire picture. If the intention of the legislator was

---

9. Further proof supporting this interpretation may be found in Exod. 22.3: '...if the stolen beast is found alive in his possession', etc.

10. Regarding this law and its meaning see, *inter alia*, G.R. Driver, *Exodus*, pp. 216-17; B.S. Childs, *The Book of Exodus*, p. 70. R. Westbrook, *Studies in Biblical and Cuneiform Law*, p. 119, explains the words תמצא בידו as referring to the person who bought the kidnapping victim from the kidnapper. However, I cannot accept this explanation, either on the basis of the wording of the law or that of its contents. The biblical syntax likewise does not allow such an explanation. And see now M. Fishbane, *Biblical Interpretation*, pp. 188-89, on the words תמצא בידו.

11. See Chapter 4: 'The Uses of או ('or') in Biblical Legal Texts'.

to state that the kidnapper must be put to death, why did he not define his law in the following form: 'Whoever steals a man...shall be put to death' (like the adjacent law, 'Whoever strikes a man so that he dies shall be put to death', Exod. 21.12)?

If we now combine the previously discussed items, we arrive at the conclusion that we must modify our earlier conclusion by stating that the law initially dealt with the kidnapping of a person and a subsequent sale to a third party. At that point, the wording was, 'Whoever steals a man and sells him shall be put to death'. Later on, when the authorities felt a need for various reasons to make the law more stringent, they added the phrase ונמצא בידו ('or is found in possession of him') at the end of the law. Thus, the peculiar wording and sequence may be explained as the result of a two-stage growth of the law.

However, in ancient times people were not prepared to delete any item in a holy text, but preferred to alter it by adding new items. In this case, they did so by inserting the words ונמצא בידו at the end of the text (as in Daube's rule).[12] As I have already mentioned, the law does not reflect the logical order of the acts entailed in the commission of the sin, but rather the order of the growth of the law.

Another proof for the existence of a less stringent stage of the law, in which one is only subject to the death penalty if one both kidnaps a person and sells him or her, appears in Deut. 24.7: 'If a man is found stealing one of his brethren, the people of Israel, and if he treats him as a slave[13] and sells him, then that thief shall die; so you shall purge the evil from the midst of you'.

There are several differences between these two laws, most of them stylistic. One difference between Exod. 21.16 and Deut. 24.7 is essential, namely, that the law in Deut. 24.7 concerns a person who commits a sin consisting of two actions: kidnapping and selling. One may thus imagine that, in the opinion of the Deuteronomic legislator, one who kidnaps another person but does not sell him is subject, not to the death penalty, but to a less severe punishment. While this case is not mentioned as such in the Book of Deuteronomy, one may arrive at that conclusion by a simple deduction.

12. Daube, *Studies*, pp. 85-86, 88, 97.
13. The Hebrew here reads *hit'amer*. Compare M. David, 'Hit'amer', regarding the root *'mr* as referring to business matters; that is, the law forbids the kidnapper from treating the victim as property. Alt notes certain texts from Ugarit in which a similar usage of *'mr* is found; see his paper, 'Zu hit'ammer'.

I will now indicate those Deuteronomic idioms which are mentioned in the law of Deut. 24.7:

1.	מאחיו מבני ישראל	one of his brethren the people of Israel
2.	והתעמר בו	if he treats him as a slave
3.	ומת הגנב ההוא	then that thief shall die
4.	ובערת הרע מקרבך	so you shall purge the evil from the midst of you

No. 1 is a typical Deuteronomistic idiom, indicative of the priorities of its ideology.

No. 2 is an idiom found only in the Book of Deuteronomy (here and in 21.14).

No. 3 is the stylistic method used for an absolute penalty statement, utilizing the form ומת (*waw* consecutive) rather than the more usual yiqtol form (מות יומת) in the passive voice.

No. 4 is a motive clause used by the Deuteronomist to encourage the people to obey to the laws.[14]

One might challenge our hypothesis by asking: How is it that the more ancient codex of the two—The Book of the Covenant—reflects a 'modern' stage of the law of kidnapping, whereas the later parallel in the Book of Deuteronomy does not? The answer is that different collections have different routes of development, depending, among other things, on local and ideological factors. One may easily see that the change in the law of kidnapping in order to make it more stringent did not have any effect on other sources (such as Deut. 24.7 and others).

The explanation we have just described is based on the conception that the law in Exod. 21.16 reflects two stages in the law of kidnapping, the later stage of which is depicted in the present law. This illustrates the legislator's attitude towards this kind of sin.[15]

On the other hand, there is another possible explanation: our previous description may be replaced by another one, stating that the two stages happened before this law was 'implanted' into the Book of the Covenant. That is, the author of the Book of the Covenant borrowed the law verbatim after it had already undergone two rounds of developments in its earlier history.[16]

14. Regarding typical Deuteronomistic phrases, see M. Weinfeld, *Deuteronomy and Deuteronomic School, passim.*

15. This conclusion follows Daube's short statement regarding the later stage represented by ונמצא בידו in the history of the law of kidnapping (*Studies*, p. 95).

16. The law allows selling a person in the event that the thief cannot pay the fine; see B. Bäntsch, *Exodus*, p. 197.

This explanation changes nothing as to our understanding of the process of creation of the law, but only regarding its place in the present Book of the Covenant. It does not even change the explanation I have given referring to the less stringent law of Deut. 24.7.[17]

ii. *The Law of the Goring Ox: Exodus 21.29-30*

A similar development is reflected in the law of the goring ox (Exod. 21.28-36), the relevant verses of which read as follows:

> When an ox gores a man or a woman to death, the ox shall be stoned, and its flesh shall not be eaten; but the owner of the ox shall be clear. But if the ox has been accustomed to gore in the past, and its owner has been warned but has not kept it in, and it kills a man or a woman, the ox shall be stoned, and its owner also shall be put to death. If a ransom is laid on him, then he shall give for the redemption of his life whatever is laid upon him.

17. In a case such as this, the formulation of the law in Deuteronomy is suitable, as mentioned, to the stage prior to the stringencies. It follows that the Deuteronomist knew an earlier version of the Book of Covenant (this possibility is already considered in the body of this chapter). Many scholars see the laws of Deuteronomy as a kind of development of and response to the existing version of the Book of Covenant, which was known to them. However, since the final version of the Book of the Covenant does not contain any less strict version of the law of kidnapping, one is forced to the conclusion that this solution is untenable. It is likewise inconceivable that the Deuteronomist took exception to the stringency of this law, because it corresponds to his own attitude toward this kind of transgression, and there seems no doubt that he would have adopted such a law had he seen it in the source before us. On the other hand, it is difficult to accept the view that the phrase 'if he treats him as a slave and sells him' is to be taken in the sense of 'he treats him as a slave or sells him', where the phrase והתעמר בו serves as an analogue to נמצא בידו. I completely reject such an interpretation; first, because the only passage, apart from Deut. 24.7, in which the root עמר is used is in the law of the captive woman: '(you shall not sell her for money), you shall not treat her as a slave, because you humiliated her' (Deut. 21.14). There, the verb התעמר ('to treat as a slave') is parallel to the proscription against selling the woman; that is, עמר is used to describe the non-humanitarian relationship expressed in the sale of the captive woman. Even in the present law, that of kidnapping, the phrase והתעמר בו ומכרו means: 'to treat him as a slave by the fact that he sold him'. Secondly, had the Deuteronomist really wished to signify two 'kinds' of transgression, as in the Book of Covenant, then in addition to the stylistic changes he had taken in the reworking of this law (see above in the text), he would have doubtless used a clear and unequivocal formula in the spirit of the hypothetical reading; 'One who steals a person shall surely be put to death', and this in his own typical style.

Verse 28 deals with the issue of an 'innocent' ox, meaning an ox that has yet not gored any person. On the other hand, v. 29 deals with an ox that already has a 'history' of goring persons. The main point of interest to us here is the relation between vv. 29 and 30.

According to v. 29, the owner of the ox is subject to the death penalty along with the ox ('and its owner also shall be put to death'). Verse 30, however, mentions the possibility of mitigating the death penalty by paying ransom.[18] This appears in the conditional phrase, 'If a ransom is laid on him then he shall give for the redemption of his life whatever is laid upon him'.

The passive form יושת 'is laid on him...whatever is laid upon him' raises some difficulties:

1. If we assume that the owner of the ox has the option to save his life by paying ransom, surely anyone involved in such an incident would choose that option, even if the ransom were very high. It is difficult to imagine that the legislator would have introduced an element of discrimination into the law by introducing different options that would differentiate between those belonging to different classes. This opposes the judicial-ethical principle described, *inter alia*, in Num. 15.16: 'One law and one ordinance shall be for you and for the stranger who sojourns with you'.

Nor can one resolve this problem by contending that the idea of equality before the law is unique and typical to the legislator of Numbers 15, because it is a general assumption in all parts of the Bible. Hence, any interpretation of a biblical law that goes against this principle must be rejected.

In addition, the above-mentioned option is to be rejected because the text speaks of the ransom as being 'laid upon him', meaning that the owner does not have the power to decide in this case.

2. Even if we assume that the option of deciding which of the two punishments (v. 29 or v. 30) is to be applied lies in the hands of the victim's family,[19] the problem still remains. This is so because, if the

---

18. According to Westbrook, *Studies*, pp. 60-61, the law of the goring ox is included among the examples of 'double laws'. However, I cannot agree with him regarding this specific law, for reasons I will mention in the following discussion (see proof no. 4 below).

19. As in the explanation of S. Paul, *Studies in the Book of the Covenant*, p. 82, that in this case the law allows the taking of ransom because it is not a regular case of murder. Paul remarks that there is no system of compensation in the Bible, because

victim's family is rich, they are likely to insist upon the option of killing the owner of the ox. If, however, they are poor, they will be more likely to choose the option of payment, unless they insist on demanding the killing of the owner of the ox which, through its owner's negligence, caused the death of one of their family. In either case there is a conflict with the principle of equality of persons before the law.

3. Even that solution which places the choice between the two kinds of punishment in the hands of the judges is to be rejected, for other reasons. According to the text of the law, the differences between vv. 28 and 29 are connected with the definition of the status of the ox; does it or does it not have a 'history' of goring any persons? Verse 29, as we have seen, is concerned with the case in which it has gored other persons in the past and its owner, despite warnings by the authorities, did not restrain the animal as ordered.

One can see from this description that the judges play no role in determining which of the two punishments is to be applied. If the case concerns an 'innocent' ox, then the judge must act in accordance with v. 28, but if the ox had a history of goring people, he has no option but to apply v. 29.

Thus, the issues of והועד בבעליו and ולא ישמרנו cannot be the basis for the differing rules applied in v. 29 and v. 30, but either for the choice between v. 28 or v. 29, or for a decision regarding the question of whether or not the owner is guilty, in which case, as in all judicial proceedings, the judge is required to search out and find the truth.

All this indicates that the law does not give the judge the right to

---

only a society with an economic system of thinking could have developed such a method. See also M. Greenberg, 'Some Postulates of Biblical Criminal Law', esp. pp. 23-24, concerning the argument that ransom is allowed in this case because the ox-owner did not personally commit the homicide, nor was it intended or premeditated. See also Greenberg, 'Ideal and Reality', pp. 120-125; and cf. J. Finkelstein, *The Ox that Gored*, pp. 29-30. Jackson, on the other hand, believes that ransom was allowed in ancient biblical law, as opposed to the prohibition against doing so at a later stage represented in Num. 35.31. See B.S. Jackson, 'Reflections on Biblical Criminal Law', esp. pp. 21-24 [= *Essays*, pp. 38-41]. From the point of view of the issue at hand, Greenberg and Jackson agree in perceiving vv. 29-30 as belonging to the same stage of the law, whereas I see them as stemming from two different stages. On the other hand, A. Phillips, 'Another Look at Murder', pp. 115-16, sees v. 30 as the result of a later development, while v. 29 was already in existence at that stage, meaning that both were in effect simultaneously. Phillips connects the creation of v. 30 with the cancellation of v. 12 as an independent law of homicide.

choose between v. 29 or v. 30, thus returning us to our original question: Who does decide?

4. It is worth noting that both ancient and modern legislators try to avoid wordings that provide a choice of options for fulfilling a certain law. This is so because such a choice may provide a way to disobey the law in general, especially in light of the fact that the authorities cannot check and try to find who has not fulfilled the law. It is therefore not surprising that even in the Bible such 'double' laws are rare.

On the basis of our discussion, one sees that the real relation between v. 29 and v. 30 lies in a different direction. I mean by this that the real relation between the two kinds of punishments is not that of options for an alternative act, because it is just a 'cover' for the real solution of the problem.

Indeed, the Talmudic Sages and the mediaeval Jewish commentators saw the word 'if' (אם) in v. 30 as a term that does not relate to an ordinary usage of a conditional sentence.[20] Regarding the phrase 'and its owner also shall be put to death', R. Abraham Ibn Ezra says, 'He is worthy to be killed, if he does not pay a ransom for his soul...as is the explanation of the phrase "an eye for an eye"...[Moreover,] this is so because the text says יומת and not ימות'. This explanation follows the *Mekilta* to Exod. 21.30 (*Mishpatim*, sect. 10).

Ibn Ezra's wording suggests that the form 'if' (אם) is interpreted as an actual law, rather than as a theoretical one. Therefore, he sees v. 29 (referring to the death penalty) as indicating, not the actual punishment, but a theoretical guideline. However, the truth is that this law needs to be interpreted in the same way as the law of kidnapping: namely, as reflecting two stages of development undergone by the law.

In the earlier period, the law of the goring ox was fulfilled according to the guidelines of v. 29, that is, 'and its owner also shall be put to death'. Later on, people began to question the justice of that system, and began to think that it was not right to kill the owner for a deed performed by his ox. Even though the case is a severe one, the owner of the ox is not directly culpable, but is at most guilty of carelessness.

At this stage an additional item (v. 30) was added to the law. By this addition, the original death penalty withered away and became a theoretical demand (compare Ibn Ezra's definition: 'he is worthy to be

20. Finkelstein, *The Ox That Gored*, p. 31.

killed', etc.). Thus, the only actual penalty is that of v. 30: 'If a ransom is laid on him'.

The period of this change may parallel the change in the law of homicide, whereby unintentional manslaughter is punished differently from murder, which is subject to the death penalty (Exod. 21.13-14), whereas previously the punishment of any killer was death (21.12).[21]

As in earlier periods, this change is accomplished by adding certain items to the holy text rather than removing any item in it. This is true in regard to our case—the law of the goring ox—in which the addition (v. 30) is defined as a condition, even though it is clearly a fictitious one. One must assume that, had the addition been worded in a positive form, it might have caused even more difficulties, for how then could one understand the relation between the two actions? It was therefore decided to use the distinctive usage of אם ('if'), but not as a real conditional.

The usage of this term is similar in Lev. 2.14: 'If you offer a cereal offering of firstfruits to the LORD', and so on. As the bringing of first-fruits to the temple is a compulsory duty, the word 'if' must be under-stood in this case to mean 'when' or 'as you bring...', and not an ordinary 'if'. The Rabbis even state in the *Mekilta* that כל אם ואם שבתורה רשות חוץ משלושה, וכ׳. 'All "ifs" in the Torah are "free" [i.e. optional], except for three: "and if you make me an altar of stone" (Exod. 20.25), which "if" actually means "when", "as soon as", etc.; "If you offer a cereal offering of first fruits to the LORD" (Lev. 2.14); "If you lend money to any of my people" (Exod. 22.25)'.

iii. *The Law of Manslaughter—Exodus 21.12-14*
The three verses of the law of manslaughter, appearing in Exod. 21.12-14, contain two different formulations of the law. We thus find here a combination from the development in two different laws. According to the earlier law, represented in v. 12, any act of killing, whether deliberate or one that occurred by accident, is punishable by death: 'Whoever strikes a man so that he dies shall be put to death' (v. 12). Alongside this, however, there are two other verses that together constitute a law in its own right, according to which the punishment of the deliberate murderer is death (v. 14), as in the previous law, but one who killed without intending to do so, as in the case of an accident, is required to

---

21. See below (2.iii) for the discussion regarding this law.

flee to the place of refuge set aside for that purpose (v. 13).

In addition to the element of intention, which is a fundamental element distinguishing the two laws, there is also a stylistic difference between the two. Verses 13-14 are formulated in a casuistic manner: 'But if a man willfully attacks another to kill him treacherously', etc. On the other hand, the previous law (v. 12) is formulated in the *particip* form, like the adjacent laws: 'Whoever strikes his father or his mother' (v. 15); 'Whoever steals a man, whether he sells him' (v. 16), and so on.

The original sequence of the casuistic law consisted of v. 14, followed by v. 13. This may be seen by the opening formula of v. 14, to which v. 13 reads as a sort of sequel—that is, its status is that of a secondary law. When the redactor of the Book of the Covenant, or an earlier redactor whose documents were used by the editor of the Book of Covenant, combined the law in such a way as to incorporate both the older law (v. 12) and the newer law (vv. 13-14), he was forced to change the order of the law, owing to both literary considerations and reasons of content. That is, had v. 14 followed immediately upon v. 12, it would have appeared as a simple repetition. By changing the order of the clauses, the unit is perceived as reflecting a seemingly unified law, in which v. 12 functions as a kind of general introduction relating to the deliberate murderer, while vv. 13-14 serve as the more detailed law. Hence, the law given in vv. 12-14 is the result of a 'growth' in at least two stages, uniting the components of the earlier law and the later law into one legal unit.[22]

iv. *The Law of Tithes: Deuteronomy 14.22-23, 24-27*

The rudimentary law stipulates that 'You shall tithe all the yield of your seed, which comes forth from the field year by year. And before the LORD your God, in the place which he shall choose, to make his name

---

22. Compare Phillips, 'Another Look', p. 116 n. 41, on the development of the law by the addition of vv. 13-14 from v. 12 alone to form the present law. H. McKeating, 'The Development of the Law on Homicide', also speaks of the development of the law of manslaughter; however, his remarks are devoted to the assembly of proofs from different parts of the Bible, especially from the historiographic sections, to confirm the development of the law of the murderer along the lines of the stages that follow from analysis of the law. McKeating distinguishes between the earlier stage of tribal law and that of centralized, monarchical law. In his opinion, the various stages of the law of manslaughter are paralleled by the testimony that arises from different texts in the Bible reflecting the development from tribal law to monarchical law.

dwell there, you shall eat the tithe...' (Deut. 14.22-23).

The act of eating the produce in 'the place which he shall choose' refers to the tithe taken from produce and especially, as stated at the beginning of the law, 'all the yield of your seed'. Further on, however, it also speaks of 'the tithe of your grain, of your wine, and of your oil, and the firstlings of your herd and flock' (v. 23).

Verse 24 raises the possibility of an alternative way of carrying out this law, reserved for those fulfilling a particular condition. This is stipulated by the verse in the words, 'And if the way is too long for you, so that you are not able to bring the tithe, when the LORD your God blesses you, because the place is too far from you, which the LORD your God chooses, to set his name there'. The distance between the person's home and 'the place which he shall choose' may cause certain difficulties in carrying the produce of the tithes to the chosen city. Before examining the solution to this technical difficulty proposed by the legislator, one must stress another point: namely, the possibility that certain places may be too far away is described in the words, 'for the LORD your God shall bless you'. That is, the fact that God's hand is generously extended over his people is reflected in the expansion of the boundaries of the country, with the result that many Israelites live at a great distance from the chosen city, creating difficulties in carrying out various ceremonies commanded by the Torah which need to be conducted at 'the place which he shall choose' (cf. the laws in Deuteronomy 12 concerning 'the place which he shall choose' and other laws to be discussed below).[23]

The practical solution proposed for that part of the population which lives too far away is articulated in vv. 25-26:

> Then you shall turn it into money, and bind up the money in your hand, and go to the place which the LORD your God chooses, and spend the money for whatever you desire, oxen, or sheep, or wine or strong drink,

---

23. Rashi interpreted the 'blessing' as referring to the quantity of produce of the particular year, making it too heavy for a person to carry. According to G.A. Smith, *Deuteronomy*, p. 194., the phrase 'when the LORD your God blesses you' does not refer to the expansion of the borders (as in the view of A. Knobel, *Die Bücher Numeri...*, pp. 264-65) nor to the blessing of the produce (Rashi and Dillman, p. 305), but is a general comment on God's blessing of his people. Smith sees this law as an additional consequence of the approach of centralization introduced by the Deuteronomist.

whatever your appetite craves; and you shall eat there before the Lord your
God and rejoice, you and your household.

The reference in v. 27 to the Levite is to be interpreted not only as
regarding the alternative option for organizing tithes for those who live
far away, but as a conclusion to the entire section of the law of tithes,
covering both the primary fulfilment of the law and to the subsidiary
clause concerning those who live far away.

A substantial question concerning the history of this law is raised by
the issue of the secondary tendency within it (vv. 24-26). On the one
hand, it is indeed possible that the entire development took place at one
stage. That is, as part and parcel of the initial law the legislator saw fit to
provide a practical solution for those who lived far away from the
chosen city. On the other hand, it seems more likely that the present law
emerged through a process entailing at least two separate stages.[24] In the
first stage, the law was observed according to the formulation in vv. 22-
23, whereas in the second stage vv. 24-26 were added for a reason
typical of Deuteronomic law, namely, that it pertained to the possibility
of geographical extension of the boundaries of the country, a theme
referred to a number of times by the author of Deuteronomy.[25]

An interesting indication of the formation of a special type of laws
taking into account the matter of the expansion of the land may be found
in the specific use of the verbs קרב ('to be/become near') and רחק ('to
be/become far') in a series of laws in the Book of Deuteronomy. In the
present law, for example, we read: 'And if the way is too long for you,
so that you are not able to bring the tithe, when the LORD your God
blesses you, because the place is too far (כי ירחק) from you, which the
LORD your God chooses, to set his name there; then you shall turn it
into money...'[26] The present law is clearly an offshoot of the reform

24. I allude here to the relation between the law of tithes and the law of the poor
tithe (vv. 28-29), an issue I do not intend to discuss here.
25. See A. Phillips, *Deuteronomy*, on Deut. 14.24, p. 101, which he sees as a new
law, albeit he sees v. 27 also as a new law.
26. The only biblical law outside of Deuteronomy that relates to the problem of
distance is that of the second Passover: 'If any man of you...is unclean through
touching a dead body, or is afar off on a journey...he shall still keep the passover to
the Lord. In the second month on the fourteenth day in the evening they shall keep it;
they shall eat it with unleavened bread and bitter herbs' (Num. 9.10-11). However,
this law twice repeats that the permission granted to postpone the passover is
restricted to the two cases mentioned, whereas one who does not belong to this

introduced by the Deuteronomist regarding his central concern—'the place which he shall choose'. The obligation to bring tithes to the central sanctuary—which in this approach is the only one—requires some sort of accomodation for those who live too far from the Temple city. Judging from the structure and formulation of these matters, it seems to me that this is indeed a new stage in the law, added at a later stage, when there were a large number of residents who did not bring tithes because of 'logistic' considerations related to the difficulties involved in getting to the Temple city, particularly when this involved carrying heavy burdens on the way there. For this reason, I believe that the clause concerning those who live too far away is in actuality a later addition, one that developed among Deuteronomic circles to counteract non-observance of the law.[27] The proposed solution suggests a more practical means of execution, utilizing the argument of distance. All this is done in order to create an appropriate 'seam' between the two parts of the law and to smooth over any roughness in their interrelationship, so as to present them as one law with two clauses.[28]

category and was 'not on a journey', but nevertheless failed to perform the passover at the proper time, 'that person shall be cut off from his people' (v. 13). Milgrom observes that consideration of one who had been far off is opposed to the generally accepted practice of the ancient Near East, where this is not a valid excuse for absence from the cult. See his interpretation of this verse in *Numbers*, p. 69. According to A. Rofé, *Introduction to Deuteronomy*, p. 17, it may be that the phrase בדרך רחוקה is a kind of extensive addition of the type that he finds in Deuteronomy (cf. n. 29 below).

27. In this respect, I reverse the order of priorities adopted in my interpretation of the law of the slave, where my primary interpretation was that both options form part of the same stage, while my alternative reading was that the continued stay of a slave in the house of the master was the result of a later development. In the case of the law of tithes I tend, as mentioned, to see the law as reflecting two distinct stages.

28. As a point of comparison to the law of tithes, one may cite the cities of refuge, mentioned in two texts in the Book of Deuteronomy. The former appears in Deut. 4.41-43, within the framework of the block of speeches of Moses in chs. 1–11. The second passage is in Deut. 19.1-10, which is in turn divided into two main sections: vv. 1-7 and vv. 8-10. Indeed, it would appear that the wording of the second part of the law of the cities of refuge is constructed on the same principle as that found in the second part of the law of tithes namely, the argument that 'If the LORD your God enlarges your border, as he has sworn to your fathers, and gives you all the land which he promised to give to your fathers' (v. 8). Thus, the need for an alternative law is explained here in terms of the expanded borders of the land, just as it is justified in the law of tithes in terms of the need for a solution to the difficulty entailed in carrying the tithes up from distant places. In the law of tithes, the proposed solution was to

v. *The Law of Animals Lost by their Owners: Deuteronomy 22.1-3*
(including a note on the formula, 'and so shall you do' [כן תעשׂה]*)*
An extremely interesting law in this respect is that in Deut. 22.1-3,
which requires that one who finds an ox or sheep wandering about
'shall take them back to your brother' (v. 1). Further on, the question of
distance is again raised,[29] when it states 'and if he is not near you, or if
you do not know him, you shall bring it home to your house, and it shall
be with you until your brother seeks it; then you shall restore it to him'.

redeem the tithes by exchanging them for equivalent monetary value, thereafter using
the money thus exchanged to purchase things needed for the celebration described in
the Temple city. In the other law mentioned, that of the cities of refuge, the solution
lies in the instruction to erect another three cities should God expand the borders of
the land. I explain the relationship between the two parts of this law in vv. 1-7 and vv.
8-10 in terms of an alternative law, which fluctuates between a smaller or larger
number of cities (that is, through the addition of three cities) in order to absorb the
unintentional manslaughters. The medieval Jewish exegete R. Moses Nahmanides
draws a distinction between the expansion of the borders mentioned in this law and
that in Deut. 12.20-25, since in his opinion the presentation in the latter is original,
unlike the case of Deut. 19.8, which deals with an additional extension of the borders
of the land. According to Phillips, *Deuteronomy*, p. 91, Deut. 12.20 reflects the
expansion of the borders during the reign of Josiah towards the direction of the
inheritance of the northern kingdom. Rofé, *Introduction*, pp. 16, 92, 98, notes that the
phrase 'lest the avenger of blood in hot anger pursue the manslayer and overtake him,
because the way is long, and wound him mortally...' (Deut. 19.6) is likewise
addressed to the need for additional cities of refuge owing to the large size of the
land. In his opinion, all three appearances of the phrase 'when he shall enlarge'
(כי ירחיב) in the Book of Deuteronomy (including 14.24, discussed in the text) are
later additions to the text. Deut. 19.8-10 expands the law of the cities of refuge in
order to bring it in line with the P document, which requires six cities. Indeed, one
might ask why the legislator raised this argument ('because the way is long', v. 6) at
this particular point, making it seem as though he were dissenting from the opinion
that one city of refuge is sufficient. But since this interpretation is inappropriate (but
see what Rofé wrote on this), it would appear that this claim in fact belongs in the
second half of the law, vv. 8-10, which speaks of the addition of three cities after God
will extend the borders. On the graduated growth of the law of the cities of refuge in
Deut. 19, see C. Steuernagel, *Deuteronomium und Josua*, p. 71. Many commentators
have noted the late date of vv. 8-10; see, for example, A.D.H. Mays, *Deuteronomy*,
p. 287. According to D.Z. Hoffmann, *Das Buch Deuteronomium*, pp. 355-57,
Deut. 19.8-9 is to be interpreted as a parenthetical remark; his remark is analogous to
the solution of the critical scholars who propose a late date for these passages.

29. As in the law of tithes and the laws of the city of refuge, and in that of
permitted flesh (Deut 12.20-25).

The double nature of the law is clear by every criterion, in that it contains both a primary means of execution, 'surely return it to your brother', and an alternative proposal, 'and gather it into your house... and return it to him'.

The issue of the actual relationship between the two possibilities for fulfilling the law arises within this context. Even in a naive and uncritical reading, the difficult question of the 'geographical' border line between the two options emerges: what distance is considered 'not close' under the wording of the law, so that the finder may claim to may realize the obligation under v. 2 and not according to v. 1? Moreover, what is the background to the claim that 'he did not know him' (v. 2)? This, it appears, is an additional option, since there is presumably no need for both conditions to be simultaneously fulfilled—that is, that the owner be both distant and not known. This is so because it makes no sense for the law to require one to immediately return a lost article to one who lives far away, even if the owner is known to the finder.[30]

Verse 3 may be interpreted as an additional, third, stage of the law, which reads, 'And so shall you do with his ass; so shall you do with his garment; so shall you do with every lost thing of your brother's, which he loses and you find; you may not withhold your help'. There can be no doubt that the formula כן תעשה ('and so shall he do') was a means of adding additional elements to existing laws.[31]

I shall now cite some other scriptural passages in which such a usage appears.

In the law of slaves in Deut. 15.17, it states, '...and to your bond-woman you shall do likewise'. It seems clear that the use of the formula here is intended to add another unit to a law that originally spoke about a male slave, now interpreted as applying by extension to females.

The same usage is found in the law in Deut. 20.15: 'Thus you shall do[32] to all the cities which are very far from you, which are not cities of

---

30. In the opinion of A. Ehrlich, *The Literal Sense of the Bible*, the words ולא ידעתו are intended to mean 'if you did not know him', the pronoun referring, in his opinion, to the animal rather than to its owners—that is, the finder does not know to whom this animal belongs.

31. Cf. Rofé, *Introduction*, p. 132, and n. 23 there.

32. As I explain further along in this discussion, the phrase כן תעשה is not used here in its usual sense: it is ordinarily used to add to the law, while here it is intended to restrict it. In principle, the very use of this formula is intended to introduce an addition to the law. Rofé already formulated this approach (*Introduction*, p. 132); this

the nations here'. The subsequent verse summarizes the law in a clear manner: 'But in the cities of these peoples that the LORD your God gives you for an inheritance, you shall save alive nothing that breathes' (v. 16). This law presents a difficulty, in that its opening is based upon the general principle that in every military action one must begin with overtures of peace. Only in v. 15 is the law explained in its later formulation, where this requirement is limited to faraway cities, while a different law, appearing in vv. 16-18, applies to nearby cities.[33]

The last verses[34] including this formula return us, in practice, to the original uses of the formula as they appear in the Book of the Covenant. The first of these is in the conclusion of the law of the sabbatical year, where it states, '...You shall do likewise with your vineyard, and with your olive orchard' (Exod. 23.11). There is no doubt that this component is to be regarded as an addition. The second case appears in the law of the first-born: 'You shall do likewise with your oxen and with your sheep; seven days it shall be with its dam; on the eighth day you shall give it to me' (Exod. 22.29). The author of Deuteronomy may have adopted the use of the phrase 'so shall you do' under the influence of the Book of the Covenant, like other influences upon him from this early collection.[35]

is a proof of his contention that the original law appears in vv. 10-14, while vv. 15-18 are an addition intended to adjust the earlier law to a reality in which there is a distinction between distant cities, to which the previous law, which was originally general, referred, and nearby cities, which Israel is obligated to destroy.

33. It does not seem to me that the 'geographical' component (i.e. near/far), which also appears here, is by chance. Hence, one may state that one of the characteristic features of the alternative laws in Deuteronomy is the parameter of distance, which is formulated using various phrases of closeness and distance, depending upon the context. I shall discuss these laws in various parts of this chapter.

34. The formula discussed here appears in negative form in Deut. 12.31: 'You shall do not so to the LORD your God...', but there does not seem to be any connection between the two idioms. It would seem that the law used this formula because of the quotation of the words of the religious seducers: 'that I also may do likewise' (v. 30), in reaction to which there appears the divine command, 'do not do so...', and so on. It follows that these words were meant to be particularly emphasized.

35. Consistent with my approach, I would observe that what we have concluded concerning the status of כן תעשה requires us to interpret in like fashion Ezek. 45.20: 'You shall do the same on the seventh day of the month for any one who has sinned through error or ignorance; so you shall make atonement for the temple'. That is, it is possible that Ezekiel's ceremony of atonement originally related to only one day, 'in the first month, on the first day of the month' (v. 18). On the other hand, there is no

We may close this discussion with the same section of the law with which it opened, namely Deut. 22.1-3. The law of lost animals contains three stages: first, a basic law, commanding one to return oxon or sheep that have strayed to their owners; second, an alternative law, applying to owners who live far away from the place where the animals were found, in which case the animal is returned after the owners appear in the place and request their lost possession; third, an extension of the law, adding to its rubric an ass, a garment or any other lost article.

Regarding the relation of v. 3 to what preceded, it is clear that we have here an expansion of the law (whether in its original form or with the addition of v. 2). It is possible that the author's tendency at this stage was to equate the applicability of the law to that of the Book of the Covenant, in that the earlier law says: 'If you meet your enemy's ox or his ass going astray, you shall bring it back to him' (Exod. 23.4).[36]

It seems to me, therefore, that one must apply here a judgment similar to that which we adopted with regard to the law of tithes. That is, just as the solution for one who lives far away from the temple city (Deut. 14.24-26) was created in response to the non-fulfilment of the law, to provide a practical possibility for its execution by the majority of the people, here too, in order to facilitate the return of lost articles, a distinction was drawn between those who live nearby and those living further away.[37]

vi. *The Law of the First-Born*

In tracing the history of the laws of the sanctity of the first-born as they are preserved in the Torah, one discovers that they emerged in two stages. Those verses which serve today as a general introduction to the

need to date the usage in Exod. 26.17 as any later than its context there.

36. According to such scholars as Smith and Driver in their respective commentaries, the law in Deut. 22 is an expansion and alteration of the earlier law of E in the Book of the Covenant. D's changes are an expansion of the law, while v. 3 is D's addition to the ancient law. However, according to Stuernagel it is actually Exod. 23.4-5 that is the later addition to the Book of the Covenant, under the influence of the Deuteronomic law; see C. Stuernagel, *Deuteronomium*, pp. 80-81.

37. Nevertheless, the question of the precise compass of the distance still remains open. See the solution proposed by the author of the *Temple Scroll* in another context, that of the law of one offering a sacrifice in the gates: 'three days distant from my Temple' (11QTemple 52.14). The distance within which it was permitted to eat a pure animal with a blemish is likewise defined as 'distant from my temple around thirty *ris*' (52.17-18).

laws functioned in the distant past as the entire 'general law'. At a later stage this 'general law' was transformed into a general introduction to the more detailed laws. This is discussed in greater detail in Part II of this book (Chapter 6).

vii. The Use of the Phrase 'Or' (אוֹ) as Indicating Development of the Laws

In Chapter 4, 'The Uses of אוֹ ('or') in Biblical Legal Texts', I discuss the function of the phrase אוֹ in biblical law. In various parts of the chapter, particularly Section 3, 'אוֹ as an Indication of the History of the Evolution of the Law', I observe that the phrase אוֹ is indicative of the development of those laws using this phrase (see that section).[38]

3. Alternative Laws Directed towards the Poor

Another group of biblical laws contains a special 'path' intended for execution by the poor. I mean to say by this that, alongside the regular law directed to all citizens, there is an alternative option intended for the poor. Such double laws, as shown in Section 2 above, emerged during the course of development of the law. The uniqueness of these specific laws lies in the fact that their alternative clause is rooted in the provision by the legislator of an alternative means of fulfilling the commandments for those who were unable to carry it out in the usual manner owing to economic distress.

I am aware of the fact that in the present discussion I have departed from the above-mentioned scheme of classification. In the first part of our discussion, the laws were classified in terms of those in which the double law was original and those in which it was not original, that is, where it derived from a later development of the law. In the present case, by contrast, I refer to the reason for the doubling of the law. I do this deliberately because in this case, as mentioned, we find a special group of laws intended for a particular sector of the population, the

---

38. One should also mention here the various types of 'motive clause', some of which are instructive for the history of the development of those laws in which this clause appears, such as that in which the motive reflects a second, later stage in the development of the law. There are also cases in which it is possible to find a number of 'levels' in the body of the motive clause itself. See the principal literature on this issue: B. Gemser, 'The Importance of the Motive Clause in the Old Testament Law'; R. Sonsino, 'Motive Clause in Hebrew Bible'.

poor. As for the textual status of the alternative clause in these laws, I tend to see the alternative addressed to the poor as a clause added over the course of time, when the legislator needed to provide a practical solution for the observance of the law by the circle of the poor.

I will exemplify this by presenting here a few such laws, without entering into discussion of each individual case. This issue is discussed in detail in Chapter 3: 'Caring for the Poor in Biblical Law'.

i. *Law of the Woman Following Childbirth: Leviticus 12.8*

There are cases in which the law anticipates *ab initio* people (or situations) for whom the fulfilment of the law as written is impossible. Such cases are referred to by the formula, '(and) if not' or the like. In Lev. 12.8, after stating that a woman following childbirth must bring a lamb as a burnt offering (together with a turtle dove or young pigeon as a sin offering), the law adds: 'And if she cannot afford a lamb...' Thus, the definitive language at the beginning is 'corrected' by the formula 'if not...' The legislator himself thereby provided an alternative means of carrying out the ritual of purification required of every woman, including poor mothers, following childbirth.[39]

ii. *The Law of the Leper: Leviticus 14.21-32*

One ought to mention in this connection the sacrifice brought by the leper following purification. This law states, 'But if he is poor and cannot afford so much, then he shall take one male lamb...' (Lev. 14.21). Comparison with the principal law concerning the purification of the leper brings out the difference: during the initial stage, involving the bringing of two live birds and cedarwood, scarlet and hyssop and the performance of related ceremonies (vv. 4-9), no difference is drawn among those of various different economic situations, presumably on the assumption that everyone is able to afford these. On the other hand, there is a clear difference in all the details of the ceremony of purification from the eighth day onwards: while a typical person must bring three lambs (two males and a female) to serve as a guilt offering, a sin

39. According to A. Bertholet, *Leviticus*, p. 41, the clause concerning the poor woman after childbirth is a kind of later addition, as indicated by the proof in the concluding formula in 12.7b. Porter, *Leviticus*, p. 95, thinks likewise, for the same reason. The latter also mentions that Lev. 1.14-17 is late, reflecting the non-priestly post-exilic cult. The offering of fowl was one of the signs of the poverty of the population at that time. The same was thought by B. Bäntsch, *Leviticus*, p. 363.

offering and a burnt offering, this is not the case of the poor person, whom the legislator allows to bring one lamb as a guilt offering (in this respect there is no difference between the poor person and a typical citizen), together with two turtledoves or two young pigeons, 'such as he can afford', for the sin offering and burnt offering (v. 22).[40]

This type of law likewise appears in the law of valuations (Lev. 27.8),[41] in the law of the guilt offering (Lev. 5.7-13), and in the law of the thief who is unable to make restitution (Exod. 22.1-2). As mentioned, these and other laws are discussed in Chapter 3, 'Caring for the Poor in Biblical Law'.

4. *Laws Doubled through the Addition of a Sanction against Non-Compliance with the Basic Law*

A certain group of laws contains a secondary component reflecting a later stage of development than the primary component of the law. In effect, this definition also fits the laws discussed above in §1b, with one crucial difference: that in the present group the second stage is intended to serve as a threat, sanction against non-compliance with the basic law. We may conclude that we have here, not two alternative possibilities, but that rather the second stage is the legislator's punitive response against non-compliance with the law.

i. *The Law of the Firstling Ass: Exodus 13.13; 34.20*
In the law of firstlings of unclean animals, we read, 'Every firstling of an ass you shall redeem with a lamb, or if you will not redeem it you shall break its neck' (Exod. 13.13; 34.20). In my comprehensive discussion of this issue,[42] I demonstrate that this law contains a single demand, to which an alternative method of execution was added over the course of time, as a sanction against those who fail to fulfil the law: the breaking of

---

40. Lev. 14.21-32 is seen by the exegetes as late, like 12.8. See, for example, Porter, *Leviticus*, p. 113; Bäntsch, *Leviticus*, p. 373, on v. 31.

41. The subject of the valuation of the poor man (Lev. 27.8) is interesting, because it is clear *ab initio*, at the time that he takes the oath, that he is unable to pay the regular required valuation. This is not the case regarding the other laws, in which the poor person's inability to stand the obligation becomes clear at a later stage than that of the obligation, or which refer to an automatic obligation, such as that of the woman following childbirth or that of the leper, in which the sacrifice is required in order for the person to escape the situation.

42. See below, Chapter 8: 'The Firstling of Unclean Animals'.

the ass's neck rather than its redemption.[43] Matters are far more transparent in the long list of laws that I discuss in the chapter on the formulation of sanctions in biblical law.[44]

ii. *Law of the Levirate Marriage.* Among these laws, there particularly stands out the law governing the refusal to carry out the demands of the law of levirate marriage. The basic rule, as stated in Deut. 25.5, reads, 'If brothers dwell together, and one of them dies and has no son, the wife of the dead shall not married outside the family to a stranger; her husband's brother shall go in to her, and take her as his wife, and perform the duty of a husband's brother to her'. In v. 7, Scripture confronts the case in which the brother-in-law refuses to perform the levirate marriage. As might be expected, things are formulated in the pattern, 'If he does not (do)':

> And if the man does not wish to take his brother's wife, then his brother's wife shall go up to the gate of the elders, and say, 'My husband's brother refuses to perpetuate his brother's name in Israel; he will not perform the duty of a husband's brother to me'...saying, 'I do not wish to take her'... And the name of his house shall be called in Israel, The house of him that had his sandal pulled off (Deut. 25.7-10).

The phrase beginning 'if the man does not wish...' can clearly be explained as an addition made at a later stage, when it became clear that the unequivocal demand of the law was not always realized, so that the

43. I discuss the true relationship between the two parts of the law *ab extenso* in Chapter 8. See also Chapter 2, 'The Formula "If he shall not (do)" and the Problem of Sanctions in Biblical Law', where I discuss the manner in which the formula 'If he shall not (do)' is used in biblical law to introduce those sanctions with which the biblical legislator threatens those who fail to carry out the law or intend not to fulfil the law.

44. Thus, as mentioned in the previous note, it is worth mentioning that there are phrases that depict, so to speak, an additional possibility to that found in the principal law, and which seem to create the situation of a double law. In practice, however, these are no more than means of emphasis. Thus, for example, in the law concerning the order of purification in Num. 19.12: 'He shall cleanse himself with the water on the third day and on the seventh day, and so be clean; but if he does not cleanse himself on the third day and on the seventh day, he will not become clean'. One should note that the phrase 'if he does not' in this passage is unnecessary, its entire function being one of emphasis. This is so because it is clear from the basic formula of the clause that the cleansing ritual described is the only way of becoming purified. One learns from this that one who does not cleanse him- or herself thus cannot become pure.

levirate marriage was not carried out. In this later stage, the formulation of sanctions is directed against those who fail to fulfil the primary thrust of the law.[45]

5. Doubling in the Laws of Sacred Things—Leviticus 27

Let us now turn to a group of scriptures in Leviticus 27, one of whose unique features is the inclusion of numerous clauses from which one gains a picture of double laws. The abundance of double laws within the context of the laws of sacred things, notwithstanding the relative scarcity of this phenomenon in biblical law as a whole, indicates the special status enjoyed by the laws of *heqdesh*.

i. The Law of One who Sanctifies a Field of Inheritance: Leviticus 27.16-21
This law opens with Lev. 27.16:

16   If a man dedicates to the LORD part of the land which is his by inheritance, then your valuation shall be according to the seed for it...
19   And if he who dedicates the field wishes to redeem it, then he shall add a fifth of the valuation in money to it, and it shall remain his.
20   But if he does not wish to redeem the field, or if he has sold the field to another man, it shall not be redeemed any more...

Hence, we learn that one who consecrates a field of inheritance can realize its sacred status in a number of ways. The point of departure is that the valuation is determined on the basis of the yield, at the rate of fifty shekels per homer of barley. For purposes of calculation, this law distinguishes between the jubilee year and the years that follow it.

If the one sanctifying the field wishes to redeem it, then 'he shall add

---

45. In practice, the sanction of stigmatizing the one who refuses to perform levirate marriage is seen as a recognition by the legislator that the original demand of the law will not be realized in the future. But whereas in the law of the firstling ass the sanction brings about material loss several times greater than the original demand of the law, in the case of levirate marriage there is no material 'loss', but only a matter of social stigma, because of the ethical dimension of such a refusal. In the extended discussion of this matter in Chapter 2, I note several different aspects of the negative attitude towards those who refuse to perform levirate marriage: from the extreme censure represented in Gen. 38, in which the refusal to discharge this obligation is described in the words 'and what he did was displeasing in the sight of the LORD' (v. 10), to the very liberal attitude displayed in the Book of Ruth (I do not mean to suggest that this is the chronological order of these passages).

a fifth of the valuation in money to it, and it shall remain his'. Should he choose not to redeem the sanctified field, or should he sell it to another person after it was consecrated, there is no longer any way to redeem it and it is lost to its owners. In such a case it becomes sacred property, and is treated '...as a field that has been devoted; the priest shall be in possession of it' (v. 21).

It follows from this analysis that we have here a double law as defined earlier, and that in practice the one sanctifying it has two (or possibly even more) possibilities of action: 'if he wishes to redeem it' (v. 19); 'if he does not wish to redeem the field...' (v. 20). It would therefore appear that the formula 'if he does not wish to redeem...' is intended to introduce the alternative option available to the owners. However, one who failed to redeem that which he sanctified is treated as if he has not fulfilled the spirit of the original sanctification, in that he did not behave as was expected of him. From an analysis of these laws, it clearly follows that the legislator saw the redemption of the field as the preferred option,[46] while one who caused a loss to the sacred things (i.e. by not paying the addition of a fifth to the valuation), in that he did not choose the path preferred by the legislator, may anticipate at least a sentimental loss, involving the loss of the particular field or animal, which will no longer return to his possession.

When we turn to the consecration of a clean animal or the like, the legislator's preference completely changes. According to vv. 9-10, for example, one is required to carry out the consecration, while any attempt to change it will lead to a double loss—of the animal sanctified, and of its substitute.

ii. *One who Sanctifies the Firstling of an Impure Animal: (Lev. 27.27)*
The law of one who sanctifies the firstling of an impure animal likewise appears in this same chapter. Even though its redemption is accomplished by paying the principel with the addition of a fifth, it states alongside it, 'if it is not redeemed, it shall be sold at your valuation' (Lev. 27.27). We thus find once again that non-redemption brings about a smaller material loss ('at your valuation').[47] The same holds true for one who sanctifies an impure animal (Lev. 27.11-13).[48]

46. See B.A. Levine, *Leviticus* (JPS), p. 196, on this verse.
47. See what I have written concerning this issue in Chapter 8, 'The Firstling of Unclean Animals'.
48. The same is true regarding one who sanctifies a house (Lev. 27.15). It should

Examination of the series of laws in Leviticus 27 indicates that, despite the fact that the phenomenon of double laws is not so widespread, there is an unusual abundance of these laws in the chapter in question. This is presumably because of the special character of the sanctification. Owing to the double possibilities proposed in these laws, it would appear that in certain cases (see above) the legislator expects the sacred object to be redeemed rather than being given to the realm of the sacred.[49] Given the particular subject—the *heqdesh*—it would appear that all the double clauses in the laws of sacred things are the original result of the basic law, rather than of a later development.[50]

6. *Evidence for Double Laws in the Ancient Near East*

The explanation suggested in this study can be substantiated by a group of laws from the Hittite laws. In these laws, the existence of two stages is explicitly defined by their author, rather than being merely a scholar's explanation, as is the case in the biblical laws.

Several items in the Hittite laws make explicit mention of the stage prior to the present law. The wording takes the form: 'formerly the punishment was x, but now it is y'. In some of these laws, the king is mentioned as the author of the reform, that is, he initiated the change in the law. In all of these laws, one can see explicit evidence of the fact that

be noted that in this series of laws the order of the options is altered, for some reason: first non-redemption, in an unclear formula, and only thereafter redemption, while in the other laws in this group the clause concerning redemption appears first. Evidently, this is no more than a stylistic variant.

49. On the other hand, the legislator is even more decisive regarding certain objects, utilizing in such cases the sense of ימר: 'he shall not exchange it' or of the root חלף: 'he shall not substitute it'. In all of these laws, the attempt of the owners to negate the duty to sanctify the object costs them twice as much—the value of the object sanctified, as well as that which the owners attempted to substitute for it. This is true both with regard to a clean animal (Lev. 27.10) and to tithes of flock and herd (v. 33; here, there appears the use of the root גאל, but in the negative form, 'he will not redeem'). It is interesting to note that in the law of the *herem* ('ban' or 'devoted thing'; vv. 28-29), the possibility of non-fulfilment of the law is so strict that the legislator assumes that the owners will not even consider such a possibility. In this case, as mentioned above, they also gain no benefit, so that their loss is only that of the object banned. The language, however, is more definitive: 'he shall surely be put to death', 'it is most holy to the LORD'.

50. For further particulars in the laws of sacred things, see Chapter 2, 'The Formula "If he shall not (do)"', etc.

certain laws in their present state reflect a second stage in the history of those laws, whereby the earlier stage was changed though substitution of a different kind of punishment. See, for example, laws 7, 9, 19, 59, 67, 91, and so on.

It is worth noting that there are some cases in the Hittite laws in which corporal and talionic penalties including the death penalty were replaced by a monetary punishment and other means, corresponding exactly to our case in Exod. 21.29-30. The two laws are §§121 and 123. Law 121 reads, 'If anyone, a free man, steals a plow and its owner finds it out, he shall put him upon the...and...Formerly they proceeded in this way, (but) now he shall give six shekels of silver and pledge his estate as security.' The same applies to §123: 'If anyone [steals a cart a...it was formerly considered] a capital crime. [Now...] he shall give three shekels of silver and pledge his estate as security.'

In law 92, corporal punishment was replaced by a payment: 'If anyone steals two beehives or three beehives, formerly (it meant exposure to) bee-sting; now he shall give six shekels of silver', and so on.[51] In laws §§166-67 the death penalty was replaced by a religious ceremony.

All this indicates that the substitution of payment for capital punishment (or the like) was an ordinary practice in the Ancient Near East.[52] Hence, our explanation regarding the phenomenon of 'double laws' is confirmed by these Hittite laws.[53]

---

51. See E. Neufeld, *The Hittite Laws*, pp. 99, 117 and n. 11. On other laws regarding the replacement of the death penalty, see p. 161.

52. P. Artsi, 'Document No. 17', cites a document from Mari in which capital punishment is replaced by a monetary penalty.

53. I have already referred to the issue of the Hittite laws as a parallel phenomenon to the biblical 'double laws' in my unpublished dissertation, Brin, 'The First-Born in Israel' (1971), *passim*, and again in my 1977 paper, 'The Firstling', *JQR* 68 (1977), p. 13 n. 33 (= Chapter 8 of the present book). Alhough the system of two stages of a law is found in the Hittite laws, the situation there differs from the biblical 'double laws': in the Hittite laws, the existence of the second stage is the result of a change in the point of view in Hittite society concerning the outlook on sin, or of economic and sociological changes; see Neufeld, *The Hittite Laws*, §§7, 51, 57, etc. It is worth noting that we do not find the existence of the two stages brought together as alternatives in the Hittite laws. Moreover, we do not find that the person involved (mentioned in the law) may choose how to fulfil the law. As I have proven in the present chapter, the variety of uses of the 'double laws' in the Bible is thus far richer than in Hittite law.

7. *Summary*

The phenomenon of 'double laws' discussed in this chapter is a general term, used to refer to different phenomena in biblical law which led to the creation of laws that have more than one means of being executed.

By the term 'different phenomena', I wish to imply that different causes and tendencies brought about the formation of double laws under various different circumstances, and that the existence of the phenomenon also had different results. Thus, for example, if we compare the history of the law of kidnapping (above, §1.b.ii) and that of the goring ox (above, §1.b.iii), we find that, despite the fact that both laws are included in the collection of laws in the Book of Covenant, the reason and consequence of the inclusion of the second, later stage are entirely different and even opposed in each case.

In the law of kidnapping (Exod. 21.16), the words 'and was found in his possession' were added in the second stage, with the intention of making the earlier law more stringent. In the above discussion, I have demonstrated that the later legislator was responding to a new reality, in which kidnappings where the victim was not sold into the possession of others had become more frequent. But since the earlier law only saw the crime as 'complete' and deserving of the death penalty if the person was both stolen and sold, this could not be true in the case of one who kidnapped without selling the victim. In this latter case, the punishment had to be lighter than the death penalty. Indeed, by a process of elimination we have analyzed Deut. 24.7 in this manner. Once the legislator decided, as mentioned, to make the law more strict, he added the words 'and was found in his possession' to fix the death penalty for kidnapping, regardless of what happened to the victim at a later stage.

On the other hand, the analysis of the law of the goring ox revealed that, whereas in an earlier stage the owner's punishment was death—'its owner shall also be put to death' (Exod. 21.29)—over the course of time, with the institution of the later stage in the law represented by v. 30, the death penalty was revoked and a more suitable, lenient punishment imposed in its place—'a ransom is laid upon him', and so on. We thus find that the results following in the case of the two 'double laws' are entirely different—in one case the later stage is stricter, in the other it is more lenient.

This contrasting development may be explained in a number of different ways, for example, by saying that one is speaking of different authors with different legal outlooks, or that the differing policies were required in response to different social needs, and so on. In the cases in question, at least, I tend to see the varying development as the result of the social situation rather than reflecting the personal predilections of the different authors or a different outlook regarding the subjects discussed in the laws.[54]

In Section 3 above I cited a series of 'double laws' whose common denominator was strictly economic: consideration of the needs of the poorer level of society. While here too, as in §2, we have the addition of a later stage in the law, all of the laws emerged later for the same reason mentioned. For this reason, I have isolated these laws in order to concentrate them within one rubric. In the cases belonging to this group, the alternatives were manifested in practice in such a way that the mainstream population needed to fulfil the basic law, while the needier sector was meant to behave in accordance with the option reserved for it.

In Section 4, I cited laws in which the emergence of a later part did not bring about an alternative method of fulfilling the law, such as we have seen in certain laws in §§1 and 2.[55] Rather, the later stage functions as a threat and sanction against those who do not fulfil that which was described in the basic law; see, for example, the law of the firstling ass.

In Section 5, we discussed a group of laws concerned with a single, unified subject—the laws of sacred things. Here, as in the example in §1, the alternative option is part of the original law—that is, it belongs to the same stage as the original option presented in the law. We thus find that, when the legislator shows preference for a particular way, generally the alternative one, he deliberately intends two means of execution. Because of factors connected with the nature of the laws of sacred things, which are insufficiently clear, these were structured *ab initio* as double laws.

However, it is worth exercising some care with regard to the definition proposed of 'double laws'. This is so because our definition

54. In the summary, I have not included the implications of §2.vii—that is, the issue of the use of the word אֹ in laws, nor the issue of the status of 'motive clauses' in connection with the development of biblical law.

55. I refer here to a number of laws discussed in §§1 and 2, where in some cases the phenomena of doubling did not bring about two alternative ways of carrying out the law. Thus, for example, in the law of kidnapping, the addition of the stringency ונמצא בידו created a new law, whose subject was the death penalty for kidnapping, without any relation to the lot of the person kidnapped.

applies to the literary expression of the law, but does not necessarily hold true as regards their practical execution. To elaborate this point: in a not-insignificant number of laws, there are indeed two ways of executing the law. For example, in §3 we found laws addressed toward the weaker members of society, while other citizens are required to fulfil the regular law in the cases mentioned. There are other double laws, such as the law of animals lost by their owners, in which there is a routine method of execution, alongside another method directed towards those that live far away from the owners.

On the other hand, at times we discovered in our discussion that the doubling of the law is theoretical rather than practical. Thus, for example, in the case of the goring ox, not both laws were actually applied, but only one: the owner of the goring ox paid a penalty. The rule 'and its owner will also be put to death' existed in practice only in very ancient times, while during the stage at which the law 'if a ransom is laid upon him' was added, this became the only punishment observed in effect. The earlier law remained as a kind of dead letter, no longer carried out in its ancient form.

The same holds true for the case of the firstling ass, in which the double law is no more than a sanction threatened by the legislator against those who refuse to carry out the law. Finally, in the case of the law of the tithe, those who lived far from the site of the temple were given an alternative way to carry out the law without being considered transgressors.

Chapter 2

THE FORMULA 'IF HE SHALL NOT (DO)' AND THE PROBLEM
OF SANCTIONS IN BIBLICAL LAW

An entire group of biblical laws contain a clause entertaining the possibility of non-fulfilment of the obligation entailed in the law in question, and its resultant consequences. In this regard, one must distinguish between two different kinds of law:

1. In those cases in which it is required that a person fulfil the instruction of the law in a natural and absolute manner, the clause '(and) if he shall not (do)' (ואם לא יעשה[ו]) refers to the person's refusal to carry out the basic law, or its non-fulfilment for some other reason.

2. This is not the case for those laws which do not involve a mandatory obligation. In such a case, the clause 'if he does not (do)'[1] calls for definition of the nature of the obligation undertaken by the individual. Since the observance of the law in question is not a mandatory obligation, the failure to perform it expressed by the clause 'if he does not (do)' does not bring about a critical situation. In such a case, the legislator is nevertheless interested in clarifying the nature of the obligation.

An example of the first type of law is that of the firstling ass, the performance of which is incumbent upon everyone who owns a first-born ass. The case of the Hebrew maid-servant is an example of the second type, since not every father sells his daughter into servitude, nor does every person buy a maid-servant; anyone who has done so is required to fulfil these conditions, and if not, such-and-such a situation is created.

Following this discussion, in a separate section, we shall examine those passages in which the legislator refers to the non-fulfilment of an obligation deriving from a law belonging to either of these two types,

---

1.   I refer below to the phrase, 'if he shall not (do)', in the abbreviated form of 'if not'; the two are identical.

whether due to economic or other reasons. That is, in certain cases the legislator is aware of the possibility that the law will not be fulfilled, not as a result of the person's deliberate will, but because its performance is practically impossible. In such a case, the legislator mandates the fulfilment of the obligation in a different manner.[2]

Finally, at the end of the chapter, we will discuss the use of the phrase 'if not' in non-legal material.

1. *Introduction: The Use of Terms of Sanction in Law and the Use of 'If Not' as a Language of Oath*

i. *On Languages of Commandment and Punishment*

It is self-evident that the described model above (i.e. the use of the clause 'if he shall not [do]' in laws) is not the only one used by the biblical legislator to threaten with punishment those who fail to fulfil the law. I will exemplify this point by citing various passages that utilize different means of achieving this object, albeit our present discussion is only concerned with the use of the formula 'if he shall not (do)' to indicate refusal to perform the law (or other non-compliance with it), and the sanction stipulated by the law in this context.

Among the verses dealing with this matter are the following:

In Exod. 19.12-13, it is stated in the imperative: 'Take heed that you do not go up into the mountain or touch the border of it', followed by the sanction, 'whoever touches the mountain shall be put to death: no hand shall touch him, but he shall be stoned or shot; whether beast or man, he shall not live'.

Analysis of this passage reveals that the proscription is phrased in absolute terms: 'Whoever touches...', with the punishment specified alongside it. Further on, the language of the prohibition is restated, clearly duplicating that which preceded: 'no hand shall touch him'; and the punishment is reiterated: 'he shall be stoned...' The multiplicity of styles and nuances seems suspect to me, suggesting a combination of different kinds of commands and prohibitions pertaining to the ban on touching the holy mountain. That is, the present text is the product of an

---

2. A comprehensive study of the use of אם, including some of the uses of אם לא, is found in M.J. Mulder, 'Die Partikel "*'im*"'. This article discusses many aspects of the word אם, but not its specific use in legal texts, including the usage אם לא.

editorial redaction of various materials of different styles used to describe the same phenomenon.

In Exod. 35.2, we read: 'Six days shall work be done, but on the seventh day you shall have a holy sabbath of solemn rest to the LORD; whoever does any work on it shall be put to death'. Here, too, we find a command (this time formulated positively) followed by a declarative formula, 'whoever does' (compare the previous 'whoever touches'), with the punishment mentioned alongside it. A more extensive formulation of command and sanction, likewise concerning the Sabbath day, appears in Exod. 31.14-15. There are also other stylistic means of expressing sanction against those who fail to fulfil the law.

ii. *'If Not' as a Language of Oath*
At this point it is worth observing the widespread use of the phrase 'if not' (אם לא), generally at the beginning of a passage, to express an obligation undertaken through an oath. There are two such idioms characteristically used in oaths: one opening with אם, 'if', whose sense is the negation of something, and the other with אם לא, 'if not', implying affirmation. I will cite several verses in which the phrase 'if not' is used in an oath:

Gen. 24.37-38: 'My master made me swear, saying...but you shall (לא אם) go to my father's house and to my kindred, and take a wife for my son'.

Num. 14.35: 'I, the LORD, have spoken: surely this (אם לא) will I do to all this wicked congregation that are gathered together against me'.

2 Sam. 19.14: 'God do so to me and more also, if you are not commander of my army henceforth in place of Joab'.

Ezek. 17.16: 'As I live, says the LORD God, surely in the place where the king dwells who made him king...in Babylon he shall die'.

In the present chapter, we will not concern ourselves with the use of אם לא as a form of oath.

2. *The Meaning of the Clause 'If he will not (do)' in Obligatory Laws*

We shall begin our discussion with the laws belonging to the former above-mentioned group, namely, those containing an obligation to fulfil the law, or in which such obligation is the result of a situation into which a person falls unintentionally (for example, the eating of meat that has died by itself or been torn).

However, we must first note that there are certain usages of '(and)...if not' that are no more than a way of indicating a direction in the law different from that depicted in the previous stages. Hence, this usage has nothing to do with the use of the same phrase to refer to non-performance of the law. I shall note several passages in which this usage appears.[3]

In Exod. 22.6-7, we find a law concerning a person who left property under someone else's care and the property was stolen: 'if the thief is found, he shall pay double'. The law then continues, 'If the thief is not found, the owner of the house shall come near to God [or: "before the judges"]'. It is clear that these verses simply outline the two possibilities with regard to the thief, option B applying whenever option A does not.

In Deut. 20.10, we find a law concerning arrangements for waging war against a city. The lawgiver wishes that one first sue for peace, 'and if its answer to you is peace...' (v. 11), and then goes on to treat the other possibility: 'but if it makes no peace with you' (v. 12).

In Deut. 24.1, in the law of divorce, we read, 'When a man takes a wife and marries her, if then she finds no favor in his eyes because he has found some indecency in her, and he writes her a bill of divorce and puts it in her hand and sends her out of his house...' The difference between this law and the previous one in terms of the use of the component 'if not' is that in this case the word 'if' does not appear in the opening phrase of the passage. However, one should note that this difference is not one of principle, but a stylistic-structural one, because in this case the alternative possibility does not come under the rubric of the rule in question: if a man marries a woman and she does find favor in his eyes, the matter ends there, that is, the marriage simply continues. The application of the present law begins directly with the second option: if the woman does not find favor in his eyes, the law determines what needs to be done for the abrogation of this marriage. This law is thus formulated in an elliptic manner; it is possible, from the rule 'if not', to reconstruct the positive option without difficulty.

Similarly, in the law of the adulterous woman in Num. 5.11-31, the oath administered by the priest to the woman begins with the words: 'If no man has lain with you, and if you have not turned aside to uncleanness, while you were under your husband's authority...',

---

3.   In the examples given in the present section, I have not distinguished between mandatory obligations and the use of this phrase in laws pertaining to voluntary obligations.

followed by, 'But if[4] you have gone astray, though you are under your husband's authority, and if you have defiled yourself...' (vv. 19-20). We may infer from this that there are two possibilities with regard to the woman's behavior. It is interesting that in this case the order is the opposite of the usual one: the negative formulation, 'if you have not (gone astray)', appears first, and only thereafter do we find the positive option, 'if' (כי here is the equivalent of אם). The options generally follow the order of 'if', and only then 'if not'.

But this usage of the phrase 'if not' is not the subject of the present chapter. We are concerned, rather, with those places in which the idiom 'if not' is used to signify non-fulfilment or refusal to comply with that which is required by the law.

i. *The Law of the Firstling Ass*

In the law concerning the firstlings of unclean animals, we read: 'Every firstling of an ass you shall redeem with a lamb, or if you will not redeem it you shall break its neck' (Exod. 13.13; 34.20). Since this is the first law in our discussion, we shall dwell upon the phenomenon in general at some length.

The law states an obligatory way of carrying it out: 'every firstling of an ass you shall redeem with a lamb'. Hence, the question arises with regard to that which is stated further on: why does the legislator allow for an alternative way of fulfilling it—'and if you will not redeem it you shall break its neck'?

But the formula we have just used is inexact, because the wording of the law is not, 'redeem...or break...' From the formulation as written, one may infer that we do not have here two equally valid ways of fulfilling the law. Rather, the second, alternative way is conditional upon the non-fulfilment of the first. Since non-fulfilment of the rule is dependent upon the choice of the owner of the firstling ass, this strengthens the view that the two ways of performing this law are not true alternatives, but that one is dependent upon the other. Moreover, an economic calculation of the respective cost of the two ways of performing this is very interesting: the value of a donkey is several times greater than that of a sheep.[5]

It is therefore more reasonable to interpret the 'alternative' options

---

4. This is an alternative usage to ואם. In practice, a variant form of אם appears in the use of כי, which is an explicit substitute for אם in laws.

5. See below, Chapter 8.

not as two different options for fulfilling the law but as a single unified demand, coupled with a sanction against one who fails to perform the law properly ('and if you do not redeem it'—'redeem' being the language of the initial imperative above—'you shall redeem with a sheep'). Since, as we noted, the value of a donkey is several times greater than that of a sheep, it is clear that what we have here is not a true alternative, but something else, namely, what I would define as a sanction directed against those who fail to fulfil the requirement of the law.

The Rabbis wisely said, 'The Torah did not say [to redeem it] with a sheep to be strict with him, but to make it easier for him' (*b. Ber.* 11a). Compare: 'The commandment of redeeming precedes the commandment of breaking its neck, as is said, "if you will not redeem it you shall break its neck"' (*m. Ber.* 2.7; cf. *Mekilta* on this verse). One can see from these remarks that the rabbis were well aware of the preferred means of execution and the lack of parity between the two methods.

Hence, we may infer from this that the phrase, 'if you will not (redeem)...' is intended as a threat against one who fails to carry out the law properly, by making the monetary loss from the refusal greater than the cost of the normal and proper fulfilment of the law.[6]

ii. *The Law of Eating Carrion or Torn Flesh*
Lev. 17.15 states that a citizen or stranger who eats meat that has died by itself or been torn by beasts 'shall wash his clothes, and bathe himself in water, and be unclean until the evening; then he shall be clean'. This is followed in v. 16 by the formula, 'if not', describing the refusal of the transgressor to bathe himself or to wash his clothes, followed by a description of his punishment, using the language: 'he shall bear his iniquity'. The nature of this punishment is not unequivocal, but is formulated in such a way as to make it clear that it refers to a divine punishment against the sinner.[7] R. Abraham Ibn Ezra emphasizes that

---

6.   The proper relationship between the two parts of the law is discussed at length at the end of Chapter 8.

7.   The phrase עון נשא appears in a series of biblical passages, and does not always have one particular sense, but is variegated. In any event, one may say that it expresses a very severe view, concerned with divine punishment and the like. At times, it would even seem from the context that it alludes to the death penalty. The following are a few passages using this phrase: Exod. 28.43 'lest they bring guilt upon themselves and die'; Lev. 5.17: '...though he does not know it, yet he is guilty and

the intention of this verse is to suggest that he may anticipate his punishment constantly, and adds: 'and he will forgive his transgression through the punishment which God brings upon him'. Regarding the identical language regarding one who eats a peace-offering outside of its proper time, he says: 'this is a punishment which the scripture does not specify'. Rashi, on Lev. 17.15, observes that the punishment will be sent at an appropriate opportunity—for example, if he eats a sacred thing or enters the Temple, and the like. More recent commentators have stressed the strictness of the language used about this punishment.[8] The question is why the legislator used such a serious threat in this case.

One may perhaps offer an explanation here which may apply as well to other laws using the above-mentioned formula: those things which are performed in the privacy of a person's own home are likely to tempt the transgressor to violate the law, thinking that it is impossible to enforce or oversee compliance or non-compliance with the law in the required manner. For this reason, the lawgiver must threaten the person with a punishment that is more severe than the monetary loss entailed in the normal execution of the law. The same is true in our case, as the general words 'he shall bear his iniquity' doubtless imply a divine sanction that is perceived as stricter than the proper fulfilment of the obligations imposed in the basic law, namely: (1) bathing in water; (2) washing his garments and 'being impure till evening'. Against these, 'he shall bear his sin' is obviously far stricter.

iii. *The Law of Levirite Marriage*

A striking example of the refusal to perform a given law is manifested in the law of levirite marriage. The basic rule is stated in Deut. 25.5, 'If brothers dwell together, and one of them dies and has no son, the wife of the dead shall not be married outside the family to a stranger; her husband's brother shall go in to her, and take her as his wife, and perform the duty of a husband's brother to her'. In v. 7, we find a confrontation with the refusal of the levirite to perform his duty; as one might expect, this is formulated with the phrase, 'and if not': 'And if the

---

shall bear his iniquity'; Ezek. 14.10: 'and they shall bear their punishment', referring to the false prophet and those who inquire of him, implying the death penalty, as alluded to in vv. 8-9.

8.   See, for example, *Sifra* on this verse, where the sages conclude on the basis of comparison to Lev. 19.8 that the meaning of the idiom is the punishment of כרת— being cut off. Cf. M. Noth, *Leviticus*, p. 132.

man does not wish to take his brother's wife, then his brother's wife shall go up to the gate of the elders, and say, "My husband's brother refuses...he will not perform the duty of a husband's brother to me"...and if he persists, saying, "I do not wish to take her"...And the name of his house shall be called in Israel, The house of him that had his sandal pulled off' (vv. 7-10).

Once again, one may ask whether this is intended as a sanction against one who refuses, or as an alternative means of fulfilling the law. That is, it is possible that the lawgiver may have assumed *ab initio* that there were two alternative options for fulfilling the law: (1) levirite marriage; (2) non-performance of the levirite marriage, entailing the ceremony of removing the shoe, and so forth (*ḥaliṣah*), signifying that there were none among the members of the family who were prepared to take the widow under their protection, so that in the final analysis she leaves the framework of the family of the deceased.[9]

From an examination of Ruth 4, we see that there were indeed actual cases in which the party involved refused to perform levirite marriage, as in the words of the redeemer. It is interesting that the wording of his refusal is reminiscent of the above basic law: 'but if he is not willing to do the part of the next of kin for you...' (Ruth 3.13). However, in his discussion with the next of kin, Boaz, presumably motivated by feelings of respect and love of peace, uses wording that does not allude to the latter's refusal to redeem: 'If you will redeem it, redeem it; but if you will not [i.e. as stated at the beginning of the passage], tell me, that I may know'. To this the redeemer responds: 'I cannot[10] redeem it for myself, lest I impair my own inheritance' (Ruth 4.4-6).

There were thus personal, social and legal reasons contributing to his refusal or inability to perform the levirite marriage. According to the description given in the Book of Ruth, nobody criticized the redeemer

9. According to Talmudic law, she was allowed to marry any man; see *m. Yeb.* 16.2. However, it is questionable whether in archaic biblical society such things were possible at all. I refer not to the question of the permission to be married 'out', but to whether such a woman could marry at all in practice.

10. The redeemer in Ruth uses the phrase יכל rather than חפץ (i.e. 'able' rather than 'willing')—i.e., unlike the legislator (and unlike the words of Boaz to Ruth, 'but if he is not willing to do the part of the next of kin for you'—Ruth 3.13). One may speculate that perhaps, according to the formula of the law in Deuteronomy, no argument of 'inability' on the part of the brother-in-law is acceptable, and that every case of non-levirite marriage is considered under the rubric of 'and if the man does not wish to take his brother's wife' (Deut. 25.7).

for his refusal to perform the levirite marriage; in the spirit of what is written there, it would appear that the process merely conti nued. In light of the demurral of the nearest redeemer, the way was paved for the next closest relatives to take his place.[11]

In the story concerning Tamar, the wife of Er (i.e. Judah's daughter-in-law), Onan's spilling of his seed on the ground is seen as a refusal to perform levirite marriage, for 'he knew that the offspring would not be his' (Gen. 38.9). The text comments in this act: 'And what he did was displeasing in the sight of the Lord, and he slew him also' (v. 10). This judgment is far stricter than the sanction demanded by the law in Deuteronomy 25.

Were we to arrange the above texts on levirite marriage in order of the seriousness with which they see the refusal to perform levirite marriage, we would find the following: the book of Ruth, the law in Deuteronomy 25, and the story of Judah and his sons.

Returning to the question of the use of the formula 'if not' in Deut. 25.7 ('And if the man does not wish to take his brother's wife...'), it is clearly possible to explain these things as justifying the sanction taken against those who violate the major thrust of the law, that is, the requirement to perform levirite marriage with the widow.[12]

---

11. On the other hand, it is possible that this passage nevertheless implies an element of condemnation of the one who refuses, in that he is designated as 'so-and-so' (פלני אלמני; Ruth 4.1), which is a survival of the erasure of his name, a kind of variant of 'And the name of his house shall be called in Israel, The house of him that had his sandal pulled off' (Deut. 25.10).

12. An echo of the status of the passage concerning the refusal to perform levirate marriage (Deut. 25.7) is implied by the language of *Sifre* on the passage under discussion: 'The commandment of levirite marriage precedes the commandment of *ḥaliṣah* [i.e. removing the sandal]'. The same phrase is used by the rabbis regarding the relation between the two clauses of the law pertaining to the firstling ass ('the commandment of redeeming precedes the commandment of breaking the neck'— *m. Bek.* 1.7; see above on this law). We may infer from this that there are not two alternatives, but one law and a response-punishment of the lawgiver for those who refuse to carry out the law. We likewise find there (*m. Bek.* 1.7) the following wording concerning the female slave: 'The commandment of designating her [i.e. for concubinage to her master] takes precedence over the commandment of redeeming her, as is stated, "...who has designated her for himself, then he shall let her be redeemed" [Exod. 21.8]' (and cf. there regarding Lev. 27.27).

iv. *The Formula of Admonition*
In Deut. 28.58-59, we read: 'If you are not careful to do all the words of this law which are written in this book, that you may fear this glorious and awful name, the LORD your God, then the LORD will bring on you and your offspring extraordinary afflictions...' I would interpret this verse as a general sanction, of the form 'if not', directed against those who violate a law or laws found in 'this book'—that is, in the codex of the Book of Deuteronomy. Compare also Deut. 28.15: 'But if you will not obey the voice of the LORD your God or be careful to do all his commandments and his statutes which I command you this day, then all these curses shall come upon you and overtake you'.

This is likewise the meaning and function of the general verse relating to the laws of the Book of Holiness: 'But if you will not hearken to me, and will not do all these commandments, if you spurn my statutes...so that you will not do all my commandments...I will appoint over you sudden terror, consumption...' (Lev. 26.14-16).

v. *The Law of one who Heard a Voice of Imprecation*
A similar formula appears in Lev. 5.1: 'If any one sins in that he hears a public adjuration to testify and though he is a witness, whether he has seen or come to know the matter, yet does not speak, he shall bear his iniquity'.[13]

One should note that, unlike the previous case, there is no double formula here; the lawgiver omitted the positive law, and sufficed with a formula of violation: 'yet does not speak, he shall bear his iniquity'. We may infer from this that the basic formulation of this law is implied in an elliptic manner[14] by the formula of violation: 'yet does not speak'. That is, it is incumbent upon anyone who hears a voice of approbation, or the like, to bear testimony, and those who do not do so violate the law and have committed a certain sin towards Heaven. Concerning such a person, the severe language is used: 'he shall bear his iniquity' (compare

---

13. Many exegetes have noted that the phrase נשא עונו may be interpreted in light of the parallel expression in v. 2 (and elsewhere) in this passage, from which it follows that the language 'and he shall bear his iniquity' is equivalent to 'and he is guilty' (ואשם). See, for example, D.Z. Hoffmann, *Das Buch Leviticus*, pp. 197-98; N.H. Snaith, *Leviticus*, pp. 47-48.

14. Cf. Ibn Ezra: 'and Scripture spoke in an abbreviated manner, and told us that the witness is required to tell, [by saying that] if he does not tell, he is subject to punishment from God, that he will bear his sin'.

the parallel verse in Prov. 29.24: 'The partner of a thief hates his own
life; he hears the curse, but discloses nothing').

To summarize this first group of laws, I will again formulate the basic
question confronting us: why do we only find clauses of this type—that
is, of 'sanction' against the non-performance of the law—in certain
specific laws (which are brought above), while they do not appear in all
laws? To sharpen our question: modern legislators routinely include
clauses of warning and punishment against those who refuse to obey the
law, whether through acts of commission or omission, in all their laws.
By contrast, in ancient laws we find that such sanctions only exist in a
very limited number of cases. It is therefore worth asking whether there
is any common denominator among those laws which do contain such a
clause of sanction. We have already suggested a partial answer to this
question above; this point shall be discussed further below, as well as in
the summary at the end of the chapter.

3. *The Significance of the Clause, 'If he will not (do)'*
in Voluntary Obligation

In those passages that relate to laws describing the obligations undertaken by a person within the framework of some sort of agreement, we
sometimes find a clause describing the status of the one undertaking this
obligation in relation to the non-fulfilment of one of the basic conditions
of the obligation. We shall now survey a series of passages belonging to
this group of laws.

i. *The Law of the Maid-Servant*
Exod. 21.7 states, 'When a man sells his daughter as a slave...' Among
the circumstances under which she may be freed, it stipulates, 'If he
does not do these three things for her, she shall go out for nothing,
without payment of money' (v. 11).

Two principal answers are given explaining the meaning of the phrase
שְׁלָשׁ־אֵלֶּה, 'these three things': one answer, given by many modern
scholars, applies it to the area of her food, clothing and conjugal rights;
the other, found in various medieval commentators and others, relates
this to the conditions of her service to her master, to his son, or of her
redemption by her master.[15] In either case, the comment, 'and if...he

---

15. See Ibn Ezra's comment on וְאִם in v. 11, and his explanation there against the
interpretation of 'three things' as alluding to food, clothing, etc.

not do' is cardinal in expressing the non-fulfilment of a primary obligation. It expresses the attitude of the legislator to the violation of the law and the sanction entailed therein: whoever does not fulfil the basic obligation, for the sake of which he bought the maidservant from her father, loses his investment: 'She shall go out for nothing, without payment of money' (Exod. 21.11).

As we noted above, among those laws which may be classified as mandatory laws—that is, which are not the result of a voluntarily entailed obligation—we sometimes find a clause articulating a sanction against one who does not carry out the law. I would interpret Exod. 21.11 as a parallel example of a sanction taken against one who does not fulfil the obligation undertaken when he acquired a Hebrew maidservant. In the case of the firstling ass, the execution of the law in the preferred manner is easier than the sanction. The same is true here: if the maid-servant is displeasing to her master, he must free her. In such a case, he at least receives her redemption money, whereas if he keeps her in his house without designating her for himself or his son (i.e. without honoring his obligation to her father), he must free her against his will, without any compensation.

The legislator was concerned about a change in the status of the servant girl from that of a concubine to that of a regular female slave, a change that would violate the conditions of her sale. It is therefore not surprising that he took into account the possibility that the master would refuse to carry out the law—an option that was not unlikely in the social situation described here, in which there existed a parallel status of female slaves without any connection to marriage. The threat invoked against the owners of female servants is intended to warn them that failure to carry out the law would bring a high cost to its violator.

ii. *The Law of Peace Offerings*
The law of peace-offerings of votive or free-will offerings states, 'It shall be eaten on the day that he offers his sacrifice, and on the morrow...but what remains of the flesh of the sacrifice on the third day shall be burned with fire' (Lev. 7.16-17). Again, as in the previous laws, this passage raises the possibility of non-fulfilment of the law, using a formula of the type, 'if not...' 'If any of the flesh...is eaten[16] on the

---

16. The 'positive' formulation, 'and if he will surely eat', is a stylistic substitute for the formula, 'and if he will not (burn)'. See below, §5, on the stylistic substitution

third day, he who offers it shall not be accepted, neither shall it be credited to him; it shall be an abomination, and he who eats of it shall bear his iniquity' (v. 18). The precise nature of this punishment is not stated, but the meaning of such language has already been made clear above in the law of one who eats carrion or torn flesh.[17] Alongside this, there are also mentioned other sins related to the eating of the flesh of the peace-offering, such as eating from the sacrifice while in a state of uncleanness (v. 20) or while unclean as a result of touching human uncleanness or an unclean animal or creature (v. 21). With regard to these two kinds of sin, the punishment is defined as כרת: 'that person shall be cut off from his people'.

One might ask the following question: for what reason did the legislator bother to impose a sanction against the non-fulfilment of the law with regard to the eating of the flesh of the peace-offering beyond the permitted time?[18] My answer is the same as before: perhaps, because the flesh is located within the private domain of the one making the offering (just as the maid-servant is in the domain of her master, and the firstling ass in the domain of its owner), there is a fear that one will be reluctant to burn it (just as the owner of the ass takes pity on the animal, and so forth).

It may be possible to draw from this the general conclusion that, when the violation of the law is easily available and feasible, the legislator threatens a severe sanction. In the two previously-mentioned cases, we learned that the punishment entailed in the sanction is greater than the loss that would occur in proper fulfilment of the law. The same is true here: in its proper execution, the owners are required to burn what remains of the offering. This is perhaps the reason why the legislator used such serious (although not always necessarily concrete) language against the violator of the law: 'he shall bear his guilt'.

In any event, it is worth noting that a parallel formulation of this rule, this time in connection with all kinds of peace offerings, appears in

of positive for negative, in accordance with the formulation of the initial clause in the laws.

17. See above concerning one who eats carrion and torn flesh, where I cited Ibn Ezra's remarks concerning the phrase, 'she will bear her iniquity' in the law of peace offerings. Compare Hoffmann, *Das Buch Leviticus*, p. 252, on v. 19, who explains, in his view, the above expression as alluding to the punishment of *karet*.

18 The sense of my question is based upon the above-mentioned fact, that in most of the laws there is no warning of any sanction at all.

Lev. 19.5-8. Verses 7-8 state, 'If it is eaten at all on the third day, it is an abomination; it will not be accepted, and every one who eats it shall bear his iniquity, because he has profaned a holy thing of the LORD; and that person shall be cut off from his people'. Hence, the general statement, 'he shall bear his iniquity', is interpreted in 19.5-8 in accordance with the punishment stated in 7.20-21.[19]

iii. *The Law of the Captive Woman*

An interesting law in terms of our discussion is that governing the beautiful woman taken captive in war. In such a case, in which one of the soldiers wishes to take her as a wife, he is required to follow a certain procedure, as detailed in the verses. In that sense, I would classify this law as belonging to the group of laws presently under discussion, namely, those stemming from a voluntary obligation. Nobody is required to marry a captive of war; however, if he wishes to do so, one is required to fulfil the stipulations of the law. In this law, too, the phrase 'if not' is used in reference to the non-fulfilment of the primary obligation: 'Then, if you have no (לא אם) delight in her, you shall let her go where she will; but you shall not sell her for money, you shall not treat her as a slave, since you have humiliated her' (Deut. 21.14). In my opinion, this law should be compared to that of the maidservant: in both cases, there is an obligation to enter into a certain form of marriage; there, too, the woman is protected, and if the man reneges or regrets his decision to marry her, he must free her; in both cases, the refusal to fulfil the obligation is cast in the form, '(and) if not...' (לא אם). The difference between the two is that the captive woman is released without any payment, so that the refusal to marry her ('if you have no delight in her') does not entail any direct or explicit sanction. Instead, the legislator simply commands, 'you shall let her go where she will'. This may be

---

19. I see a parallel to the subject under discussion, the law of peace offerings, in Deut. 23.22. As in the case of the peace-offerings, the votive offering is of course not an obligation; nevertheless, one who has taken a vow is required to fulfil it. The formulation in this law is different from that discussed here, in that it does not contain the formula, 'if one does not do', and the like. One may see this as a variant formula: 'When you make a vow to the LORD your God, do not put off fulfilling it, for the LORD your God will require it of you, and you will have incurred guilt'. It seems to me that this is a short formula, similar to the type, '(and if you do not do), and you will have incurred guilt'.

classified as exhortative and persuasive rhetoric, such as is often found in the formulation of laws in Deuteronomy.[20]

iv. *The Group of Laws in Leviticus 27*

Leviticus 27 contains a large group of laws dealing with consecrated things. The common denominator of all these laws is that they belong to the type of 'double laws',[21] in addition to the relationship between the two components of these laws being formulated in the form, 'and if he will not (redeem)', and so on.

We may infer from this that the clause, 'if he does not wish to redeem' (e.g. v. 20), represents a different option regarding the manner of redemption than does the original law: 'if he wishes to redeem...' It follows as a matter of course that the sequel to this clause, 'But if he does not redeem', implies a certain sanction against the owners, whose field 'shall not be redeemed any more...the field ...shall be holy to the LORD, as a field that has been devoted; the priest shall be in possession of it' (vv. 20-21).[22]

From the spirit of the laws of consecration, it would appear that the clause, 'if not', serves a different function from the usual. It no longer refers to the non-performance of the obligation to consecrate, but specifically refers to those cases in which the person *wishes* to fulfil the original obligation ('will not redeem' = to fulfil the original consecration). The sanction thus appears in the usual form of, 'if not', but the true picture is revealed by the verb 'redeem'.[23]

---

20. In the law of the slave in Lev. 25.47-55, Scripture refers to the form of subjugation and the ways of freeing. In this law, there likewise appears the formula, 'If he has not been redeemed in any of these ways, he and his children with him shall go free in the jubilee year' (v. 54). The function of the phrase 'if not' in this passage may be explained as intended to clarify what is meant to be concluded from the first part of the law, namely, that the fact that the slave did not succeed in redeeming himself, nor did any of his relatives manage to redeem him, does not prejudice his right to be freed in the general redemption of the jubilee year. It is self-evident that the language 'if not' does not serve in the law in question as an introduction to any sort of sanction.

21. On this concept, see above, Chapter 1.

22. See Levine, *Leviticus* (JPS), p. 198.

23. On the other hand, the lawgiver is even more decisive regarding certain objects. In these cases he uses the verbs ימר: 'he shall not exchange it' or חלף 'he shall not substitute for it'. In all of these laws, the attempt to violate the committment to consecrate the animal or object in question will cost the owners double—the thing

In all other laws of the Bible referring to a voluntary obligation, there is not a single case in which one finds a sanction imposed against the non-fulfilment of an obligation. One should nevertheless note that one does find formulae using the phrase, '(and) if not', in other laws as well, in a different usage. In section 5 below, we shall examine the status of the phrase, '(and) if not' in such passages.

4. *The Combination 'If Not' and its Substitutes for Designating Inability to Fulfil the Law*

In another group of laws, we find this clause used in relation to the inability of the person to fulfil the law. Within the context of our present discussion, this does not refer to cases of refusal to fulfil the law, but to those in which the person is unable to do so, generally speaking owing to economic reasons.[24]

In Lev. 27.1-8, in the law of consecrations, we find the phrase, 'And if a man is too poor (ואם מך הוא) to pay your valuation, then he shall bring the person before the priest, and the priest shall value him; according to the ability of him who vowed the priest shall value him' (v. 8). The general clause, 'If he is too poor to pay your valuation', is clearly an alternative to the phrase 'if not', just as the lawgiver could have written ואם לא תמצא/תשיג ידו ('if his means do not suffice'). We thus find an economic consideration introduced into the law of assessments, which now determines what is to be done and serves as a substitute for the assessment based upon membership in a particular group of age and gender, which is ordinarily the basis of classification used by the law.[25]

---

consecrated and that which the owners tried to exchange with it. Thus also with regard to a clean animal (v. 10) and tithes of flock and herd (v. 33; here there is also the use of גאל, although in the negative expression, 'it shall not be redeemed'). It is interesting that in the law of the ban (vv. 28-29), the possibility of non-fulfilment of the law is so strict that the lawmaker does not even allow for deliberation on the part of the owners. In this case, there is no choice given, and the material loss is only of the object that was banned; nevertheless, the language used is much more decisive: 'he shall be put to death', 'it is totally consecrated to the LORD'.

24. I discuss these and other similar verses in Chapter 3.

25. Change in the demands of the law because of the involvement of a poor person also appears in the law concerning a pledge in Deut. 24. In v. 12, it states, 'And if he is a poor man, you shall not sleep in his pledge', which is a limitation, that the one holding the pledge is exempt from *prima facie* if the one referred to is not a poor person; but see the discussion of this verse below (Chapter 3 §3).

A particularly interesting case is that of the law of one who seduces a virgin (Exod. 22.15-16). According to the statement of the law, one who seduces an unbetrothed virgin and lies with her is required to take her as his wife. But it may impossible to fulfil this obligation because of the father's refusal to give her to him ('if her father utterly refuses to give her to him'[26] is an alternative wording to 'if he will not [do]' mentioned above). In such a case, the seducer 'shall pay money equivalent to the marriage present for virgins'. Within the context of our present discussion this law is unique, because the inability to fulfil the law is not the result of an economic handicap or the like, but of the interference of a third party. It is interesting to note that even in this case, as in the group of laws mentioned above, the sanction is heavier than proper fulfilment of the law. In the normal execution of the law, the seducer must marry the woman; should it be impossible for him to do so owing to the father's refusal, he is nevertheless required to pay the bride-price without enjoying the benefits of having a wife.[27]

5. *The Formula, 'If...' as an Alternative Language for Non-Fulfilment of the Law, and the Use of 'If Not' for Emphasis Per Se*

It should be noted that clauses of the above-mentioned type can be formulated using the word 'if', and not necessarily 'if not', as we have seen thus far. The difference between the two formulae depends upon the manner of formulation of the primary clause. If it takes the form of a 'do not do' command, then the formula of the violation or non-fulfilment of the law appears in a 'positive' clause: 'and if...' Hence, in the laws of consecration of an animal to God (Lev. 27), in the case of a clean animal, the commandment is formulated in a negative way, 'he shall not substitute anything for it or exchange it, a good for a bad, or a bad for a good' (v. 10). This reflects the tendency of the legislator to

---

26. Compare the discussion of Exod. 7.26-27 below, §6.

27. A special law using the formula 'if not' in the laws of debt appears in Deut. 22.2, regarding the case of one who found an ox or sheep wandering about: 'And if he is not near you, or if you do not know him...' One should note that this is not an example of the formulation, 'if he does not do' (or the like, which is the subject of our discussion); in any event, see the discussion in Chapter 1 above, 'Double Laws in the Bible', in which I discuss other laws in which the lawgiver proposed alternative solutions for those who were unable to carry out the basic law, such as vv. 24-26 in Deut. 14, in which there is a proposal for an alternative way of observing the law of tithes by one who lives far from the chosen city.

insure that the consecration be carried out strictly, where the sanctified animal is perceived as bearing a special status. The violation of the consecration (i.e. its non-fulfilment, or the refusal to fulfil the obligation entailed) is formulated in a 'positive' manner (together with the sanction): 'And if he makes any exchange of beast for beast, then both it and that for which it is exchanged shall be holy'. This should be compared with the sanction found in the law of the firstling ass: 'if you will not redeem it you shall break its neck'. In the case of the firstling ass, the sanction is greater than in the chapter of consecrations, in that there the loss is only one animal in addition to that consecrated, whereas the value of an ass is equivalent to three sheep.[28]

Other examples in which the phrase '(and) if' is used as a secondary language in relation to the phrases of 'if not', which is brought as the main language, appear, for example, in the law of one who strikes a pregnant woman. The language in Exod. 21.23 is: 'if any harm follows', which is used as a secondary clause to the main law, 'and yet no harm follows'—and so on in many other similar cases.[29]

It is worth noting that there are yet other cases in which the phrase, 'if not', functions in a different manner from that described in this chapter.[30] See, for example, Num. 19.12, 'He [i.e. the one who gathers the ashes of the red heifer] shall cleanse himself with the water on the third day and on the seventh day, and so be clean; but if he does not cleanse himself on the third day and on the seventh day, he will not become clean'. It should be noted that the clause beginning 'if he does not' is totally superfluous in this verse, its entire function being one of emphasis. One may already infer from the formulation of the primary clause that the way to achieve purity is through the purification ceremony described, from which one may clearly infer that one who does not do so cannot become clean.

---

28. On a series of additional laws in Lev. 27, in which non-fulfilment of obligation is formulated with the phrase 'if' rather than 'if not', see above, §3, concerning the use of alternatives in laws designating a voluntary obligation.

29. This law is cited here only to exemplify those cases in which the primary clause is formulated with the phrase 'if not' (or the like), while the secondary clauses is formulated 'if'. However, there is no connection to the main question of this chapter: the designation of non-fulfilment of the law and the sanction against it.

30. In addition to the use of the phrase 'if not' for the beginning of oaths, as mentioned above, §1.

6. *Languages of 'If Not' in Non-Legal Material*

Even though our main concern in this chapter is the status of the phrase 'if not' in legal contexts, it is worth examining the use of this combination in certain non-legal textual contexts.

The term 'if not' is used in a variety of narrative material. In the story of the servant of Abraham (Gen. 24), Abraham's instructions to the servant state, 'But if the woman is not willing to follow you, then you will be free of this oath of mine' (v. 8). Similar language is used in v. 41: 'and if they will not give her to you, you will be free from my oath'.

In 1 Sam. 12.15, we read, 'But if you will not hearken to the voice of the Lord, but rebel against the commandment of the LORD, then the hand of the Lord will be against you and your fathers'. Jeremiah says to Zedekiah, in Jer. 38.17-18, 'If you will surrender...then your life shall be spared...But if you do not surrender to the princes of the king of Babylon, then this city shall be given into the hands of the Chaldeans.'

A like formula appears in the command to conquer and settle the land: 'When you pass over the Jordan...then you shall drive out all the inhabitants of the land from before you, and destroy all their figured stones...and you shall take possession of the land and settle in it...But if you do not drive out the inhabitants of the land...' (Num. 33.51-55).

In the story of Dinah's brothers in Shechem, the brothers told the people of Shechem the conditions under which they might marry, with the formula: 'that you will become as we are and every male of you be circumcised...and we will dwell with you...But if you will not listen to us and be circumcised, then we will take our daughter, and we will be gone' (Gen. 34.15-17).

In Jeremiah's prophecy concerning the 'household of the king of Judah', the prophet turns to the royal house with the demand to behave with justice and righteousness:

> Do justice and righteousness, and deliver from the hand of the oppressor him who has been robbed. And do no wrong or violence to the stranger, the fatherless, and the widow...For if you will indeed obey this word, then there shall enter the gates of this house kings who sit on the throne of David...But if you will not heed these words, I swear by myself, says the LORD, that this house shall become a desolation (Jer. 22.3-5).

I would like to discuss in some depth the chapter concerning the tribes of Gad and Reuben: 'So Moses said to them, "If you will do this, if you will take up arms...But if you will not do so, behold, you have sinned

against the LORD; and be sure your sin will find you out"' (Num.
32.20-23). In light of their obligation, 'but we will take up arms, ready to
go before the people of Israel...We will not return to our homes until the
people of Israel have inherited each his inheritance' (vv. 17-18), Moses's
words confirm their obligation in the form of a condition: 'If you will do
this, if you will take up arms...', and so on. (v. 20). The conditional
formulation of Moses' words, which are intended to repeat the
obligation, may also include the formula 'if not' (v. 23). In that case, the
sanction is, 'you have sinned before the LORD; and be sure your sin will
find you out'. This language is reminiscent of what is stated in the law of
one who eats peace-offerings on the third day (Lev. 7.18), or of one
who has not washed affected clothing and bathed in water in the law of
one who eats carrion and torn flesh (Lev. 17). In all these cases, the
sanction is implied in its definition as a sin against God, 'he shall bear his
iniquity'. Even though it does not include any explicit definition of the
nature of the punishment, this threat is very serious.

The text in Numbers 32 is also indicative of the significance of the
sanction clause in laws. The obligation is preserved here, and in connection with its repetition there appears a double formula: positive ('if')
for a case of fulfilling the obligation, and negative ('if not') in relation to
its non-fulfilment. It is thus that one needs to understand the relevant
wording of the law: in those places where the clause regarding sanctions
was preserved, it is based upon an understanding of a negative
condition, directed to one who does not fulfil the law.

In Exod. 7.26, we find the divine commandment addressed to
Pharaoh: 'Let my people go, that they may serve me'. These words
may easily be understood as tantamount to law (although they are presented, as I said, as divine commandments, with all the suitable
differences that apply). It therefore should not be surprising that,
alongside the specific divine command, one finds a sanction imposed
against refusal to obey: 'But if you refuse to let them go, behold, I will
plague all your country with frogs' (Exod. 8.2). In my opinion, the
phrase 'if you refuse' is to be seen as parallel to 'if not' (if a person does
not do as required by law, then...). This constitutes an appropriate
parallel in the realm of the narrative to the legal material in the Bible:
non-response to the law for these or other reasons will bring in its wake
one or another sanction.

From all of the above passages, we may conclude that the phrase 'if
not' is used to complement the explicit use of the phrase 'if' and the

like. These phrases clearly indicate the ambience of a legal situation concerning the fulfilment of obligations phrased with the word 'if...', or of non-obedience to the obligation conveyed by the phrase 'if not'. The fixed legal ambience of all of the uses of 'if not', even in non-legal material, teaches us that those who formulated these passages drew their language from fixed usages whose source lay in the legal realm. Since we find a relationship to the non-fulfilment of the law in a series of laws, it is clear that these passages are the result of a basic knowledge of the law. We therefore receive confirmation of the legal status of the formula 'if not' even from its quasi-legal use in the non-legal material.

7. *Summary*

In this chapter, we have discussed the meaning and status of the clause, 'if he shall not (do)' in biblical law. We found that this formula appears in a number of mandatory laws, as well as in a number of laws concerning voluntarily undertaken obligations. The phrase 'if not' is interpreted in these laws as a warning of the sanction by which the lawgiver threatens those who do not properly fulfil their obligations.

In several places, I questioned why phrases of sanction appear specifically in these laws, and suggested an answer to this question. It seems to me that there are a number of reasons for the absence of such clauses in other laws:

First, it seems to me that a certain role is played by the usual factor of the lack of unity and completeness in the biblical collection, a factor that expresses itself in various ways concerning many different subjects. We therefore cannot infer anything in particular from the fact that the clause in question is absent in other laws.

Secondly, relating to what I said in the previous paragraph, one must remember that, in a body of laws created by a large number of authors, there are in any event different practices concerning this point. On the other hand, the reason for incorporating a clause threatening sanctions, as regards those laws brought into this discussion, is likely to differ from one law to another. Nevertheless, I wish to repeat a particular line, which I mentioned above in several cases:

In several of the discussions of specific laws, I suggested the conjecture that those acts performed in the privacy of a person's home may tempt a person to violate the law, thinking that it is impossible to supervise whether or not he or she has done what is required. In other words, in matters subject to the direct responsibility of the individual, where one is unobserved by any strange eye, one is more likely to be tempted not to fulfil the obligation imposed by the law. This is the case with regard to the firstling of the ass which, because it is an unclean animal and hence not offered upon the altar, might have led some people to think that one could avoid performing the redemption required by law. For this reason, the lawgiver needed to threaten a punishment several times more severe than the loss incurred through the regular execution of the law: 'Every firstling of an ass you shall redeem with a lamb, or if you will not redeem it you shall break its neck' (Exod. 13.13). It follows from this that, as a general rule, the lawgiver threatens serious punishment whenever violation of the law is likely. A sign of this strictness is that the loss to the owners resulting from the sanction is greater than the cost to the owners would be were they to fulfil the law in the normal way. The same is true of the law of peace offerings (which are subject to the control of the owners), in which the eating of the sacrifice is limited to the day of the sacrifice and the following day, whereas that which is left on the third day must be burnt. Again, perhaps because the flesh is found in the possession of the one offering (like the firstling ass in the hands of its owners), there is a suspicion that one may wish to avoid burning it (just as the owners will not wish to lose their ass).

Such an explanation likewise applies to the laws of voluntarily undertaken obligations—see above, §3—such as those regarding the law of the maid-servant. In this case, the legislator warns the owner that, if he does not fulfil his original obligation to the maid servant, he will lose his right to present her for redemption and will need to free her without any compensation.

There may be a common denominator or a number of common elements among those laws containing a sanction clause; however, apart from what I have just mentioned, I have not found any. I have no doubt that the lack of unity or consistency, which I have also noted in this summary, also plays an important role in the incorporation of certain laws and the omission of others from the group under consideration.

Chapter 3

CARING FOR THE POOR IN BIBLICAL LAW

In several biblical laws we find a clause pertaining to the person's inability to carry out the law. It should be noted that these do not pertain to refusal to perform the law,[1] but rather to a situation in which the citizen is unable to perform them, generally speaking by reason of economic hardship. In this chapter we shall examine a number of laws containing a clause of this type, observing its manner of use and the alternative ways of execution proposed in the law. In other parts of the chapter, we shall discuss a series of texts which see the poor person as requiring special protection, an approach that took the form of specific legislation for the poor.

1. *Leniencies in the Laws for Economic Reasons*

In the law of valuations, we read, 'When a man makes a special vow of persons to the LORD at your valuation, then your valuation of a male shall be...fifty shekels of silver...If the person is a female, your valuation shall be thirty shekels. If the person is from five years old up...If the person is from a month old up to five years old...' (Lev. 27.2-6). The list of valuations is arranged by order of age, each age group containing a separate 'valuation' for males and females.

However, at the conclusion of the list of valuations by age and gender, it states, 'And if a man is too poor to pay your valuation, then he shall bring the person before the the priest, and the priest shall value him; according to the ability of him who vowed the priest shall value him' (v. 8). That is, the primary law regarding the valuation of one who had vowed 'a special vow of persons to the LORD at your valuation' (27.2) is unequivocal, the amount of the valuation being based exclusively upon

---

1.   As in the subject of Chapter 2: 'The Formula "If he shall not (do)" and the Problem of Sanctions in Biblical Law'.

the age and sex of the person. The economic clause, 'And if a man is too poor to pay your valuation', is a simple textual variant of the formulae 'if he does not';[2] the legislator could just as easily have written, 'and if he does not have'. Thus, for example, in the law of the woman after childbirth in Lev. 12.8, it states, 'And if she cannot afford a lamb' (see below).

In v. 8 an economic consideration is introduced, which is henceforth the criterion for payment instead of membership in a group by age and gender, the usual basis for classification used by the law. On the basis of the position of the verse in question it is clear that, notwithstanding the fact that it utilizes masculine language, it also refers to the case of a female who is unable to afford the sum required for her valuation. The law uses the masculine form simply because this is the usual practice in the wording of biblical laws.

There are some cases in which the law anticipates *ab initio* that there will be certain people for whom (or situations in which) it is impossible to carry out the law as written, relating to these with the formula, '(and) if he does not' (or the like). Thus, in Lev. 12.8, after stating that the post-natal mother needs to bring a lamb as a burnt offering (and a turtledove or pigeon as a sin offering), it adds, 'and if she cannot afford a lamb'. The categorical language is thus 'corrected' by the use of the formula 'if he does not', the legislator thereby responding to the question of the manner of execution of the law requiring the purification of every new mother (*yoledet*), including poor women. Compare here also Lk. 2.24, on the sacrifice bought by the mother of Jesus.

One should mention in this connection the matter of the sacrifice brought by the leper when he becomes purified from leprosy (Lev. 14.21): 'But if he is poor and cannot afford so much, then he shall take one male lamb...' A comparison with the principal law relating to the purification of the leper brings out the difference: with regard to the first stage, that of the bringing of two living birds and cedarwood and scarlet stuff and hyssop wood and the related ceremonies (vv. 4-9), there is no difference among individuals of different economic situations—presumably based upon the assumption that everyone is able to afford them. However, from the eighth day onwards there is a difference in the ceremonies of purification: whereas the typical citizen must bring three lambs (two males and one female) for a guilt offering, a sin offering and

---

2.   This is the formula of the clause relating to the non-fulfilment of the law, which I analyze in Chapter 2 §4.

a burnt offering, this is not so in the case of the poor person. The legislator allows the latter to bring a single lamb as a purifying guilt offering (here too there is no difference between the poor person and the typical citizen), while the sin offering and burnt offering are in this case performed with two turtledoves or two pigeons, 'such as he can afford' (v. 22).

It should be noted that the phrase 'such as he can afford' in v. 22 evidently refers to the two alternatives of turtledoves and pigeons. Otherwise, this verse presents a difficulty, because it might seem that the legislator raises the possibility that, if one cannot afford even these fowls, one is exempt from bringing them—an interpretation not supported by the present wording of the text.

Further along in this law, in vv. 30-31,[3] Scripture again mentions the difference between turtledoves and pigeons, together with the phrase 'such as he can afford', as mentioned previously in v. 22.[4]

On the other hand, in v. 32 it states in summary manner: 'this is the law for him in whom is a leprous disease, who cannot afford the offerings for his cleansing'. It is clear that the use of the term 'who cannot afford' in this verse is similar to its use at the beginning of the chapter with regard to the poor leper ('but he if he is poor and cannot afford so much'). A general usage of this type likewise appears in the law of the woman following childbirth, 'and if she cannot afford a lamb' (Lev. 12.8), in which her neediness is clearly defined in terms of the size of the sacrifice required, 'a lamb'. Similarly, in the law of valuations, 'and if a man is too poor to pay your valuation...and the priest shall value him; according to the ability of him who vowed the priest shall value him' (Lev. 27.8), the extent of his economic difficulty is stated precisely ('too poor to pay your valuation'), while the solution is likewise clearly formulated in terms of the extent of the economic ability

3.   The phrase 'as much as he can afford' (אות אשר תשיג ידו) does not appear in the LXX or the Peshitta, and some scholars tend to see it as an addition borrowed from v. 30. Compare the interpretations of A. Bertholet, *Leviticus*, p. 48; A. Ehrlich, *Randglossen*, p. 49.

4.   See the interpretation of D.Z. Hoffmann, *Leviticus*, pp. 405-406. According to Hoffmann, the phrase אשר תשיג ידו (or the like) in vv. 22, 30 and 31 refers to the relationship between turtledoves and pigeons. In his view, pigeons are cheaper than turtledoves, the latter being a larger bird; the legislator allows the poor to make do with the smaller (and thus cheaper) pigeon. Regarding v. 31, he believes that the verse comes to stress that one may not bring one turtledove and one pigeon, but two of the same kind of those which 'he can afford'.

3. *Caring for the Poor in Biblical Law* 77

of the specific person making the oath. In this case Scripture likewise utilizes the root נשג, (to afford): 'according to the ability of him who vowed...'

Hence, we find that the law of the leper presents us with two different usages of the term השיג יד: on the one hand, inability to bring an offering as required; on the other hand, a secondary meaning, in the context of the choice between turtledoves and pigeons on the basis of which is the cheaper of the two in terms of one's economic ability ('such as he can afford'). It is superfluous to add that these two usages are totally different from one another.[5]

5. The idiom השיג יד appears twice more in the Bible: in Num. 6.21 and in Ezek. 46.7. In Num. 6.21, we read of the Nazirite. 'This is the law for the Nazirite who takes a vow. His offering to the Lord shall be acording to his vow as a Nazirite, apart from what else he can afford; in accordance with the vow which he takes, so shall he do according to the law for his separation as a Nazirite'. The phrase 'apart from what else he can afford' is intended to imply that the offering in question for the conclusion of the Nazirite state is a kind of minimal obligation, and that the Nazirite with greater wherewithal may add to the offering as much as he can afford. See the interpretations of Rashi and Nahmanides; cf. Milgrom, *Numbers*, pp. 50, 355-58. Ibn Ezra interpreted the above idiom as indicating an obligation on the part of the Nazirite 'that he shall give in accordance with his wealth, and also according to the days of his oath, be they many or few'. That is, the amount specified in the verse is a kind of minimum (as we interpret it), while one who can afford more should bring in accordance with his more fortunate economic situation. The Sages inferred from this that, if the Nazirite is unable to afford the minimal payment of his vow, the community is obligated to help him to defray his obligation. See *b. Tem.* 10a; and cf. Milgrom and other exegetes for the rabbinic sources concerning the assistance given to Nazirites by the leaders and wealthy members of the community, such as *m. Naz.* 2.5; Josephus, *Ant.* 19.294, and cf. Acts 21.24. Examination of the literal meaning of Scripture here reveals that, unlike other uses of the idiom השיג יד, this refers to a person with economic wherewithal, rather than one who is lacking. On the late character of the usage...מלבד ('apart from...')', see I. Knohl, 'Sabbath and Festivals', pp. 144-46, in an appendix to the article. Knohl discusses the late date of the formula מלבד, attributing it to the stage of redaction of the Torah. He believes that, even outside of the Torah, the formula only appears in texts from the time of the Exile and thereafter. I shall not enter here into a substantive critique of his view per se. On the text of this passage, which also includes additions, see also B. Bäntsch, *Numeri*, p. 482.

In Ezek. 46.7, the phrase השיג יד is mentioned in the formula '...and with the lambs as much as he is able'. Whereas the components of the meal offerings that accompany the bull and the ram, mentioned in the new-moon offering of the prince, are formulated exactly, 'as a cereal offering he shall provide an ephah with the bull and an ephah with the ram' (Ezek. 46.7), the compass of the meal offering offered

One might ask whether this double usage is a matter of chance, or whether it may teach us something about the history of the creation of the text, which was not composed all at once, but is probably the outcome of the work of several different redactors, of which this is one result.

Another text that struggles with the question of the economic situation of the poor person appears in the law of the guilt-offering in Leviticus 5. At the beginning of the law, the regular offering to be brought by a person who has committed one of the transgressions listed in that verse is detailed. Thus, in v. 6: 'and he shall bring his guilt offering to the LORD for the sin which he has committed, a female from the flock, a lamb or a goat, for a sin offering'. The legislator here takes account of the person who is unable to shoulder the financial burden, allowing him to suffice with a less expensive sacrifice. The sages designated this sacrifice as 'the ascending and descending offering' (קרבן עולה ויורד), because it considers the economic ability of the one making the offering, going up or down accordingly: 'But if he cannot afford a lamb, then he shall bring, as his guilt offering to the LORD for the sin which he has committed, two turtledoves or two young pigeons, one for a sin offering and the other for a burnt offering' (v. 7). The wording here formulates the choice as a variant between a lamb and two turtledoves or two pigeons, unlike the case of the leper who is purified, where the same matter is presented as a given reality, 'such as he can afford'.

with the sheep is subject to the decision of the prince, according to what is available to him, his means and his wishes. It is interesting that, even in the offering of the Sabbath, which includes lambs in addition to goats, the meal offering accompanying the lambs is formulated in similar language: 'and the cereal offering with the lambs shall be as much as he is able' (v. 5). Perhaps this reflects a special consideration related to the nature of the offering of a lamb. In any event, on the basis of the parallel in v. 5, the phrase 'which he can afford' relates to the means of the prince, in the same spirit as its use in the chapter of the Nazirite, and is not a question of usage in the sense that I use it in the present work. There is no basis for Fabry's suggestion that a distinction should be drawn between מצא יד, which refers in his opinion to one who is unable to give anything, and the usage הישׂ יד, to one who is restricted in payments beyond a certain amount. See H.J. Fabry, 'דל', *TDOT*, III, p. 219. On the interchangable usage of the terms דל and אין ידו משׂנת, see Lev. 14.21, where both terms are used to describe the poverty of an individual. Perhaps we have here a 'double reading' (and see above, where there is an exegetical attempt to explain the necessity of the two languages).

Further along, in v. 11, the case is given of one for whom even the previous leniency is insufficient: 'But if he cannot afford two turtledoves or two young pigeons, then he shall bring, as his offering for the sin which he has committed, a tenth of an ephah of fine flour for a sin offering'. Rabbi Abraham Ibn Ezra interprets the compass of this sacrifice as enough food for one person for one day. It would seem that he meant to say here that the law gives the poor person the maximum possible consideration, in that the amount demanded is one that is feasible even for the poorest members of society. R. Moses Nahmanides thought that such a leniency was invoked here because one is speaking of a person who 'errs in the path of the commandments', rather than of one who has committed a sin culpable of excision (*karet*)—that is, a capital sin. Nahmanides' attention would seem to be directed primarily towards the nature of the sin, rather than towards the economic consideration.[6]

In light of our analysis of the economic clause relating to the status of the one making the offering, one may ask two questions: (1) For what reason did the legislator trouble to introduce the economic factor specifically in these cases? Why is it that in other laws, whose fulfilment also involves a certain element of economic difficulty, there is not a similar solution offered to this problem? (2) What happens to an individual who is unable to fulfil the law even in its 'corrected', considerate form? The law is not formulated in an absolutely liberal formula, such as 'the poor man shall give as much as he can afford', a wording that would have allowed for a total exemption in those cases where necessary. In the present formulation of the laws, there would still be cases in which a poor person would remain in a state of impurity because of being unable to perform the purification ceremony under any circumstances.[7]

6.   See Levine, *Leviticus, ad. loc*. Levine suggests a parallel in Phoenician inscriptions, describing an offering of this type in Carthage of the fourth and third centuries BCE.

7.   The case of the law of valuations is somewhat different, in that nobody asked the poor person to volunteer to pay the valuation. Precisely in this case, the calculation is maximalist: 'and the priest shall value him; according to the ability of him who vowed the priest shall value him' (Lev. 27.8)—which may even go to the extent of a total exemption. This consideration may also have come into play in the law of the Nazirite, which is likewise on the order of a voluntary obligation. I refer to the sages' interpretation of Num. 6.21; cf. n. 5 above. It is quite possible that considerations of this type likewise came into play in certain obligatory laws, such as those of the guilt

I have found yet another variant of the clause concerning inability to carry out the law for economic reasons in Exod. 12.4, in the law of the passover celebrated in Egypt. It states there, 'and if the household is too small for a lamb, then a man and his neighbor next to his house shall take...'[8] I see this as another manifestation of the principle that the law provides an alternative option for those who are unable to carry out the primary command. However, this case differs from the preceding ones in two points: (1) There is no formula 'and if he does not', but rather it states, 'and if the household is too small...' On the basis of the contents of the statement, this language would appear to be a substitute for the previous one. (2) Although no explicit economic reason is given here,

---

offering or of the purifying leper. However, we have noted in our analysis that the legislator took into account the economic hardship of those involved only up to a certain limit. It follows that it is incorrect to assume that if the poor cannot afford even the minimum prescribed (namely, the third level mentioned in the law of the guilt offering, Lev. 5.11, 'a tenth of a ephah of fine flour for a sin offering'), that they may then fulfil their obligation by bringing an offering of what they have. If the author of Lev. 5 reduced his demands from a lamb to a turtledove, and thereafter to a tenth of an ephah of grain, what are we to say of the case of the leper? In that case, there was a concession to economic need in the reduction of the sin offering and burnt offering from two lambs for to two turtledoves, but the legislator makes no concessions either regarding the birds and the other materials used in the ceremony of purification, or in the one lamb required for the guilt offering. One might therefore suggest that the maximalist degree of consideration implied in the law of valuations, and the almost maximal one in the law of guilt offerings, on the one hand, and on the other, the refusal to make any concessions in regard to the lamb for the guilt offering in the law of the leper, are the product of a different legislator, less considerate of the economic situation. Or, alternatively, perhaps we have here a different approach by the same legislator, who adopts different positions as a result of his varying outlooks concerning the nature of the specific obligations in question. That is, it may be that in his opinion leprosy is a situation so filled with impurity that one cannot forego certain minimum demands of the one being purified, for otherwise the impurity cannot be removed. If this view is correct, it is impossible for the poor person who cannot afford a lamb to ever become purified. See Ibn Ezra on Lev. 12.6: 'If the priest does not atone for him, he shall not become pure'. This may be why, in his opinion, the legislator was concerned to assure that even a poor woman can become pure after childbirth, since otherwise she would be likely to remain impure due to her economic inability to bring the obligatory offering. See also Levine, *Leviticus* ('Olam ha-Tanakh), on this verse, pp. 36, 85. For a survey of the stature of the poor people (דל) who are not identical with the poor (עני), see Fabry, 'דל', pp. 219-20.

    8.   Josephus notes the minimal number of ten people needed for ritual purposes (*War* 6.423).

we do have one that is vaguely similar to it, in that the question of the number of members of the household being too few to make it possible to eat an entire lamb is also, in the final analysis, an economic reason. However, matters were not formulated in terms of their poverty ('and if she be too poor', etc.), but through an indirect formula relating to the uneconomical nature, so to speak, of 'wasting' an entire lamb on a small family.

A formula taking into consideration a certain person's inability to make the payment required by law likewise appears in the Dead Sea Scrolls. In 1QS 7.6-8, it states, 'If a man defrauds the community of the Yahad, causing a deficit in its funds, he shall make it good. But if he lacks the means to pay it, he is to be penalized for sixty days.' What is interesting in this source is that even in a case involving an actual sin the legislator is willing to take into consideration the economic situation. In this respect it differs from biblical law, in which the legislator's liberality is only expressed in general laws concerning purification and the like, the legislator being unwilling to exhibit leniency or consideration in the case of sin. But compare the law of the thief who was caught and was unable to pay double, below in Section 2.[9]

2. *Consideration of Economic Situation in the Formulation of Alternative Options in the Laws*

In the law of the thief, we read, 'but if the sun has risen upon him [the thief]...he shall make restitution; if he has nothing, then he shall be sold for his theft' (Exod. 22.2). The thief is obligated to pay the penalty fixed by the legislator; if he is unable to pay, the basic obligation is realized in an alternative manner—namely, by sale into slavery.[10]

On the one hand, we find here a further case of a law that considers the inability of the poor to execute the law as written, owing to

9. In another sense, there is a similarity between this law in the *Rule Scroll* and that of the thief, in that in both cases the monetary penalty is exchanged for a different type of obligation. In the Bible it is by slavery, whereas here it is by expulsion from regular membership in the society of the Yahad. In Chapter 2 above, I cite the case of a man who seduces a virgin and cannot fulfil the requirement of the law to marry the girl because of the father's objections. See the discussion there, Chapter 2 §4.

10. Many exegetes have already commented that this verse was originally located after Exod. 21.37; thus, for example, Bäntsch, *Exodus*, p. 197. But this does not change anything for our purposes, in that the subject discussed there is the fixing of an alternative method of fulfilling it for one who is unable to fulfil the original law.

economic exigencies; on the other hand, because of the serious nature of the matter, involving a crime of theft, the proposed alternative is simply another way of attaining the same economic punishment. For this reason, I have not included this law among those in the first part of this chapter.

The economic formula discussed in Section 1, 'but if he cannot afford...', which appears in the law of the woman purifying herself after childbirth, as well as in other similar languages, repeats itself in a similar formula concerning the male in Lev. 25.28: 'But if he has not sufficient means to get it back for himself...in the jubilee it shall be released'. These phrases appear in the law of the sale of a homestead because of economic misfortune ('if your brother becomes poor'). But even though the reason given is economic, as in the law of the post-natal woman, there is a difference between the two 'and if not' clauses. The law of purification of the woman after childbirth, that of the purification of the leper, and the law of the guilt offering brought for certain specific transgressions, all relate to a general obligation. By contrast, in Leviticus 25, the corresponding clause is intended to indicate an additional option concerning automatic redemption during the jubilee year, referring to the case of one who is unable to raise the requisite sum to redeem the homestead which has been sold—either personally or through a relative.

Early redemption, and in its absence automatic redemption in the jubilee year, are also mentioned in the law of the poor person who was sold into slavery due to economic straits. The same solutions are stated in such a case, albeit in compulsory language: 'after he is sold he may be redeemed' (Lev. 25.48).

3. *Laws Directed to the Poor*

In this section, I shall mention a number of laws initially introduced by the legislator as applicable to the poor alone. In these cases, the economic disabilities of this social group led to the creation of laws intended to show preference to the poor, granting them special privileges in certain areas.[11] I should note that in the present chapter I do not intend to discuss the laws of gifts to the poor, such as those of the

11. It is generally accepted in scholarship that these verses are to be seen not as actual laws but as ethical exhortations with an explicit social tendency. That is, one is not concerned here with laws that can be enforced by the authorities, but with an appeal to the heart of people to behave in accordance with the norm depicted.

corner of the field, gleanings, the forgotten sheaf, and the like. In the law in Deut. 24.10-11 concerning the pledge, it states,

> When you make your neighbor a loan of any sort, you shall not go into his house to fetch his pledge. You shall stand outside, and the man to whom you make the loan shall bring the pledge out to you.

The instructions contained in the law in question are extremely clear. The intention is to protect a man who was forced to leave one of his tools as a pledge; the legislator formulates his regulations in such a way that the poor person will not be embarrassed in front of the members of his household. The regulation barring the creditor from entering the house of his debtor should be interpreted as a prohibition preventing a person from determining which object to take as a pledge. This decision is left to the debtor.

The entire situation is somewhat puzzling. One would have expected that one who needed help from another person and was forced to guarantee a debt by leaving a pledge would go to the home of the creditor in order to arrange the matter, and among other things would bring the object that had been agreed as a pledge. The understanding of this anomaly is evidently rooted in the particular social situation in which the matters are embedded, which we are unable to evaluate precisely.[12]

Further on in this law, in vv. 12-13, it states, 'And if he is a poor man, you shall not sleep in his pledge...you shall restore to him the pledge that he may sleep in his cloak and bless you; and it shall be righteousness to you before the LORD your God'.

Concerning the logic of the law in question, one may well ask whether it is a special instruction to the poor, or whether in practice it is intended to apply to anyone who has given a pledge. If the pledge was given in exchange for a loan, one is presumably dealing with a person who is in difficult financial straits, requiring him to take a loan from the rich person and needing to guarantee it by means of the pledge in question.

---

12. For the resolution of this puzzle, see I.L. Seeligmann, 'Loans', p. 191, and his explanation there of the two opinions regarding the time for taking the pledge. In brief, Seeligmann sees the seizing the pledge as a reaction to non-payment of the debt. Josephus explained the law in question in this manner (*Ant.* 4.268); cf. Rashi *ad loc.*, who stresses that a pledge is not a security given against the loan, but an object taken by the creditor once the borrower has failed to make good on payments. This may help to resolve the puzzlement I noted above concerning the substantive question as to why the creditor comes to the house of the borrower rather than vice versa.

It follows that the phrase 'and if he is a poor man' is superfluous.[13]

In any event, whether the law is meant to apply only to the poor people among those who gave their pledge to the creditor,[14] or whether in practice it applies to all debtors (as in the formula of the law in the Book of Covenant, Exod. 22.25),[15] this law is one that establishes a special arrangement for the poor people (who give pledges), at least in the formal sense. The legislator assumes that the person holding the pledge will not make improper use thereof, and hence it is forbidden for the creditor to sleep in it. It is likewise explicitly stated that one must

13. According to Seeligmann, the words 'and if he is a poor man' are super-fluous; the author may have included them because he sought a way to connect the law with that in Exod. 22.25. The peculiar formulation may have led Josephus to the mistaken conclusion that one is speaking in vv. 10-11 of a wealthy person, as opposed to the 'other', who is a poor borrower (*Ant.* 4.269). Cf. I.L. Seeligmann, p. 195 n. 34.

14. Compare Nahmanides on this verse: 'He is called a poor man when he has not another pledge like it, but if he had two tools of the same kind, he may take one and return one, whether he is a poor man or a wealthy one, with much property'. According to this opinion, the law deals only with one who is truly poor, and does not apply to one who has given a pledge for purposes of securing the loan.

15. There are some scholars who see this as the source of the law in Deuteronomy. In the law in Exodus, we read, 'If ever you take your neighbor's garment in pledge, you shall restore it to him before the sun goes down; for that is his only covering, it is his mantle for his body; in what else shall he sleep? And if he cries to me, I will hear, for I am compassionate' (Exod. 22.25-26). It should be noted that the instruction here applies to all acts of pledge taking, and not only the case in which 'he is a poor man'. However, it clearly follows from the formulation of the law that, in the opinion of the legislator, all those who give pledges against their loans are poor. Note the motive clause, 'for that is his only covering, it is his mantle for his body; in what else shall he sleep?' Furthermore, the rule in Deuteronomy states that the creditor may not sleep with the pledge of the poor, because the latter needs it for a cover in which to sleep. There is no such prohibition in the Book of the Covenant, but instead there appears an explicit statement concerning a general obligation to return the pledge to whoever has given one, so that the poor person may sleep in the pledge. It should further be noted that, whereas Deuteronomy states '...and bless you; and it shall be righteousness to you before the LORD your God' (Deut. 24.13)—that is, that the blessing of the poor person will bring positive divine blessing upon the creditor— in the Book of the Covenant there appears a similar motif in the opposite direction: 'And if he cries to me, I will hear, for I am compassionate' (Exod. 22.26). That is, the cry of the poor to God will bring the divine curse down upon the creditor. Cf. the law of the wages of the hired man in Deut. 24.15: 'lest he cry against you to the LORD, and it be sin in you'.

return the pledge every evening, so that the poor may sleep in their garments. It is unnecessary to add that this law is totally removed from the setting of a commercial way of life, since it would be impossible for life in a commercial society to be conducted in such a manner. This law, which is unique to the pledge belonging to a poor man, complements the approach that is already well known from the law of prohibition of interest—namely, the non-commercial and non-economic nature of the laws of the Torah, as has already been noted by several scholars.[16]

In Deut. 24.14-15 we find another law granting special rights to the poor members of society:

> You shall not oppress a hired servant who is poor and needy, whether he is one of your brethren or one of the sojourners who are in your land within your towns; you shall give him his hire on the day he earns it, before the sun goes down (for he is poor, and sets his heart upon it); lest he cry against you to the LORD, and it be sin in you.

The phrase given as justification, 'for he is poor, and sets his heart upon it; lest he cry against you to the LORD, and it be sin in you', speaks for itself. The very fact of the hired laborer (and his like) being poor entitles him to special protection on the part of the legislator.[17] In the view of the legislator, the day labourer is presumed to be poor, and his employer is proscribed from holding on to the payment due him for his work: 'the sun shall not set on it'. The reason provided by the legislator is a double one; on the one hand, as mentioned, he notes his economic status: 'for he is poor'. On the other hand, he observes that which follows from this—namely, that the poor man will turn towards God, bringing guilt upon the one who postpones paying his wages.

---

16. See M. David, 'The Codex Hammurabi', especially pp. 153-55, 157, concerning Mesopotamia, which was commercial and highly developed, as opposed to the non-commercial character of ancient Israel. Compare with this the interpretation of Driver, *Deuteronomy*, on Deut. 24.10ff. E. Neufeld, 'The Prohibition Against Loans' and M. Gamoran, 'The Biblical Law' wrote in a like vein.

17. Nahmanides, on Deut. 24.14, 'You shall not oppress a hired servant', states, 'Scripture speaks here in terms of what actually happens. There are many stated concerning how things happen, such as "If you loan money to the poor"'. Further on, he cites the *Sifre* on this verse: 'If so, why does it say, "the poor and destitute…"'? I am quicker to punish [offenses regarding] the poor and destitute than [those against] any other person'. It follows that his approach to this verse is that the formulation is contingent, in that it applies to everyone—exactly opposite to the approach he formulated in Deut. 24.12-13, and compare above, n. 14.

The same holds true of the law prohibiting loaning on interest. It should be noted that the opening phrase in the law in the Book of Covenant (Exod. 22.24) already indicates that the legislator (again) formulates his words in a manner giving preference to the poor members of society: 'If you lend money to any of my people[18] with you who is poor, you shall not be to him as a creditor, and you shall not exact interest from him'. The proper interpretation of this law would seem to be, not that it fixes any special behavior towards the poor, but that it speaks in terms of the actuality of events as he understands them; to use the phrase used by the sages, 'Scripture spoke in terms of that which happens'. That is, since those who need loans are generally poor, the legislator imposed certain limitations upon creditors, such as that against acting like a creditor towards the poor or the prohibition against taking interest. One must again remember that one is speaking of the situation in a non-economically oriented society, as noted above. I refer by this to the fact that the legislator seems unaware of the possibility of a loan being made upon a purely commercial basis, such as a loan between merchants. A similar law appears in Deut. 23.20-21.[19]

The law in Deut. 15.1-11 prescribes the abrogation of all debts in the sabbatical year. The immediate consequence of this law is the need for the legislator to be alert to the potential refusal of those who have money from loaning to the poor during the year immediately preceding the year of release: 'Take heed lest there be a base thought in your heart, and you say, "The seventh year, the year of release is near", and your eye be hostile to your poor brother, and you give him nothing, and he cry to the Lord against you, and it be sin in you' (Deut. 15.9). Just as the author of the Book of the Covenant commands, 'If you lend money to any of my people with you who is poor' (Exod. 22.24), the Deuteronomist states here the need to forego commercial considerations and to allow the poor to use the money belonging to the wealthy as a

---

18. Some scholars see the idiom את עמי ('my people') as a variation on the language את העני ('the poor'). See Bäntsch, *Exodus*, p. 202; Seeligmann, 'Loan', p. 198, stresses that עם is sometimes used in the social sense as a synonym for the poor members of society, a usage that differs from the national meaning of the term.

19. Most scholars see the law in Deut. 23.20-21 as later than that of the Book of the Covenant, and based upon it. See, for example, Neufeld, 'The Prohibition', pp. 409-10; even Gamoran, 'The Biblical Law', p. 132, thinks that the laws of interest in Deuteronomy are the latest among the laws of interest. Seeligmann, 'Loan', p. 203, concurs with this.

loan. The legislation of the author of the Book of Covenant is likewise formulated in an explicitly non-commercial manner: 'you shall not be to him as a creditor, and you shall not exact interest from him' (22.24). These two laws are essentially two halves of the same coin, concerned with laws specially for the poor, written with the concern that their rights be given preference above commercial considerations (such as the matter of interest, which is the usual motivation for loaning money in a commercial society, or the unwillingness to undertake high risk loans, the hypothetical consideration of the loaner as the sabbatical year approaches). Both legislators call for maximal consideration of the poor above any other factor.[20]

In the same context, we also find laws barring the oppressing of the stranger (Exod. 22.20 and 23.8; cf. also Lev. 19.33-34) or afflicting the widow and orphan (vv. 21-23), both of which contain a motive clause.[21] But whereas the former mentions Israel's being strangers in Egypt, the latter utilizes a formula that we have already seen in connection with the law of the pledge, namely, that God responds to the cry of the needy and curses one who takes advantage of the weak: 'and they cry out to me, I will surely hear their cry; and my wrath will burn...' (vv. 23-24). Compare the use of the root צעק in the law concerning the pledge: 'and if he cries to me, I will hear, for I am compassionate' (v. 26), and again in the matter of payment of the hired labourer (Deut. 24.15): 'lest he cry against you to the LORD, and it be sin in you'.[22]

One should remark that the laws exemplified here are taken from the immediate literary context—that is, that they belong to a continuous unit in Exodus 22–23.[23] One might also note that most (and perhaps all) of the laws I have cited in the present chapter are formulated in a negative manner, in the sense that they protect the poor by preventing such-and-such an act being done to them. This may also explain the surprise that I

20. According to Seeligmann, 'Loan', p. 198, the words referring to interest in the law in Exod. 22 are to be treated as an addition. In this article, Seeligmann demonstrates that the model of loaning with interest is a later model, as opposed to that of a loan with a pledge, which first appears only in Lev. 25.

21. On the motive clause in biblical law, see Gemser, 'The Importance of the Motive Clause'; R. Sonsino, *Motive Clause*.

22. Compare the statement in n. 15 on the difference among the reasons given in the laws concerning the substance of the appeal to God, and the consequent difference in results.

23. Without entering into details of the claim that there may be more than one unit here, the boundaries of the text are: Exod. 22.20–23.9.

expressed above: is it only forbidden to oppress the stranger, and is one only to refrain from afflicting the orphan and the widow?! The answer is that the legislator mentioned them in particular because, as the weakest members of society, they are most subject to economic and other pressures. For this reason, they are granted protection over and above that granted to others by virtue of a special law, even though the proscriptions mentioned in these laws are generally speaking applicable to all. Rashi explained well: 'The same applies to every person, but the Scripture spoke in terms of that which happens [in fact], because they have little strength and they are commonly oppressed'.[24]

In this context, one should mention two other laws that are brought in this section: 1. 'nor shall you be partial to a poor man in his suit' (Exod. 23.3);[25] 2. 'You shall not pervert the justice due to your poor in his suit' (v. 6).

The common denominator of these two laws (and of those other laws brought together with them) is their concern with appropriate behavior in the judicial realm. These laws are likewise couched in a negative form, as are most of the laws concerning the poor that have been cited in Section 3 of this chapter, as I have already noted.

Despite the superficial impression, there is no contradiction between the two laws: the law 'You shall not pervert the justice due to your poor in his suit' continues in practice the line raised in the law of the poor people which we discussed earlier. That is, the protection of the rights of the poor is given by the lawgiver in that context and place in which there is danger that the poor are liable to suffer discrimination. The uniqueness of this verse is therefore only in the specific realm discussed, and not in the idea itself.

The other law ('nor shall you be partial to a poor man in his suit') is extremely important, in that it draws a clear line between the call to show preference for the poor by the protections granted them through a series of laws, and the warning not to automatically favor individuals in legal disputes simply because they are poor. This is a kind of opposite counterpoint to the argument in Wisdom literature: 'Do not rob the poor, because he is poor, or crush the afflicted at the gate; for the

24. His interpretation of 'You shall not afflict any widow or orphan' (Exod. 22.21).

25. Various scholars have proposed reading the verse as וגדל לא תהדר בריבו ('And a great one you shall not favor in his judgment'; i.e., adding a ג to the word דל). See Fabry, 'דל'.

LORD will plead their cause and despoil of life those who despoil them' (Prov. 22.22-23).[26] That is, one who is likely to be prey to the powerful simply because of poverty is equally not to be preferred in judgment simply because of poverty. A parallel and more complete law[27] appears in the formula of the Book of Holiness: 'You shall not be partial to the poor or defer to the great, but in righteousness shall you judge your neighbor' (Lev. 19.15).

26. The importance of this verse lies in its presentation of the defense of the poor and destitute both in the social arena ('Do not rob the poor') and in the legal arena ('or crush the afflicted at the gate'). The motive clause, 'for the LORD will plead their cause...' reminds one of the legal background ('their cause') and the type of divine intervention, which is also mentioned in the motive clauses in the laws, as discussed above.

27. In that he warns against showing favor to any social group, poor and great alike.

Chapter 4

THE USE OF 'OR' (אֹו) IN BIBLICAL LEGAL TEXTS

The phrase 'or' (אֹו) is used frequently in the Bible to indicate various possibilities that exist concerning the subject under discussion in a given text, to variegate the examples brought, or for other purposes. However, the term אֹו is most commonly used in legal texts. We shall examine below the manner in which אֹו is used in these texts, in order to clarify the broad spectrum of meanings that follow from this usage.

The word אֹו is frequently used in legal texts within the framework of the development of a given law, complementary to or parallel with the term אִם ('if'), in order to indicate the beginning of secondary clauses in the law, alongside כִּי, which serves as the primary opening phrase in many laws.[1] Compare Exod. 21.28-32: 'When (כִּי) an ox gores a man... but if the ox...if a ransom...[or] (אֹו) if it gores a man's son or daughter', and so forth; Exod. 21.35-36: 'When (כִּי) one man's ox hurts...or (אֹו) if it is known...';[2] Lev. 4.22-23: 'When a ruler sins...[or] (אֹו) if the sin...is made known'; Lev. 5.1-3: 'If any one sins in that...or (אֹו) if any one touches an unclean thing...or (אֹו) if he touches human uncleanness...'; vv. 21-22: 'If any one sins...or (אֹו) has found what was lost...'

Other usages appear in such texts, alongside these formal usages. We shall survey below the verses that are concerned with law, and observe the tendencies of the use in these cases. At the end of the chapter, we shall discuss the use of the letter *waw* in the sense of 'or'.

1. See, among other things, S.E. Loewenstamm, '*Mishpat*', p. 626.
2. According to Daube, the phrase 'or if it is known that the ox has been accustomed to gore in the past' (Exod. 21.36), and '[or] if it gores a man's son' (v. 31; and the combination at the end of the laws), indicates that this is an addition to the laws. See D. Daube, *Studies*, pp. 85-86, 106. On the other hand, note the reason cited by Loewenstamm for the use of the phrase 'or' in these writings ('*Shor nagah*', p. 604).

1. אוֹ *to Extend the Applicability of the Law*

One of the uses of the term אוֹ is to support idioms of option for male and female. This formula is used to indicate that, regarding the subject under discussion, the same rule is applicable for both sexes; e.g., 'a man or woman' (Num. 5.6; Deut. 17.2; etc.).

The same holds true for the entire complex of laws pertaining to slavery. It states regarding one who smites his servant, 'When a man strikes his slave, male or female...' (Exod. 21.20)—that is, the female slave is mentioned in concert with the male. This is done to clarify matters, so that one will not gain the impression that the term עבד refers only to a male slave.[3] This may be in contrast to some law that is not extant which speaks of a male servant alone. Such phrases as 'or female slave' appear in Exod. 21.26, 27 and 32 as well.

Among other matters, the law of the slave mentions his marriage to a wife given him by his master. This law states that the offspring, 'sons or daughters', belong to the master; therefore, if the slave wishes to be released, his wife and children must remain with the master (Exod. 21.4). Had this verse used the phrase 'sons' alone, people might think that only male children[4] have some continuity with the master's household, whereas daughters are not included under this rubric. Hence, this phrase informs us that the law is the same in both cases. Here, too,

---

3.   The general rule concerning this matter, according to the approach of the rabbis, appears in *Mekilta de-Rabbi Yishma'el; Neziqin*, ch. 6, p. 269: 'Since all damages in the Torah are taught in general, and Scripture detailed one of them, in that it equated women to men...R. Josiah said: Why does it say "a man or a woman"? Because it says...I only know [that this applies to] a man. To a woman from whence? The Torah says, "a man or a woman". The verse equated the woman to the man regarding all damages in the Torah'. We may assume that these remarks apply generally to the entire legal system, and that their method was to infer from that which was explicit to that which was not explicit. On the other hand, my interest in those laws which include the formula of option is somewhat different, in that I apply it to the laws that include such a formula, and take note of the significance and the reason for its appearance.

4.   Compare, for example, the interpretations of the phrase, 'and has no son', in the law of levirate marriage (Deut. 25.5). Some interpreted the word בן as referring here specifically to a male offspring; see Driver, *Deuteronomy*, p. 382, as against others, who interpreted: 'and he has no seed'. LXX translated בן as σπέρμα; likewise, the rabbis, in *b. B. Bat.* 109a: 'a son and a daughter are the same concerning levirate marriage'; cf. *b. Yeb.* 22b; 35b.

one may also suggest the second proposal previously invoked, namely, that in formulating matters thus, the legislator intended to polemicize against those legal approaches in which only the sons, and not the daughters, remain. This applies equally well to Exod. 21.28, 29.[5]

The same tendency of invoking a broader meaning may be seen in the law of damage caused by grazing animals. The law refers to the destruction of 'a field or vineyard' (22.4) by an animal. Here, too, Scripture presents alternatives, so that the law will not be understood as applying to excessively narrow cases, for example, that one is speaking here only of one who sends an animal to feed in the field of other person implying that, had it been sent to graze in a vineyard or some other place of growth which is not considered a field, the act would not constitute a transgression.[6] The phrase 'he shall make restitution from the best in his own field and in his own vineyard' (Exod. 22.4) is to be understood in a like manner; the phrase ומיטב ('and the best') is used in the sense of או מיטב · ('or the best'). On the use of *waw* (usually translated as 'and') in the sense of א ('or'), see the end of this chapter.[7]

5. Hizkoni explains the reference to the woman, as well as the separate reference to son and daughter in Exod. 21.31, as intended to neutralize the possible claim by the owner of the ox that the woman injured wandered about too much (in that she ought not to have been in public places where oxen pass), or that the son and daughter were not properly supervised by their father. For this reason, the verse specifically mentions that the law applying to them is the same.

6. This reflects the non-formalistic approach of the Bible, as opposed to the system of Roman law. Thus, for example, in Gaius, *Institutiones*, Book IV, *De Actionibus*, §11, we find that *X*, who brought suit against *Y* who destroyed his vines, lost the case because the *Law of the Twelve Tablets* speaks of the destruction of 'trees'. Since he did not phrase his suit thusly, he lost. See F. de Zulueta, *The Institutes of Gaius*, p. 235; see also R. Yaron, *Roman Law*, p. 4.

7. See *Mekilta de-Rabbi Yishma'el*, Neziqin §14, p. 296: '"When a man causes a field or vineyard to be grazed over" [Exod. 22.4]—to hold him accountable for each one separately. "A field or vineyard"—just as a vineyard bears fruits, so [this refers to] a field that bears fruits'. Likewise, in *Mekilta* to Exod. 22.5 (Neziqin §14, p. 297): '"Or the standing grain"—even the tree is implied by this; "or the field"—[you might think he is culpable] even if it licked the dust or even if he had tools within his stacked grain and he lit it? The Torah states, "or the standing grain or the field". Just as the field is...so is the standing grain...'

R. Meir Loeb Malbim (19th cent.) interprets the *Mekilta*'s reading of Exod. 22.5 as follows: 'The word א is brought for division by kind; for were the text to say "the stacked grain and the standing grain and the field", you would think it spoke of these alone. But once it says "or the standing grain", it makes a general division, and

At the beginning of the law of the pit, we find a formula of option: 'When a man leaves a pit open, or when a man digs up it and does not cover it...' (Exod. 21.33). This may be interpreted as combining the two possible manners in which the pit, which is the site of the accident referred to in this law, was 'created'. The law is applicable whether the pit is 'new'—that is, the result of digging by that person, who thereby caused this accident, or whether it is 'old'—that is, it had been dug previously and closed up, and was now reopened, resulting in the accident. The use of the formula of option in this discussion may therefore be seen as extending the applicability of the rule so as to encompass all types of harm caused to animals that fell into the pit (whatever may have been the time of 'creation' and form of the pit).[8]

The formula of option appears a number of times in the bloc of passages in Leviticus 5: 'If any one sin in that he hears a public adjuration to testify and though he is a witness, whether (אוֹ) he has seen or (אוֹ) come to know the matter...' (Lev. 5.1). The definitions of the option are utilized in order to incorporate a wider range of cases in which the witness was involved in an adjuration: through knowledge, seeing, hearing and the like.[9] Subsequently, in vv. 21-22, there appear a

anything which resembles one of the [items] considered falls under its rubric'. His remarks here follow the rule he established in his tractate *Ayelet ha-Shaḥar*, §214: 'The word אוֹ likewise indicates the division into kinds, so that when it says "אוֹ"...it is intended to make a *general division*' (my emphasis); see there for his sources. A comprehensive discussion of the sages' views concerning the word אוֹ appears in Malbim, *ha-Torah veha-Miẓvah*, ibid., on *Parshat va-yiqra* (Leviticus), §312.

8. See *Mekilta de-Rabbi Yishma'el*, Neziqin §11, p. 288: '"When a man leaves a pit open" [Exod. 21.33]—I only know of the case where he leaves it open. From whence do I know [that it applies] should he dig it? Scripture says, "or when a man digs"'. Cf. *b. B. Qam.* 49b, where they ask: 'For what reason does Scripture say, "When he leaves open...or when he digs". If he is culpable for leaving open, how much more so for digging?!', etc. Cf. *Tosafot* to *b. Sanh.* 45a, s.v. *mah bor.*

9. In *Sifra* to Lev. 5.1-4, we find a distinction drawn regarding the uniqueness of the use of אוֹ in this passage, and its comparison to other passages using a similar technique. Compare the text in *b. Šeb.* 33b: 'From whence do we know that it speaks there only of monetary suits? Said R. Eliezer: It states "or"s here and it states "or"s in the case of a pledge [Lev. 5.21-24]. Shall we say that, just as the "or"s spoken of in the case of a pledge only speaks of monetary suit, so too the "or"s stated here only speak of monetary suit? Let the "or"s mentioned in the case of a murderer be a proof: they are "or"s and they do not speak of...One draws an analogy from those "or"s with which there is an oath from "or"s with which there is...The "or"s of a murderer...the "or"s of the unfaithful wife...which are "or"s'. Cf. also *b. Šeb.*

number of possibilities of trespass of faith: 'by deceiving his neighbor in a matter of deposit or security, or though robbery, or if he has oppressed his neighbor or has found what was lost and lied about it'. Compare also v. 23 for other formulae of option.[10]

We have found formulae of option used in a series of laws in explicitly priestly texts. Thus, in the definition of the sister for purposes of the laws of incest, we read, '...the nakedness of your sister, the daughter of your father or the daughter of your mother, whether born at home or born abroad' (Lev. 18.9).[11]

In the law of sacred things, it is forbidden to substitute or exchange an animal that has been consecrated, in whatever direction the substitution may be made: 'good for a bad or a bad for a good' (Lev. 27.10).

The priest who is unfit to perform sacred service is defined on the

34a: 'Rabbah bar Ulla challenged this: "or" "or"? [The case of] oath shall prove, for they are "or"s', etc.

10. The same is true regarding the obligation to lift up an animal which has fallen down by the way (Deut. 22.4): 'your brother's ass or his ox', as well as regarding animals which have been lost, in which the law requires that one return to their owner 'your brother's ox or his sheep' (Deut. 22.1). However, the legislator did not content himself here with this formula of option, but added an expanded formula, in which there is a conglomeration of alternatives: 'And so you shall do with his ass; so you shall do with his garment; so you shall do with any lost thing of your brother's' (v. 3). This expanded formulation, brought in a sort of anaphora, is extremely strange; had this law been incorporated within the Book of the Covenant, the legislator would have presumably used the formula of option 'or', rather than that used here, which is perhaps strictly in the style of the Book of Deuteronomy (cf. Deut. 3.21; 4.5; 7.19; 12.4, 30, 31; 15.17; 20.15; for more on the matter of the Book of Covenant, see the end of this chapter). Even in the matter of the means of release of the Hebrew servant in the version of Leviticus, there is a formula of option: 'one of his brothers may redeem him, or his uncle, or his cousin...or a near kinsman...or if he grows rich he may redeem himself' (Lev. 25.48-49). Earlier, regarding one who bought a servant, a similar formula is brought: 'and sells himself to the stranger or sojourner with you, or to a member of the stranger's family' (v. 47).

The law of manslaughter (Num. 35.16-18) is likewise formulated in a broader manner through the help of a formula of option. Thus, we find here alternative descriptions of the vessel: 'with an intrument of iron...or with a stone in the hand...or with a weapon of wood', as well as of the motivation of the murder: 'from hatred...or in enmity...But [or] if he stabbed him suddenly without enmity, or hurled... without lying in wait...or used a stone...(vv. 20-23).

11. Similarly, in the definition of one who entices others to idolatrous worship (Deut. 13.7): '...or your son, or your daughter, or the wife of your bosom, or your friend...', etc.

basis of the blemishes from which he suffers, which are listed in a formula of option: 'a man blind or lame, or one has has a mutilated face or a limb too long, or a man who has...or a hunchback, or a dwarf, or a man...with crushed testicles' (Lev. 21.18-20). Similarly, the parallel list concerned with ritual impurities of the priest, in Lev. 22.4-9, reads: '...who is a leper or suffers a discharge...[or] whoever touches anything...and whoever...', and so on. Further on, we even find a formula of option defining the types of blemish that disqualify an animal from being fit for an offering: 'animals blind or disabled or mutilated or having a discharge...' (v. 22).[12] The defining 'boundaries' of leprosy in Lev. 13.47-49 are defined in like manner: 'in a garment, whether a woolen or a linen garment, in warp or woof...or...or...or...' (and likewise in vv. 51-53).

Even the ways through which one becomes defiled by contact with a dead body are formulated in this stylistic technique: 'Whoever in the open field touches one who is slain with the sword, or a dead body, or a bone of a man, or a grave...' (Num. 19.16; cf. v. 18). There are still other passages in priestly writings that are formulated thus.

We thus find that the use of a formula of option to define an extended meaning is manifested, apart from explicitly legal texts (laws of damages and the like), in priestly texts. I believe that this latter practice reflects the fact that priestly texts are also in fact a certain kind of legal text. It should nevertheless be noted that the formula of option in these priestly texts is brought in far longer form (that is, in strings containing numerous units, of the type 'or...or...or...') than those in regular laws. Perhaps this reflects the priestly version of the use of the formula of option.

2. אוֹ *to Facilitate Clarification of the Law*

In the above-cited verses, we found that the formula of option is used in order to lend broader meaning to the subject under discussion. We have even noted the ways in which this extention is expressed. In the present

---

12. K. Elliger, *Leviticus*, p. 296, observes the dependence of Lev. 22.22-23 upon 21.18-20, which is formulated, in his opinion, in a rhythmic and original manner. He understands 22.23 to be an addition, noting, among other signs, the disappearance of the formula אוֹ (which still appears in 21.18). 22.24 is understood as a text that was enlarged later, among the proofs of which is the use of the conjunctive *waw* instead of אוֹ (as in ומעוך וכתות ונתוק וכרות, etc.).

section, I shall cite several examples in which the formula of option is used alongside (or instead of) the above use, for other purposes. These occasionally differ, depending upon the nature of the text under discussion.

An interesting meaning follows from the use of אֹו in the law of one who smites a slave and kills him. It is stated there that if he dies 'under his hand, he shall be punished'—'But if the slave survives a day or two, he is not to be punished; for the slave is his money' (Exod. 21.20-21). The formula of option clarifies the principle of the requirement of a certain interval between the beating and the slave's death. Were the legislator to have contended himself with formulating the interval, 'but if he survives for a day...', we would face difficulty in interpeting the meaning of this restriction upon the interval. Such a formula would allow for three possible interpretations: (1) a day, specifically, so that a period less than this does not fall under the rubric of the law; (2) a day or less; (3) a day or more. But since any law must be formulated in a clear and unambiguous manner, the legislator used a formula of option, thereby clarifying his intention entirely.[13] It is true that the phrase, 'dies under his hand' helps us to make an antithetical comparison to the matter of the interval, but the direction and tendency of the law are clarified further (or entirely) by means of the formula of option: if the slave dies immediately (i.e. within a day), the one smiting—the owner—is culpable; if, however, he remains alive for a day or more, he is not culpable.[14]

Another law in which one sees a similar formula is that in Deut. 17.6 and 19.15, where the need for a certain number of witnesses to convict a person is clarified: '...on the evidence of two witnesses or of three witnesses'. The number two alone could have provided us with an

13. According to A. Kahana, the phrase 'a day or two' is to be seen as a combination of two variant texts, which were combined into one formula in the extant version of the law (*Commentary to Exodus*, ad loc.).

14. Abraham Ibn Ezra compares the phrase, 'but if a day or two', with 'on the evidence of two witnesses, or of three witnesses, shall a charge be sustained' (see the related discussion in the body of this chapter), seeing both as expressing the same principle: 'This is what is said: "a day or two", and like it, "on the evidence of two or three witnesses"' (see his commentary to Exod. 21.21). Hizkoni (in his commentary to Exod. 21.21) likewise compares the two laws. S.D. Luzzatto, following the sages, attempts to interpret the meaning of the idiom, arriving at the conclusion that it refers to a time period that is close to one day and to two days—that is, at least one day and one night (i.e. a 24-hour period); see his *Perush la-Torah*, ad loc.

absolute number of witnesses required; for what reason then does it say, 'two or three witnesses'? Both verses explicitly state, 'a single witness shall not prevail...'; 'he shall not be put to death on the evidence of one witness', and so on. It follows from this that it is clear that the court is not to heed the testimony of less than two witnesses, but that if there are more than this, the court is to fix the ruling on the basis of their cumulative testimony. It therefore seems to me that the sense of the idiom giving the option 'two or three' is two or more.[15] For another interpretation of this idiom, see below, in the next section.

One may infer from other passages that the use of the formula of option 'A or B' may imply, not only of A and B alone (as in the examples of male slave/female slave; son/daughter, etc.), but that one

15. R. Yaron believes that the formula 'x or $x+1$' in the law is intended to indicate that x is not meant as an exact number, but that the law is applicable both in the case of x and greater than it; see his Review of *Les lois assyriennes*, by G. Cardascia, p. 556. Compare Jackson, who surveys the structure 'x or $x+1$' extensively, arriving at the conclusion that the portion 'or $x+1$' is the outcome of the tendency of a later law to achieve completeness and clarity regarding the subject of the law (J.B. Jackson, *Essays*, ch. 6: 'Two or Three Witnesses', pp. 153-71, esp. pp. 158, 161, 168). See also the summary of Loewenstamm, who believes that such phrases as 'if he survives a day or two' and 'two witnesses or three witnesses' reflect everyday patterns of speech (Loewenstamm, *Comparative Studies*, pp. 443-44). But perhaps the expression may be interpreted another way? The formula, 'two witnesses or three witnesses' presents a certain difficulty for the sages and the traditional commentators. We read in *b. Mak.* 5b: 'Rabbi Akiba said: "on the evidence of two witnesses or of three witnesses". If testimony is sustained by two, why did the verse specify three? The third witness was added here, [not to diminish his responsibility,] but to render it as serious for him, and to make his legal liability equal to that of the others. In *b. B. Bat.* 160b, this verse was invoked as referring to two kinds of documents: 'two [witnesses are required] for a simple writ, and three for one that is tied'. Compare also Rashi to Deut. 17.6. According to Nahmanides, two witnesses are sufficient if there is not a third one, but if there are three, one must bring the third. Ibn Ezra explains the idiom as referring to a case in which the testimonies of one pair of witnesses contradict another, in which event the group of three witnesses is decisive. S.D. Luzzatto, like Ramban, infers from this combination that it is a mizvah to seek more and more witnesses—that is, to bring as many witnesses as possible, so as to clarify the matter.

According to Y. Yadin, one may infer from CD 9.16-20. that the death sentence 'on the testimony...or of three witnesses' is applied by the Qumran sect following an accumulation of three separate cases of transgressions punishable by death, where in each case there is only one witness; but there are also other interpretations of this. See Y. Yadin, *The Temple Scroll*, I, pp. 290-291 (and bibliography there).

may even derive from this a broader picture than from A and from B together. In other words, it is a way of expressing a comprehensive inclusion of details concerning the matter at hand. To this type belong the formulae of option that appear in the law of guardians (Exod. 22.9-14). There are listed here various kinds of animals that need to be watched: 'an ass or an ox or a sheep or any beast to keep'. This is an expanded formula of option, encompassing the entirety of all domestic animals. The 'broad' nature of the oath taken may be seen from the statement: 'whether he has not put his hand to his neighbor's property' (29.10). This declaration already appears in the previous law (29.7). The meaning of the idiom, 'his neighbor's property' is extremely wide. Hence all possible objects that are subject to watching are encompassed therein, even beyond those explicitly mentioned in v. 9.

The matter of the 'destiny' of the animal given to be watched is likewise expressed in a formula of option: 'and it dies or is hurt or is driven away' (v. 9). The three possibilities mentioned here are incorporated within the framework of the law and, according to my approach, we find that, by virtue of this formula, even the other negative things that can happen to animals are included here automatically. See also v. 13, in the law of the borrower, in which the destiny of the animal left with a person is expressed by the formula of option 'is hurt or dies';[16] in my opinion, here too the other possibilities are all included, even though only two possibilities (among the three mentioned in the previous law) are mentioned here. Regarding this, compare the law of one who steals an animal, in which there appear two formulae of option: 'If a man steals an ox or a sheep, and kills it or sells it' (Exod. 21.37). The first option is concerned with the species of animal stolen, while the second formula includes two possibilities, slaughter or sale (while still alive) of the animal stolen. The picture that follows from this formula of option is of an animal that cannot be returned to its owners in proper condition, either because it has been slaughtered or because it is no longer in the thief's possession. This clear picture is also created by virtue of the formula of option.

16. A document from Nuzi contains a parallel to the biblical law of the animal that was harmed. There appears there a formula that is a *hendiadys*, from which it follows that the biblical idiom, 'and it is hurt or dies' may be seen as a formula of the type 'hurt and dies'. But see the remarks of S.M. Paul, who finds it preferable to explain the expression as a phrase indicating alternatives (*Studies*, pp. 94-95 and n. 6, and see the bibliography there).

3. אֹו *as Indicating the History of the Formation of the Law*

A third type of formula of option originated, in my opinion, in a development that occurred within the framework of a particular law. I shall exemplify this by the practice of making a hole in the ear of a slave. In Deut. 15.17, we read: 'and thrust it through his ear into the door', while in Exod. 21.6 it states: 'he shall bring him to the door or the doorpost'—that is, a formula of option mentioning either the door and the doorpost. Unlike the above-mentioned passages, it seems to me that this formula does not merely entail an expansion of its applicability (although this is also included *ipso facto*, that is, not only the door, but also the doorpost, is considered a proper object for performing the ritual awling); rather, given the parallel in the Book of Deuteronomy, which retains only a part of the formula, it seems reasonable to assume that the formula of option emerged during the process of creation of the law. That is, in one source the formula was 'door' (as clearly reflected in the formula from Deuteronomy regarding our matter), whereas in another source the reading was 'doorpost'. The two versions are united in Exodus 21, in which the two previous versions are combined into one version, through a formula of option. One may also possibly 'forego' one stage if we conjecture that the formula of option was formulated at the same time that the reading 'doorpost' emerged, thus describing it as involving two stages rather than three.

The passage in Exod. 21.18 concerning an argument between two men, in which one smites his fellow 'with a stone or with his fist', can likewise be explained in a similar manner, that is, that there was one version reading 'with a stone' and another 'with his fist', and the formula of option combined the two. Here too, one may entertain the possibility that the formula of option was already present in the original stage, its tendency being to expand the meaning of the verse, so that it would not be interpreted as dealing specifically with a stone per se.[17]

I explained earlier that the formulation of the number of witnesses (Deut. 17.6; 19.15) is analogous to 'but if he survives for a day or two'

---

17. The broad approach, according to which the formula of option ought to be interpreted, is well represented in the remarks of the sages in *Mekilta de-Rabbi Yishma'el*, Neziqin §6, p. 269: '[Might we think that] with a stone or his fist he is held culpable, and by any other thing he is exempt? The Torah states "or with a stone held in the hand", etc. This teaches that he is not held culpable until he strikes him with an object that is capable of killing' (that is, not only with a stone or with his fist).

(in the law of one who smites his servant so that he dies): that is, the testimony of one witness is not accepted, but that of two or more is accepted. However, this interpretation seems to me somewhat weak, since in the case of one who smites his slave one needs to mention 'a day or two' in order to clarify the meaning of the law (i.e. one day or more), whereas here it is explicitly stated, 'a single witness shall not prevail' (Deut. 19.15), from which it logically follows that two are permitted.[18] It therefore seems preferable to me to accept another interpretation, similar to that which we learned concerning the door or the doorpost, the stone or the fist, and the like, namely, that we have here a law that is combined from two different levels. According to one approach, one must bring two witnesses for purposes of testimony, while according to another approach one needs three; both versions appear in the combined formula. This solution is facilitated by the use of a formula of option, which does not seem to play a real function in the explication of the law save for the sustaining of the choice per se. It is clear, however, that this choice is in fact of no significance with regard to practical matters. On the contrary, the attempt to sustain that which is written herein is likely to confuse, however you look at it: if two witnesses are sufficient, for what reason does one need three? And if three are required, why are two mentioned?

4. *Auxiliary Conclusions*

i. The formula of option discussed in this chapter is not unique to Israel. Even an extremely superficial examination will reveal its use in other law codes of the ancient Near East. Thus, for example, in the Laws of Eshnunna, §40 concerns one who purchased a male-slave, a female slave, a bull or any merchandise; §49 speaks of the theft of a male or female slave; §50 speaks of different functionaries: a ruler, the prince of the canal, or another official; and so on and so forth.

18. The version of Num. 35.30, 'If any one kills a person, the murderer shall be put to death on the evidence of witnesses; but no person shall be put to death on the testimony of one witness', proves that it is sufficient to state that one witness is inadeqate, to make it clear that the law is decided by at least two witnesses. According to G. von Rad, Deut. 19.15, 'a single witness shall not prevail...', should be seen as the original formula, while everything about two or three witnesses is a much later exegetical expansion. He also finds a number of levels within this expansion (*Deuteronomy*, p. 128).

In the *Laws of Hammurabi* §6, we hear of a temple or a palace; §7 speaks of so-and-so who bought or received into his possession silver or gold or a male servant or a female servant or a lamb or a sheep or an ass or any other thing; §8 concerns a bull or a sheep or an ass or a boat, and so on in other laws.

In any event, one may note that the existence of formulae of option *per se* does not necessarily imply that all the varieties of use enumerated above existed there. Rather, it seems to me that here it is no more than a technical use.

ii. The biblical passages containing the formula of option are generally speaking found within the legal sections of the Torah. Of all the collections of laws, it seems to me that the Book of the Covenant (Exod. 21–23) is richest in expressions of this type. This leads one to the conclusion that this is yet another of a series of stylistic-ideological features characteristic of the code of the Book of Covenant. The term אוֹ ('or') is used more extensively in the Book of Covenant (28×) than it is in the law-code of Deuteronomy (26×), despite the fact that the latter is several times larger than that of the Book of Covenant.

5. *Appendix: Waw in the Sense of 'Or' in the Bible*[19]

We may expand the circle of passages that fall under the rubric of our study by including certain legal texts in the Bible in which *waw* appears in the sense of 'or'. I will enumerate here a number of such passages; it is not my intention to provide a comprehensive list of all the uses of *waw* as 'or', but simply to note some exemplary texts.

The very existence of *waw* in such a status may make sense from analysis of the texts in which this form appears. Thus, in Exod. 21.15, 'Whoever strikes his father and his mother (וְאִמּוֹ) shall be put to death'. It is clear that the intention is not only that one who strikes both of them is to be considered a sinner, but that וְאִמּוֹ is understood here in the sense of 'or his mother'; see Rashi's comment *ad loc.*, 'either one or the other'. This was evidently likewise also the intention of Ibn Ezra when he said that '[the word] "strikes" serves for the other'—that is, that this verse

---

19. On the problem of *ù* in Akkadian, which may sometimes be interpreted as a conjunction and at others as articulating an alternative ('or'), see R. Yaron, *The Laws of Eshnunna*, pp. 15-16. Cf. Paul, *Studies*, p. 94 n. 6, concerning the Akkadian *ù* and its parallels in Hebrew.

is to be read as if it were written 'one who hits his father and/or (hits) his mother'. This is in fact the interpretation of all the exegetes and the translations (such as the LXX). This is likewise stated in the *Mekilta* (to Exod. 21.17): 'Meaning both of them together, and meaning each in their own right', and so on. Compare also *Sifra, Qedoshim* (to Lev. 20.9): 'Might it be that he is not accountable until he curses both of them at the same time?...'[20]

Such a use of *waw* may also be present in the following verse[21]— Exod. 21.16, 'Whoever steals a man, whether he sells him or (ונמצא בידו) is found in possession of him', and so forth. The double formulation (he is sold and/or he is found in possession) is intended to teach that the punishment for kidnapping is death, whether the victim was sold or whether he continued to hold the person. It is clear that the *waw* in the word ונמצא is not to be interpreted as a conjunctive *waw* (= and), for if he sold him he cannot continue to hold him; it follows that ונמצא is equivalent to 'or he is found'.[22]

But there are also substitutions of *waw* for או that emerge through comparison of the Masoretic text with other versions. The substitutions may involve ואו for או or vice versa. Thus, in Lev. 22.28, 'and whether the mother is a cow or a ewe, you shall not kill both her and her young on one day'. In the Samaritan text and in several manuscripts of the Septuagint, the reading there, instead of שור או שה, is ושור ושה ('a cow and a ewe'). Likewise, in 11QTemple 52.6, 'a cow and a ewe, it and its young, you shall not sacrifice on one day'. A similar phenomenon appears also in 11QTemple 64.8, 'according to two witnesses and according to three witnesses', while in the Masoretic tradition the same law reads, 'according to two witnesses or according to three witnesses'

---

20. On the reading of *abiša ù umiša* as either 'her father and her mother' or 'her father or her mother' in the *Laws of Eshnunna* §§26–28, see Yaron, pp. 96-97. For a comparison to the problems that arise in Exod. 21.15, see *ibid*. n. 62, where there are further parallels to this subject. On the equation of *waw* with או or the like in rabbinic literature, see Malbim, *ha-Torah veha-Miẓvah*, II, pp. 1024-25.

21. We find there an interesting situation, in which this usage of *waw* appears in a small collection of three consecutive verses: 'Whoever strikes his father or his mother... whether he sells him or is found in possession... Whoever curses his father or his mother' (Exod. 21.15-17). Cassuto, in his commentary, compares the *waw* of ונמצא בידו to the *waw* of ואמו; see Cassuto, *Commentary, ad loc.*

22. See what I have written on this subject above, Chapter 1, §2.i.

(Deut. 19.15; cf. 17.6).[23] Finally, in 11QTemple 65.9 we read, 'the father of the young woman or her mother', while the biblical parallel, in Deut. 22.15, is 'the father of the young woman and her mother'.

23. But in 11QTemple 61.6-7, the law of the witnesses appears a second time, this time adhering to the Masoretic formula, 'according to two witnesses or three witnesses', etc. In a comprehensive study of the *Temple Scroll*, I explain the author's approach regarding verses that appear more than once in the scroll. See Brin, 'The Bible in the Temple Scroll'.

Chapter 5

BIBLICAL LAWS IN THE DEAD SEA SCROLLS

Continuing my earlier work on the *Temple Scroll*,[1] I shall now discuss a
series of texts from the Dead Sea Scrolls that illuminate the approach of
the sect to biblical law, and the manner in which these laws were
reworked within the sectarian framework. The texts to be discussed
concern the laws of passover, the laws of incest, and laws pertaining to
prophets and prophecy. Within the framework of this chapter, I intend
to explain the image of biblical law reflected within the Qumran
documents, and thereby reconstruct the growth of the law within the
framework of the sect's writings. Towards this end, we shall attempt to
understand the reasons that led the sectarian authors to deviate from the
position of the original biblical law. All this, as I said, will be exemplified
in terms of three issues, the first two taken from the *Temple Scroll* and
4Q251, and the latter taken from a new document, published only
recently (4Q375). The laws encompass a variety of subjects: laws of the
festivals (Passover), laws of marriage and forbidden relations, and the law
of the prophet (the source of which is in Deut. 13.2-6).

1. *The Law of Passover*

In the *Temple Scroll*, 11QTemple 17.6-9, the law of the Passover
appears as follows:

ועש[ו [בארבע]ה עשר בחודש הראישן [בין הערביים]	6
פסח לה' [וזבחו לפני מנחת הערב וזבחו [במועדו(?)]	7
מבן עשרי[ם] שנה ומעלה יעשו אותו ואכלוהו בלילה	8
בחצרות [ה]קודש והשכימו והלכו איש לאוהלו	9

1.   See G. Brin, 'Linguistic Notes'; *idem*, 'The Bible as Reflected in the Temple
Scroll'; *idem*, 'Concerning some Uses'.

(6) [And let] them [keep] on [the four]teenth of the first month, [in the evening],

(7) The LORD's [passover]; and they shall sacrifice before the evening sacrifice. And they shall sacrifice [(it) at its appointed time (?)]

(8) from twent[y] years old and upwards they shall keep it; and let them eat it at night

(9) in the courts of [the] ho[l]y (place). And they shall rise early, and every man shall go to his tent [   ].[2]

This law is composed in an explicitly mosaic fashion, following the author's usual approach, which has been demonstrated by Yadin in detail in his edition of the scroll, and which I have shown in my articles.[3]

Let me exemplify my remarks with regard to the law in question:

The material on line 6: '[And let] them [keep] on [the four]teenth of the first month, [in the evening]', is taken from Num. 9.3: 'On the fourteenth day of this month, in the evening, you shall keep it at its appointed time...you shall keep it'. Compare v. 2: 'Let the people of Israel keep the passover at its appointed time'.

The statement in v. 8, 'from twent[y] years old and upwards', does not appear in any of the traditional biblical texts concerning the subject of Passover, but is a well-known biblical phrase, used in the matter of the half-shekel, the census and elsewhere. Compare Exod. 30.14: 'Every one who is numbered in the census, from twenty years old and upward, shall give the LORD's offering'; Num. 1.3: 'from twenty years old and upward, all in Israel who are able to go forth to arm, you and Aaron shall number them, company by company'; and other passages.[4]

The statement further on in line 8, 'they shall keep it', likewise appears in Exod. 12.47 in the context of performing the Passover: '(all)...shall keep it'.

At the end of line 8, we read, 'and let them eat it at night', following the statement made in Exod. 12.8, 10 about the Passover of Egypt: 'They shall eat the flesh that night...and you shall let none of it remain until the morning, any thing that remains until the morning you shall burn'.

Line 9: 'And they shall rise early, and every man shall go to his tent', is clearly influenced by Deut. 16.7: '...and in the morning you shall turn and go to your tents'.

2.   Yadin, *Temple Scroll*, II, pp. 73-74.
3.   Brin, 'The Bible as Reflected'; and in 'Concerning', *passim*.
4.   See Brin, 'The Formula, "From...and Onward..." '.

i. *The Choice of Sources for the Law of Passover*

The above survey indicates that the author utilized biblical sources, combined in mosaic fashion within his textual framework. The manner by which he chose these for the law in question, as he did with regard to other laws, indicates his great expertise in the sources and his deliberate choice of those that were most suitable to his purpose. By tracing the method through which he sifted out those which he chose to use, we may learn something of his ideas.

Let us open our discussion with line 6. The Bible contains a series of different texts concerning the subject of the Passover sacrifice, from among which our author chose Num. 9.2-5. The principal subject of this passage is the second Passover, the regular Passover being invoked in this text only in order to define the unique status of the second Passover. This fact makes us question the reason as to why, of all the texts concerned with Passover, our author specifically used this relatively marginal one.

Let us briefly survey the other texts on Passover that he could have used, and his probable considerations for rejecting them. Exodus 12 is primarily concerned with the Passover celebrated in Egypt at the time of the Exodus. Thus, even the more general verses in this chapter are 'contaminated' by the concerns of those texts that are unique to the Passover of Egypt—namely, the preparation of the Paschal sacrifice on the level of the family. But since our author adopted a post-Deuteronomist approach, whose very essence demanded a ceremony connected to the Temple, he refrained from beginning his words with Exodus 12.

The law in Leviticus 23 is quite brief and does not examine the subject of the sacrifice in any detail, even though this is the focus of his approach. Hence, he merely states there in a single isolated verse: 'In the first month, on the fourteenth day of the month in the evening, is the LORD's passover' (Lev. 23.5; the same text appears, with minor changes, in Num. 28.16).

The text in Deuteronomy combines the Passover and the Feast of Unleavened Bread, in a formulation that is both extensive and homiletical. Hence, it is likewise unsuitable for the author of this scroll, who needs to give a brief but comprehensive description of the festival. This, despite the fact that in terms of the method of executing the sacrifice the author follows the approach of centralization, which requires the bringing of the sacrifice to the Temple city.

In light of all these factors, the deliberate choice of the text in Num. 9.2-3 becomes clear. This text includes a brief order to make the Passover, preparatory to the primary law of this text, which is concerned with the second Passover. The identification of our text with Num. 9.3 is further supported by the fact that, of all the biblical passages concerning Passover, only here does there appear the linguistic construction 'on the fourteenth day of the month (בחדש)', also used by the *Temple Scroll* (in Lev. 23.5 the wording is לחדש). Moreover, in the LXX to v. 3 there likewise appears the phrase 'in the first (month)' = τοῦ πρώτου, as in the scroll.[5]

The invocation according to the instruction of God (27.1) is addressed to the entire people. This text in any event represents the general-national aspect, and not merely the priestly-cultic. This is shown by the use of the plural form: 'they shall sacrifice' (l. 7) and presumably also, 'let] them [keep]' (l. 6), as well as 'they shall keep it and let them eat it...and they shall rise early, and every man shall go to his tent' (ll. 8-9).

ii. *The Time for Offering the Passover Sacrifice*
The time for the sacrifice is formulated in our text as 'and they shall sacrifice before the evening sacrifice', whereas in the Bible it states, 'in the evening you shall keep it' (Num. 9.3; cf. Lev. 23.5, and also Exod. 12.6, regarding the Passover of Egypt). Compare also Deut. 16.6: 'there you shall offer the Passover sacrifice, in the evening at the going down of the sun, at the time you came out of Egypt', which we shall discuss further below. The Rabbis ruled that the Passover sacrifice is offered after the daily afternoon sacrifice (*m. Pes.* 5.1). Thus, the scroll took a clearly different approach, presumably representing the position of one of the sects of the Second Temple period.

iii. *The Time of Eating the Passover*
Regarding the question of the time of eating, the scroll states, 'let them eat it at night' (l. 8), similar to the requirement of biblical law, 'they shall eat the flesh that night' (Exod. 12.8). Note the continuation of that same verse, 'And you shall let none of it remain until the morning, anything that remains until the morning you shall burn' (v. 10), and compare 'They shall leave none of it until the morning' (Num. 9.12). While this latter text in fact refers to the second Passover, it is clear that it follows

5.   In the Masoretic tradition, the phrase בחדש הזה appears in v. 3, while (בחדש) הראשון appears in v. 1.

the observances of the first Passover, from the statement there:
'according to all the statute for the passover they shall keep it' (v. 12).
In Deuteronomy, following the instruction about the time for the
sacrifice ('in the evening at the going down of the sun'; cf. above), we
read that its eating follows immediately upon the sacrifice: 'and you shall
boil it and eat it at the place...and in the morning you shall turn and go
to your tents' (16.7). We thus find that, apart from the stylistic differences, there is no difference on this point between the demands of the
Temple Scroll and those of other sources.

There would thus seem to be no difference between the rabbis and the
Scroll regarding the time of its eating, even though there are some
rabbinic sources which prescribe as a precaution that it be eaten before
midnight. This does not, however, change the law in general, which is
faithful to the biblical command allowing it to be eaten all night long.[6]

iv. *The Place for Eating the Sacrifice*
'Let them eat it at night in the courts of [the] ho[l]y (place)' (ll. 8-9). In
addition to the issues of the times for the offering and eating of the
sacrifice discussed above, the scroll also refers to the place where the
sacrifice is to be eaten. According to it, one is required to eat the flesh
of the sacrifice 'in the courts of the holy place'—that is, within those
Temple precincts where non-priests are permitted to enter. In that
respect, the biblical sources differ greatly from the statement made in the
scroll. Some passages, such as Leviticus 23, Numbers 9, and the like, do
not mention the question of place at all, while Exodus 12, which is
concerned with the Passover of Egypt, speaks of it being offered and
eaten in the homes of the families.

Of all of the sources in the Torah, only the Book of Deuteroomy
refers explicitly to the question of place. Consistent with its approach in
all of its laws, it applies the rule of the centrality of cult to Passover as
well. In our case, the legislator does not suffice with a 'positive'
instruction, but begins with a negative phrase: 'You may not offer the
passover sacrifice within any of your towns which the LORD your God
gives you' (Deut. 16.5). Note the formula, 'you may not' (לא תוכל),

---

6. See B.Z. Wacholder, *The Dawn of Qumran*, pp. 50-51. According to
Schiffman, the scroll allows eating the sacrifice all night long, while *Jubilees* only
allows it until midnight (L. Schiffman, 'The Sacrificial System', pp. 224-25).
However, J.C. VanderKam has already shown that there is no difference between
Jubilees and the *Temple Scroll* regarding this matter ('The Temple Scroll', p. 229).

which is typical of the Deuteronomistic author: 'you may not put a foreigner over you, who is not your brother' (17.15). One should note that in this law, too, the positive imperative ('you may indeed set as king over you...') precedes the negative.[7]

The positive instruction of the law of passover in the Book of Deteronomy is: '[You may not offer]...but at the place which the LORD your God will choose, to make his name dwell in it, there you shall offer the passover sacrifice, in the evening at the going down of the sun, at the time you came out of Egypt. And you shall boil it and eat it at the place which the LORD your God will choose...' (Deut. 16.5-7). This rule applies both to the time of the sacrifice—that is, in the evening at the going down of the sun—and to the locale of the sacrifice and the eating: 'but at the place which the LORD your God will choose...there you shall offer the passover sacrifice...And you shall boil it and eat it at the place...' (16.5-7).

The dependence of the author of the *Temple Scroll* upon this source is clear, as he also wishes to carry out the ceremony at the Temple, reflecting the influence of the Deuteronomic source. Following the appearance of the Deuteronomist, there no longer existed any other options for performing rituals in Judaism save through the system of centralization.

The rabbis interpreted the imperative in Deuteronomy such that the actual performance of the Passover offering must take place within the Temple, but its flesh may be consumed anywhere within the walls of Jerusalem (*m. Zeb.* 5.8).[8] The rule in our scroll that the sacrifice must be eaten 'in the courts of [the] ho[l]y (place)' (l. 9) thus creates a requirement not mentioned in Scripture, and seems to create an open confrontation with the accepted halakhah as expressed by the rabbinic Sages.

One might claim there is a certain sectarian element present here, not only in terms of the contents, but even in terms of the manner of formulation: the phrase, 'courts of the holy place' (בחצרות הקודש) does not appear at all in the biblical laws of Passover. Moreover, an examination of the frequency of the use of the idiom הקודש-X ('x of the holy') reveals this as a common stylistic element of the scrolls. S. Talmon has recently published a number of fragments of sectarian

---

7. On the formula לא תוכל in Deuteronomy and its manner of reworking in the *Temple Scroll*, see Brin, 'Linguistic Notes'.

8. See Wacholder, *Dawn*, pp. 50-51.

texts from Masada, two of which contain idioms of this type: ;קודשי ת[
הודיעו יום קודש.[9] The phrase לשער מרום הקודש likewise appears in 4Q500
line 4,[10] and there are many other like examples.

In addition to the fact that the use of קודש in the conjunctive is frequently repeated in the literature of the scrolls, and particularly that the
phrase 'and let them eat it at night in the courts of [the] ho[l]y (place)'
does not at all appear in the parallel biblical law, this usage also betrays
the late nature of the text. Moreover, the idiom חצרות קודש appears only
once in the Bible in a language similar to that discussed: 'and those who
gather it shall drink it in the courts of the sanctuary' (Isa. 62.9)—itself a
verse dating from the end of the Babylonian Exile, or possibly even
from the beginning of the period of the Return. This is further evidence
for the late date of the text in question.

To all these points one must add the following data: the use of חצר in
the plural form חצרות (and not חצרים, which has a different history)
appears within the Bible in reference to the holy[11] (the Tabernacle, the
Temple and the like) only in later literature. The term חצרות appears in
two passages in the book of Kings: 'in the two courts of the house of
the Lord' (2 Kgs 21.5; 23.12). Apart from there, the term חצרות only
appears in Nehemiah and Chronicles; a group of patently late passages
from the Psalms also makes use of this term. It follows from all this that
the unique use of חצרות to describe portions of the Temple appears
primarily in passages from the time of the Exile and that of the Return.
This is a clear indication of the period of the author of the *Temple
Scroll*. It is well known that the date of a given author may be
determined on the basis of his own independent usages, rather than by
means of analysis of those portions of his text which he copies
unchanged from existing works. But as this passage in the law of
Passover is a complete novellum on his part, which does not rely upon
any biblical text, it is not surprising that he expresses himself regarding
this matter in a language characteristic of the later period.

A parallel to the obligation to eat the Passover in the holy precincts,
which as mentioned does not appear in the Bible, appears in *Jubilees*
49.16-17. This source not only mentions the place where the eating is to

9.   S. Talmon, 'Fragments', pp. 279-80.
10. According to M. Baillet, *Discoveries*.
11. The noun חצרות appears once in Exodus, but not in relation to the subject of
holiness: וימותו הצפרדעים מן הבתים מו החצרות ומן השדות ('The frogs died out of the
houses and courtyards and out of the fields'; Exod. 8.9).

take place, but justifies it while polemicizing against the other point of view. It states,

> And they shall not eat it outside the sanctuary of the LORD, but before the sanctuary of the LORD...And every man shall eat it in the sanctuary of your God before the LORD from twenty years old and upwards; for thus is it written and ordained that they should eat it in the sanctuary of the LORD.[12]

This wordy formulation is indicative of the effort made by the author of *Jubilees* to stress the idea of eating in the realm of the Temple. But his words also indicate that to date this demand had not been fulfilled, but that the Passover sacrifice was customarily eaten 'outside of the Temple of the LORD'. It would therefore seem that this passage represents a confrontation with the idea formulated in Deuteronomy 16, and particularly with an exegetical approach such as that cited previously in the name of the rabbis, that allowed eating the passover anywhere within the city walls. It is interesting to note their emphasis that the method of execution which they propose involves following that which was written and commanded ('for thus is it written and ordained...'). Is this a form of polemic, or did the author of *Jubilees* perhaps know of a binding, normative text that required this, such as the command in the *Temple Scroll*; or perhaps he referred to that scroll itself—thereby implying that he saw it as obligatory.

Similarly, regarding the idiom, 'from twenty years old and upwards' (l. 8), one might say that the phrase in *Jubilees* 49.17 also knows of this practice, but that it first brings the full biblical version, 'All the congregation of Israel shall keep it' (Exod. 12.47), and alongside it mentions the range of ages, as stated. Moreover, it uses phrases such as 'everyone who is numbered in the census' and the like, thereby identifying the biblical source from which these circles drew their formulation. The absence in the *Temple Scroll* of the biblical phraseology referring to the entire congregation (Exod. 12.47) serves to emphasize the tradition of the circle represented by the author of the scroll.

There is no doubt that in both these sources—the *Temple Scroll* and the *Book of Jubilees*—the wording reflects the sectarian interpretation noted here. One may also trace the development of the idea which found expression in this demand: one of the changes that took place in the text was from the consumption of the Paschal sacrifice by *all* of the

---

12. Compare with the English version in VanderKam, *The Book of Jubilees*.

people to its consumption by *adult males* alone. This change is rooted in the fact that the author of the scroll required that the Passover sacrifice be eaten in the holy precincts. But the statement in column 39 implies that entrance into the middle courtyard is restricted to adult males, 'from twenty years and upwards':

> a woman and a child shall not (?) enter it until the day that he shall fulfil the law [   ] for himself (?) to the LORD, half a shekel, a statute for ever, a memorial in their settlements; the shekel is twenty (?) gerahs. And when they shall collect the half-she[k]el of each of them [   ] for me, only then will they enter, from the age of twenty…(39.7-11)[13]

It follows that neither women nor youths below the age of twenty were allowed in the middle courtyard. On the other hand, a male who is more than twenty years old and has brought his contribution of a half-shekel is allowed to enter.

Hence, the statement that participation in the meal of the Passover sacrifice is restricted to those over twenty years of age can have only one meaning, namely, that women do not participate in the passover sacrifice, because in the sectarian literature this age range relates to males alone. This is particularly true with regard to the subject of entry to certain areas of the Temple precincts (= the middle courtyard).

Apart from the range of ages which, as mentioned, refers only to males, males have an additional claim: namely, the use of the plural form חצרות to refer to the place of eating. This term was specifically used because the adult males (who had paid the half shekel) were permitted to enter two courtyards,[14] namely, the outer and the middle one, whereas the women were only allowed to enter the outer one (11QTemple 40.6: '[and] to their daughters and to the aliens who we[re] born [   ]…').[15]

We must conclude from this that the instruction to eat the passover offering 'in the courts of the holy place' (17.8) must be interpreted as implying that it is to be eaten by men alone, as opposed to the biblical statement that 'all the congregation of Israel shall keep it' (Exod. 12.47). This verse instructs future generations to continue to observe that which they have been told concerning the Passover of Egypt, which was

13. Yadin, *Temple Scroll*, II, pp. 166-67.

14. Wacholder's statement (*Dawn*, pp. 50-51) that eating is permitted in all three courtyards has no basis in fact.

15. Yadin, *Temple Scroll*, II, p. 170.

consumed within a family framework (Exod. 12.6, 7, 11, 14).[16]

To summarize our discussion of the Passover offering: the author of the *Temple Scroll* constructs his own words about the Passover sacrifice by gathering the relevant biblical texts. As he has a rich collection of verses concerning Passover available, he is able to choose those verses which best enable him to present the ideas that he wishes to disseminate. He begins with a relatively marginal verse, Num. 9.2-3, and concludes with a passage from Deuteronomy, much of his approach being based upon the principle of the Deuteronomic idea.

Alongside this mosaic work, he constructs his own teaching, which he attempts to demonstrate by making maximal use of biblical verses. In their absence, he sketches his words by using sources from the circle close to him, or even through his own independent composition.

In this manner, he turns the general demand for the observance of Passover into a sectarian and parochial observance. Moreover, his words are constructed in tandem with other statements from other parts of his work. This is true regarding his refusal to allow women or children to participate in the Passover celebration, as they are unable to enter certain parts of the Temple.

2. *Laws of Prohibited Marriages in the Temple Scroll*

Column 66 of the *Temple Scroll* contains a table of proscribed marriages. The table is incomplete, ending with the truncated phrase, 'A [man] shall not take', without preserving the continuation of the text. As a result, we know neither which prohibition the text is alluding to there, nor what additional proscriptions might have been recorded further on in the scroll. Further evidence of the truncated nature of this list is that it does not include all those components that we would expect to find in a list of this sort:

16. On the difference between the Passover observed in Egypt and that of subsequent generations regarding this point, see in *Mekilta*: 'This teaches that the Passover in later generations came "mixed"'—that is, not separated by families, as it was in Egypt. Cf. *Targ. Ps.-J.* to this verse, and Rashi's comment to Exod. 12.47: 'Because he says regarding the Passover of Egypt "a lamb for each house", [i.e.] that they were counted by families, one might think that the Passover of generations is the same way. Scripture says, "all the congregation of Israel shall do it".'

לוא יקח   11

איש את אשת אביהו ולוא יגלה כנף אביהו לוא יקח איש את אשת   12

אחיהו ולוא יגלה כנף אחיהו בן אביה או בן אמו כי נדה היא   13

לוא יקח איש את אחותו בת אביהו או בת אמו תועבה היא לוא   14

יקח איש את אחות אביהו או את אחות אמו כי זמה היא לוא   15

יקח איש את   16

בת אחיהו או בת אחותו כי תועבה היא לוא יקח   17

(11) A man shall not take
(12) his father's wife nor shall he uncover his father's skirt. A man shall not take
(13) his brother's wife, nor shall he uncover his brother's skirt, be it his father's son or his mother's son, for this is impurity.
(14) A man shall not take his sister, his father's or his mother's daughter, for this is an abomination.
(15) A man shall not take his father's sister or his mother's sister, for it is wickedness. A man
(16) shall not take
(17) his brother's daughter or his sister's daughter, for it is an abomination. A [man] shall not take[17]

i. *The Nature of the List of Prohibitions*

At the outset, we should note that parallels to the present list exist in several places in the Bible, such as Leviticus 18 and 20. These are referred to in the exegetical literature as incest lists, that is, lists containing precise definitions of prohibited sexual connections. These lists (Lev. 18, 20, and others) thereby also serve to indicate forbidden marital unions; however, as mentioned, this is not their primary intention, but rather an offshoot thereof.

On the other hand, in the text in question the partial list is presented as a list of prohibited marriages, as may be seen by its consistent use of the phrase 'shall not take'—לא יקח—the root לקח clearly referring to matters of marriage.[18]

Hence, assuming that the continuation of the list (on fragmented column lxvi and on column lxvii, which is blank) had the same stylistic feature (יקח), it is clear that the list did not include such types of abominations as homosexuality or sexual connections between human beings and animals,[19] since in such cases it would obviously be

17.   Yadin, *Temple Scroll*, II, pp. 298-300.

18.   See my remarks on this in Brin, 'The Bible as Reflected', p. 197.

19.   On the other hand, it may be that the list continued up to a certain point using the formula, 'he shall not take', and from that point onward included other kinds of

impossible to use the phrase 'to take'. Is one to see in this nicety—the focus on prohibited marriages rather than with prohibited sexual relations per se—a continuation of the general approach of the author of the *Temple Scroll* to these sensitive subjects?

To elaborate, the *Temple Scroll* contains a law stating that one who laid with his wife is forbidden to enter the temple city for three days (45.11-12). A parallel passage in the *Damascus Covenant* reads, 'Let no man lie with a woman in the city of the sanctuary, so as to convey uncleanness to the [city of the] sanctuary with their impurity' (CD 12.1-2). Whereas the latter text refers to sexual relations between a man and (any) woman, the author of the *Temple Scroll*, who is more sensitive regarding this subject, reads 'his wife'. The same nicety appears in the Samaritan Pentateuch to Lev. 15.18: 'If a husband lies with his wife (ואשה כי ישכב איש אותה) and has an emission of semen, both of them shall bathe themselves in water, and be unclean until the evening'. This is an alteration of the Masoretic reading, ואשה כי ישכב איש אתה('If a man lies with a woman').[20]

To return to the list of prohibited marriages in col. 66: in my opinion, this (or similar) lists represent the 'law' referred to by the scroll in the law of the seduced maiden: 'If a man seduces a virgin who is not betrothed, but is fit for him according to the law (והיא רויה לו מן החוק)... and she shall be his wife...' (66.8-11). As the legislator requires the seducer to marry the girl, he adds the condition (to which the ancient biblical legislator was not sensitive) that the two of them, the man and the maiden, must be fit to create a marriage connection between them under law: that is, that they do not belong to the category of those included in the list of proscribed marriages. Yadin quite properly

sexual transgressions. In any event, in CD 5.7-11 the sin of lying with a menstruant woman is mentioned alongside violation of the proscription against marriage with the daughter of a brother or sister; the text from 6Q reads, אש[ר ישכבעם] [אל ישכב] איש עם [זכר משכבי]אשה ('[who sha]ll lie with [ ] [a man shall not lie with] a man in the manner of lying with [a woman]'). One may see here a collection of sexual prohibitions, in which in both lines there are mentioned two kinds of prohibited intercourse, of which we do not know the nature of the former, while the latter is clearly concerned with homosexual intercourse. See M. Baillet, 'Les Petites Grotetes', p. 130. Discussion of a new text—4Q251—concerning prohibited sexual unions will be found in section 3 of this chapter.

20. It is surprising that, according to the approach of this scroll, a woman was not proscribed from entering the sanctuary city after lying with her husband. Moreover, no mention is made here regarding the necessity to bathe herself.

mentions the parallel rabbinic law concerning 'one who is fit to him' (ראויה לו), but it seems to me more important to note the remarks of the *Mekilta* to Exod. 22.15-16 on the sequel to this passage:

> 'He shall give the marriage present for her, and make her his wife' [Exod. 22.15]: Scripture speaks of one who is fit to be his wife (ראויה לו), to exclude a widow to a regular priest, a *netinah* to an Israelite, or an Israelite woman to a *natin* or *mamzer*.

One may add to this that *Sifre* 119, on Deut. 22.29, states,

> 'And she shall be his wife': this teaches that he must 'drink out of his vessel' [i.e. 'lie in the bed he has made'], even if she is lame, and even if she is diseased with boils. If he found in her some unseemly thing, or if she is not allowed to marry into Israel, might you think that he is still allowed to keep her? Scripture says: 'She shall be his wife': one who is fit to him (הראויה לו; and cf. *m. Ket.* 3.5).

In both these texts, a clear line is drawn between those matters which the legislator does not see as upsetting the requirement that the man marry the maiden with whom he has lain, and those situations in which the legislator does not allow him to carry out the unequivocal requirement of biblical law, that the rapist or seducer marry the maiden without any option on his part. The latter situations pertain to prohibitions derived from other biblical laws. It therefore follows that the rabbinic texts (from *Mishna*, *Mekilta* and *Sifre*) and that from the *Temple Scroll* use the phrase 'suitable to him' and the like. In particular, the formula used by the scroll, '...according to the law', is directed toward one thing: the compatibility between the case at hand (i.e. a particular man and woman) and the list of prohibited marriages found in other passages. However, I do not intend to say by this that the two texts necessarily refer to identical lists.

ii. *The Order in Which the Prohibitions on Column 66 are Mentioned*

Temple Scroll	Leviticus 18	Leviticus 20	Deuteronomy 23	Deuteronomy 27
father's wife	father's wife	father's wife	father's wife	father's wife
brother's wife	sister	sister		sister[21]
sister	paternal or	maternal or		mother-in-law
paternal or	maternal aunt	paternal aunt		
maternal aunt	brother's wife	brother's wife		
fraternal or				
sorietal niece				

21. In the LXX, the reading here is 'his father's or mother's sister'.

Comparison of the above lists reveals that the order in the list in the *Temple Scroll* is dictated by the following principles:

The list begins with the prohibition concerning the father's wife, because this is the point which the author had reached in his exposition of the laws of the book of Deuteronomy. This discussion appears in Deut. 23.1, which mentions the prohibition against marrying one's father's wife. There are no further prohibitions concerning this subject in that chapter; the author of the *Temple Scroll*, consistent with his approach,[22] goes on from there to copy from another place in the book, ch. 27.

One may discern the underlying logic of this method of arranging the components of the list: the opening was dictated, as said, by the place reached by the author in Deuteronomy, while thereafter things are arranged in a series of links:[23] father's wife, brother's wife, father's (or mother's) sister, brother's (or sister's) daughter.

The second relation proscribed in the list is the brother's wife. Here our author abandons the approach of Deuteronomy, which does not have such a prohibition. On the contrary, according to the law of levirate marriage, the brother is required to marry his dead brother's widow if he left no offspring. We thus find a direct conflict between Deuteronomy and the approach to this subject taken by the author of the scroll.

The third prohibition in the list is that of the sister. In this case, the order is prescribed by the second text in Deuteronomy concerned with forbidden sexual relations: Deuteronomy 27, the list of those who are cursed, which includes a number of incest prohibitions. However, unlike the *Temple Scroll* (and Deut. 23.1: 'he shall not take'), this does not constitute a list of prohibited marriages.

The list in Deuteronomy 27, like Deuteronomy 23, opens with the

---

22. See Yadin, *Temple Scroll*, I, and compare Brin, 'The Bible as Reflected', pp. 206-209, concerning the author's approach whereby on the one hand he follows the order of Scriptures in Deuteronomy, which constitutes his basic text in this portion of the scroll, and on the other hand he gathers additional related texts by his own order of subject matter. The texts that complement the complex of different subjects are brought from other sections of Deuteronomy, which are not an immediate continuation of the section quoted, as well as from other biblical books, most usually from the Torah. The author thereby creates a series of 'scrolls' arranged by subject.

23. On the system of association in the scroll, see Brin, 'The Bible as Reflected', pp. 206-209, 223-24.

father's wife, continuing from there to the proscription of the sister. However, in the scroll it appears after the prohibition of the brother's wife, which does not appear in Deuteronomy due to the law of levirate marriage, which requires one to marry one's brother's wife under certain conditions. There is hence no doubt that levirate marriage was not practiced among the circles of the author of the *Temple Scroll*; otherwise, the prohibition of the brother's sister would not have been included in their official list.

According to a number of traditions of the LXX to Deut. 27.22, the prohibition there refers to the father's or mother's sister rather than to one's own sister; in any event, this is the next prohibition appearing in the list in the scroll.

The prohibition against lying with one's mother-in-law appears thereafter in Deut. 27.23, but not in the fragment of the list that we have in the scroll.

From what we have stated thus far, it is clear that the reason for dealing with incest prohibitions at this particular place in the scroll, as well as the manner of its formulation ('a man shall not take'), is based upon the order with which the author of the scroll deals with texts from Deuteronomy, in the course of his reworking of that book. Thus, after dealing with the law of the betrothed virgin (Deut. 22.28-29), he went on to the law in 23.1; from there, he continued, as was his practice, to yet another passage in the book dealing with the same subject, namely, Deuteronomy 27.

The final link in this chain is the prohibition against marrying one's niece, the daughter of either one's brother or one's sister. But as is well known, there is no such prohibition in the Bible.[24] On the contrary,

---

24. The circles of the sect were witnesses to the lack of such an explicit prohibition in the Bible. In order to justify their own approach, they read in the *Damascus Covenant*, 'And they take each man the daughter of his brother and the daughter of his sister, and Moses said, do not approach the sister of your mother to uncover her, for she is the nakedness of your mother' (Lev. 18.13). But although the rules against incest are written for men, they also apply to women. When therefore a brother's daughter uncovers the nakedness of her father's brother, she is [also his] near kin' (vv. 7-11). That is, as there was no explicit prohibition of this connection, they arrived at proof of it through exegesis of the relevant verses. To this one must add that, despite the fact that a work such as the *Temple Scroll* existed in the sect, the prohibition against taking the niece was not cited from it. This fact helps us to determine the question regarding the status of the *Temple Scroll*. That is, since there is a relationship between the two compositions, and despite the fact that the *Temple*

rabbinic literature contains various statements praising one who marries his sister's daughter; but there were doubtless differences among the various Jewish sects regarding this point, as has already been noted by numerous scholars.[25]

As mentioned, the Bible contains two basic texts dealing with matters of incest: Leviticus 18 and 20. The lists included there are extremely detailed. Since, as mentioned, the question of the fraternal (or sorietal) niece does not appear, one should note that the other four links which appear in the list in the *Temple Scroll* do appear in the two lists in Leviticus.

The order of the units mentioned in Leviticus 18 and 20 are relatively similar;[26] that is, if one ignores certain other components, the inner order of the prohibitions mentioned in both lists is the same in both cases: father's wife, sister, paternal or maternal aunt, brother's wife.

We may conclude from this that the list in the scroll differs from both incest lists in that the brother's wife appears in second rather than fourth position.

iii. *Definition of the Prohibition*

The dominant verb used in the scroll is יקח, 'to take'. In Deut. 23.1, from which our author took the beginning of his initial involvement in his subject, it states: 'a man shall not take his father's wife'.

Scroll represents itself as being written by Moses, the author of the *Damascus Covenant* did not see fit to quote the *Temple Scroll* as if it were the Torah. To this fact we may add Stegemann's remark concerning the scarcity of copies of the *Temple Scroll* found in Qumran, which we would have expected to find in greater numbers had the work indeed been considered as a full substitute for the Torah; see there further on this subject. To this one may now add the consideration which I mentioned, without relation to Stegemann's approach to the status of the scroll and the time of its composition. See H. Stegemann, *The Origin of the Temple Scroll*, pp. 235-56.

25. See now J. Sussman, 'The History of Halakhah and the Dead Sea Scroll', p. 35 n. 113. Yadin, *The Temple Scroll*, I, p. 372, sees a connection between the prohibition of the sorietal niece and that against the fraternal aunt. In his opinion, this is demonstrated by the fact that in CD 5.7-11 the prohibition against marrying one's sister's daughter is justified by the biblical proscription against marrying one's father's sister, while in 11QTemple 66 the two proscriptions appear alongside one another. One should also note that the prohibition in the *Damascus Covenant* is formulated using the phrase לקח, as in the *Temple Scroll*, that is, as referring to matters of marriage.

26. There are not a few differences between these two lists, both in relation to the wording, the order, and the composition itself.

In Deuteronomy 27, by contrast, the prohibition is defined using the language, 'Cursed be he who lies with...'

In Leviticus 18, the formula in all four units is: 'You shall not uncover the nakedness of...' (ערות...לא תגלה).

In Leviticus 20, there are three different kinds of formulae: ואיש כי ישכב ('the man who lies with...'—for the father's wife); ואיש אשר יקח ('if a man takes...'—brothers wife, sister); וערות...לא תגלה ('you shall not uncover the nakedness of...'—father's sister).

In contrast to all these, the *Temple Scroll*, as mentioned, utilizes a uniform pattern: 'a man shall not take'. We therefore find that the scroll is concerned with marriage connections, while in all other texts the emphasis is upon specific sexual prohibitions. To be more precise, the formulation in the units concerning the brother's wife and the sister uses the verb לקח, as in the scroll. Is the difference in the definition of the prohibition in the two texts in Deuteronomy, using the verb לקח with regard to the father's wife (23.1), on the one hand, and שכב (27.20), on the other, and similarly in relation to the sister (27.22), significant? That is, did the author of Deuteronomy intend, in practice, to refer to different kind of prohibitions?

It may be that the answer to this question is positive. However, given the state of the extant material, it is impossible for us to define the nature of that difference. On the other hand, the stylistic variation among the various transgressions in Leviticus 20 may indicate that that list was composed from a number of different sources, the hallmark of this being the lack of unity regarding the definition of the prohibition, which is the main subject of these lists.[27]

iv. *Motive Clause in the List of Prohibitions*
One of the striking stylistic signs of the list in question is that all of its components are accompanied by a motive clause.[28] We shall now trace the formulation of the motive clause for each one of the components.

The list opens with the father's wife, the motive for the prohibition being given as, 'nor shall he uncover his father's skirt'. The prohibition

27. Daube, *Studies*, sees Lev. 20 as a text that developed gradually, each time an additional level being added. He notes the location of these levels on the basis of the type of relation, the use of verbs, and other matters. See *Studies*, pp. 78-82, and see p. 78 for close conclusions concerning Lev. 18 and Deut. 27.

28. On the term 'motive clause' and its function in law, see B. Gemser, 'The Importance of the Motive Clause'; R. Sonsino, 'Motive Clause in Hebrew Bible'.

itself is formulated, as mentioned, using the phrase '[a man] shall not take'. As we have here a list of proscribed marriages, the wording of the motive follows the tendency of the language in Deuteronomy 23. On the other hand, in Leviticus 18 all four phrases are formulated, 'You shall not uncover the nakedness of...' We thus find that the wording of the motive in our list is reminiscent of the formulation of the prohibition in Leviticus 18. The language of the clause in that verse continues, 'it is your father's nakedness' (Lev. 18.8). In Leviticus 20, the transgression is formulated using the verb שכב, 'to lie with', while the motive clause resembles Leviticus 18: '[he] has uncovered his father's nakedness' (20.11).

Regarding the prohibition of the brother's wife, the scroll continues consistently in both parts: לקח ('to take') in the prohibition, and גלה ('to uncover [nakedness]') in the motive. Here, however, the motive clause contains an additional item: 'for this is impurity', that is, there are two motive clauses here.

In Leviticus 18, as mentioned, the transgression is formulated in terms of גלה, the clause reading, 'she is your brother's nakedness' (v. 16).

In Leviticus 20, the transgression is formulated using the word לקח, while the motive clause is as in the previous component: 'he has uncovered his brother's nakedness' (v. 20). Here too, an additional motive clause appears, similar to that in the scroll to the point of identity with: 'it is impurity' (נדה הוא).

Between these two texts, the elements of the clauses are arranged in chiastic order:

In Lev. 20.21: 'If a man takes his brother's wife, [a] it is impurity; [b] he has uncovered his brother's nakedness'.

In the *Temple Scroll*: 'A man shall not take his brother's wife, [b] nor shall he uncover his brother's skirt...[a] for this is impurity'.

This clearly indicates that the author of the *Temple Scroll* drew this component of his list from Leviticus 20, for the following reasons: (1) only here[29] is the prohibition formulated with the verb לקח, a point that was suitable to his needs; (2) the language of both motive clauses is similar to the point of identity; (3) the order of the elements in the two clauses is chiastic: a–b b–a. In ancient literature, this is a clear sign that two passages bear a relation of quotation to one another.[30]

---

29. Lev. 18.16 states, ערות אשת אחיך לא תגלה, 'you shall not uncover the nakedness of your brother's wife'.

30. See G. Brin–Y. Hoffman, 'On the Use of Chiasmus in the Bible'.

The prohibition of the sister contains a brief motive clause: 'for this is an abomination' (תועבה היא).[31] This belongs to the same type of motive clause as the second clause in the previous prohibition, that of the brother's wife: 'for this is impurity'. In Leviticus 18.9, no motive clause at all appears in this case, while 'it is an abomination' appears in v. 22, in the law of homosexuality.

The similarity to the list in Leviticus 20 is also made clear in this case. Here too, the prohibition is defined as 'if a man takes...',[32] while the motive is 'it is a shameful thing (חסד הוא),[33] '...he has uncovered his sister's nakedness'. That is, there are two motive clauses, the first of which is identical to that in the scroll in terms of its stylistic type.

In the case of the proscription of the paternal or maternal aunt, we find the motive clause: 'for it is wickedness'. In Lev. 20.19, the motive clause belongs to the first type: 'for that is to make naked one's near kin'; in Lev. 18.13-14, we find a similar language: 'for she is your father's near kinswoman...for she is your mother's near kinswoman'. The phrase, 'it is wickedness' (זמה הוא) appears there in the discussion of

31. The fifth prohibition in the list in the scroll—that against taking the daughter of ones brother or the daughter of ones sister—likewise ends with the phrase 'it is an abomination'. On the one hand, this is like the second language in the motive clause ('it is an abomination'—re the sister); on the other hand, it is a formula like that of a causal phrase.

32. In my opinion this point is central, because throughout the list in Lev. 20 the verbs used are different: שכב, קרב, גלה, etc. On the other hand, the language of לקח ('to take') only appears in relation to a woman and her mother, a sister, and the brother's wife. Two of these three cases are brought in the scroll. We thus find that, in addition to the other proofs I have cited above, this is an important indication that the author of the scroll utilized the text in Leviticus 20 as the continuation of that which began according to Deut. 23.1. It should be noted that in the *Sifra* on this verse, a distinction is drawn regarding the distinction between לקח and שכב. See *Sifra* §110 to Lev. 20.14, concerning the prohibition against taking a woman and her mother: 'in all of them it says "lying with" and here it speaks of "taking", to teach you that he is only culpable if it is done in the manner of marriage'.

33. The definition given in the scroll, 'it is an abomination', is similar to the language in Lev. 20.13 in the law regarding one who lies with a man as with a woman ('both of them have committed an abomination'). It is interesting to note that throughout the long list of Lev. 20 only three usages of לקח (see above) are accompanied by a motive clause of the second type. On the other hand, in the law of homosexuality, and also regarding one who lies with his daughter-in-law, there appears a type similar, though not identical, to this: 'both of them have committed an abomination' and 'they have committed incest (*tebel*)'.

a woman and her daughter. The language of the clause used in the scroll comes from Lev. 18.17 in the law of the woman and her daughter, as well as from Lev. 20.14, albeit in the latter the familial connection is defined as 'a woman and her mother'. The phrase זמה ('wickedness') appears there both in the motive clause and as the purpose of the punishment: 'that there may be no wickedness among you'.

v. *The Nature of the Punishment*
Consonant with the nature of the list which, as mentioned, defines prohibited marriages, there is no mention made of punishment. In this respect, it is similar to Leviticus 18, which defines the prohibitions without mentioning any sanctions. On the other hand, the list in Leviticus 20 contains a detailed list of the punishments anticipated for those who violate these prohibitions, regarding the same family connections as are mentioned in the scroll.

In any event, it is worth stressing that, whereas the author followed the available text of Leviticus 20 regarding his formulations and motive clauses, this was not so regarding the question of punishment. However, it does not seem to me that his practice was influenced by Leviticus 18 in this respect. Rather, the identical principle underlying the two lists, that of mentioning in principle the prohibition, led to a similar solution: the absence of any explicit punishment.

The following are the punishments listed in Leviticus 20 in our cases:

In the matter of the father's wife, it states, 'both of them shall be put to death, their blood is upon them' (v. 11).

For the brother's wife, 'they shall be childless' (v. 21).

Concerning the sister, we find two languages of punishment: 'they shall be cut off in the sight of the children of their people'; in addition, it says regarding the brother, 'he shall bear his iniquity', while regarding the paternal or maternal aunt, 'they shall bear their iniquity'.

We thus find three central phrases of punishment for the two transgressors. Only in the case of the sister does there seem to be some hesitation regarding the fact that two texts were preserved. According to one, both of them are subject to punishment, while the alternative formula speaks of punishment of the man alone.

We also need to distinguish between humanly executed punishment and punishment by God, but I do not intend to discuss this subject here. In any event, only in the case of the father's wife does the formulation clearly seem to be one of punishment by human hands ('both of them shall be put to death, their blood is upon them', 20.11).

3. *Prohibited Unions in 4Q251*

The seventh fragment of 4Q251 presents us with a unique text within the context of laws of incest.[34] I shall here copy the text and thereafter discuss several matters relating to it, following the general lines of the previous discussion.

1	על עריות [...]
2	אל יקח איש את א[חותו בת אביו או בת אמו...אל יקח איש]
3	את בת אחיו ואת בת א[חותו לאשה...אל ינל]
4	איש את ערות אחות א[ביו ואת ערות אחות אמו ואל תנתן אשה לאחי]
5	אביה ולאחי אמה [לאשה...]
6	אל ינל איש ערות [...]
7	אל יקח איש בתי (?) נ (?)[...]

(1) Concerning immoral unions [...]

(2) A man should not marry his si[ster, the daughter of his father or the daughter of his mother...A man should not marry]

(3) the daughter of his brother or the daughter of his si[ster...He should not uncover]

(4) the nakedness of the sister of his fa[ther or the sister of his mother. Nor should a woman be given to the brother of]

(5) her father or to the brother of her mother [as a wife]

(6) A man should not uncover the nakedness of [...]

(7) A man should not take the daughter of (?) [...]

1. This fragment contains the introductory phrase 'concerning immoral unions', which may serve as a general heading, the like of which is found neither in the *Temple Scroll* nor in any other source.

2. The order of the components is: sister, fraternal or sorietal niece, [paternal or maternal] aunt, [paternal] and maternal uncle, and two prohibitions whose formula is truncated. It is clear in this case that the order differs from that of the *Temple Scroll* in that the sister appears together with the niece, and only thereafter, rather than preceding it, does there appear the paternal aunt.

3. As we have demonstrated above, *Temple Scroll* 66 consists of a list of prohibited marriages, for which reason it uses the fixed opening, 'he shall not take'. The present document, by contrast, does not utilize a

---

34. The text was examined according to the following editions: E. Tov, *Dead Sea Scrolls on Microfiche*; R.E. Eisenman and J.M. Robinson, *A Facsimile Edition of the Dead Sea Scrolls*. The reconstructions and English translation are based primarily upon R.E. Eisenman and M. Wise, *The Dead Sea Scrolls Uncovered*, pp. 200-205.

uniform language of proscription. Alongside the phrase אל יקח ('he shall not take', ll. 2, 7), we find אל יגל ('he shall not uncover', l. 6, as well as [3-4]); there is no doubt that there was also at least one other formula of prohibition, as follows from lines 4-5: [...ל אשה תנתן ואל] (['...Nor should a woman be given to the brother of] her father or to the brother of her mother [as a wife]'). Even if we assume that the suggested reconstruction of line 4, ל אשה תנתן ואל ('Nor should a woman be given to') is incorrect, it is clear that the subsequent formula in line 5, '...to] her father or to the brother of her mother [...]' indicates the use of different verbs from those found in the prohibition appearing previously in the document (compare to all these the previous discussion, in the section concerning the languages of prohibition used in the *Temple Scroll*).

4. Lines 4-5 contain a unique sort of prohibition, in that it is directed towards the woman. According to this, the woman is proscribed from marrying her uncle, whether on her father's or her mother's side. One should note that this prohibition corresponds to the proscription of one's fraternal or sorietal niece, which appears explicitly in this document. Furthermore, the incest lists in Leviticus 18 and 20 are directed only towards males, whether in the explicit prohibitions or in the general introduction to these prohibitions: 'None of you shall approach any one near of kin to uncover nakedness; I am the LORD' (18.6). The parallel list in Leviticus 20 contains no parallel general opening.

In general, the biblical formulation does not directly address the woman regarding the transgression of specific sexual prohibitions, since the male was presumably seen as responsible for initiating the act. The woman is in fact addressed in one case: 'neither shall any woman give herself to a beast to lie with it: it is perversion' (Lev. 18.23), and 'If a woman approaches any beast and lies with it, you shall kill the woman and the beast' (20.16). That is, only when the other 'partner' to the sexual act is an animal does the formulation of the biblical author impose the prohibition upon the woman. Why did the author of our document deviate from the biblical sources to impose this prohibition upon the woman, unlike all the other sources—particularly in light of the fact that he thereby duplicates the prohibition of the niece, that was already included in his list of prohibitions?

This may stem from the fact that the sect saw the rule prohibiting the fraternal and sorietal niece as a central one, distinguishing it from the rest of Israel (note above the admiration expressed in the circles of the

rabbinic sages for one who marries his niece!). For this reason, they saw
fit to emphasize the prohibition through means of this mutual and
redundant formulation.

An indication of the unique status of this prohibition appears, in my
opinion, in the statement in the *Damascus Covenant*: 'And they take
each man the daughter of their brother and the daughter of his sister,
and Moses said, "do not approach the sister of your mother to uncover
her, for she is the nakedness of your mother" (Lev. 18.13). But
although the rules against incest are written for men, they also apply to
women. When therefore a brother's daughter uncovers the nakedness of
her father's brother, she is [also his] near kin' (CD 5.7-11). This source
'filled in' that which was missing from the explicit prohibitions of the
Torah by deriving it logically from another prohibition (that of the
maternal aunt); that is, this conclusion was derived through means of
hermeneutical exegesis.

Moreover, the 'active' formulation of 4Q251 here finds its parallel,
both ideologically and in terms of contents. That is, the argument
advanced in the *Damascus Covenant*, 'But although the rules against
incest are written for men, *they also apply to women*', implies that the
prohibitions of Leviticus 18 and 20 are to be understood not only as
explicitly written, regarding the males, but that one ought to draw
analogous conclusions in the opposite direction as well. By their
rhetorical question, 'When therefore a brother's daughter uncovers the
nakedness of her father's brother, she is [also his] near kin...' (vv. 10-
11), they clearly indicate that they consider the prohibitions as if they
had also been formulated from the viewpoint of the woman, and not
only that of the man.

In light of all these elements of similarity, I have no doubt that the
author of 4Q251 came from the same circles as the author of the
Damascus Covenant. We may conclude from this that the document in
question faithfully reflects the approach of the Judaean Desert sect.

5. In addition to all these, one should take note of the sectarian nature
of the language used in the document. I refer to the fact that its
formulations are dominated almost exclusively by the form: אל יקטל איש.
Thus, אל יקח/ינל איש (ll. 2, 6, 7), and presumably also [אל ינל] איש את
[...בי]א]אחות ערות (ll. 3-4). Such usages appear neither in *Temple Scroll*
66 nor in the two principal incest lists in the Bible (Lev. 18, 20).

Moreover, the formula of אל יקטל איש appears in the other fragments
of 4Q251 as well. Thus, line 2 in frag. 2: [...ם] צואי[...] אל; line 3: אל

[...]א[ששים ובבגדים אש[...]; line 4: ש מאהלו[ ] אל[ ]; line 5: אל יעל איש בהמה; etc.
Frag. 3 line 3: א[ל יז איש מזרע אהרון]; frag. 5 line 2 [...] אל יאחר איש כי; line
5: אל יאכל א[י]ש חטים חדשים.

We find that 4Q251 maintains a consistent system of formulation of
commandments in the negative. One might add to this the fact that no
similar formulation appears anywhere in the Bible, including those
sections concerned with law.

A similar formula appears only in the following verses: Exod. 16.19,
איש אל יותר ממנו ('Let no man leave any of it till the morning'); Exod.
16.29, אל יצא איש ממקומו ('let no man go out of his place'); Exod. 19.24,
'do not let the priests and the people break through (אל יהרסו לעלות) to
come up to the LORD'; Exod. 34.3, 'and let no man be seen (וגם איש
אל ירא) throughout all the mountain; let no flocks or herd feed (אל ירעו)
before that mountain'; Exod. 36.6, 'let neither man nor woman do
anything more (אל יעשו עוד מלאכה)'.

One should note that, while all of these verses do in fact contain
instructions formulated in a negative way, none of them is an actual law,
but each of them refers to singular events referred to at that point in the
text. In a smaller group of laws, the pattern אל תקטל appears in the
second person; thus Lev. 11.43: אל תשקצו את נפשתיכם ('You shall not
make yourselves abominable'); Lev. 25.14: אל תונו איש את אחיו ('you shall
not wrong one another'). However, this use is also dissimilar to the use
of אל יקטל in this context.

On the other hand, in the Qumran literature this is the dominant
formula. I shall cite here a few formulae from the *Manual of Discipline*
and from the *Damascus Covenant* that utilize this approach:

In 1QS 6.1, 'Let no man accuse (אל יביא איש) his companion before the
Congregation...'; 6.10, 'Let no man interrupt (אל ידבר איש) his companion before his speech has ended'; CD 10.10-11, 'let no man bathe
(אל ירחץ איש) in dirty water'; 10.14-15, 'Let no man do (אל יעש איש) work
on the sixth day from the moment when the sun's orb is distant by its
own fulness from the gate'; 11.5, 'Let no man walk (אל ילך איש) after a
beast to pasture it outside his town more than two thousand cubits', and
many others.[35]

In light of all the above, it would appear that 4Q251 is a kind of
appendix and addition to the *Damascus Covenant* scroll. The other

---

35. On the subject of the word אל, see E. Qimron, 'אל in our Early Sources',
pp. 473-82; *idem, The Hebrew of the Dead Sea Scrolls*, pp. 80-81.

fragments (frags. 1–6) contain clear and specific repetitions of the *Damascus Covenant*.

4. *Issues concerning Prophets (Studies in 4Q375)*

i. *Introduction*

The Hebrew Bible contains a number of laws concerning prophets and prophecy, and the Qumran literature likewise has a very definite attitude towards issues relating to prophecy. It is clear that the members of the sect expected the reappearance of prophecy, following its disappearance sometime during the Second Temple period. For this reason, their writings included laws and other material concerning prophets.[36]

Extremely significant material relating to this issue appears in 4Q375, recently published by Strugnell.[37] The first fragment of this text consists of three sections dealing with prophecy, while the second fragment describes a ritual of atonement conducted in the Temple. Given the present state of the document, and particularly the fact that both fragments are written on the same scroll, one must accept Strugnell's opinion that the two fragments are related to one another, that is, that the ritual is meant to be performed following the appearance of the people at 'the place which the LORD your God will choose', so as to clarify whether the prophet in question is to be executed or allowed to stay alive.

The first fragment presents two basic concepts concerning prophecy: (1) that one is required to obey God's commandments which are announced 'by the mouth of the prophet' (ll. 1-4); (2) that a prophet who attempts to persuade the people to leave God's commandments and ways must be put to death. Parallels to these two laws, dealing with two opposite sides of prophecy, appear in the Bible.

The second section is followed by a third section without any explicit parallel in the biblical material, certainly not in any legal text. Lines 4-9 refer to the reaction of the tribe '[that] he comes from' (אשר] הואה ממנו[), which opposes the decision to execute its prophet, demanding that he be

---

36. Regarding the issue of prophecy see Brin, 'Biblical Prophecy in Qumran Literature'.

37. J. Strugnell, 'Moses-Pseudepigrapha at Qumran'. The spaces in the text copied are based upon Strugnell, albeit some of them have no confirmation from the copy of the document found in his article. I suggest below some modifications to his reconstructions.

released. It is implied that, notwithstanding the severe accusation leveled against the prophet that he persuaded the people to leave God's ways, it seems to be sufficient to point to his past deeds (ll. 6-7: for he is...a [fai]thful prophet'; נביא) [נ]אמן הואה) as a valid justification for his release.

This situation is very strange, because opposition to the execution of a false prophet contradicts the laws found in Deuteronomy 13. Even stranger, this opposition is not based upon denial of the accusation per se, but refers instead to the positive elements in the prophet's past history.

The law concerning the seducer prophet, which appears in Deut. 13.2-6, reads as follows:

> If a prophet arises among you, or a dreamer of dreams, and gives you a sign or a wonder, and the sign or wonder that he tells you comes to pass, and if he says, 'Let us go after other gods', which you have not known, 'and let us serve them', you shall not listen to the words of that prophet or to that dreamer of dreams; for the LORD your God is testing you, to know whether you love the LORD with all your heart and with all your soul. You shall walk after the LORD your God and fear him, and keep his commandments and obey his voice, and you shall serve him and cleave to him. But that prophet or that dreamer of dreams shall be put to death, because he has taught rebellion against the LORD your God, who brought you out of the land of Egypt and redeemed you out of the house of bondage, to make you leave the way in which the LORD your God commanded you to walk. So you shall purge evil from the midst of you.

The identical law appears in 11QTemple 54.8-18, with very slight textual variations. Some of these changes are typical of the *Temple Scroll*, such as the use of the first person in speech attributed to God, and the like. The fact that the author of 4Q375 does not make these changes indicates that he elaborates the biblical text without the 'intermediacy' of such works as the *Temple Scroll*. On the other hand, as I shall show below, he is very close to the *Temple Scroll* regarding other issues, both textual and otherwise.

Through comparison with the text of Deuteronomy 13, it is clear that the wording of lines 4-5, even though worded as if it is the beginning of the subject, is actually based upon the final part of the law of the prophet in Deuteronomy 13. Unlike the biblical formula, 'but that prophet or that dreamer of dreams shall be put to death' (Deut. 13.6), its wording is, 'but the prophet who rises up...' (l. 4), which is an introductory formula. We can see from this that the author combines here two separate textual elements: the beginning of the biblical text and its middle. That is, his wording was based upon v. 2, 'if a prophet arises among you...', combined with v. 6, 'but that prophet...' However, since the structure of the words is based upon v. 6, he must alter the middle part of the verse, which originally refers back to v. 2, so as to make it stand independently. But v. 6 does not contain any accusation against the prophet, because one already appeared at the beginning of the section: 'Let us go after other gods, which you have not known, and let us serve them' (v. 3). Thus, the author decides to utilize the causal clause, which in the Bible appears immediately after the order to execute the prophet, which is transferred in such a way as to become part of the prophet's definition: '...who rises up and preaches among thee [apostasy so as to make thee] turn away from thy God'.

In the Bible: '...shall be put to death, because he has taught rebellion against the LORD your God, who brought you out of the land of Egypt and redeemed you out of the house of bondage, to make you leave the way in which the LORD your God commanded you to walk'. יומת כי דבר סרה על ה' אלהיכם.

In 4Q 375: '...and preaches among thee [apostasy so as to make thee] turn away from thy God, he shall be put to death'. ודבר בכה [סרה להש]יבכה מאחרי אלוהיכה יומת

The exchange of these components led to an additional change: instead of accusing the prophet of uttering words of apostasy against God, as in the biblical text, the text here accuses him of uttering words of apostasy to the people, persuading them to abandon God's ordinances. This phenomenon finds parallels in other compositions, such as the *Temple Scroll*. In any event, as a result of the above-described change, the author was unable to use the other part of the biblical verse, which describes God in these words: 'who brought you out of the land of Egypt and redeemed you out of the house of bondage' (v. 6).

Such accusations are leveled against a prophet in two biblical passages. In Jer. 28.16, in a prophecy against Hananiah ben Azzur, we read, 'This very year you shall die, because you have uttered rebellion (סרה) against the LORD'. In the next chapter, it is stated against Shemaiah, '...for he has spoken rebellion (סרה) against the LORD' (29.32). In both cases, one finds an application of the laws of Deuteronomy 13 combined with those of Deuteronomy 18.

In 4Q375, the details of the accusation stemming from the prophet's speech of apostasy are worded slightly differently from their biblical counterpart. Instead of 'to make you leave the way in which the LORD your God commanded you to walk' (Deut. 13, 6), we read '[so as to make thee] turn away from thy God' (l. 5). A similar accusation appears in CD 6.1-2: '...and because they prophesied falsehood so as to turn Israel away from God'. There too, as in 4Q375, this wicked behaviour is ascribed to false prophets. By contrast, the positive way is described as follows: '...all those...shall enter into the Covenant before God to obey all his Commandments so that they may not abandon...' (1QS 1.16-17).[38]

While the biblical description concludes with this, 4Q375 contains an additional element, without parallel in the Bible: the 'appeal' of the prophet's tribe against his execution. Such a practice or law is unknown in the Bible.

ii. *Textual-Philological Exegesis of Fragment 1 i*

Fragment 1 i:

את כול אשר] יצוה אלוהיכה אליכה מפי הנביא ושמרתה	1
את כל החו]קים האלה ושבתה עד ה' אלוהיכה בכול	2
לבכה ובכו]ל נפשכה ושב אלוהיכה מחרון אפו הגדול	3
להושיעכ]ה ממצוקותיכה והנביא אשר יקום ודבר בכה	4
סרה להש]יבכה מאחרי אלוהיכה יומת [ ]וכיא יקום השבט	5
אשר] הואה ממנו ואמר לוא יומת כיא צדיק הואה נביא	6
נ]אמן הואה ובאתה עם השבט ההואה וזקניכה ושופטיכה	7
א]ל המקום אשר יבחר אלוהיכה באחד שבטיכה לפני	8
ה]כוהן המשיח אשר יוצק על ר[ו]אשו שמן המשיחה	9

(1)...thou shalt perform all that] thy God will command thee by the mouth of the prophet, and thou shalt keep (2) [all these sta]tutes, and thou shalt return unto YAHWE thy God with all (3) [thy heart and with al]l thy soul and (or: then) thy God will turn from the fury of His great anger [(4) so as to save th]ee from [all] thy distress.

But the prophet who rises up and preaches among thee (5) [apostasy so as to make thee] turn away from thy God, he shall be put to death. But, if there stands up the tribe (6) [which] he comes from, and says 'Let him not be put to death, for he is righteous (or: truthful), a [(7) fai]thful prophet is

---

38. According to Strugnell, 'Moses-Pseudepigrapha', p. 229, the phrase 'to make thee] turn away from thy God' (l. 5) is a non-biblical elaboration of Deut. 13.6, 'to make you leave the way'. However, I have already explained the author's difficulties in using the biblical wording of accusation against the prophet in Deut. 13.6. Moreover, the use of להש[יבכה (l. 5) is intended to match the key-word in the document: ושבתה (l. 2); ושב (l. 3). The author uses this word under the influence of 2 Kgs 23.25-26.

he', then thou shalt come, with that tribe and thy elders and thy judges,
[(8) t]o the place which thy God shall choose among one of thy tribes,
into the presence of [(9) the] anointed priest, upon whose head poured the
oil of anointing.

Our document opens with the demand that the people obey God's
instruction as transmitted by the true prophet:[39]

...thou shalt perform all that] thy God will command thee by the mouth of
the prophet, and thou shalt keep [all these sta]tutes, and thou shalt return
unto YAHWE thy God with all [thy heart and with al]l thy soul and (or:
then) thy God will turn from the fury of His great anger [so as to save
th]ee from [all] thy distress.

Such a demand does not appear in the text of Deuteronomy 13. A
parallel text containing such a demand for obedience to the true prophet
(which the people refused to obey) appears in *Pesher Hosea* (4Q166 ii
3-5): 'But they forgot God who [...] They cast His Commandments
behind them which He had sent [in the mouth of] His servants the
prophets, and they listened to those who led them astray, and they
revered them...'.[40]

Only thereafter, in lines 4-5, does there appear the issue of the seducer
prophet, based upon Deuteronomy 13, elaborated as described above:
'But the prophet who rises up and preaches among thee [apostasy so as
to make thee] turn away from thy God' (ll. 4-5).

In my opinion, it may be demonstrated that lines 1-3 also originated in
Deuteronomy 13. Deut. 13.1 constitutes the concluding formula of the
final section of Deut. 12: 'Everything that I command you shall be
careful to do; you shall not add to it or take from it'. However, in
4Q375 this motif appears at the very beginning of the first subject—the
true prophet—which precedes that of the seducer prophet. It is
interesting to note that 11QTemple 54.5-7 likewise cites Deut. 13.1
before the law of the seducer prophet. In both 4Q375 and the Temple
Scroll, Deut. 12.29-31, of which 13.1 is the concluding formula, is not

39. A contrasting phrase to this appears in 1QH 4.15-18, 'and they set before
them the stumbling block of their sin. They come to inquire of Thee from the mouth
of lying prophets deceived by error who speak [with strange] lips to Thy people, and
alien tongue...For [they hearken] not [to] Thy [voice], nor do they give ear to Thy
word'.

40. See J.M. Allegro, *Discoveries*, V, p. 31, 4Q166 ii 3-5. This passage deals with
the issue of disobedience to the true prophet and following after the false prophets.
See also my previous note, and cf. Brin, 'Biblical Prophecy'.

used.[41] That is, in both texts 13.1 appears without the previous section, which serves as its immediate context. However, in the *Temple Scroll* Deut. 13.1 is still used as the concluding formula (for the law of vows). Thus, the author of the *Temple Scroll* has substituted Deut. 13.1 for the original ending of that law (Num. 30.17).

The wording of this section of our document is as follows:

> (1)...thou shalt perform all that] thy God will command thee by the mouth of the prophet, and thou shalt keep (2) [all these sta]tutes, and thou shalt return unto YAHWE thy God with all (3) [thy heart and with al]l thy soul and (or then) thy God will turn from the fury of His great anger (4) [so as to save th]ee from [all] thy distress'.

Examaniation of the begining of this section clearly reveals that it is essentially an elaboration of Deut. 13.1: 'Everything that I command you you shall be careful to do, you shall not add to it or take from it'. Moreover, if we take into account the various versions found in parallel sources, ancient translations, and the like, the resemblance to 13.1 becomes even more pronounced. Thus, according to the Samaritan version, the Peshitta, the Septuagint (most manuscripts), and the Vulgate, the text begins in the singular rather than the plural: 'God commands thee' (מצוך) rather than 'you', in the plural (מצוה אתכם). Our document likewise follows this reading.

Comparison of these texts reveals that we have here the same text as Deut. 13.1, with the difference that the first-person speaker of Deuteronomy is converted into the third person. This is opposed to the usual manner of elaboration of the *Temple Scroll*, in which third-person speech is converted into first-person speech uttered by God.

The author may also have been influenced by other Deuteronomic texts concerning the obligation to follow the instructions of the true

---

41. Deut. 13.1 essentially closes the previous section, but despite this comes at the beginning of a chapter, as against the ancient Jewish division into *parashot*, in which the break comes after 13.1. Thus, the mistake made by Langton in dividing the Bible into chapters has ancient roots, as seen in our document. Both the author of 4Q375 and Langton (and possible also the *Temple Scroll*, but see above) see in 13.1 the beginning of a unit rather than an ending point. In modern Bible translations (English, German, etc.), ch. 13 starts with v. 2 of the MT, seeing v. 1 as the conclusion of ch. 12, which is correct from the exegetical point of view. However, there are some commentators who, through a complicated process of reconstruction of the history of the chapter, see 13.1 as a beginning; see, for example, S.R. Driver, *Deuteronomy, ad loc.*

prophet, such as Deut. 18.18, 'and he shall speak to them all that I command him'.

The phrase 'everything (הדבר, singular) that I command you, you shall be careful to do' in Deut. 13.1 appears in our document in the plural: 'and thou shalt keep [all these sta]tutes (חוקים)'. The same holds true for 11QTemple 54.5-7: כול הדברים אשר אנכי מצווכה אותמה היום תשמור לעשות ('all the things that I command you concerning them this day, you shall take care to perform them...').

The closing phrase in Deut. 13.1, 'you shall not add to it or take from it', is not used in our document, because it serves as a concluding formula, whereas our author uses that verse as an opening formula, as I have demonstrated above.

In the opening verse here, our author adds the phrase, 'by the mouth of the prophet' (l. 1). Moses' first-person speech in Deut. 13.1, typical of Deuteronomic style, is converted into third-person speech spoken by God, 'thou shalt perform [all that] thy God will command thee by the mouth of the prophet' (l. 1), facilitating the description of God as lawgiver. The author continues from there quite naturally to relate how God's commands have come to the knowledge of the people, namely, by means of the prophet. In this way, he is able to differentiate between the true prophet and the prophet who preaches apostasy to the people in order to dissuade them from obeying God's commands.

All this is useful to the author, who intends to present a full range of laws regarding prophecy, based upon Deuteronomy 13. On this basis, he states that the true prophets are God's intermediaries, charged with conveying his instructions to the people, thereby completing the Torah.[42]

The author then describes the deeds of the seducer prophet in legal terms, using the appropriate section in Deuteronomy 13 with some changes owing to his method of elaboration.

In lines 2b-3, which continue lines 1-2a, he writes' 'and thou shalt return unto YAHWE thy God with all [thy heart and with al]l thy soul'. This is an elaboration of Deut. 13.4-5: 'for the LORD your God is testing you, to know whether you love the LORD with all your heart and with all your soul. You shall walk after the LORD your God and fear him, and keep his commandments and obey his voice, and you shall serve him and cleave to him'. But whereas in the Bible the text speaks about

---

42. Regarding the proofs from the scrolls for such a role of the prophets, see Brin, 'Biblical Prophecy'.

the nature of the trial posed by the seducer prophet, demanding that the people reject his ideas and act in accordance with God's commands, in our document the author transfers this section to the beginning, making it a description of the aim of true prophecy announced 'by the mouth of the prophet' (l. 1).[43]

Lines 3b-4: 'and (or: then) thy God will turn from the fury of His great anger [so as to save th]ee from [all] thy distress', is an expression composed by the Qumran author. This illustrates the difficulty he experienced in arranging this material, in that he needed to speak of God's decision to cancel his planned punishments within the framework of this positive section. The author drew upon Deut. 13.18, '...that the LORD may turn from the fierceness of his anger', changing God's name from *YHWH* to *Elohim* (I will deal below with his approach towards the use of the divine names).

The author now turns to the issue of the seducer prophet as such. I already described above his method of organizing this passage, altering the syntax of v. 6 and refraining from describing the prophet as 'that prophet', because in this case it is not the same kind of prophet as that spoken about by the author at the beginning of the passage.

In lines 5b-7, the author focuses his attention on the appeal brought by the prophet's tribe against his execution: 'But if there stands up the tribe [that] he comes from, and says, "Let him not be put to death, for he is righteous (or: truthful), a [fai]thful prophet is he"'. The idiom, 'if there stands up the tribe' (וכי יקום השבט) is derived from the beginning of the law of the seducer prophet, 'if a prophet arises among you' (Deut. 13.2) and such passages as 'a scepter (or: tribe, שבט) shall rise out of Israel' (Num. 24.17), which likewise appears in Qumranic writings (1QM 11.6; CD 7.19-20).

The idea of associating the prophet with a particular tribe ('the tribe [that] he comes from') is not a biblical one. Hence, we must inquire into its origins. I believe that this idea is also based on Deuteronomy 13, but utilizing an exegesis representing the author's own understanding rather than the original intent of the biblical text.

---

43. I therefore cannot accept the reference cited by Strugnell, 'Moses-Pseudepigrapha', p. 228. Proof of my position may be found in the fact that the source of the following section ('and God shall return', etc.) is also in Deut. 13. Moreover, the use of divine names in our document, which I will deal with later, further supports the biblical reference that I have mentioned above concerning this section.

Deut. 13.2 reads, 'If a prophet arises among you'. This wording led our author to explain the text as referring to a prophet who comes from among you (מקרבך), that is, from a certain circle of people. One of the biblical phrases used to describe such a 'circle' is 'tribe'; cf. the use in line 8, 'among one of thy tribes'.

Notwithstanding the fact that the Bible does not draw any connection between prophets and specific tribes per se, there are many passages that betray a local flavour of prophecy. Thus, mention is made in 2 Kings 2 of 'sons of the prophets' from Jericho (v. 5 and 15), and others that dwell at Beth El (v. 3). In 1 Kgs 13.11 there is 'an old prophet in Beth-el' (cf. v. 25: 'told it in the town where the old prophet dwells'). Alongside this, another 'man of God...who came from Judah' (2 Kgs 23.17) is mentioned. Jonah ben Amitai is described as 'the prophet who was from Gat-Hepher' (2 Kgs 14.25). Jeremiah's rival, Hananiah ben Azzur, is defined as 'the prophet from Gibeon' (Jer. 28.1). The controversy concerning Amos's prophecy likewise bears a local tone. The authorities in Beth-el try to drive him back to Judah: 'O Seer, go flee away to the land of Judah, and eat bread there, and prophesy there' (Amos 7.12).

It is clear that these prophets were not connected to particular tribes as such, as would seem to be implied by our document. Nevertheless, all of these texts do carry a local connotation, which in turn implies connection to the tribe. Hence, the idea expressed in our document that the tribe wishes to protect its own prophet is logical.

Moreover, a connection between prophets and tribes does appear in Talmudic literature. Thus, *b. Suk.* 27b: 'There was not a single tribe in Israel that did not produce prophets'; *t. Suk.* 1.9: 'There was not a single tribe in Israel that did not raise up a prophet'. This idea also appears in the Pseudepigrapha. In *Lives of the Prophets* 5.1, Hosea is identified as stemming from the tribe of Issachar; in 6.1, Micah from Ephraim; in 8.1, Joel from Reuben; in 11.1, Nahum from Simeon; in 13.1, Zephaniah from Simeon, and so on.

The tribe's appeal here includes the words, 'Let him not be put to death', which openly contradicts the wording of this selfsame law, 'he shall be put to death'. This is reminiscent of the episode in Jeremiah's trial, in which the accusers demand, 'this man deserves the sentence of death' (Jer. 26.11),[44] while Jeremiah's defenders (or perhaps the final

---

44. Regarding the situation of the passages in Jer. 26, see Brin, *The Prophet in his Struggles*, pp. 33-55.

verdict) states, 'this man does not deserve the sentence of death' (v. 16). Were it not for the use there of מות as a noun, that passage would have been identical to the form in our document. See also Deut. 17.6, 'a person shall not be put to death on the evidence of one witness'; Deut. 24.16, 'Fathers shall not be put to death for the children, nor shall children be put to death...'; Lev. 19.20, '...They shall not be put to death'.

The significance of these passages is that they are articulated in judicial contexts. Two of them even have the same construction as the sentence in our document: ...לא יומת...כי (Lev. 19.20; Deut. 24.16). It is worth adding that most of these parallel texts are taken from Deuteronomy, which is the source for most (and perhaps all) of the phrases in this document.[45]

The Bible does contain one case of opposition to the carrying out of a death penalty. During the battle against the Philistines, Saul adjures the people not to eat until the victory against the Philistines is achieved. His son, Jonathan, unknowingly violated that oath. The identity of the violator is discovered through the oracular use of the Urim and the Thumim, and he is supposed to be executed, in accordance with Saul's oath to execute whoever is found to have violated the oath. The people intervene on his behalf, crying, '"Shall Jonathan die, who has wrought this great victory in Israel? Far from it! As the LORD lives, not one hair of his head shall fall to the ground..." So the people ransomed Jonathan, that he did not die' (1 Sam. 14.45).

But despite the fact that we do find there an incident of intervention on the part of the people to stay an execution, the two incidents are not identical, nor even similar. In the case of Jonathan, there was no violation of a substantive law of the Torah, but rather unintentional transgression of a royal oath. The people's intervention led to the cancellation of the execution, but may in no way be defined as an attempt to countervene an explicit law. For other parallel cases, see the end of this chapter.

The argument brought by the tribe on behalf of its prophet is worded

45. The phrase used by the tribe, 'Let him not be put to death', explicitly contradicts the statement of law, 'But the prophet who rises up and preaches among thee [apostasy so as to make thee] turn away from thy God, he shall be put to death'. This is reminiscent of the contradiction between the statement by the serpent, 'You shall surely not die', and God's command, 'you shall not eat of the fruit of the garden...lest you die' (Gen. 3.3-4).

as follows: 'for[46] he is righteous (or: truthful), a [fai]thful prophet is he'. The statement about his being 'righteous' does not necessarily relate to his prophetic career or personal history, but may simply mean that the accusation against him is not true, that he is the 'righteous' party (צדיק) in this particular case (cf. Deut. 25.1). On the other hand, the phrase 'a [fai]thful prophet is he' clearly relates to his calling as a prophet.

There are many sources in the Bible for the former phrase; thus, 'he is righteous' (Ezek. 18.9).[47] On the other hand, the latter phrase is without parallel in the Bible, albeit there are a number of phrases that are similar. To cite a few texts using similar phrases: it is said regarding Samuel that 'Samuel was faithful (נאמן, or "established") as a prophet of the LORD' (1 Sam. 3.20). The connection among God, prophets and faithfulness is likewise found, among other places, in 1 Chron. 20.20: 'Believe in the LORD your God, and you will be established (והאמנו); believe His prophets, and you will succeed'. See also below on the connection between God's characteristics and those of the prophets.

Concerning the argument used by the tribe making the appeal, it is illuminating to compare God's statement about Moses, 'If there is a prophet among you...Not so with my servant Moses; he is entrusted (נאמן = faithful) with all my house' (Num. 12.6-7). This term refers to Moses' prophecy, as may be seen from the sequel, 'with him I speak mouth to mouth...' (v. 8). The use of the term 'faithful' in such a central text regarding prophecy and its definition may indicate an important source indicative of the direction of the thinking of the author of our document. In the LXX to Num. 12.7, נאמן is translated as πιστός. To this one should add Strugnell's remark concerning the phrase προφήτην πιστόν (נביא נאמן) in 1 Macc. 14.41, referring to the future prophet.[48]

Another interesting phrase is that in Isa. 1.26, '...the city of righteousness, the faithful city' (קריה נאמנה), combining both components of the persona of the prophet found in lines 6-7. Such usages are likewise found in Hab. 2.4, 'but the righteous shall live by his faith'. It is

---

46. Regarding the space, see above, n. 37.

47. Strugnell, 'Moses-Pseudepigrapha', p. 229, compares this with Isa. 41.26: 'Who declared it from the beginning, that we might know, and beforetime, that we might say, "He is righteous"'. However, it is not clear whether this refers to the prophet or to God himself. Moreover, 'righteous' is not a term typically used to define a prophet, so that this verse in Isaiah is no proof that it is ascribed to a prophet.

48. Strugnell, 'Moses-Pseudepigrapha', p. 229.

interesting that, in dealing with this passage, PesHab 8.1-3 reads, 'This concerns all those who observe the law in the house of Judah, whom God will deliver from the House of Judgement because of their suffering and because of their faith in the Teacher of righteousness'. Note the astonishing parallel to our document created by the presence of all three basic components: righteousness, faithfulness and the 'House of Judgment'. In our document, righteousness corresponds to the High Court to which the tribe, accompanied by others, appeals: 'then thou shalt come, with that tribe and thy elders and thy judges, [t]o the place which thy God shall choose'. (See below for the manner in which the law in Deut. 17 is reworked in this document.)

Psalm 19.10 includes both components, 'the ordinances of the Lord are true, and righteous altogether', as do other similar biblical texts. But in general, one may state that the idioms אמת וצדק or אמת וצדקה are found less frequently in the Bible than in the smaller corpus of Qumranic writings.

The sectarian literature frequently contains phrases concerning faithfulness, truth and righteousness, for example, CD 9.22-23: 'two faithful witnesses'; 9.21-22: 'if they are faithful'; 3.19: 'and He built them a sure (lit. faithful) house'. Compare also its use in a liturgical text: 'a faithful shepherd' (1Q34[b] 3 ii 8).[49] In 11QTemple 56.3-4, discussing Deut. 17.10-11, the biblical text is modified through the addition of the word אמת—'and declare to you truly'—which is also one change introduced by the author of the *Temple Scroll* into the law of the high court. A similar usage appears in 4QShirShabb: אמת [ו]צדק (4Q404 5 6); רוחי דעת אמת [ו]צדק (4Q405 19 4); ...אמת וצדק עולמ[י (4Q405 20 ii 21-22 5).[50] Finally, in 1QM 4.6 we find the form: אמת אל צדק אל.

The use of 'faithfulness', sometimes in texts referring specifically to prophecy(!), is typical of the literature of the Second Commonwealth. Thus, in Sir. 46.13-15: 'Sanctified of the LORD in the prophetical office, Samuel, who acted as judge and priest...Because of his truthfulness they sought the prophet (חזה), and the seer (רואה)[51] was also found reliable in his words'. Samuel is thus described by the terms prophecy, seer and

49. DJD, I, pp. 152-54.
50. C. Newsom, *Songs of the Sabbath Sacrifice*, pp. 252, 293, 303.
51. It is worth noting that the edition of Ben Sira published by the Academy of the Hebrew Language (Jerusalem, 1973) records that the root אמן appears 24 times in the various passages, 11 of which are in the same conjugation (*niphal*) as the usage with which we are dealing here.

faithful.[52] In Sir. 36.20-21 the prophets are referred to in general: 'Give testimony to the first of Thy works, and establish the vision spoken in Thy name. Give reward to them that await for Thee, that Thy prophets may be proved trustworthy'. The term 'be proved trustworthy' (יאמינו, from the root אמן) here means that they will be acknowledged as faithful, because their predictions are fulfilled. The term 'faithful' also refers to Abraham (44.20, who is given the title 'prophet' in Gen. 20.7). Job is likewise called 'prophet' (49.9): 'He also made mention of Job among the prophets who maintained all the ways of righteousness'.[53] Here, there only appears the term צדק (righteousness) without 'faithful', but in Job 34.2 there appears the phrase 'a faithful friend'.

It is worth pointing out that the blessings recited over the reading of the *Haftarah* in the synagogue uses very similar phrases: 'God...who has chosen good prophets and desires their words which were said in truth (באמת)...who chooses the Torah...and the prophets of truth and righteousness (אמת וצדק)'.[54] These terms originated during the Second Commonwealth period, as has been shown by students of the history of Jewish liturgy.[55] Prophets are referred to with terms of faithful, truth and righteousness, which resemble those in the present document.[56]

52. In Charles's edition of Ben Sira, רועה ('shepherd') is seen as a misreading for רואה ('seer').

53. Regarding Job's 'prophecy', see *S. 'Ol. R.*, ch. 21.

54. Further on in that passage, phrases are used referring to God which are very similar to those said about the '[true and faithful] prophets': '...faithful God... whose words are all of truth and righteousness. You are faithful, O God...and Your words are of truth are faithful...for You are a faithful king...God who is faithful in all His words'. These phrases of righteousness, truth and faithfulness make the description of the prophet in the tribe's argumentation very similar to that of God. I have already cited the phrases of righteousness and truth relating to God from the scroll literature, and there are many more. See, for example, 1QH 1.31, '...in all Thy works of truth and [in all thy] righteous [judgements]''; 4.40, '...for You are (the) truth and all Your deeds are in righteousness'; 1QM 13.3, 'Blessed be all those who [serve] Him in righteousness and who know Him by faith', etc.

55. See J. Heinemann, *Prayer in the Talmud*, pp. 228-29, regarding the early date of these blessings. He states that the blessings of the Haftarah were formulated earlier than the seven benedictions of the Sabbaths. On p. 227, he sees them as having derived from the benedictions of the High Priest. On p. 34, he explains that they were composed in opposition to the numerous false prophets of that period, e.g., the visions included in the Apocrypha. See also D. Flusser, 'Sanctus und Gloria'.

56. The use of phrases of truth and righteousness in relation to the biblical prophets also appears in Josephus' writings. In *Apion* 1.37-39, he defines the differences

To return to our document: after mentioning the appeal of the tribe (ll. 5-7), there follows the instruction: 'then thou shalt come, with that tribe and thy elders and thy judges, [t]o the place which thy God shall choose among one of thy tribes,[57] into the presence of [the] anointed priest, upon whose head poured the oil of anointing'.

One might ask whom this text is addressing. Until now, the addressee was Israel, who hears the laws. However, the lawgiver here calls upon the addressee to come with the tribe bringing the appeal 'and thy elders and thy judges', suggesting that the local elders and judges are likewise referred to in the second person. It may be that here too the text refers to Israel, the sense being that the people are to come '[t]o the place which thy God shall choose', together with their leaders and judges, all of whom will accompany the appealing tribe. Thus, the entire procedure is to be performed on the general national level, owing to the highly sensitive nature of the issue at stake: a prophet who has spoken against God, thereby leading Israel astray, and whose tribe nevertheless supports him.

Another sign of the general, public nature of the procedure appears in the second fragment (1 ii), in which the high priest conducts a certain ritual reminiscent of that of the Day of Atonement, at the end of which, after studying the hidden laws (הנסת[רות ממכה), it states, 'And he shall come forth before a[ll the leaders of] the assembly. And this [...]' (ll. 8-9). If these two fragments in fact belong to one sequence, it seems probable that the phrase, 'then thou shalt come' refers in fact to the entire nation, with its leaders. If this interpretation is not accepted, 'thou' may simply refer to all those who were present at the incident in which the prophet appeared and heard the protest of the tribe. However, the words 'thy elders and thy judges' mitigate against this interpretation, which cannot

---

between the Jewish Canon and the Hellenistic writings. Among the advantages of the Bible, he mentions the existence of an uninterrupted line of prophets, as well as the fact that all of the biblical literature was written with righteousness—two factors which he finds missing in the Hellenistic writings. He adds that the interruption of the line of prophecy during the Persian period diminished the value and importance of post-biblical Jewish writings. In *Ant.* 10.35, Josephus defines Isaiah as a truthful prophet who, because he knew that he never uttered a single false word, recorded his prophecies so that their truth might be revealed in the future. Josephus adds that the same applies to the other prophets.

57. Regarding the space in the text, see above, n. 37.

be connected with an individual or a random group, but suggest a
national, or at least tribal, context.

I would like to add that the reference to the elders and judges is
suitable to a national affair. Thus, for example, in the ceremony of the
covenant in Josh. 23.2, we read, 'Joshua summoned all Israel, their
elders and heads, their judges and officers'. A similarly impressive
picture appears in Deut. 29.9: 'You stand this day all of you...the heads
of your tribes, your elders, and your officers'. In the ceremony of
blessing and cursing in Josh. 8.33, there participate 'all Israel... with their
elders and officers and their judges', and so on. Our author uses these
and other such phrases to convey the special atmosphere appropriate to
such an event.

Moreover, if up until this point the basic biblical text used by the
author as a source for both kinds of prophets, the true prophet and the
seductive false prophet (ll. 4-5), was Deuteronomy 13, from line 7
onwards the basic text used is Deut. 17.8-13, the law describing the high
court. This law states that if one does not know how to rule in a
particularly difficult case, 'then you shall arise and go up to the
place...and come to the Levitical priests...' (vv. 8-9). The word used
there is ובאת ('you shall arise' or 'you shall come'), which is likewise
used at the beginning of the new stage in our document. In Deut. 17.9,
however, it may refer to the local judge who has difficulty in deciding a
knotty case, or to one of the litigants in a judicial dispute which cannot
be resolved by the local judges. As our author utilizes the biblical text in
a somewhat different sense than the original, he must add a few phrases
of his own formulation that are absent in the original. By so doing, even
though he attempts to write in the biblical manner, he betrays his own
later style.[58]

In lines 8-9, it is written: '[t]o the place which thy God shall choose
among one of thy tribes, into the presence of [the] anointed priest'.
Although he uses the general wording of Deuteronomy 17, the author
inserts two changes: (1) he reads, 'the place which thy God shall
choose', rather than 'the place which the LORD your God will choose'
(Deut. 17.8); (2) the location of the phrase regarding 'the place which...
shall choose' is different than in the biblical source.

The second change is a result of the fact that the author adopted a
principal law with an opening formula specifically concerned with

---

58. Regarding this consideration, see Brin, 'The Bible as Reflected', p. 212.

difficult cases for a completely different issue: a legal appeal concerning a seducer prophet. He thus needed to scrap the original opening formula and compose a substitute one suitable to his case. He thereby lost the original location of the phrase, 'the place...', which he was then forced to place in his rewriting of v. 9, rather than in v. 8 as in the original.

Regarding the former change, the phrase used there, 'the place which thy God shall choose', does not appear in any biblical text; Deut. 17.8 reads 'the place which the LORD your God will choose'. The phrase, 'among one of thy tribes', added in line 8, reflects the influence of Deut. 12.14, which is the only biblical text using it.

The change in God's name from ה' אלהיך (Deut. 17.8) to אלוהיכה (l. 8) is clearly a result of the author's policy regarding God's names. Thus:

יצוה אלוהיכה	1
ושבתה עד ה' אלוהיכה	2
ושב אלוהיכה	3
להשיבכה מאחרי אלוהיכה	5
יבחר אלוהיכה	8

One can clearly see here that there is an overwhelming majority of uses of the name Elohim (five times) as against that of YHWH (once; but even in that instance it does not appear alone, but as part of the double name YHWH *Elohim*). Moreover, in all of those texts in which God is referred to as the actor or author of certain deeds, the name used is *Elohim*. Again, in all of those phrases which were composed by the author, rather than those copied from the biblical text, the name used is *Elohim*. Thus, in line 1, God's first-person speech, 'that I command you' (Deut. 13.1), is changed to the third person, using the name *Elohim*, 'thy God will command thee' (l. 1); in line 3, 'then thy God will turn from the fury of His great anger' is a reworking of Deut. 13.18, '...that the LORD may turn from the fierceness of his anger'. The author thus changed both the status of this sentence (as described above), as well as altering God's name from YHWH to Elohim. Line 8, 't]o the place which thy God shall choose', is, as stated above, a variation based upon either Deut. 17.8, 'the place which the LORD your God will choose', or 17.10, 'from that place which the LORD will choose'. In either case, the name YHWH is dropped, consistent with the author's general tendency.

The only appearance of YHWH (in its dual form: YHWH *Elohim*) is in ll. 2-3, 'and thou shalt return unto *YAHWE* thy God with all [thy heart and with al]l thy soul.' This is an elaboration of Deut. 13.4-5, '...with all your heart and with all your soul. You shall walk after the LORD your God and fear him'. Thus, even this usage is not really his own, but is copied from a biblical source, which in this case he left unaltered.

In fragment 1 ii, the name YHWH again appears, in the phrase 'and shall study a[ll the laws of] YAHWE' (ll. 7-8). As in the previous example (1 i 2-3), the author evidently feels that a phrase which speaks about the commandments—that is, the laws of God—ought to be worded with the Ineffable Name. Hence, this case is like the previously-mentioned one from fragment 1 i, with certain changes required by the different contents and usage in these two examples.

Let us now return to our line-by-line exegesis of the text, resuming where we left off. A new idiom is used in line 7: 'then thou shalt come with that tribe and thy elders...' The phrase generally used in biblical Hebrew to describe going in company is: ו (ובאת אתה) ...Thus, for example, Gen. 6.18; Exod. 3.18; Ezek. 38.15, etc. Here, however, we find a different construction:ובאת עם... It should be noted that the form בא עם does appear in the Bible in this sense in a few rare instances (Gen. 29.6; Ps. 26.4; Est. 5.14), and in a few post-biblical texts. More often, the idiom בא עם is used in connection with a quarrel, a dispute, litigation, or the like; thus, Isa. 3.14, 'The LORD enters [lit.: comes] into judgment with the elders and princes of his people'; Job 22.4, 'Is it for your fear of him that he reproves you, and enters (lit.: comes) into judgment with you?'

Our author may have chosen this construction in order to refer, on the one hand, to, the entire nation who go together,...ו ובאתה אתה; and, on the other hand, the one who appeals: ובאת עם. Thus, the first group is described in accordance with the usual biblical method (...ובאת...ו...ו...), to indicate a series of groups going together. All of these accompany the latter group, that opposed to the execution of the prophet, their act of going being described in the variant form (ובאת עם), in order to help the author to distinguish the status of each group.[59]

Another interesting combination of verb and preposition appears in the same context: 'then thou shalt come, with that tribe...before [the] anointed priest' (ll. 7-9). The form 'to come before' (בוא לפני) is a very rare one in the Bible, appearing only in certain contexts unrelated to the usage in our case, all of which have the sense of priority in time or in space. Thus, in 2 Sam. 20.8, 'and Amasa came to meet them [lit. "came

59. I have found one text with בוא עם in the *Songs of the Sabbath Sacrifice*, 4Q402 1 2, '...as they came with the God [...' See Newsom, *Songs*, p. 149.

before them"]', where the text describes the position of Amasa in
relation to Joab and his men, and does not imply any relation of
authority or the presentation of a legal matter, as it does in the case of
our document. The same holds true for 2 Sam. 19.9, '...and all the
people came before the king'. Their coming before him has no connection with the king's status, but simply indicates their assembling
round him following Absalom's death. This description contrasts with
another one regarding their earlier behaviour, 'and the people stole into
the city that day as people steal in who are ashamed when they flee in
battle' (v. 4). Their rallying around the king came about in wake of
Joab's condemnation of David.[60]

The other uses of the phrase 'to come before' relate to cultic
purposes, and are intended to describe Moses, Aaron or others coming
before God. Thus in Exod. 34.34: 'but whenever Moses came in before
the Lord to speak with him'; 28.30: 'and they shall be upon Aaron's
heart when he comes before the LORD'; 1 Chron. 16.29, '...bring an
offering and come before him'. In the parallel text, Ps. 96.8, we read,
'...bring an offering, and come into his courts' (cf. LXX to 1 Chron.
16.29); Ps. 100.2: '...come before him with singing'; Ezek. 46.9, 'When
the people of the land come before the LORD', and so on.

There are still other cases in which בוא לפני is used in the sense of
approaching or being accepted by God, and the like. Thus, in Ps. 79.11,
'Let the groans of the prisoners come before thee'; 88.3, 'Let my
prayer come before thee'. Yet other texts using this phrase in reference
to God have the sense of bringing a case before his judgment, 'This
will be my salvation, that a godless man shall not come before him'
(Job 13.16).

Only in the book of Esther is the phrase בוא לפני used in connection
with a person (Est. 8.1), but even in that context the phrase means 'to
be allowed to get closer to the king', and does not have the sense of an
individual or dispute being brought before the authority (king, judge) for
a decision. As for Est. 9.25, ובבואה לפני המלך, 'but when she came before
the king', this is an admittedly difficult text. Scholars usually see it as
referring to Esther's approaching the king to ask him to cancel Haman's
orders. (Thus according to some ancient translations. The LXX, however,
ascribes this action to Haman. Others understand it as an indefinite

---

60. The compound phrases, בוא ויצא לפני ('come [and] go out before'), whether
they appear together or separately, have a different meaning, and are hence irrelevant
for our discussion; for that reason, I do not discuss such passages here.

Studies in Biblical Law

phrase, i.e., when Haman's order came under the king's review; cf. the commentaries on this passage.) It may be that this text actually means, 'to bring a case before the decision of the authority'. If so, this is the only example of such a usage in the Bible; it will be remembered, as is well known, that the book of Esther is extremely late.[61]

On the other hand, this locution is used extensively used in rabbinic literature, in the sense of 'to come before an authority, teacher and the like, for a ruling or decision' (that is, the same usage as in our document). Thus: 'as they came before the court' (*m. Roš Haš.* 1.5); 'as the case came before R. Aqiba' (*m. Yeb.* 12.5); 'he then came before the court' (*m. B. Bat.* 10.6); and many more, as this is a common idiom in the Talmudic compositions.[62]

The Bible utilizes other idioms to express the same idea, especially עמד לפני, 'to stand before...' Thus, Num. 27.22: '...he took Joshua and caused him to stand before Eleazar the priest'; 27.2: 'And they stood before Moses and before Eleazar the priest'; Gen. 41.46: 'And Joseph was thirty years old when he stood before Pharaoh'; and many other like phrases.[63]

---

61. Est. 1.19 reads, 'If it please the king, let a royal order go forth...that Vashti is to come no more before king Ahashuerus'. In this case, the phrase refers to her approaching of the king and the continuation of her marital bond with him, as the following passage reads, 'and let the king give her royal position to another that is better than she'. Compare also v. 11, 'to bring Queen Vashti before the King'. See also 2.12, 13, 14, 15.

62. The substitution of the preposition לפני ('before') for other prepositions is typical of later biblical literature and of post-biblical literature; e.g. 1 Chron. 16.37, 'to serve always before the Ark'. See also 11QTemple 56.9 in the context of the law of the supreme court, in which the phrase לשרת לפני ('to serve before [Me]') appears instead of לשרת שם ('to serve there' [i.e. in the chosen place]).

63. Three passages from 1 Kgs 1 yield a seemingly different picture, in that these passages do contain the phrase בוא לפני המלך ('to come before the king'). However, a straightfoward reading of these passages reveals that the (later) meaning discussed here is not used in them. Verse 23 reads, 'and he (the prophet Nathan) came in before the king'. However, the passage begins, 'Nathan the prophet came in. And they told the king, "Here is Nathan the prophet". And when he came in before the king...' This indicates that the text simply describes Nathan's approaching the king in stages. Similarly, the phrase in question describes the moment at which he reached the king. In v. 28, we find a similar phrase, 'Then King David answered, "Call Bathsheba to me". So she came into the king's presence.' As in the previous passage, the phrase is used in the sense of 'to approach the king', especially in this text, where the approach was the result of the king's own initiative. It should be noted that the text expresses

The significance of this point regarding the phrase, 'then thou shalt come...into the presence of [lit., 'before'] [the] anointed priest' (1 i 7-9) is the following: our author, while utilizing the law of the high court in Deuteronomy 17, needs to alter it, because he uses it in a different manner than the original. In so doing, he must compose a phrase to bridge this gap, which is more likely to be worded in his own style. Thus, whereas in the Bible it says, 'You will come...to... and to...', he writes, 'then thou shalt come...before [the] anointed priest', a more usual manner of expression in his own day.

In this context, I would like to note an interesting usage of בוא לפני in the *Temple Scroll*. In 58.18-19, it is written, 'And he [the king] shall not go out [to war] until he comes before the high priest, who shall inquire for him by the judgment of the Urim and the Thummim'. This is a further indication of the late language of the *Temple Scroll*, which has hitherto not been noted in the research.

To continue with our document: '...before [the] anointed priest, upon whose head poured[64] the oil of anointing' (ll. 8-9). This text clearly refers to the high priest.[65] Thus, in addition to the above-mentioned signs regarding the national significance of this entire issue—namely, that all Israel must be present in the special appeal of the tribe regarding the fate of its prophet—the fact that the author introduces an explicit change from the basic text regarding the procedures of the supreme court (Deut. 17), by demanding that the high priest himself be in charge of that case, indicates the great severity and importance with which he

---

the same idea through two parallel phrases: 'so she came into the king's presence', and immediately thereafter, 'and she stood before the king'. The same holds true of v. 32, 'King David said, "Call to me Zadok the priest, Nathan the prophet..." So they came before the king.'

64. Regarding the space in the text, see above, n. 37.

65. As is known, the procedure of anointing by pouring oil on the head during the ceremony of inauguration is only mentioned regarding Aaron (Exod. 29.7; Lev. 8.12). For a general statement most similar to the phrase in our document, cf. Lev. 21.10, 'The priest who is chief among his brethren, upon whose head the anointing oil is poured'. All the components of our verse appear here, with the following exceptions: there he is described as 'chief among his brethren', whereas in 4Q375 he is called 'the anointed priest'; the word משחה appears in 4Q375 in a different construction, משיחה. Compare also 1QM 9.8, '...and they shall not profane the anointing (משיחה) of their priesthood with the blood of nations of vanity'. This construction does not appear in the Bible; it is, however, used in the Talmudic literature, indicating its late date. Compare *m. Men.* 6.3; *m. Hor.* 3.1; 3.2.

views the matter.[66] In the Bible, we read, '...and coming to the Levitical priests and to the judge who is in office in those days, you shall consult them and they shall declare to you the decision' (Deut. 17.9). It should be observed that this text is worded in very general, undramatic terms; the authorities from the High Court are referred to in the plural, and identified as belonging to two groups: 1. 'the Levitical priests'; 2. 'the judge who is in office in those days'. The minor key used here suits the everyday and ordinary matters that the law speaks about there— 'between one kind of homicide and another, one kind of legal right and another, or one kind of assault and another, any case within your towns...' (17.8)—whereas in our document the procedure is devoted to a unique case of an appeal against the fulfilment of the demand of the holy law on the part of one tribe.

iii. Textual-Philological Exegesis of Fragment 1 ii

The ritual described in the second fragment is strongly reminiscent of the ritual of the Day of Atonement (see below), and is a further sign of the extraordinary nature of the event dealt with in our document. The text of the fragment reads:

Fragment 1 ii

1

2

3   והזה   ולקח [פר בן בקר ואיל אחד

4   באצב[עו על פני הכפורת   [ ]

5   לחטאת האי[ל   ] ושעיר עז[י]ם האחד אשר

6   לחטאת יק[ח ושחט אותו וכ]פר בעד כול העדה ואה[רון יזה מן הדם

7   לפני פרוכת [המסך ונגש ע]ד לארון העדות ודרש את [כול מצוות

8   ה' לכול [   ]הנסת[רות ממכה ו]י[צא לפני כ]ול ראשי אבות

9   העדה הזה [ ] ל[ל]

Fragment 1 ii

(1-2)[...] (3) and he shall take [one bullock, a son of the herd, and one ram...and he shall sprinkle] (4) with his fin[ger on the surface of the Kapporet...]...[...] (5) the flesh of the ra[m...] one go[at which is] (6) for a sin offering shall he ta[ke and he shall slaughter it and he shall]

---

66. The wording of the law in Deut. 17.8-13 was known in Qumran, as it appears in full in 11QTemple 56.1-11. The main features of that law and its vocabulary are a verbatim copy of the biblical text, with certain differences of style and contents suitable to the method of the Qumran author; none of these changes resemble the spirit of 4Q375. Regarding this law in the *Temple Scroll*, see G. Brin, 'The Bible as Reflected', pp. 184-85.

make atonement on behalf of all the assembly. And Aa[ron (or: afterwards
he) shall sprinkle part of the blood] (7) before the veil of [screen and shall
draw near t]o the Ark of the Testimony, and shall study a[ll the laws of]
(8) YAHWE for all [...those things that have been con]cealed from thee.
And he shall come forth before a[ll the leaders of] (9) the assembly. And
this [...

The ceremony performed by the anointed priest consists of various ritual
acts: animal offerings, sprinkling of their blood and inquiring of God's
ordinances 'that have been con]cealed from thee'.

Let us first attempt to clarify the textual and ideological background
of this fragment, beginning with the issue of sacrifices. The extant
fragments of this passage mention a ram and a goat, but the missing
sections leave room for other sacrificial components, as well as alluding
to the act of sprinkling blood.

The ceremony of the Day of Atonement detailed in Leviticus 16 lists,
as the sacrifice brought by Aaron, a bull for a sin offering and a ram as
a burnt offering, and two goats for a sin offering and a ram as a burnt
offering of the people.

The wording in lines 5-6, 'one go[at which is] for a sin offering',
clearly indicates that there was more than one goat involved here as
well; as stated in line 6, 'and he shall] make atonement on behalf of all
the assembly'. The most plausible conclusion is that lines 5-6 refer to
one of the two (?) goats brought by the people. Thus, the missing lines
1-3 may have mentioned the sacrifices brought for 'the anointed priest'.

The offering of the people's goat is the last act mentioned before the
priest (who is not explicitly named in the extant fragment) approaches
the ark and begins his inquiry concerning the laws of YHWH. By
contrast, in the ceremony of Leviticus 16 the bringing of the burnt
offering is the final act mentioned. In this context, one should add that
line 5 makes mention of '...] the flesh of the ra[m...'[67] This suggests
that the priest performs some act regarding the ram—either his own
burnt offering or that of the people—prior to the bringing of the sin
offerings, whereas in the Bible both these burnt offerings are sacrificed
after all of the acts related to the sin offerings have been completed and
after the second goat of the people is sent into the desert.[68]

---

67. The term 'the flesh of the ram' appears in the Bible only once, upon the
inauguration of Aaron, in Exod. 29.32.

68. Strugnell, 'Moses-Pseudepigrapha', p. 230, is mistaken in his statement that

Line 6 reads, '[and he shall] make atonement on behalf of all the assembly'. A similar idiom is found several times in Leviticus 16: 'and he shall make atonement for himself and for his house' (vv. 6, 11, 17); 'and make atonement for himself and for the people' (v. 24); and in further passages in Leviticus, in Ezekiel and in Chronicles. From this point of view, as well, our text resembles certain texts in Leviticus, especially that concerning the Day of Atonement.

After the slaughtering of the goat of the people, the document mentions the sprinkling of its blood 'before the veil of [holiness] (l. 7)'. I prefer this reconstruction to Strugnell's 'before the veil of [screen]', for two reasons: first, because the usage of הקודש (= holiness) as a *nomen rectum* is typical of the sect's writings; second, because the phrase פרכת הקודש (the veil of holiness) appears in Lev. 4.6 (and in v. 17, according to one Hebrew manuscript, the Samaritan Pentateuch, and the LXX).

Both of these verses contain phrases very similar to those appearing in the document: v. 6, 'and the [anointed; see v. 5] priest shall dip his finger in the blood and sprinkle part of the blood seven times before the Lord in front of the veil of the sanctuary [or: holiness]'; v. 17, 'and the [anointed] priest shall dip his finger in the blood and sprinkle it seven times before the Lord in front of the veil (or: the holiness; see above)'. According to Strugnell, our document reads, 'And Aa[ron shall sprinkle part of the blood] before the veil of [the holiness] and shall draw near to the Ark of the Testimony' (ll. 6-7). On the basis of the previous mention of the sacrifices, as well as that of the veil and the Ark of the Testimony, I believe that Strugnell's reconstructions are in principle correct, with the exception of 'screen', for which I prefer 'holiness'. The reconstruction 'and A[aron' in l. 6 is also not certain; I would prefer: '[afterwards he shall sprinkle]' (ואח]ר יזה). The reference to Aaron detracts from the general legal nature of this text and limits it to the period of the desert, something which I see as contrary to the general tendency of the author.

It is worth noting that this kind of blood sprinkling is not mentioned in the ceremony of the Day of Atonement in Leviticus 16. Sprinklings on and before the *kapporet* are mentioned in v. 15,[69] as are acts of

Lev. 16 does not describe the destiny of the goat, as seen by the clear description in v. 24.

69. His reconstruction in ll. 3-4, 'and he shall sprinkle] with his fin[ger on the surface of the kapporet' is reasonable, in that it clearly agrees with the description of the various kinds of sacrifices offered on the Day of Atonement, as well as with the blood sprinkling described there, vv. 14-15.

sprinkling on the altar in vv. 18-19. On the other hand, the sprinkling of blood before the veil is mentioned in Lev. 4.6-17, which deals with the sin offering brought in atonement for wrongdoing on the part of the high priest (Lev. 4.3-12). The second section of this chapter deals with a sin offering brought for the people's sin, 'If the whole congregation of Israel commits a sin' (vv. 13-21). Both ceremonies are conducted by the anointed priest, as in our document. Perhaps the author used the same wording to refer to sprinkling here because he thought that in this case the type of sin (i.e. that of the seducer prophet) was similar to that of the nation (and of the anointed priest) mentioned in the book of Leviticus.

The description of the ceremony of the Day of Atonement in 11QTemple 26.3-13 mentions the two goats of the people, including a comparison of the fate of the goat with that of the bull (ll. 7, 9). Column 27 mentions the continuation of the ritual: following the offering of the goat and the sending of the second live goat into the desert, it states, 'Then he shall offer the bull and the [ra]m and the [male lambs, according to] their ord[inance,] on the altar of burnt offering' (ll. 3-4). This is evidently a sequel to 25.12-16 regarding the sacrifice of the day: 'You shall make a burnt offering thereon to the Lord, one bull, one ram, seven male lambs a year old, [...] one male goat for a sin offering, besides the sin of atonement' (ll. 12-14). In ll. 15-16 we read, 'And for the sin offering of atonement you shall offer two rams for burnt offering, one shall be offered by the high priest for himself and his father's house'. In this respect, the approach of the *Temple Scroll* follows Num. 29.8. Regarding the sin offering, this passage says, '...besides the sin offering of atonement' (v. 11), probably alluding to Leviticus 16.

All this indicates that our document's approach differs both from that of the Bible and from the *Temple Scroll*, which in this case closely resembles the Bible.

Following the sprinkling of the blood of the goat 'before the veil of [holiness]' (l. 7), the priest approaches 'the ark of the testimony and shall study a[ll the laws of] YAHWE for all [...those things that have been con]cealed from thee. And he shall come forth before a[ll the leaders of] the assembly. And this [....]' (ll. 7-9). This implies that the act of studying the scriptures is to be performed before the ark of the testimony. The fact that no one else is permitted to enter this holy place shows that the studying of 'the concealed' (נסתרות) is to take place between God and the high priest alone, in the Holy of Holies, without the involvement of any other person. Only afterwards does the high priest go out 'before a[ll the leaders of] the assembly' (ll. 8-9).

Since the high priest is required to interpret the scriptures in order to know the decision he needs to reach for that case, it is clear that he himself does not initially know what the law is. Hence—assuming that the reconstruction '[that have been con]cealed from thee' is correct—this phrase is to be understood as referring to their concealment, not only from the people, but even from the high priest himself. Perhaps we may deduce from this that there are two levels of 'concealed things': one, those which are concealed from the people, but which the *doresh hatorah* and other leaders of the sect know how to solve; two, those to which neither the ordinary people nor the leaders know the solution. As noted, even the leader required a special ceremony, like that described in the document, to decipher them. In the cases of the second level of secrets, only the high priest, but not the regular *doresh hatorah* such as in 1QS 6.6, were able to reveal these *nistarot* and give God's answer to these who need it.

Moreover, if Strugnell's reconstruction is correct regarding the connection between דורש and נסתרות, viz. 'and shall study (ודרש) a[ll the laws of] YHWH for all [...those things that have been con]cealed from thee', similar phrases appear in other parallel texts. Thus, 1QS 8.11-12, 'and the interpreter (הדורש) shall not conceal from them, out of the fear of the spirit of apostasy, any of those things hidden (נסתרות) from Israel which have been discovered by him'. Against the wicked people it is said, 'They have neither inquired nor sought after Him concerning His laws that they might know the hidden things in which they sinfully erred' (1QS 5.11). Finally, regarding God who knows all the 'hidden things', we read in Deut. 29.28, 'The secret things belong to the Lord our God'. The same idea is expressed in the Qumran prayer, 'You know the secret things and the reve[ealed]' (4Q508 2).

All this would indicate that the appeal to the anointed priest reflects the great severity of the issue at hand. Moreover, it seems to me that the special ceremony resembling that of the Day of Atonement serves a double function: on the one hand, it is one the signs of the unique and difficult incident; on the other, the mention of the Ark of the Testimony and of the study of hidden things in its proximity alludes to one of the reasons for the ceremony. Since the Torah scroll was in the ark or in its vicinity (see Deut. 31.6, 29 and CD 5.2-3, 'but David had not read in the sealed Book of the Law which was inside the Ark of the Covenant'), the ceremony is arranged so as to enable the priest to read by approaching the Book of the Law.[70]

The priest's study or examination of 'a[ll the laws of] YHWH' (ll. 7-8) is designated here, as is usual in the sect's literature, by the term דרש. The use of this verb to refer to the study of Scripture was evidently coined only in the late biblical books (Ezra and Chronicles).[71] The sect had a special office known as *Doresh Hatorah*; see for example 1QS 6.6. In CD 6.7 there is an 'identification' of the *Doresh Hatorah*, which reads, 'and the Staff is the Searcher of the Law'. A different 'identification' appears in 7.18, 'and the Star is the Searcher of the Law';[72] and in 4QFlor. 1.11, 'He is the Branch of David who shall arise with the Searcher of the Law'. Albeit, in the case discussed in our document, the one performing the 'expounding' is the high priest, from which we may infer that this differs from the regular routine of expounding described in the other biblical passages, being an unusual event.

However, 1QS 5.8 is an important passage, showing that the searching out of scriptures by the (ordinary) priests was a usual procedure in the life of the sect, albeit not implying the involvement of the high priest in a one-time ceremony, as in our document. 1Q29 5-7 2 contains a similar phrase regarding the priest, ידרוש הכוהן לכל רצונו ('and the priest will study according to his desire'; on the connections between 4Q375 and 1Q29, see below).

The task of the priests in expounding the Torah follows from 1QS 5.7-12. The text begins: 'Whoever approaches the council of the community shall enter the covenant...to return with all his heart and soul to every commandment of the Laws of Moses in accordance with all that has been revealed of it to the sons of Zaddok, the keepers of the covenant and seekers (דורשי) of His will' (ll. 7-9). As against this, evildoers are described as '...men of falsehood who walk in the way of wickedness...They have neither inquired nor sought after Him concerning His laws that they might know the hidden things in which

---

70. Regarding the connection between the unique ceremony and the act of studying of the Law, see Strugnell, 'Moses-Pseudepigrapha', pp. 232, 246. On the passage from the *Damascus Covenant*, see J. Vanderkam, 'Zadok and the SPR HTWRA HHTUM', p. 565.

71. A. Hurvitz, *The Transitional Period*, p. 134.

72. In the two latter passages the 'identification' is only for purposes of the *pesher*, and is not a significant idea in the sect's philosophy.

they have sinfully erred. And matters revealed they have treated with insolence' (ll. 11-12).[73]

We therefore see that the study of the Law included both the hidden and revealed things as the basis for the behaviour of the members of the sect, which was one of the elements that distinguished them from the wicked people. However, this does not refer to the function of the high priest in special ceremonies such as that known to us from our document. It seems that, under extraordinary circumstances, the high priest assumed the task of studying the scriptures.

In the context of literature from the period, we find the 'hidden things' mentioned in Ben Sira, in reference to the figure of Isaiah: 'and saved them by the hand of Isaiah...Unto eternity he declared the things that shall be, and hidden things before they come to pass' (Sir. 48.20-25). God is defined in 42.19 as 'He who declares what is past and what is future, and reveals the profoundest secrets'. The parallel use in both these verses of נהיות ('past') and נסתרות suggests that the latter refers to future events. Compare also v. 18: 'He searches out the deep...and all their secrets He surveys; for Jahweh possesses all knowledge and sees what comes unto eternity'.

In another passage, Ben Sira states, 'Meditate upon that which thou must grasp, and be not occupied with what is hidden'. The idea here is that these are issues and subjects from which ordinary human beings are excluded from dealing; only God and those who are 'appointed' to such issue are allowed to treat them (3.22). We have already seen that God 'surveys all their secrets'. Only those who are authorized to do so, such as the 'expounders of Torah' in the sect, are fit to do so.

Let us now return to our document: the tribe's appeal against the explicit law regarding the seducer prophet will be determined by what is found by (or revealed to) the priest after he studies the hidden things (l. 8). This is reminiscent of the wood gatherer in the Bible, who was put into custody by Moses, who did not know how to deal with the case, 'because it had not been made plain what should be done to him' (Num. 15.34). This differs from our case, in that there is an explicit law stating that the penalty for the seducer prophet is death—a law that is reiterated in this document.

Moreover, in the case of the wood gatherer one might say that there was a question as to whether the type of labour in question was to be

---

73. Regarding the 'revealed' and 'hidden' things, see Schiffman, *The Halakhah at Qumran*, pp. 75-76.

considered a profanation of the Sabbath. However, our case has no such mitigating features. Indeed, the argument offered by his tribe in his defense relates to his positive past history, and not to the refutation of the present charge per se. Again, in the case of the wood-hewer, the question might have related to the form of the death penalty, which is not stated explicitly in the law, so that they detained him until receiving God's instructions. This again does not apply to our case.

On the other hand, in the incident of the blasphemer (Lev. 24.10-16), this form is also repeated: 'And they put him in custody, till the will of the Lord should be declared to them' (v. 12). However, this may be because there was no law which suited that specific case. This is suggested by the fact that, in addition to the decision regarding that specific person, the general law regarding this matter is proclaimed here. This is similar to other cases, such as the law of inheritance of daughters, announced in connection with the incident of the daughters of Zelophehad (Num. 27.1-11). The present case is yet again different, as the law of the seducer prophet is already well known.

Lines 8-9, 'And he shall come forth before a[ll the leaders of] the assembly', relate to the role of the priest after he has finished studying that stated in Scripture before the ark of the testimony. The phrase יצא לפני ('to come out' or 'go before') appears in the Bible in a military sense: 'Fear not...tomorrow go out against them' (2 Chron. 20.17); or to indicate the action of a leader who goes before the people, for example, 'and that our king may...go out before us' (1 Sam. 8.20). There is, however, a third, cultic meaning, which seems to be the connotation intended here by our author. Exod. 28.35 reads, '...and its sound shall be heard when he goes into the holy place before the Lord, and when he comes out, lest he die'. Hence, this idiom is intended to describe the entrance of the high priest into the holy precincts and his departure from them. Compare, especially, the description of the movements of the high priest in and out of the Sanctuary during the Day of Atonement ritual—the same ceremony as that dealt with by our document, 'There shall be no man in the tent of meeting when he enters to make atonement in the holy place until he comes out...Then he shall go out to the altar which is before the Lord...and he shall...come forth and offer his burnt offering...' (Lev. 16.17-18, 24). Similarly, Ezek. 46.9-10: 'When the people of the land come before the Lord at the appointed feasts...he...shall go out by the south gate...and he...shall return by the north gate...each shall go out straight ahead. When they go in, the prince shall go in with them; when they go out, he shall go out.'

Our author may have preferred to conclude the section about the priest with a wording parallel to that describing the initial appearance before him of the two sides, the tribe and all the people. Thus, just as it initially says, 'then thou shalt come...before [the] anointed priest' (1 i 7-9), it concludes with the similar wording, 'And he shall come forth before a[ll the leaders of] the assembly' (1 ii 8-9).

The final line contains only a single word beyond the description of the priest's approaching the people: וזה ('And this...', l. 9). Strugnell suggests that the priest's proclamation of the verdict concerning the prophet begins here. If this is so, we have here the beginning of a formula similar to that of Deut. 15.2, 'And this (וזה) is the manner of the release'.

iv. *The Tribe Intervenes on Behalf of the Prophet*

A striking feature of our document is the intervention of the tribe on behalf of its prophet: 'Let him not be put to death, for he is righteous (or: truthful), a [fai]thful prophet is he' (1 i 6-7). I do not agree with Strugnell's interpretation that the text relates to a dispute as to whether or not this person is in fact a true or a false prophet.[74] The falsity of this interpretation is supported by the overall contents of this document. We have already noted above that the issue is joined concerning a seducer prophet, rather than a false prophet. The remarks offered by the tribe in his defence refer to the prophet's past good record: 'for he is righteous (or: truthful), a [fai]thful prophet is he'. This is reminiscent of the seducer prophet in Deuteronomy 13, which presents the prophet in terms of his past, 'If a prophet arises among you, or a dreamer of dreams, and gives you a sign or a wonder, and the sign or wonder which he tells you comes to pass...' (vv. 2-3). Nevertheless, the lawgiver insists there that the people not follow such a prophet, 'but that prophet or that dreamer of dreams shall be put to death' (v. 6). It follows from this that the appeal of the tribe here challenges an explicit biblical law.

Moreover, were Strugnell's identification of this situation correct, the author would have based his description upon Deuteronomy 18, which is specifically concerned with the issue of the true or false prophet, rather than on Deuteronomy 13, which concerns a seducer prophet.

It is worth noting that, during the period relatively close to that of our

---

74. Strugnell, 'Moses-Pseudepigrapha', p. 246.

author, Philo wrote that the execution of a prophet or other public leader who acts sinfully against God is to be expedited by the authorities without bringing him to trial (*Spec. Leg*, 1.55). There is no doubt that this is based upon the law of the seducer prophet in Deuteronomy 13.[75] One may ask whether, by emphasizing that he is not to be brought to trial, Philo is polemicizing against an idea similar to that encountered in this document.

v. *Biblical Laws concerning Prophets*
The Torah contains two legal rubrics concerning prophets: Deuteronomy 13 and 18. Further light is shed upon the subject by Numbers 12, in which the prophecy of Moses is compared to that of the other prophets: 'If there is a prophet among you, I the Lord make myself known to him in a vision, I speak with him in a dream. Not so with my servant Moses; he is entrusted with all my house. With him I speak mouth to mouth, clearly, and not in dark speech' (vv. 6-8).

The question here (in Numbers 12) concerns the level of the prophets and the extent to which they approached the level of Moses, who achieved the closest possible contact with God.

Apart from the Torah, the issue of prophecy explicitly appears in two texts from the prophetic books: Jeremiah 28 and Ezekiel 14. In Jeremiah 28, during the course of the debate between Jeremiah and Hananiah, Jeremiah says,

> The prophets who preceded you and me from ancient times prophesied war, famine, and pestilence against many countries and great kingdoms. As for the prophet who prophesies peace, when the word of that prophet comes to pass, then it will be known that God has truly sent the prophet (v. 8-9).

The definition implied by these words of Jeremiah contains an elaboration and exegesis of the law of prophecy in Deuteronomy 18. In any event, the issue dealt with here is not among those dealt with in our document.[76]

Ezek. 14.1-11 poses the question of the status of a prophet who prophesies to persons who have worshipped idols, '...and I will stretch out my hand against him, and will destroy him from the midst of My people Israel and they shall bear their punishment. The punishment of

---

75. See the edition of F.H. Colson (LCL, Vol. 7), *ad loc.*
76. See Brin, *The Prophet*, pp. 94-104.

the prophet and the punishment of the inquirer shall be alike' (vv. 9-10). This passage deals with the death penalty imposed upon a prophet who does not fulfil his task properly. According to the contents and wording there, the issue is not a judicial punishment, but one that is divinely sent.[77]

The common denominator of Ezekiel 14 and our document is the behaviour of the prophets in relation to God and to the mission imposed upon them. In both cases, the prophets in question are to die in punishment for neglecting their tasks. The difference between the two texts is that Ezekiel does not relate to the issue from a judicial viewpoint, and that the sin is also different. In 4Q375, the prophet is punished for attempting to bring the people into apostasy, while in Ezekiel the prophet is not involved in worshipping idols, but followers from among the people are, and the prophet's sin is defined in terms of a willingness to respond to such sinners.

vi. *The Relation Between 1Q22, 1Q29, 4Q376 and 4Q375*

Strugnell has noted the connections between the document under discussion here and three other texts, two from Cave 1 and one from Cave 4: 1Q22, 1Q29 and 4Q376.

It seems to me that the text known as *The Sayings of Moses* (1Q22) bears no relation to the issues discussed, apart from one point pertaining to the ritual of the Day of Atonement described therein. But while the ritual discussed there is the ordinary ritual of the Day of Atonement, conducted at its regular time on the tenth day of the seventh month, in the case of our document the ritual resembles that of the Day of Atonement, but is in fact a special ceremony intended to determine the fate of the prophet.

In 4Q376 the anointed priest (or his deputy, according to Strugnell's suggestion) is mentioned, as are certain kinds of sacrifices (1 i) ('one young bull and a ram'). In 1 ii the appearance of the priest is mentioned, the text reading, 'until the priest finishes speaking' (l. 2). Another common denominator appears in l. 3: 'and thou shalt keep and perform all that he (the priest) shall tell thee', which resembles the beginning of 4Q375, '...thou shalt perform all that] thy God will command thee by the mouth of the prophet, and thou shalt keep all these sta]tutes'. In both texts, the people is asked to keep and to obey the laws or

---

77. Brin, *Studies in Ezekiel*, pp. 64-70.

instructions. But whereas in 4Q375 the laws are given 'by the mouth of the prophet' (1. 1), in 4Q376 this function is fulfilled by the priest: 'until the priest finishes speaking...and after [the cloud (or light?)] has been removed...' (ll. 2-3). Only thereafter does there appear the order, 'and thou shalt keep and perform all that he (the priest) shall tell thee' (l. 3). Since the priest is earlier referred to as one who speaks 'before the eyes of the entire assembly', I ascribe to him the giving of God's instructions here.

I cannot, however, concur with Strugnell's proposal that the fate of the prophet in 4Q375 is mentioned thereafter. My rejection is based on the following: even if he is correct, in 1Q29, in substituting והנבי[א ('and the prophet') for והנ[ו and המדבר סרה ('who utters rebellion') instead of המדבר שבה, his attempt to 'plant' these words from 1Q29 into 4Q376 cannot be proven, even if these two texts have certain words and subjects in common.

Let us add that the next section of 4Q376 is concerned with the activity of the king (prince) while in a military camp, while another concerns his going to war against a besieged city, and so on. All this indicates that this document consists of different subjects, so that there is no proof that it is an organic continuation of 4Q375.

As for 1Q29, while it does contain several idioms that resemble our text, and on the other hand shares certain points in common with 4Q376, I do not see it in principle as a text that can solve the problems of our document.

vii. *The Date and Underlying Situation of the Composition of 4Q375*
On the basis of our analysis, 4Q375 may be dated around the Hasmonean Period. This date is supported both by the paleographical evidence[78] (which gives a latest *terminus ad quem*), as well as by the linqustic findings. Our analysis revealed that, even though the author relied extensively upon Deuteronomy 13 and 17 in fragment 1 i, and upon Leviticus 16 in fragment 1 ii, he filled in the gaps, for which there was no suitable text, with his own independent writing. Such additions may help to uncover the exact time at which he wrote.

Those phrases which may be instructive regarding the author, his time and his circle, are the following:

78. See Strugnell's proofs in his article, 'Moses-Pseudepigrapha', pp. 224-26.

1 i 5-6	'the tribe which he comes from'	השבט [אשר] הואה ממנו
1 i 7-9	'Then thou shalt come before [the] anointed priest'	ובאתה...לפני [ה]כהן המשיח
1 i 9	'the oil of anointing'	שמן המשיחה
1 ii 7-8	'and shall study [all the laws of] YHWH'	ודרש את [כול מצוות] ה'
1 ii 7-8	'and shall study...[those laws that have been conce]aled from thee'	ודרש...[ ] הנסת[רות ממכה

I believe that these linguistic proofs, together with the ideological-content ones (including the author's behaviour regarding the use of divine names), lead us to the definite conclusion that this document stemmed from the Judaean Desert sect. The main innovation of this document in relation to the biblical sources is two-pronged:

1. The appeal by the 'tribe' against an explicit law of the Pentateuch that is well known to the sect, and which is itself cited in that same document.

2. The conducting of a special ceremony resembling the atonement ritual of the Day of Atonement, in order to solve the complicated case.

Nowhere else in the Bible do we find a similar appeal against an explicit law. The closest analogous case is that of the widow from Tekoa in 2 Samuel 14. The woman recounts her family affairs to King David, mentioning that during the course of a quarrel one of her sons killed the other, so that now her entire family demands the blood of the fratricide: '"Give up the man who struck his brother, that we may kill him for the life of his brother whom he slew"; and so we[79] would destroy the heir also. Thus they would quench my coal which is left, and leave to my husband neither name nor remnant upon the face of the earth' (v. 7). David, acting as both king and judge, instructs her, 'Go to your house, and I will give orders concerning you'. After the widow repeats her request that 'my son be not destroyed', he assures her, 'As the LORD lives, not one hair of your son shall fall to the ground' (vv. 8-11).

Despite the fact that he was dealing here with a case of murder, which explicitly calls for the execution of the murderer, David sends the evildoer free without any kind of punishment. Even if one were to contend that the death, because it occurred during the course of a violent quarrel, falls under the rubric of manslaughter, David's decision does not fit the stipulations of Exod. 21.13 either.

79. See Brin, 'Working Methods of Biblical Translators'.

One might argue that during the time of David these laws perhaps were not in existence. But such a statement must likewise be rejected, in view of the relatively early date of some of these laws. One very ancient statement speaking against bloodshed from a theological point of view reads, 'Whoever sheds the blood of man his blood shall be shed, for God made man in his own image' (Gen. 9.6).

We must therefore return to our earlier conception concerning David's action, stating that David acts here as an authority who may pardon a convicted person outside of the normal legal framework, notwithstanding the unequivocal rule of the law. In our document, the sect seems to have 'granted' to the high priest the same right of pardon that David took upon himself, or which was one of his privileges. That is, in the event of a protest on the part of the tribe, the high priest was allowed to come to such a decision if he received such an answer from God following the performance of the special ritual.

Another case worth mentioning here involves the affair of the concubine at Gibeah. The inhabitants of that town in Benjamin raped to death the concubine of a certain person who had enjoyed hospitality in their town. The entire nation of Israel asked the inhabitants of Gibeah to surrender the perpetrators of this crime 'that we may put them to death, and put away evil from Israel' (Judg. 20, 13), but the Benjaminites refused and hence Israel declared war against that tribe.

In that case, as in our document, the tribe acted in defence of individuals who were subject to a mandatory death penalty for their crime. But in our document the nation is asked to bring the case '[t]o the place which thy God shall choose' in order to solve the problem, invoking God's help for this severe event by using an extraordinary ceremony. On the other hand, in Judg. 20.27-28 the people inquire the word of God through Phineas son of Eleazar, the high priest. In that case, Phineas announces the success of their campaign against the rebellious tribe in the name of God. Hence, despite certain similarities, the two cases are entirely different.

viii. *The Reasons for Introducing the Case in our Document*
One may well ask why the author dealt with this case in our document. As I have shown elsewhere, the sect was intensely interested in the issue of prophecy,[80] and there is no doubt that it anticipated the reappearance of prophets. For example, in 1QS 9.11 we read, '...until there shall

---

80. See Brin, 'Biblical Prophecy in Qumran Literature'.

come the prophet and the messiahs of Aaron and Israel'. The very fact that the *Temple Scroll* deals with the law of prophecy in Deuteronomy 13 and 18, and that two documents from Cave 4 (4Q175 l. 5-8 and a variant in 4Q158 6.6-10) deal with the law of prophecy in Deuteronomy 18, is further indication of this fact.

The present text presents the law of the seducer prophet on the basis of Deuteronomy 13, with the innovation of the possibility of appeal by the tribe to whom the prophet belongs. The excuse raised by the tribe refers to his being a true prophet, 'for he is righteous (or: truthful), a [fai]thful prophet is he' (ll. 6-7). As we have noted above, they did not deny his accusation 'so as to make th]ee turn away from thy God', but claimed that his past righteousness may stand him in good stead to defend his present deeds. It is as if to say, even the present deeds of such a person can be explained, given his past, as being performed as a divine mission, as will be proven in the future.

One must reiterate that it is not only their opposition to his execution that openly contradicts the law of the Torah. Their defence based upon his past 'righteousness' likewise opposes the stipulations of Deut. 13.2-3, which specifically states, 'If a prophet arises among you, or a dreamer of dreams, and gives you a sign or a wonder, and the sign or wonder which he tells you comes to pass, and if he says, "Let us go after other gods", which you have not known, "and let us serve them"...'.

This law clearly speaks about a faithful prophet—that is, one whose former predictions have been found to be fulfilled. Nevertheless, the lawgiver warns the people, 'You shall not listen to the words of that prophet' (v. 4). It is interesting that our author uses certain of those signs which are part of the definition of the incident as a mitigating factor in defense of the prophet. His polemic against the law is thus both explicit and systematic.

This is also indicated by the following: as we have seen above, the author deliberately alters the beginning of the law regarding the prophet. One of the changes is that he does not describe the prophet's past, which *is* included in the biblical law, 'and gives you a sign or a wonder, and the sign or wonder which he tells you comes to pass' (vv. 2-3). It would seem that this change was a significant one, needed for the defence of the prophet by the 'tribe'. Such a defence would have been impossible had he copied the law as it appears in the Bible.[81]

---

81. Regarding other changes in the elaboration of this law, see above.

One should add to this the fact that, as already indicated above, the phrase of justification of the prophet, 'for he is righteous (or: truthful), a [fai]thful prophet is he' (vv. 6-7), suits the language of the sources from the later Second Temple period. This kind of justification illustrates, in my opinion, the author's positive attitude toward that prophet.

We now turn to the more basic question as to what this is all about. Why does our author protect the seducer prophet by means of the 'tribe'?

The fragmentary state of our document prevents us from knowing precisely the priest's decision as to the ultimate fate of this prophet. However, it is not impossible that, as a result of the ceremony performed by the high priest, the incident ends with an official announcement of his innocence. This being so, the historical background of this 'law' may be as follows: the prophet symbolizes one of the leaders of the sect, and this incident depicts one more expression of the polemic between the sect and the leaders in Jerusalem. I propose the present conjecture concerning the circumstances that may have constituted the background of the document under discussion with great caution.

We know that Jerusalem did not recognize the sect's leaders (see *Pesher Habakkuk*, *Pesher Hosea*, etc.). This document thus represents a polemic concerning the figure of a spiritual leader of the sect, who was defined by the official leadership in Jerusalem as a false prophet, while the Qumran sect evaluated him in very positive light. Our author formulated the background to the specific polemic in formal legal style. Towards this end, our author had no compunctions against formulating two wordings that contradict an explicit biblical law:

1. In the definition of the prophet, he omitted the reference to the sign or wonder (Deut. 18.2-3) that the prophet had given in the past, since he needed this as a positive justification, rather than as part of the definition of the seducer prophet.

2. He invented a new law, stating that in cases such as this there is a right of appeal by the circle close to the prophet, 'the tribe [which] he comes from' (ll. 5-6, possibly an allusion in our case to his sect); the authority for the final decision is the high priest, who may arrive at a godly verdict after conducting this unique ceremony.

4. *Summary*

In this chapter we have discussed three biblical laws as they appear in texts from Qumran. We observed that in the Passover law of the *Temple Scroll*, the author utilized a whole series of literary techniques in order to lend to this law a biblical semblance and appearance. Towards this end, he made use of an entire series of writings from the Bible, part of which are indeed concerned with Passover. Each of these is used in an independent and arbitrary way, according to the result of his own plan, so that, for example, he takes a certain passage from the law of the second passover and uses it in a suitable way such that the new law concerning the (regular) passover is based upon it. I have discussed the reason for this choice in my study. He adds to these the obligation to go to the Temple and to eat the sacrifice there, doing so, on the one hand, under the influence of the author of Deuteronomy, and on the other hand, expressing the approach that this sect and others saw fit to emphasize regarding the Passover sacrifice (the matter appears, for example, in the book of *Jubilees*). The author's entire intention is to advance the manner of presentation of the law by the sect and in accordance with its principles; at the same time, the author makes every effort to assure that everything will be seen as being required by the Torah. This is why the author 'stitches' together the material of his writing so as to be composed predominantly of biblical phrases. The tendency thereby described is that the development expressed in the sectarian text is essentially a direct continuation of that required by the Torah, even though thereby the nature of the biblical material was itself altered, taking on a sectarian cast.

In the second discussion, regarding the list of incest prohibitions in the *Temple Scroll*, we arrived at similar conclusions. The author of the *Temple Scroll* based the sectarian framework of these prohibitions upon the biblical text in Leviticus 18 and 20 as well as, of course, upon the basic text in Deuteronomy, to which their own words always returned. In this framework, too, there is expressed the sectarian world-view with regard to the subject discussed, in such a manner that there is included here the sectarian text against marrying the niece, which has no biblical basis, and the like.

Document 4Q375 from Qumran, discussed in the fourth section, is an example of the usage of legal material, the law of the prophet in Deuteronomy, in a new, non-biblical context. Here, too, the author attempts to express his teaching while using combinations of biblical fragments, so that finally there is created a new text, in which the author concentrates the sections expressing his outlook regarding the subjects under discussion. I have also attempted to explain that, in practice, this reflects an attempt to explain actual events in the life of the sect and its world-view while presenting them as biblical legal material.

Part II

LAWS OF THE FIRST-BORN

INTRODUCTION

This part of the book contains six chapters, in which I bring a series of studies concerning the subject of the first-born. In the first four chapters I treat the laws of the first-born in the Bible, the law of the firstling of clean animals, the law of the firstling of unclean animals and the first-born of human beings. In all of these, there are discussions regarding the sanctity of the first-born and various expressions used in connection to the various objects in human beings and beasts. In the closing chapters of this section of the book, I treat the laws of inheritance of the first-born, that is, the civil aspect of the first-born, as opposed to the religious aspect, which was the subject of the earlier discussion. Here, the status of the first-born regarding inheritance and the question of the father's authority to alter the preferred status of the first-born are discussed. Likewise discussed are the questions of the size of the first-born's share of the inheritance according to various approaches. This group of chapters concludes with a chapter concerning the first-born of the king and his status regarding the inheritance of rulership and the authority of the royal house.

The subject of the first-born is a central one in biblical literature, expressed in a variety of aspects: social, legal, religious and others. In my new book, *Issues in the Bible and the Dead Sea Scrolls* (Hebrew; Tel Aviv: Ha-Kibbutz ha-Meuḥad and Tel-Aviv University, 1994), I include a number of studies relating to this problem. The first section of this book, 'On the First-Born', contains seven chapters representing various aspects of the subject of the first-born, particularly the social ones. The following are the titles of the chapters included:

1. The First-Born of the Father and the First-Born of the Mother in Scripture
2. The Status of the First-Born in Genealogical Lists
3. Methods of Transferring Family Hegemony and their Connection to Arrangements of Birthright

At the beginning of my presentation I discuss the social aspects of the birthright. In my studies, I deal with various different forms of marriage, primarily polygamous, and their connection to the status of the first-born. In another chapter, there is a discussion of biblical geneologies and the issue of the position taken by the first-born. It follows from this study that, even though the first-born assumes a position of primacy in the genealogical listings, this is recorded in a variety of ways, from which one may learn of the history of those families and the position of the first-born in them.

The institution of the birthright is not only a formality, but also carries with it concrete powers with regard to the family property and the status of hegemony generally. In this context, one may ask such questions as: is it possible to dismiss a first-born? What happens if the first-born dies? Who takes his place in the order of family hierarchy? Is it possible to appoint one of the sons as first-born? and other similar subjects. The relationship of the father to the first-born is likewise a topic for discussion within this context.

Since the sources acknowledge a superiority of the first-born that finds expression in a variety of avenues, it is worthwhile examining the reasons given by biblical writers for the preferred status of the first-born.

The latter chapters deal with texts of various different literary types relating to social, historic and geographical aspects of the question of the birthright and familial hegemony. In this framework, I discuss texts pertaining to the sons of Isaac, the sons of Jacob, and the sons of Joseph.

By contrast, in the chapters dealing with the first-born in the present book, my interest is to present the legal aspects of this subject. This discussion, as mentioned (see above), consists of two parts, religious and civil.

The Laws of the Sanctity of the First-Born:

Exod. 13.2	Exod. 13.11-13	Exod. 22.26-29	Exod. 34.19-20
	A		
קדש לי כל בכור פטר כל רחם בבני ישראל באדם ובבהמה לי הוא	והעברת כל פטר רחם לה'		כל פטר רחם לי
	B		
	וכל פטר שגר בהמה אשר יהיה לך הזכרים לה'		וכל תקנך תזכר פטר שור ושה
	C		
	וכל פטר חמר תפדה בשה ואם לא תפדה וערפתו		ופטר חמור תפדה בשה ואם לא תפדה וערפתו
	D	**D**	
	וכל בכור אדם בבניך תפדה	בכור בניך תתן לי	כל בכור בניך תפדה
		B	
			כן תעשה לשרך לצאנך שבעת ימים יהיה עם אמו ביום השמיני תתנו לי

Note: The letters A, B, C, D indicate the internal structure of the law in Exod. 13.11-13. All those other laws whose structure is identical to this passage have not been marked at all, while those places that are marked (Ex. 22.26-29; Num. 18.15-18) indicate the relationship of the structure of those passages to that of Exod. 13.11-13.

A Comparative Table

Lev. 27.26-27	Num. 18.15-18	Deut. 15.19-23

A

כל פטר רחם
לכל בשר אשר
יקריבו לה' באדם
ובבהמה יהיה לך

Lev. 27.26-27	Deut. 15.19-23
אך בכור אשר	כל הבכור אשר
יבכר לה' בבהמה לא	יולד בבקרך
יקדיש איש אתו אם שור	ובצאנך הזכר
אם שה לה' הוא	תקדיש לה'
	אלהיך לא תעבד
	בבכר שורך לא
	תגוז בכור צאנך
	לפני ה' אלהיך
ואם בבהמה הטמאה ופדה	תאכלנו שנה בשנה
בערכך ויסף חמשתו עליו	וג'
ואם לא יגאל תמכר בערכך	

D

אך פדה תפדה את בכור האדם

C

ואת בכור הבהמה הטמאה
תפדה ופדויו מבן חדש תפדה
בערכך כסף חמשת שקלים בשקל
הקדש עשרים גרה הוא

B

אך בכור שור או בכור כשב
או בכור עז לא תפדה קדש
הם את דמם תזרק על המזבח ואת
חלבם תקטיר...ובשרם יהיה לך כחזה
התנופה וכשוק הימין לך יהיה

Chapter 6

THE DEVELOPMENT OF THE BIBLICAL LAWS OF THE FIRST-BORN

The laws governing the sanctity of the first-born of humans and of animals appear seven different times in the Torah, in addition to other references in passing to the sanctity of the first-born, such as Num. 3.11-13, 45-51 and 8.16-18. These laws describe the laws pertaining to various categories of first-born (of both human and animal). The more detailed of these passages may be divided into four basic sections:

1. a general law,[1] expressing the principle of the sanctity of the first-born among human beings and animals;
2. the law of the firstling of clean animals;
3. the law of the firstling of unclean animals;
4. the law of the first-born of human beings.

1. The General Status of the Passage in Exodus 13.1-2

Exod. 13.1-2 states, 'The LORD said..."Consecrate to me all the first-born; whatever is the first to open the womb among the people of Israel, both of man and of beast, is mine"'. This verse constitutes a 'general rule', without being followed immediately thereafter by any details, as is customary in the laws of first-born (see above). Instead, the passage immediately following Exod. 13.2 deals with the law of unleavened bread, and only after the conclusion of this passage is there another section dealing with the laws of the first-born (vv. 11-15). This arrangement of the chapter shows that there is no substantial connection

---

1. I have deliberately refrained from calling this an 'introductory formula', because that would suggest a specific embodiment of the law, in which there is first a general opening sentence, followed by an elaboration of those details composing the given law. This is not, in my opinion, the original situation. In order better to understand this matter, I also use other terms, such as: the 'general verse', the 'general version', etc.

between 13.2 and 13.11-13.[2] Had there been no 'general rule' in 13.11-13, one might have seen 13.2 as serving this function, appearing separately from the other sections of the law of the first-born because of some literary consideration. However, since v. 12a constitutes the 'general part' of this law, serving as an introduction to 13.11-13 (see more on this below), we must conclude that Exodus 13 contains two separate sections addressing themselves to the laws of the first-born.

It seems to be me that the reason why the 'general rule' appears alone in Exod. 13.1-2, without any detailed clauses, is because the author of the chapter already had vv. 11-13 at hand, and therefore saw no need to repeat the general text that he brought at the beginning of the chapter.[3]

Even if one accepts the opposite view—namely, that all of Exodus 13 is unified—this does not affect our description of the status of 13.1-2 as a 'general law of the first-born' which appears without any elaborating clauses.[4] One should note that, among all the laws of the first-born, this phenomenon appears only in Exod. 13.1-2.

According to the classical documentary hypothesis, 13.2 belongs to the P source. Yet according to our analysis this is precisely the most ancient source (see below), refuting the approach of the documentary theory (in Wellhausen's version, for example), which would make this passage latest in time.

2.   It is interesting that a traditional exegete such as D.Z. Hoffmann sees Exod. 13.2 as representing a different picture from that in vv. 11-13. He believes that, in the approach of this verse, there is reflected a different situation of the law of the first-born of humans than that in the parallel law in Exod. 13.13 (see his *Leviticus*, II, p. 270). R. Samuel b. Meir (Rashbam) sees 13.2 as an instruction regarding the service of the first-born in the sanctuary. According to his approach, the clause regarding their redemption reflects a stage subsequent to the 'general law'.

3.   The general nature of 13.2 has also been noted by the rabbis, so that when discussing this verse they applied the homiletical principle, כלל שהוא צריך לפרט ('a general rule that needs to be detailed'; cf. *b. Bek.* 19a; *Tanḥuma, Bo'*, 11; *Yal. Shim'.* 1.214). G. von Rad sees vv. 11-13 as the elucidation of the formula in v. 2 (*Old Testament Theology*, II, p. 408 n. 10); cf. M. Fishbane, *Biblical Interpretation*, p. 182.

4.   We would then need to explain 13.1-2 as the general introduction to the law, whose specific law appears in 12b-13; however, without noticing that a general introduction was already brought in v. 2, the author mentions it again in v. 12a.

2. *The Status of the Phrase, 'You Shall Set Apart to the Lord all That First Opens the Womb' (Exodus 13.12a)*

I would likewise interpret Exod. 13.12a, 'you shall set apart to the LORD all that first opens the womb', in a general sense (that is, as applying to humans and beasts), as mentioned above. This is so, even though prima facie the verse seems to deal with a particular type of first-born, and not with all first-born. The arguments in support of this interpretation are the following:

Exod. 13.11-13 presents an entire complex of laws of first-born:

> And when the LORD brings you into the land of the Canaanites...you shall set apart to the LORD all that first opens the womb. All the firstlings of your cattle that are males shall be the LORD's. Every firstling of an ass you shall redeem with a lamb, or if you will not redeem it you shall break its neck. Every first-born of man among your sons you shall redeem.

Thus, vv. 12b-13 encompass all three types of first-born: clean animals, unclean animals and human beings. Hence, the phrase 'you shall set apart to the LORD all that first opens the womb' ought to be seen as a 'general law'—both because of its appearance at the beginning of these 'types', and because of the general phrase '...all that first opens the womb'.

Further proof may be obtained by comparison of Exod. 13.12-13 with its closest parallel, Exod. 34.19-20:[5]

Exodus 13		*Exodus 34*	
12a	you shall set apart to the LORD all that first opens the womb.	19a	All that opens the womb is mine
12b	All the firstlings of your cattle that are males shall be of the Lord's.	19b	all your male cattle the firstlings of cow and sheep,
13	Every firstling of an ass...	20	The firstling of an ass...
	Every first-born of man...	21	the first-born of your sons...

5.   The similarity of the two verses is likewise accepted by the advocates of the documentary hypothesis, who identify both as belonging to J. However, there are others who see Exod. 13.11-13 as having undergone Deuteronomic redaction, albeit scholars are divided as to the degree to which this redaction left an impression upon the present text of the verse. See J. Wellhausen, *Prolegomena*, p. 88 (according to whom the Deuteronomic editing already begins in 13.3-10), and G. Beer, *Exodus, ad loc.* Bäntsch (Exodus, *ad loc.*), by contrast, thinks that the Deuteronomic redaction of this chapter is from vv. 11-16. Compare also A.H. MacNeile, *Exodus*; G.B. Gray, *Numbers*; M. Noth, *Überlieferungsgeschichte*, p. 51. On the Deuteronomic redaction of this chapter, see also M. Caloz, 'Exode XIII, 3-16'.

By placing these texts opposite one another, one clearly sees that the general phrase, 'All that opens the womb is mine' (34.19a), is parallel both in terms of location and language to 'you shall set apart to the LORD all that first opens the womb' (Exod. 13.12a). It follows that the interpretation of v. 12a as being concerned only with the first-born of humans[6] is incorrect.

By the same token, one must reject the interpretation that claims that both halves of v. 12 refer to the firstlings of clean animals (such an interpretation may perhaps be implicit in a section of the *tefillin* from Qumran, והעברת] כל פטר [רחם בבהמת]ך אשר יהיה לך הזכרים ל]ה',[7] whereas in the Masoretic text we read והעברת כל פטר רחם לה' וכל פטר שגר בהמה הזכרים לה'.... As both parts of v. 12 are united in the Qumran version, the entire verse [and not only 12b] deals with the firstling of clean animals). Compare also Rashi's first comment on the phrase *sheger behameh* (12b), Stade,[8] Kaufmann[9] and others. The proponents of this idea (with the exception of Stade, on whom see n. 8) may have based their position upon the latter half of the verse, having thought that the entire verse speaks about the firstling of clean animals, possibly based upon the conjunctive, 'and all the firstlings of your cattle'. Moreover, the verb והעברת ('shall be set apart', literally, 'you shall transfer over to') seems to apply to both halves of the verse—or perhaps they did not observe the appearance of a general statement of the law of the first-born in most of these laws. On the other hand, Nahmanides is correct (in his commentary to Exod. 13.12), as are Bäntsch,[10] Morgenstern[11] and

6. Such as the view expressed in Bacon (see Bäntsch, *Exodus*, pp. 111-12); cf. Rashi's second explanation in *sheger behema* (*s.v.* 12b), Cassutto, *Commentary to Exodus*, and others.

7. DJD, III, pp. 150-51.

8. B. Stade, *Biblische Theologie*, pp. 170-71. He also interprets the idiom 'all that opens the womb' in this manner each time it appears, because it is untenable to assume that Israelite religion requires the giving of the human first-born to God. To this claim, one may answer that (1) in the appearances of the 'general law' in parallel scriptural passages, there are some cases in which the first-born of humankind is mentioned explicitly alongside the firstling of animals; (2) the requirement that one give the first-born of humans to God is not in itself a clear proof of its being sacrificed, nor of any other extreme interpretation; cf. below, Chapter 9.

9. Kaufmann, *History*, I, p. 146.

10. *Exodus*, pp. 111-12.

11. J. Morgenstern, 'The Oldest Document', p. 85.

others,[12] in stating that 12a refers to the first-born of both human beings and beasts.

Morgenstern[13] invokes further proof that 13.12a also deals with the first-born of humans, namely, that v. 13 instructs one to redeem the first-born of human beings. He interprets this clause as neutralizing the instruction in 12a; if human first-born were not included in the general rule of v. 12a, there would have been no need to alter the rule here.

3. *The 'General Formula' in Laws of the First-Born*

From what I have explained above, it may be seen that four of the seven scriptural passages dealing with the sanctity of the first-born contain a general phrase concerning the first-born of both human beings and beasts:

1. Exod. 12.2: 'Consecrate to me all the first-born...both of man and of beast'.
2. Exod. 13.12a: 'You shall set apart to the LORD all that first opens the womb'.
3. Exod. 34.19: 'All that opens the womb is mine'.
4. Num 18.15: 'Everything that opens the womb of all flesh, whether man or beast, which they offer to the LORD, shall be yours...'

These general phrases speak equally of the first-born of both human beings and beasts, using such phrases as 'consecrate to me', 'set apart to the LORD', and the like, to express what one is required to do with the first-born. It seems to me that they thereby express an earlier stage in the development of the laws of the first-born.

In three passages, a general formula of this type is absent: Exod. 22.28, Lev. 27.26-27 and Deut. 15.19-23. In the case of Exod. 22.28, this absence may be connected with the special character of this verse (see below). In Lev. 27.26-27, the absence of such a general statement is traceable to the fact that this law is in practice not an independent law, like the other laws of the first-born, but a kind of reference to these laws, in the course of a discussion of sanctified things. In Deut. 15.19-23, the 'general law' is missing because this passage deals only with the firstling of clean animals, and does not include the full gamut of laws of

12. Caloz, 'Exode XIII, 3-16', p. 45.
13. Morgenstern, 'The Oldest Document', p. 85.

the first-born as is found in the parallel sections; there was thus no reason to include a general law concerning the first-born of human beings and beasts (both clean and unclean).

4. *The Relation of General Formulae to Specific Languages in the Laws of the First-Born*

i. *In All of the Laws of First-Born*
In most of the laws of first-born and firstlings, one finds a general formula commanding one to consecrate the first-born of human beings and of beasts to God. In one of these, the general formula appears alone, unaccompanied by any detailed clauses (Exod. 13.2; see above, §1). In the other three cases, the general formula appears at the beginning of the laws of the first-born, followed by specific clauses treating the various kinds of first-born or firstlings separately. It follows that, within the formulae of the laws as given, the above-mentioned general phrase functions as an introduction, the other clauses constituting the elaboration of this introductory formula.

Considered in these terms, one might think that the general phrase and its detailed clauses were initially composed as one law, following the logical model of progressing from the general to the particular. However, it seems to me that the development of the laws of the first-born should be understood as divided into two distinct stages: during the first stage, there was only a 'general law' for both human beings and beasts, while at a second, later stage, the detailed rules were added. The distinction between the two stages in the history of these laws emerges from a comparison of the languages of consecration stated in the general law, as compared with that found in the specific laws. Thus, for example, the general law in Exod. 34.19 states, 'All that opens the womb is mine'. This verse is concerned with establishing the connection to God of all of the various kinds of first-born and firstlings (this is roughly the significance of the other parallel phrases). On the other hand, in the specific law concerning the first-born of human beings it states, 'All the first-born of your sons you shall redeem' (v. 20). The term 'redeem' (תפדה) signifies the severing or releasing of the first-born from his connection to God. Hence, the detailed clause nullifies or reverses what was stated in the general law, supporting my contention that the specific clauses originated in a later stage than the general law.

It therefore seems to me that there first appeared a general law, which established in principle the attachment to God of all kinds of first-born—both human beings and beasts. Only at some later point were there added at one time all of the additional clauses, serving as a kind of elaboration of this general law, establishing separately the different requirements pertaining to each of the types of first-born. However, I do not wish to imply by this that, at the stage during which the general law existed without any elaboration, it was a kind of dead letter which was not carried out at all. Rather, we must assume that its execution was probably different from that which was later stipulated by the detailed laws—as was indeed the case regarding human first-borns. This point is demonstrated in our separate discussion of the history of the laws of the human first-born.

One should note that, of all the laws of first-born and firstlings, that recorded in Exod. 22.28-29 is closest to the language and spirit of the general law. This is illustrated by the fact that this passage does not contain any clause specifically mentioning the redemption of the first-born of human beings. On the contrary, it states there that the first-born of clean animals are to be treated in the same manner as one does the human first-born:[14] 'the first-born of your sons you shall give to me. You shall do likewise with your oxen and with your sheep...you shall give it to me'.[15]

It therefore seems to me that this law was the earliest among all the laws of the first-born, and was closest in time to the general law. It is interesting that it is precisely this passage which contains no general introductory clause at all[16]—a fact that may stem from the

---

14. H. Holzinger, *Exodus, ad loc.*, reads here בכור מקנך ('the firstling of your herd') instead of בכור בניך ('the first-born of your sons')—presumably in order to make the law 'free' of the subject of the human first-born. However, his reading is groundless, as may be demonstrated from the phrase 'you shall do likewise with your oxen', indicating that it previously spoke of some kind other than oxen and sheep, as this would be included under the rubric of 'the firstling of your herd'. Cf. W. Zimmerli, 'Erstgeborne und Leviten', p. 463.

15. One must add that this verse does not say that one must do to human beings as one does to animals, but the opposite. Many exegetical difficulties have been caused for those who understood the verse in the opposite direction, as may be seen from an examination of the exegetical and scholarly literature pertaining to our subject. Cf. Fishbane, *Biblical Interpretation*, pp. 181-83.

16. The suggestion by Morgenstern, 'The Oldest Document', pp. 82-83, that one should read the original version of the verse as if it had a general introduction, 'Whatever is the first to open the womb is Mine'—does not seem correct.

similarity of the verse, in terms of both language and contents, to the general law.[17]

ii. *On the Use of the General Law in Numbers 18.15*

In Num 18.15, we find a unique version of the general law: 'Everything that opens the womb of all flesh, whether man or beast, which they offer to the LORD, shall be yours'. The uniqueness of this wording derives from the fact that it is addressed to the priest (like the other matters mentioned in this chapter; see there vv. 1, 2, 5, 8, etc.). As the laws of the first-born—including their details—are generally addressed to the father of the first-born or to the owners of the firstling animal, one can see in the use of the general rule in this text clear traces of an attempt to adjust it to the main thrust of the chapter.

The general rule begins, 'Everything that opens the womb of all flesh, whether man or beast...', following the usual formulation of the general rule. This is followed by a correction, by means of an addition in accordance with the spirit of the chapter: 'shall be yours'—that is, the priest's. One likewise learns from its sequel of the gap between the ancient, original use of the law, and its use in the context of instruction to the priests.

Verse 16 reads, 'Nevertheless, the first-born of man you shall redeem, and the firsting of unclean beasts you shall redeem'. According to the wording of this verse, the priests are obligated to redeem the first-born in question. Yet in the other passages concerning the laws of first-born, the instruction to redeem is addressed to the father of the human first-born and to the owners of the firstling ass. It has therefore been suggested that one should read here תִּפְדֶּה (*tapdeh*) rather than תִּפְדֶּה (*tipdeh*; thus BH[3] and Stamm[18]), that is, that you shall collect its redemption price.[19] Yet in fact it seems to me that even in Numbers 18

See further in the body of this chapter.

17. R. de Vaux (*Ancient Israel*, pp. 442-43) notes the similarity between Exod. 22.28-29 and Exod. 13.1-2, from which he arrives at various conclusions concerning the nature of the law in question.

18. J.J. Stamm, *Erlösen und Vergeben*, p. 12 n. 3.

19. Thus also the interpretation of Ibn Ezra: 'you shall take his redemption [money]', and also on v. 17, albeit there he brought an additional interpretation: 'and many interpreted that "redeem" [refers] to the Israelite', that is, these 'many' thought that there is a change of person in the middle of this chapter, such that part of the verse refers to priests, and another part to Israelites (see above, in the body of this chapter).

the wording is addressed to the father and the owners, as in the other laws of the first-born, without taking into account that the law here has been incorporated within a special framework addressed to priests.

There is nevertheless nothing to prevent one from seeing Numbers 18 as a unified law, the hesitations revealed in its formulation being the result of the combination of two different kinds of material—the ancient and the more recent—which was performed, in my opinion, in one stage. From what we have explained above, it follows that Num. 18.15-18 is later than the other laws of firstlings. This late date is likewise reflected in the fact that the law of the firstling ass included in the other laws of the first-born has been expanded to include the firstlings of unclean beasts.[20]

5. *The Order of Components in the Laws of the First-Born*

From the various comparisons we have conducted among the laws of the first-born, it becomes clear that the order of the basic formula is as follows: a general introduction, the firstlings of clean animals, the firstling of unclean animals, the first-born of human beings. This order appears in Exodus 13 and 34 as well as in Leviticus 27.

In Exodus 22, the human first-born is mentioned first, and only thereafter the firstling of clean beasts. There is thus a change here compared with the earlier pattern. It is interesting that this order corresponds to that in Numbers 18: a general introduction, first-born of human beings, firstlings of unclean beasts, and firstlings of clean beasts.

One should mention that the essential difference between these two patterns lies in the position of the law of the first-born of human beings. In those passages in which the clause concerning the human first-born appears at the beginning (for whatever reason), the position of the law of the firstling of unclean animals is likewise changed, so that it remains adjacent to it.[21] This in turn affects the position of the law of clean

---

20. According to the classical documentary hypothesis, Num. 18 belongs to P, and as such is understood to be late. My remarks regarding the relative lateness of the law in Num. 18 stem from an examination of the verse itself with its various elements, without any connection to the question of origin.

21. A place where there is in fact a law concerning the firstling of unclean animals. The LXX to Exod. 20.29 mentions καὶ τὸ ὑποζύγιόν σου, 'to your ass', which is not brought in the Masoretic text. Thus, according to the approach of the Septuagint, the law of the firstling ass was equated with that of the firstling of cattle and flock.

animals. One should mention that in Neh. 10.37 as well, the law of the firstling of unclean beasts is adjacent to that of human first-borns, following the order of their appearance in Numbers 18, and evidently being influenced by that passage. The proximity of the details concerning the first-born of human beings and the firstling of the unclean beasts in all of these models is substantive, deriving from the development of the laws of the first-born.

However, one must assume that the version of the LXX does not refect the original text of this verse. Evidently, the authors of the Septuagint attempted to add this detail of the firstling ass on their own, in order to complete the picture of the law—that is, so that it would include all of the details found in the other laws (Exod. 13 and 34; Num. 18). The arguments for the derivative nature of the reading of the LXX are the following: (1) in some of the laws of firstlings, not all of the 'kinds' appear. Compare above regarding Exod. 13.2, Deut. 15.19-23 and elsewhere. There is therefore no need for all of the details to appear in each of the laws of firstlings. (2) Analysis of the order of elements of these laws indicates that the first-born of humans and the firstling of unclean beasts always appear together, while according to the LXX these first-born appear separately, flock, herd, etc. being mentioned between them.

Chapter 7

THE FIRSTLING OF CLEAN ANIMALS

1. *Introduction*

Within the overall complex of the laws of sanctification of the first-born, the law of the male firstling of clean animals occupies a fixed place, one that is not absent in even one case.

There are various testimonies that suggest that the sacrifice of the firstling of clean animals is an ancient ceremony, one which, according to one biblical account (Gen. 4.4), goes back to the very beginnings of human history.[1] That passage states that Abel's sacrifice included 'the firstlings of his flock', although there is nothing there to indicate a specific requirement to bring these offerings.[2]

According to some scholars, one ought to accept the evidence of that verse concerning the date from which the sanctification of firstling animals was practiced. In other words, this ritual form was already practiced in hoary antiquity, being intended to offer thanks to God for the fertility of the offspring of the flocks,[3] or as a ceremony of

---

1. A.S. Hartom, 'First-Born'; N.H. Ben-Shammai, 'First-Born', p. 692.

2. The identification of Abel's offering as 'the firstlings of his flock' is intended to indicate their high quality. This is likewise the purpose in mentioning the first-born of animals in the *Sib. Or.* 3.578: 'And firstlings of the flock and of the fat sheep'; 3.626: 'an offering to God of hundreds of bulls and firstlings of sheep'.

3. H. Ringgren, *Sacrifice in the Bible*, p. 46; if this is so, the law of the sanctity of the firstling serves as a specific case of the law of the first-fruits which are sanctified to God (cf. p. 51). On the weakness of the comparison between the first growth of vegetation and firstlings of living creatures, see R. Campbell Thompson, *Semitic Magic*, p. 221. One should note that different kinds of 'first' are grouped together with one another in one verse in Exod. 22.28-29: 'the fulness of your harvest and the outflow of your presses (plant life)...the first-born of your sons (human life)...your oxen and your sheep (animal life)'. On this verse, see the discussion below.

protection against the evil spirits which scheme against the flocks.[4] This law continued to be observed in Israel until the time of the Second Temple. On the other hand, testimony concerning the offering of firstlings outside of Israel[5] is extremely sparse.[6]

2. *The Reason Given for the Sanctity of Firstlings and the Applicability of the Law of Firstling Animals*

The sanctification of firstling animals within Israel is proclaimed in the Bible in two different ways:

a. through the statement that firstlings in Israel were sanctified when the first-born of Egypt were struck;

b. through the law of sanctification of the first-born.

a. There are various passages declaring that the first-born 'of man and beast' in Israel became sanctified to God when he struck dead all the first-born in the land of Egypt. However, these passages do not elaborate the nature of this sanctification, but simply state the fact of the relationship of the first-born to God: 'they shall be mine'; 'I consecrated for my own' (Num. 3.13; 8.17).[7] Neither do these sources distinguish between the firstlings of clean animals and those of unclean animals, a distinction that exists in the laws of the first-born.

On the other hand, nowhere in the laws of the first-born does one find the above-mentioned reason for the sanctification of the first-born

---

4.   W. Eichrodt, *Theologie*, I, pp. 74-75. See also S.A. Loewenstamm, *The Tradition of the Exodus*, pp. 82-84.

5.   Hockel's citations of the sources concerning the offering of firstlings of the flock according to the *Iliad* as 4.102; 4.120; 23.864 (*Christus*, p. 25) are incorrect. Cassuto states ('The Second Chapter of Hosea', p. 121) that the Canaanites offered the firstlings of the flock to their god, but does not cite any source for this.

6.   According to T. Gaster, 'The Service of the Sanctuary', p. 578, the *peṭer*, that is, the first-born sacrifice, should be included among the types of offerings known to us from Ugarit—all this based upon the appearance of the form *dpṭry* in one Ugarit text, *UT* 71.9. J. Gray concurs with his opinion ('Cultic Affinities', p. 211). But of course one cannot infer anything from this owing to the truncated nature of the entire text, so that one cannot even ascertain its contents.

7.   Campbell Thompson, *Semitic Magic*, p. 221, believes that the connection to the plagues of Egypt (Num. 3) was drawn by J (one should note that advocates of the documentary hypothesis generally ascribe this verse to P!?), whereas according to E the reason for the sanctity of the firstlings is connected with the Binding of Isaac (!!).

explicitly stated, with the exception of Exod. 13.14-15, which is a kind of 'intermediate verse' between the two approaches. That verse does mention the smiting of the first-born of Egypt as the reason for the sanctity of the first-born,[8] and even mentions the manner in which this sanctification was executed:

> For when Pharaoh stubbornly refused to let us go, the LORD slew all the first-born in the land of Egypt, both the first-born of man and the first-born of cattle. Therefore I sacrifice to the Lord all the males that first open the womb; but all the first-born of my sons I redeem (v. 15).

The relationship of Exod. 13.14-16 to the law of the first-born in vv. 11-13 is quite clear.[9] In v. 14, a substantive connection is drawn between the two passages through the question of the son: 'And when in time to come your son asks you, "What does this mean?" you shall say to him...' The word 'this' (זאת) refers in this context to the law of the first-born; thus *Targ. Ps.-J.* to Exod. 13.14, which translates מה זאת ('what is this') as מה דא מצוותא דבכוריא ('What is this commandment of first-borns?').

b. As mentioned, the male firstling[10] of clean animals occupies a fixed place within the framework of laws of the first-born. Albeit, this type of firstling is not referred to as 'firstling of clean animals', but through other terms.

There are some places in which Scripture uses very general language, such as 'all the firstlings of your cattle' (Exod. 13.12). It is clear from the context that this refers to the firstlings of clean animals, since this expression appears after the general introductory phrase referring to the totality of first-born among both human beings and beasts,[11] and before specifying the firstling ass and the first-born of human beings.

In the other laws, firstlings of the kind discussed are referred to by various terms, as follows: by means of a general formula: 'all the

---

8. For another aspect of this matter, see below, n. 34.

9. On the description of vv. 14-16 as the result of Deuteronomistic editing, see above, Chapter 6 n. 5.

10. It is interpreted thus in most sources. It is clear from this that the law of firstlings was only applicable to half of those calving for the first time, as one may assume that in half of the cases a female was born first, so that there would not be any firstling from this animal (i.e. neither the firstling female nor the male which follows it). On the odds of birth of males and females among animals, see L.J. Cole, 'Sex-Ratio', p. 421.

11. See above, Chapter 6.

firstling...of your herd and flock' (Deut. 15.19, and also 12.6, 17; cf. Neh. 10.37); and by means of specific terms: 'the firstling of a cow', 'the firstling of a sheep', 'the firstling of a goat'[12] (Num. 18.17, etc.).[13] It follows that those animals included under the rubric of 'clean beasts' come from both the flock and the herd, that is, cows, sheep and goats.

Josephus' definition (*Ant.* 4.70-71) is extremely general: 'that which opens the womb of all those fit for sacrifice'. By contrast, Philo classifies the male firstlings of animals into two groups: (a) firstlings of domesticated animals, suitable for human use and service; (b) specific species: oxen, sheep and goat when they are pure (without blemish) will be sacrificed[14] (*Spec. Leg.* 1.135).

Philo's remarks may express an exegetical attempt to explain the difference between those verses which speak in general terms (such as: 'all the firstlings of your cattle', Exod. 13.12; or 'for all the first-born are mine...I consecrated for my own all the first-born, both of man and of beast', Num. 3.13),[15] and those which enumerate the specific firstlings: ox, sheep, and so on. He derives from this a compromise position: the other kinds were intended for the priests, but were not sacrificed. However, Philo's suggestion is lacking in substance, for the rubric of this law contains no more than flock and herd, whose specific species are then enumerated. Indeed, Talmudic halakhah specifies that the requirement to offer the firstlings of pure animals applies only to animals of the herd and flock (thus according to *m. Bek.* 2–6 and elsewhere). Compare also *m. Bek.* 4.7: 'If one is suspected of neglecting the law of firstlings, one does not take from him the flesh of deer' (i.e. even though the law of firstlings does not apply to game animals, one suspects that he might sell the flesh of first-born calfs as vennison; see

12. The word צאן appears in Exod. 22.29 as a specific noun, but also appears elsewhere as a generic noun; see Deut. 15.19, where both meanings of צאן appear in the same verse.

13. Also in Exod. 34.19; Lev. 27.26. The phrase בכור שה, mentioned in Lev. 27.26, refers either to a sheep or a goat when it appears together with the word שור. There is likewise the idiomatic expression שה כשבים ושה עזים (Deut. 14.4, and compare Num. 15.11).

14. According to B. Stade, *Biblische Theologie*, I, p. 170. The general formula, 'whatever is the first to open the womb', allows us to conjecture that the law of firstlings originally included a greater variety of kinds than these, which are expounded in the specific laws as referring to flock and cattle.

15. This may also have influenced his interpretation of the general wordings appearing at the beginning of the laws.

Albeck, *Mishnah, ad loc.* Compare also *b. Bek.* 33a: "Just as the gazelle and hart are exempt from the law of firstlings...').

3. *The Meaning of the Laws of Firstlings of Clean Animals*

Let us now turn to a discussion of the various specific instructions contained in the laws of firstlings.

> Exod. 13.2: 'Consecrate to me all the first-born; whatever is the first to open the womb...'
>
> Exod. 13.12: 'All the firstlings of your cattle that are males shall be the LORD's'.
>
> Exod. 34.19 is almost identical (in Exod. 13.15, v. 12 [see above, p. 182] is explicated, 'Therefore I sacrifice to the LORD all the males that first open the womb').
>
> Exod. 22.28-29: 'The first-born of your sons you shall give to me. You shall do likewise with your oxen and with your sheep...you shall give it to me...'
>
> Num. 18.16: 'But the firstling of a cow, or the firstling of a sheep...you shall not redeem; they are holy'.
>
> Deut. 15:19: 'All the firstling males...you shall consecrate to the LORD your God; you shall do no work...You shall eat it...before the LORD your God'.

In all of the above sources, expressions such as 'to the LORD', 'give to the LORD', 'sanctify to the LORD', and the like, are used regarding first-born. According to Exod. 13.15, which interprets vv. 11-13,[16] these expressions seem to allude to the fact of the sacrifice of the firstling of pure animals, albeit in some of these laws the form of sacrifice required is not stated explicitly.

The phrase, 'I sacrifice' (Exod. 13.15) does not refer to a specific type of sacrifice,[17] because [the verb] זבח is a generic term, liable to appear within the framework of a variety of different cultic activities, for example, a burnt-offering (Exod. 20.24) or a peace-offering (Lev. 19.15).

In another section of these laws, more explicit expressions are used regarding the form of sacrifice of the firstling of clean animals. Hence, the law in Numbers 18 opens with the general formula, 'Everything that opens the womb of all flesh, whether man or beast, which they offer to

---

16. See above, §2 of this chapter.

17. M. Haran, 'Priesthood; Priestly Gifts', p. 42, interprets the phrase in this verse, 'therefore I sacrifice', as applying specifically to the זבח (i.e. peace-offering).

the LORD, shall be yours' (v. 15). It then goes on to state the law regarding the firstling of pure beasts (vv. 17-18):

> But the firstling of a cow, or the firstling of a sheep, or the firstling of a goat, you shall not redeem; they are holy. You shall sprinkle their blood upon the altar, and shall burn their fat as an offering by fire, a pleasing odor to the LORD; but their flesh shall by yours, as the breast that is waved and as the right thigh are yours.

This clearly refers to a ritual form, namely, that after the burning of the inner parts and the sprinkling of the blood upon the altar, the flesh is considered as a gift to the priests.

In the covenant of Nehemiah, we find the same practice as in Numbers 18 regarding the firstlings of clean animals: '...also to bring to the house of our God, to the priests who minister in the house of our God, the first-born of our sons and of our cattle' (Neh. 10.37). Presumably, the 'bringing' to the priests involved the burning of the organs upon the altar and the giving of the flesh to the priests.

In the very ancient law found in Exod. 22.28-29, we read, 'You shall do likewise with your oxen and with your sheep...you shall give it to me'. According to Wellhausen[18] and others,[19] this speaks of a peace-offering whose flesh is consumed by its owners. Exodus 13 and 34 are interpreted in like fashion.

One should note that the underlying principle of this interpretation (like that of Robertson-Smith) is that the institution of the shared meal is seen as the earliest stage of the Israelite sacrificial cult, which is hence likely to entail a peace-offering rather than a burnt-offering.[20]

But even without returning to basic assumptions concerning the history of the Israelite cult, it seems to me that these laws do not refer to a peace-offering; rather, the form of sacrifice alluded to in these laws ('give to me', 'to me', etc.) involved a total gift to the realm of the holy, that is, one is speaking here of a burnt-offering.[21] One may also interpret

18. *Prologomena*, pp. 72, 152-53.

19. Compare, for example, Driver, *Exodus*, on Exod. 22.28-29.

20. Albeit Wellhausen himself admits the antiquity of the burnt-offering, although not in the context of firstlings (*Prologomena*, p. 69). However, recent studies of the history of Israelite sacrifice suggest a measure of reserve regarding this approach, that is, toward the necessity to see all ancient sacrifices as embodying the sacred shared meal. Compare R.J. Thompson, *Penitence and Sacrifice*, p. 62, and earlier Kaufmann, *History*, I, p. 563.

21. According to H. Holzinger, *Exodus*, on Exod. 22.28-29, p. 93 (and cf. Gray,

these laws as referring to priestly gifts: namely, that the organs are burnt
upon the altar while the flesh is divided among the priests,[22] as in the
law of the firstling in Numbers 18 (as I have shown above).

The former interpretation is based upon an analysis of the phrase
'given to the LORD', which appears here. No one would deny that the
expression '*X* gave to *Y*' implies an unconditional gift. The same holds
true for gifts to the sacred: 'The first fruits of your grain, of your wine
and of your oil, and the first of the fleece of your sheep, you shall give
him' (Deut. 18.4), that is, an absolute gift of the Israelite to the priest, in
which the one giving does not retain any rights of benefit. Likewise, in
Exod. 30.12: 'they shall give...to the LORD'; 30.13: 'shall give the
LORD's offering' (i.e. the half shekel); Num. 15.4: 'of the first of your
coarse meal you shall give to the LORD'.

One may also understand the significance of the phrase 'given to the
LORD' on the basis of the usage in Num. 18.12: 'All the best of the
oil...of what they give to the LORD, I give to you'. Its transfer from the
realm (of God) to that of (the priests) is clearly indicated by the use of
the phrase, 'give to'.

One might add that nowhere in the Bible is the subject of the peace-
offering described by the term 'giving to God'.[23]

A further argument supporting our interpretation is to be found, in
my opinion, in the similarity of this passage—both in terms of subject
matter and literary style—to the laws of the first growth of plant matter.
'You shall not delay to offer from the fulness of your harvest and from
the outflow of your presses. The first-born of your sons you shall give
to me. You shall do likewise with your oxen and with your sheep...'
(Exod. 22.28-29). All commentators agree that מלאתך ודמעך (here
translated as 'the fulness of your harvest and the outflow of your

Sacrifice, p. 24, based upon the phrase, 'give to the LORD').

22. J. Morgenstern, *Rites of Birth*, p. 173, simultaneously interprets the type of
sacrifice mentioned in Exod. 13.12; 34.19; 22.29 in two different ways: as a burnt-
offering and as a priestly gift.

23. It is worth noting the difference in use of language between the law of tithes in
Deut. 14.22-27 and that in Deut. 26 (and compare also Deut. 14.28-29). According to
the law in Deuteronomy, the regular tithe is eaten by its owners, the verb נתן not being
used in this chapter. While the realm of the sacred does indeed benefit from certain
portions, the prime beneficiaries are the owners; as against that, concerning the poor
tithe it states, 'giving it to the Levite, the sojourner, the fatherless, and the widow',
since it is actually removed from the possession of the owners.

presses') are gifts to the holy[24] from the first of the grain and wine (albeit they disagree regarding the exact meaning of these terms). The owners do not derive any benefit from the process of their being given to the holy. The same is likewise true, by inference, regarding the firstling of ox and sheep, which are mentioned in close proximity. This being the case, Exod. 22.28-29 is to be read as presenting gifts to the holy realm of the type of the 'first' of plant life, (of human beings) and of clean animals.

On the other hand, this proximity of subject can also support the latter interpretation mentioned above, namely, that the firstlings of herd and flock were brought as gifts to the priest (and not as a burnt-offering) after the inner organs were consumed. This is so, because the 'fulness of your harvest' and 'outflow of your presses' are likewise priestly gifts. In any event, this context does not provide any support to the view I have rejected, namely, that this law is to be interpreted as referring to a peace-offering.

On the basis of all that has been explained above, we may conclude that the law in Exod. 22.28-29 concerning the giving of the firstling of the ox, and so on, to God, as well as the laws in Exod. 13.12 and 34.19 stating that the firstlings of pure animals belong to 'the LORD', all refer to the bringing of these firstlings to the holy place as a burnt-offering, or as priestly gifts following the burning of their inner organs.

One should also note that some scholars,[25] including some who support the classical documentary hypothesis,[26] understand the above

---

24. See the commentaries to this verse, and also Haran, 'Priesthood', p. 42.

25. Compare M.M. Kalish, *Leviticus*, p. 620, who states that the laws of firstlings in Exodus refer to a burnt-offering, unlike the other laws (Num. 18; Deut. 15). Compare also the view of D.Z. Hoffmann, *Commentary to Deuteronomy*, II, p. 260; Kaufmann, *History*, I, p. 146. Note the repeated emphasis in Kaufmann upon the offering of firstlings as burnt-offerings in the early laws, owing to the sacred nature of the taboo in these laws. For this reason, one ought not to speak in this context, in his opinion, of peace-offerings.

26. Bäntsch, *Exodus*, on Exod. 13.12, states that this refers to a total sacrifice of the firstling of the clean animal, based upon the term והעברת ('you shall set apart'), which he interprets as implying 'offering up by fire'. One may counter this by the following arguments: (1) the phrase והעברת is taken from the 'general law', and refers to all types of first-born mentioned in that law; see above, Chapter 6. (2) This phrase does not mean offering by fire. See below, on the meaning of languages that speak of sanctification. It is also interpreted as a burnt offering by Thompson, *Penitence and Sacrifice*, p. 209; and cf. Holzinger, *Exodus*, p. 93; Morgenstern, *Rites of Birth*,

laws as speaking of a burnt-offering—whether explicitly or by implication—as against Wellhausen.

Let us now turn to other verses concerning laws of firstlings.

It is impossible to infer precisely the law of the firstling of pure animals from Lev. 27.26, because the statement concerning firstlings is cited there in connection with various other kinds of consecration. What is stated there is that, because of its essential sanctity as a firstling,[27] one may not sanctify a firstling with any further consecration: 'But a firstling of animals...no man may dedicate; whether ox or sheep, it is the LORD's'. Nothing is said there regarding the manner of offering the firstling; on the other hand, the phrase 'it is the LORD's' is reminiscent of the terminology used in Exod. 13.2, 12 (= 34.19).[28]

A different picture of the law of firstlings of clean animals emerges from the Book of Deuteronomy. The subject appears there several times: once in a detailed law in Deut. 15.19-23, while in other references—Deut. 12.6, 17; 14.23—the firstlings of herd and flock are included among other sacred gifts to be brought to 'the place which the LORD your God will choose'. The law in 15.19-23 only includes the firstlings of pure animals,[29] whereas in those sources discussed previously the subject appears within the context of other kinds of firstlings (see above).

Two kinds of expressions are used regarding the ritual form of offering the first-born according to the approach of Deuteronomy. The former is similar in wording to those formulae that have already been discussed in the previous laws: 'you shall consecrate to the LORD your God'. Thereafter, it is explicitly stated one what one needs to do with the firstling:[30] 'you shall do no work with the firstling of your

p. 173. Cassuto may also think similarly, in his *Commentary to Exodus* (on Exod. 22.29); cf. M. Weinfeld, 'Deuteronomy—The Present State', p. 261.

27. Compare Mendelssohn's interpretation in the *Bi'ur*, and A. Bertholet, *Leviticus, ad loc.*

28. On the other hand, the law in Lev. 27 resembles that of Num. 18 in that it uses a general language regarding the impure animal: that is, it speaks of unclean animals generally, and not only of the firstling of the ass, as in more ancient laws (see below, Chapter 8, on the laws of the unclean firstling animal).

29. This likewise includes the subject of the blemished firstling clean animal, which is to be eaten in the gates like ordinary flesh. This law has no parallel elsewhere in Scripture.

30. Some scholars believe that the passage in Deut. 15 is not unified, and that v. 19 and vv. 20-23 were originally separate from one another. Verse 19 is the original

herd,[31] nor shear the firstling of your flock'.[32] This is followed by the main point: 'You shall eat it, you and your household, before the LORD your God year by year at the place which the LORD shall choose'.[33]

The plain sense of this verse is that it refers to the consumption of the flesh of the firstling-sacrifice by its owners. The requirement is that it be consumed at the place that God has chosen—that is, in the Temple city. According to this view, the eating takes place in the context of a public ceremony to be performed once a year. This is the sense of the phrase, 'You shall eat it before the LORD your God year by year', in which 'before the LORD' implies pilgrimage to the Temple. It therefore seems likely that the bringing of the firstlings was combined with the pilgrimage of the Festival of Spring; this is likewise the season in which the flocks give birth. We cannot reasonably assume that the legislator would demand a further pilgrimage close to the time of the pilgrimage connected with the festival of spring. We therefore find that, according to

law, and only later were vv. 20-23 added, in the Deuteronomic spirit of centralization of the cult. See G. von Rad, *Studies in Deuteronomy*, 17; F. Horst, *Gottes Recht*, pp. 105-106. However, I have no doubt that v. 19 did not stand by itself, because vv. 20-23 provide the concrete details of the order of sacrifice and so on needed by this law. Proof of this is that the author of Deuteronomy does not cite the law of the first-born of humans and of unclean animals, because his only interest there is with the unique method of sacrifice (that described in vv. 20-23!). Regarding these firstlings, there was no change in the spirit of the outlook of Deuteronomy. See below for the continuation, and n. 35 below.

31. In the opinion of D. Jacobsen, *The Social Background*, p. 236, the pohibition against shearing the firstling of the flock or performing labour using the firstling ox comes instead of the requirement to give them to God completely on the eighth day. According to this view, it would follow from the overall context of his words that the picture of the law in Deut. 15.19-23 is later than that of Num. 18 (according to Kaufmann); or that perhaps the gift to the priests (Num. 18.17) is not understood by him as a gift to God. He differs on this latter point from the classical documentary hypothesis.

32. Gray, *Sacrifice*, p. 34, sees this as the double solution of the Deuteronomist to the question of the firstling clean animal: on the one hand, the firstling belongs to God (for which reason certain labours involving the firstling are prohibited to the owners); on the other hand, the benefit from the sacred feast is that of the owners alone (after offering up the fat and giving of the blood).

33. See F. Horst, *Gottes Recht*, p. 117; and also pp. 104-105, on the concentration of firstling sacrifices during the springtime. In his opinion, it continued to be brought on additional occasions during the course of the year.

the approach of Deuteronomy, the appearance in the Temple city during the festival of spring involves an additional function, namely, the bringing of firstlings.[34]

34. Contemporary exegesis notes the placing of the law in Deut. 15.19-23 adjacent to 16.1-8, which speaks of the law of Passover. On the basis of various conjectures, exegetes concluded that at a certain stage the two laws constituted one complex, in the sense that the bringing of the firstlings took place specifically on Passover. The same holds true for Exod. 13.12-13 and 34.19-20, whose proximity to the laws of Passover has likewise been noted by scholarship. See also M. Caloz, 'Exode XIII', p. 59; and H. Guthe, 'Das Passahfest', p. 227. Guthe even thinks that Deut. 16.1 originally dealt with Passover rather than with the Feast of Unleavened Bread, as in the present formulation of the verse. Likewise, approximately, P. Volz, *Die biblische Altertümer*, p. 146; and see also F. Blome, *Die Opfermaterie*, pp. 394-95 and n. 23 (and other literature cited there).

According to this approach, these laws reflect the ancient practice of shepherds who offered the firstlings of their flock in the springtime (A.H. MacNeille, 'First-Born', p. 264). Further along, he explains the nature of Passover as the festival of the annual offering of the firstlings of the flock. One who explains matters in this way ipso facto removes all independent life from the plague of the first-born, making it but one of the explanations of an ancient practice. Thus Eichrodt, *Theologie*, I, pp. 74-75. On the entire question, see Loewenstamm, *The Tradition of the Exodus*, pp. 80-94.

Wellhausen demonstrated that the connection between the offering of the firstlings of animals and Passover only exists in later sources belonging to P, and in Exod. 13.11-16, a section that in his view has undergone Deuteronomic editing. Wellhausen thereby arrives at the theory that the historicization of Passover first appears in D, and that this ritual was originally connected with fertility of the flock and did not have any historical meaning (*Prologomena*, pp. 86-88). As for the theory that the Passover offering as such was a firstling, see Pedersen, *Israel*, III-IV, pp. 410, 703; Robertson Smith, *Religion*, p. 463, while according to J.G. Frazer, even human sacrifices were practiced specifically on Passover (*The Golden Bough*, IV, pp. 175-77).

As against all this, one should note that, despite the extensive detail with which the Passover offering is described in Exod. 12, it is nowhere stated there that the paschal lamb is a firstling; it is difficult to imagine that such a basic detail would simply disappear. It therefore seems to me that the connection alluded to here is artificial and fabricated (for further proof, see Loewenstamm, *Tradition*, p. 82). On the refutation of the connection between the Passover offering and the firstlings, see also R. de Vaux, *Ancient Israel*, p. 489. He notes, among other things, that Exod. 22.28-29 is not at all proximate to the laws of Passover, while Exod. 34.19 refers to the Festival of Unleavened Bread rather than to Passover. Horst, *Gottes Recht*, p. 110, likewise rejects any attempt to draw such a connection.

In my opinion, (1) the passover sacrifice was not made with the firstling; (2) without any connection to this, the author of Deuteronomy requires that the firstlings of clean animals be brought to the chosen city in an annual public ceremony (evidently

All this appears in Deuteronomy in place of the private practice that had previously been customary, according to which whoever owned a firstling clean animal offered the firstling to the realm of the holy on the local altars close to its birth (Exod. 22.29, 'on the eighth day'; Exod. 13.12, without mentioning any specific time).

Thus, the picture of the law obtained from this source suits the basic framework of the laws of Deuteronomy, namely, a public-national character, suitable for and involving cultic, ritual ceremonies. The form of the ritual here likewise reflects something of the atmosphere of Deuteronomy—that is, the peace-offering in the chosen city, whose benefit is enjoyed by the owners—since it does in the case of other sacred gifts, such as tithes, which in Deuteronomy are likewise consumed by their owners in the Temple city, as opposed to their character as gifts to the Levites in Numbers 18, for example.[35]

But it may also be that this law is intended to remove the firstling from the realm of the priesthood. In other words, that which is treated explicitly as a priestly gift according to the tendency of priestly circles is, according to the approach of Deuteronomy, transferred to the realm of the owners. Hence, we find that the law of the firstling in Deut. 15.19-23 fits the Deuteronomic approach both in terms of the nature of the text (i.e. transition from local sanctuaries to a central sanctuary) and in terms of its primary tendency, namely, to reduce the numerous priestly gifts.

Traditional exegesis found difficulty with this law and attempted to harmonize it with the law in Num. 18.17-18.[36] Rashi made some explicit

on the festival of spring, as stated above). Things are not thus in other sources. However, this has nothing to do with the Passover offering, as shown by the fact that, among the details of the Passover sacrifice in Deuteronomy (ch. 16), there is no mention of the fact that the animals in question were firstlings.

35. It follows from this that the reason why the laws of the first-born of humans or of unclean animals are not mentioned is that these laws did not change in relation to what was stated in earlier sources, since the question of 'the place which the Lord will choose' or the like did not arise regarding them.

36. In this regard, there are those who seek to interpret the law in Deut. 15.19-23 as if it referred to the firstling of the flock (i.e. the first one born in a particular flock or the first one born in a specific season), while there are others who wish to interpret the phrase בכור in that same verse as referring to the one born second, following the one that opened the womb (sic). It is clear that none of these interpretations fits the simple meaning of the law. For the same reason, Hizkoni interprets Deut. 15.19 as applying to a female first-born (sic). See also the polemical remarks directed against these

statements about this: ' "You shall eat it" (Deut. 15.20): this is addressed
to the priest, for we have already found that it is among the priestly
gifts, whether it be perfect or blemished, as stated, "but their flesh shall
be yours" (Num. 18.17)'. Similarly, R. Abraham Ibn Ezra: ' "You shall
eat it"—he that is fit to eat it, as I have explained (that is, the priest).'
The other traditional commentators interpret this along similar lines.

Details of the execution of the law of firstlings during the Second
Temple period appear in Philo (*Spec. Leg.* 1.135), Josephus (*Ant.* 4.70-
71) and in greater detail by the rabbinic sages in Tractate *Bekhorot* in
both the Mishnah and the Talmud, and in other rabbinic sources.
Compare, for example, *m. Zeb.* 5.8: 'The first-born...are less-stringent
sacred things...their slaughtering [takes place]...the firstling is consumed
by the priests'; *m. Bek.* 5.2: 'An Israelite is not to be counted together
with a priest over the firstling'; *t. Bek.* 3.15: 'One does not count
towards the firstling except for a group which is composed entirely of
priests'; and many similar sources.

We therefore find that, according to the approach of the rabbis, the
ultimately binding form of the law is that which took shape in Num.
18.15-18 (and likewise by the laws in Exod. 13.12; 22.29; 34.19,
according to the view that these speak about priestly gifts—see above).

In Tob. 1.6-7 (long version), mention is made of Tobias' pilgrimage to
Jerusalem. We find there that, among other sacrifices, he brought
firstlings to be given to the Aaronide priests as a sacrifice upon the altar.
One may infer from this that a 'sacrifice upon the altar' refers to the
sprinkling of the blood and the burning of the fat upon the altar, while
the flesh is given to the priests, as explicitly required by the law in Num.
18.17-18.[37]

One should mention that Tobias emphasizes here that he alone performed the pilgrimage to the Temple, while the others sacrificed to the
calf at Dan; in 5.14 (short version), Tobias went up to Jerusalem
together with others, and offered both firstlings and tithes of grain, 'and
they did not err in the error of their brethren'. The error referred to is
their failure to make pilgrimage to Jerusalem, which is evidently not

interpretations in Ibn Ezra to Deut. 15.19; and cf. Hoffmann, *Commentary to
Deuteronomy, ad loc.*; M. Kasher, *Torah Shelemah*, XIV, pp. 192-93.

37. The shorter version of Tob. 1.6 contains an extremely truncated list of the
priestly gifts in which, among other matters, the subject of firstlings is missing. See
below (in the text) for the reference to firstlings even in the short version, so that one
may not draw any conclusions from the absence of reference to them in 1.6.

specifically directed to their failure to carry out the law of firstlings, since there are even mentioned additional priestly gifts in this verse.

4. *Summary: Laws of the Firstlings of Clean Animals*

It seems clear from the above survey that the laws governing the firstlings of pure animals reflect several different forms of cultic behavior, such as the ritual of burning organs upon the altar and the consumption of the flesh by the priests, or on the other hand the ritual consumption of holy things by their owners in the holy city.

Moreover, if the laws in Exodus 13 (= 34) and 22 are interpreted as referring to burnt-offerings (see in the previous section), then the sources reflect three different cultic forms with regard to the offering of firstlings of pure animals. Advocates of the documentary hypothesis sought to see the differences among these various cultic forms as reflecting a development that found expression in the sequence of sources. According to this approach, JE is the earliest source, as is well known, while P is the latest source. This being the case, according to JE (i.e. Exod. 13.12; 22 and 34) the firstlings were literally offered up as burnt-offerings. In the second stage (D), they were eaten by the owners, while in the third stage (P), they were given as gifts to the priests.[38]

According to another approach—that of Wellhausen and others[39]— the form of sacrifice stated in JE is to be interpreted within the general framework above as a shared meal, that is, as a peace-offering. In that case, the evolution is: consumption by the owners in the local cities (JE) or in the central sanctuary (D), while in P it is transformed into a priestly gift. For a refutation of this interpretation, see what I have written above concerning these verses.

Kaufmann, who, as is well-known, advocates a different order of sources, sees the evolution of the laws of firstlings as follows: he interprets JE as above as referring to a burnt-offering, but sees the final stage as D—its consumption by the owners in the Temple city.

In contrast with all these approaches, I do not believe that the different forms of the ceremony stem from an earlier or later date, nor that they reflect development from one form into another. The existence of different forms of execution of the law of firstling clean animals raises

---

38. E.B. Cross, *The Hebrew Family*, p. 111-20. For further literature, see above in the commentary to the various passages (and in the notes).

39. See above.

the question of the reality reflected by this difference. One ought to point out that, together with the differences in the execution of the law, there is also a common element to the different sources concerning the firstling of pure animals, namely, the 'general law'. As I have shown above in Chapter 6, most of these laws contain a general portion, which serves in the context of the given text as an opening formula, followed by the clauses that detail the various kinds of first-born. An analysis of this subject reveals that the 'general law' was originally an independent and exclusive element. This law established the basic principle by which the firstling of animals (and the first-born of human beings; but see on this below, Chapter 9) belong to God. This belonging to God was known since earliest times; it is surprising that, at the later stage, when the detailed clauses were added, it became clear that there was a difference among the laws. These differences would seem to have stemmed from the interpretation given to this general principle in practice, in accordance with the tendency and leanings of different circles (whether these were the representatives of different local temples or the like). We therefore find that the differences reflect different social tendencies.

Indeed, the picture of the law given in Numbers 18, for example, clearly reflects the tendency of people associated with the Temple, whose leading interest was to augment the property of the priesthood, and whose understanding of the firstling of clean animals as a gift to the priesthood brought them a fixed tax, which nicely supported the need of the Temple and its workers. By contrast, the law of firstling animals in Deuteronomy incorporates the overall tendency of the book as shown above, namely, the limitation of priestly gifts, the celebration of general public festivals instead of private customs, eating in the Temple city, and the like.

Comparison of the law of firstlings with the law of tithes or with other laws will bring out the fact that the issue of different means of execution of a given law is not typical specifically of the law of the firstlings, since in these other laws the sources likewise differ from one another regarding the different means of execution. A careful examination may reveal that the differences in execution in the law of tithes, for example, correspond to the range of differences that we have observed in the laws of firstlings. Nevertheless, we do find a unique and independent phenomenon portrayed regarding the laws of the firstlings, namely, the matter of the 'general law', which expresses the basic demand in principle which is identical in relation to all of the sources: 'Whatever opens the womb...is mine'. This is stated before the diverse laws are separated according to their different executions. We therefore find that, despite the differences in the specific manner of executing the demand, all of them were directed toward the fulfilment of the same general statement, 'it is mine'.

From what I have stated, it follows that there is no justification for the conjecture that the manner of execution during the Second Temple period was specifically based upon Num. 18.15-18 simply because this was the latest source, according to this approach. I reject this theory for two reasons:

1. I have already show above an exegetical possibility, according to which the earliest laws of the Book of the Covenant (and others) already see the sacrifice of the firstling as a priestly gift, as in Num. 18.17-18.

2. It is possible to explain the domination of the method of execution of Num. 18.17-18 on the basis of the fact that this passage reflects a Temple tradition that superceded the tradition reflected in Deut. 15.19-23, owing to considerations of prestige, historical reasons and the like. And all this is unrelated to questions of earliness or lateness.

On another source relating to the firstlings of animals, see below, at the end of Chapter 9, in the discussion of the first-born of human beings.

Chapter 8

THE FIRSTLING OF UNCLEAN ANIMALS*

The present chapter is concerned with the firstling of unclean animals, and is divided into three sections. The first deals with the question of applicability, that is, to which firstlings the law refers. The second section is an analysis of the law itself, according to the various texts concerning the firstlings of unclean animals. The third examines the problem of duality of execution that appears in two biblical passages (Exod. 13.13; 34.20).

1. On the Question of Applicability— The Ass or All Unclean Animals?

The subject of unclean animals appears in several of the laws concerning the first-born,[1] and includes two sorts of reference: in some of the laws specific mention is made of the firstling of the ass (Exod. 13.13;[2] 34.29; and the LXX to Exod. 22.29),[3] while in others the wording is general,

---

* See also the discussion above, Chapter 1, §4: 'Laws Doubled through the Addition of a Sanction against Non-Compliance with the Basic Law'.

1. It does not appear in the Masoretic text of Exod. 22.28-29 (see below, n. 3), nor in Deut. 15.18-23, for the reason that there is no change on this point in Deuteronomy with regard to the ancient law, since the question of bringing to 'the place which the LORD your God will chose' does not apply. I discuss this point above, in Chapters 6 and 7.

2. Note that in the Peshitta there appears, instead of the words 'firstling of an ass', the more general רחמא דבעירא (i.e. 'the firstling of livestock'). Perhaps his purpose was to make this conform to Num. 18.15, which speaks of the firstlings of unclean animals in general, albeit according to the Peshitta there is no reference to an unclean animal.

3. We may assume that the Septuagint does not here reflect the original version. It would appear that the translators tried to fill in this detail concerning the firstling of an ass on their own, so that the form of the law would be complete, that is, so that it

speaking only of the firstling of unclean beasts (Num. 18.15; cf. also
Lev. 27.27).

A certain exegesis of the oldest laws concerning firstlings may be seen
in Neh. 10.36. Within the framework of Nehemiah's covenant, the law
of the first-born is mentioned as follows: 'to bring to the house of our
God, to the priests who minister in the house of our God, the first-born
of our sons and of our cattle, as it is written in the law, and the firstlings
of our herds and of our flocks'.

If the act of 'bringing' to the house of the LORD (v. 36) applies also
to the first half of v. 37, this passage contains two different instructions:
(1) to bring to the house of God the first-born of our sons and the
firstlings of our cattle (vv. 36b-37); (2) to bring to the priests in the
house of God the firstlings of our herds and of our flocks (v. 37). Since
'the firstlings of our herds and of our flocks' refers to clean animals,
one must conclude that the first section refers to the first-born of human
beings and firstlings of unclean animals. In addition, one can see from
the wording of the law that it refers to firstlings of all kinds of unclean
cattle,[4] and not only that of the ass.[5] In the fact that some of the sources

would include the same details as found in the other laws (i.e. Exod. 13; 34; Num. 18).
The proofs of the secondary nature of the LXX are the following: (a) in several of the
laws concerning the first-born, not all types of first-born of human beings or of cattle
are included, for example, Exod. 13.2, Deut. 15.19-23 and elsewhere. It is therefore
not imperative that all details should appear in every single law concerning the first-
born. (b) an analysis of the order of the components in the laws of first-born indicates
that the first-born of human beings and the firstlings of unclean animals always
appear together, while in the LXX these two are separated, ox, sheep, and so on
interrupting between them.

4. Ibn Ezra, Mezudat Zion, M. Zer Kabod (*Commentary on Ezra and
Nehemiah*); cf. Malbim, *Bible Commentary, ad loc*. But the latter concludes from this
separation that the firstlings of unclean animals need not be brought to the Temple, in
contrast to the firstlings of herd and flock, which must be brought to the Temple. On
the other hand, W. Rudolph asserts that 'and our cattle' in this verse does not have a
specific meaning, and might indeed refer to an unclean animal, although one cannot
make any final determination regarding the meaning of this term (*Ezra und Nehemia*,
pp. 178-79). Rudolph sees v. 37b, ואת בכורי בקרינו וצאנו, as a gloss inserted to
explain the term ובהמתנו. Accordingly, he sees ובהמתנו as originally referring to clean
firstlings. See also L.W. Batten, *Ezra and Nehemiah*, p. 378. To prove his
interpretation, he notes the words ככתוב בתורה, which are out of place in the verse,
suggesting that the words בכורי בקרינו are a later addition to the original verse.

5. See A.M. Weiss, *Each Generation and its Exegetes*, p. 51; H. Tchernowitz,
History of the Halakah, III, p. 134; Y. Kaufmann, *History*, IV, p. 335; M. Fishbane,

deal with the firstling of the ass alone, I see ancient evidence of the domestication of the ass as the first stage in the domestication of unclean animals, in that when the law concerning the firstling was instituted the only animal available to represent the group of unclean animals was the ass. This coincides with Ibn Ezra's interpretation of Exod. 13.13,[6] 'Israel (in those days) had no other unclean cattle except the ass'. Thus the law of Num. 18.15, which does not mention the firstling of the ass but instead uses the firstling of unclean beasts,[7] represents an extension of the ancient law[8] concerning the firstling of the ass to apply as well to other kinds of unclean domestic animals.[9] Such is the position in Nehemiah 10.

Another way of explaining the difference in applicability is to interpret the position of Numbers 18 (as well as Lev. 27 and Neh. 10) as reflecting an independent tradition held in some sanctuaries. This tradition understands the law as dealing *ab initio* with the firstlings of all unclean animals. This was done for two reasons: (1) in order to fulfil the demand of the ancient 'general rule'[10] concerning the first-born, which states in an inclusive wording, 'you shall set apart to the LORD all that

Biblical Interpretation, pp. 213-16.

6.   According to Thomsen, the law of the firstling ass reflected an ancient ritual whose meaning was no longer understood by the time the law was put into written form (P. Thomsen, 'Esel'). Pedersen (*Israel*, III-IV, pp. 317-18) ascribes the law concerning the firstling of the ass to the importance of that animal in everyday life, for which reason it is mentioned among those laws whose purpose is the dedication of firstlings. On the other hand, its inclusion in the framework of the law took place at too late a stage of history to be sanctified by actually being sacrificed. For a similar solution, see E. Nielsen, 'Ox and Ass in the Old Testament', p. 274.

7.   The general form is found even in Lev. 27.27, but one must remember that Lev. 27 is not an actual law of firstlings.

8.   Num. 18.15-18 reflects a later stage in the law of firstlings.

9.   Luzzatto states that the verse (Exod. 13.13 and its parallels) speaks of the usual case, but that in practice all types of cattle need redemption. See G.B. Gray, *Sacrifice in the Old Testament*, p. 24 n. 1. This is the common interpretation among scholars; cf. the various commentaries to Num. 18.15, 17, and cf. Kaufmann, *History*, I, p. 147; Elliger, *Leviticus*, on Lev. 27.27; and Hartom, 'First-Born'. Those scholars who adhere to the Documentary Hypothesis see the matter as a change made by P (and Neh. 10), when compared with the ancient laws of JE.

10.   I see the opening formulae of the laws of the first-born (Exod. 13.12a; 34.19; Num. 18.15) as reflecting an ancient stage in which this part comprised the entire law. Only later on in history were other details added concerning the various types of first-born. See on this problem above, Chapter 6.

first opens the womb' (Exod. 13.12); 'whatever is the first to open the womb...is mine' (v. 2). Just as all the various kinds of clean animals are included under the rubric of this law, so are the unclean ones. (2) In order to augment the income of the priesthood—a tendency that is likewise expressed in various rules concerning firstling clean animals. It is obvious that, if the law of redemption of the firstling is applied to all kinds of unclean animals, and not only to the firstling ass, the portion of the Temple is increased.

This attempt to widen the applicability of the law from the ass to all unclean animals also appears in the writings of Josephus and Philo. After speaking of the firstlings of those which 'are appointed for sacrifices', Josephus mentions 'the other (kinds) of cattle'. It is clear that his interpretation relies upon Num. 18.15, which takes the more general point of view. In so doing, Josephus overlooks other laws that mention specifically the firstling of an ass (*Ant.* 4.70-71).

Philo, on the other hand, speaks explicitly about the redemption of firstlings of unclean animals, such as horses, asses, camels, and so on (*Spec. Leg.* 1.136). In §248, he deals with the firstling of unclean animals generally, without specifically mentioning the ass. This exegesis was likewise adopted by the Karaites.[11]

It can nervertheless be seen that these attempts to widen the application of the law did not become the usual way of executing the law. That this approach was not the dominant or determinative concept during the Second Commonwealth and thereafter can clearly be seen from rabbinic sources. Thus, the ancient command concerning the firstling of the ass was the only one that remained in effect.

In *b. Bek.* 5b-6a we find a polemic directed against the interpretation of the term 'firstling of an unclean animal' (as in Num. 18:15)[12] to include the firstling of horses and camels.[13] In *t. Bek.* 1.3, we even find the explicit statement, 'Of all unclean cattle only the ass is subject to the law of the firstling'. One should give special attention to the somewhat puzzling remarks of R. Meir (*t. Bek.* 1.4): 'R. Meir used to say: Whoever

11. Thus, for example, *Keter Torah* by Aaron ben Elijah of Nicomedia to Exod. 13.13; Tchernowitz, *History of the Halakhah*, III, p. 134 n. 20; I.M. Grintz, 'First-Born', p. 697.

12. See Rashi to *b. Bek.* 5b-6a.

13. This is similar to Philo's opinion (see above). The same polemic is found in *Mekilta* to Exod. 17.8, where it is also directed against the dedication of the firstlings of horses and camels.

observes the law concerning the firstling of the ass is considered as if he had observed the law concerning all kinds of unclean animals'. These words may be understood as a compromise between the more general formulation of the law as 'all unclean animals', and the other sources which explicitly mention only the firstling of an ass.[14]

Since the rabbis have interpreted the law as applying to the firstling ass alone, they deem it necessary to explain why the first-born of asses are different from other first-born, and so on. Their answers, 'It is the LORD's command' (*Mek.*, Beshalaḥ, 1), or 'It is a decree of Scripture' (*b. Bek.* 5b), indicates that they have no rational explanation for this identification. Hence, they must have seen the sources using the general description as a stylistic alternative to the specific law concerning the firstling of the ass.

2. *The Various Ways of Redeeming the Firstling of Unclean Animals*

In addition to the question of applicability, there is another difference among the various laws of the first-born, namely, the method of redemption.[15] Exod. 13.13 and 34.20 mention two alternative methods of redemption: 'Every firstling of an ass you shall redeem with a lamb, or if you will not redeem it, you shall break its neck'. By contrast, in Num. 18.15 only one manner of redemption is described: 'and the firstling of unclean beasts you shall redeem' (concerning Lev. 27, see below).[16]

Thus, Exod. 13.13 and 34.20 explicitly state that the redemption of an ass is to be performed with a lamb, while Num. 18.15 speaks in general

14. Concerning other rabbinic sources, see H. Albeck, *Mishnah: Seder Qodashim*, p. 153, Introduction to *Masekhet Bekhorot*; cf. the sources cited by Kaufmann, *History*, IV, p. 135.

15. It is clear that I thereby omit one stage in the history of this law, since the 'general law' (see n. 10 above) deals with the first-born of human beings and cattle (clean and unclean). In all of the opening formulae, it is stated that all first-born must be given to God. This demand has been interpreted as applying in practice to the firstlings of clean animals, which are to be sacrificed in fact. But what about unclean animals? It seems to me that these were given to the Temple authorities (*heqdesh*) as property, to serve as draught animals, for trade, and the like.

16. Neh. 10.37 mentions 'the firstling...of our cattle', meaning the firstlings of unclean animals (see above, §1). Since they must be brought to the Temple (vv. 36-37), a kind of redemption in the Temple must have been intended here. Cf. the similar situation in Lk. 2.22-23.

terms, 'and you shall redeem', without prescribing any specific method.[17] The following verse reads, 'And their redemption price (at a month old shall you redeem them) you shall fix at five shekels in silver', and so on. One may ask whom or what is referred to by the possessive pronoun in the form ופדויו ('and their redemption price'), v. 15 speaking of both the first-born of human beings and of the firstlings of unclean animals, both of which must be redeemed. Neh. 10.37 is of no help, since this verse makes no mention at all of redemption.[18] While Leviticus 27 does deal with redemption, it does so in a special context (see below), which does not help us to identify the object of the possessive pronoun in Num. 18.16.

One explanation is that v. 16 applies the same method of redemption to both human first-born and the firstlings of unclean animals,[19] both of which are redeemed with five shekels.[20] But this cannot be accepted, for the sum mentioned in Num. 18.16—five shekels—is the same as that specified in Num. 3.47 for Israel's first-born in the desert. Even the form בערכך ('your valuation') corresponds to the 'valuation' of a person between one month and five years of age (Lev. 27.6). It is therefore clear that Num. 18.16 refers only to the first-born of humans, mentioned at the beginning of v. 15,[21] so that Numbers 18 does not contain any specific method for redeeming the firstling of unclean animals.[22]

17. *Targ. Ps.-J.* to Num. 18.15 mentions the redemption of the firstling of an unclean animal with a lamb; it is clear that this was influenced by Exod. 13.13.

18. Here one finds no explicit use of nouns or verbs derived from פדה. Rather, this requirement is logically derived from the context and subject matter.

19. Gray (*Numbers*, p. 231) states that the possessive pronoun in ופדויו ('and their redemption price') alludes to human first-born, albeit in the present arrangement of Num. 18 it might likewise refer to the firstling of unclean animals. He therefore surmises that the law of the firstling of unclean animals should have appeared after v. 16, or that this law is a later addition within the original framework of 18.15-18 (cf. n. 22 below).

20. This is A. Schalit's opinion in his short comment on *Antiquities*, Book 4 n. 42a (Hebrew edition); likewise Frazer, *The Golden Bough*, IV, p. 173. However, he contends that Num. 18.15 refers to the firstling of all kinds of unclean animals except for the ass, which must be redeemed with a lamb.

21. The common interpretation in ancient and later exegesis is that v. 16 refers to the redemption of human first-born alone.

22. Note that, due to the difficulty in understanding v. 16 as referring to the firstling of an unclean animal, there is a tendency to see it as having been moved from its original position, or as a later interpolation. See M. Noth, *Numeri*, p. 120; B. Bäntsch, *Numeri*, p. 556; and cf. n. 19 above.

Perhaps the lack of a specific law concerning the manner of such redemption may be explained on the basis of the development that took place in the law, from the ass to all species of unclean animals. This necessitated the use of the general form, תפדה ('you shall redeem'), because the value of each species varied according to its particular kind, and so forth. Perhaps the law of Lev. 27.11-12 was applied here, in which the redemption price of unclean animals is determined in each case through the specific valuation by the priest, whereas the valuation of a human being in that same text is fixed by law according to age and sex. The relationship existing between Numbers 18 and Leviticus 27 is thus additional evidence to justify the interpretation that Num. 18.16 applies only to the human first-born.

In Lev. 27.26-27, we read, 'But a firstling of animals, which as a firstling belongs to the LORD, no man may dedicate; whether ox or sheep, it is the LORD's. And if it is an unclean animal, then he shall buy it back at your valuation, and add a fifth to it; or if it is not redeemed, it shall be sold at your valuation'.

This law may be interpreted in one of two ways:

1. The first possibility, as stated in v. 26, is that one cannot sanctify the firstling of a clean animal because it is already holy by virtue of being a firstling. In the case of the firstling of an unclean animal, v. 27 states how to deal with it in general, without referrence to any special sanctification. According to this explanation, the law of redemption of firstlings of unclean animals in Leviticus 27 differs from that in Numbers 18. While the latter requires only that one pay the value of the firstling, the former requires payment of its value plus a fifth; otherwise, it is given over to the priest.

2. The second possibility is that vv. 26 and 27 are integrally related.[23]

---

23. An interesting interpretation has been suggested by Nahmanides, Abarbanel and D.Z. Hoffmann (p. 406), in their comments *ad loc.* According to them, the law of firstlings of unclean animals includes the ass alone, whereas the firstlings of other unclean animals that were dedicated are treated like any other unclean animals that were sanctified (note especially the law in Lev. 27.11-13).

Rashi is more extreme, thinking that Lev. 27.27 does not deal with a firstling at all, since he assumes that the law of the firstling of unclean animals exists only with regard to the ass. Moreover, the term *bekor* is not even mentioned in that verse (v. 27). See Mendelssohn, *Bi'ur, ad loc.* opposing this interpretation. In my opinion, vv. 26-27 is to be seen as one literary unit: 'But a firstling of animals, which as a firstling belongs to the LORD, no man may dedicate, whether ox or sheep...And if it is an unclean animal...' From my discussion above, it is clear that I can accept neither

Whereas v. 26 states that the firstling of a clean animal cannot be further sanctified, v. 27 speaks of one who sanctifies the firstling of an unclean animal, over and above its intrinsic holiness as a firstling. According to this explanation, there would be no difference between Leviticus 27 and Numbers 18 regarding the usual form of redemption. The difference described in this verse is limited to that case in which there is a special sanctification of the firstling. In that case, the special holiness is nullified by adding an additional fifth of its value to its valuation.[24] Only if it is not redeemed is it sold by the priests (to others) at its 'valuation', that is, the redemption cost of a firstling of an unclean animal that has not been specially sanctified (Num. 18). But while in the usual case the firstling remains in its owner's possession after being redeemed at its valuation, in the other case, that of the firstling that has been dedicated for an additional sanctification, it remains in the owner's possession only if it has been redeemed at its value plus a fifth.[25]

Comparison with the law concerning one who dedicates a non-firstling unclean animal found in the same context (Lev. 27.11-13) indicates that the difference between the two laws lies in the order of priorities. In the case of one who dedicates an unclean animal, the first priority is to give the beast to the Temple; otherwise, the Temple will

Rashi's extreme exegesis nor Nahmanides'. Rashi's solution must be rejected because of the organic connection of v. 26 with v. 27, which speaks of a firstling of unclean animal. Nahmanides' solution is a harmonistic one, whose purpose is to resolve the above-mentioned problem—the ass alone or all unclean animals. Moreover, since the details of Lev. 27 partially overlap with those of Num. 18, these solutions are to be rejected.

24. Mendelssohn (*Bi'ur* to Lev. 27) sees this text as an additional means for redeeming the firstling of unclean animals; similarly, P. Heinisch, *Leviticus*, pp. 124-25. A. Bertholet contends that the law concerning the firstling of unclean animals is different, because the Israelites used to act according to the law of the regular unclean animal which was sanctified (27.11-13), or that the law refers to a clean animal that has suffered a physical defect (*Leviticus*, pp. 98-99.)

According to Bäntsch, this text refers to a situation in which one is unable to redeem the animal with a lamb, in which case one must add a fifth to its value, unlike Exod. 13.13 and 34.20, which in such a case require the beheading of the animal. See also K. Elliger, *Leviticus*, p. 387. This interpretation cannot be accepted for several reasons: first of all, because it does not fit the wording of the law in Lev. 27, in which paying the fifth is seen as the first possibility; moreover, to the contrary, if the firstling is not redeemed, it must be sold to someone else at its valuation alone.

25. See below, at the end of §4, concerning the LXX to Exod. 13.13. My solution here is somewhat similar to that of the LXX to that verse.

pass it on to the possession of another lay person. The alternative possibility is the redemption of the beast by paying its value plus one-fifth. The reverse order prevails in the case of the dedication of the firstling of an unclean animal (v. 27). Redemption by paying its value plus a fifth constitutes the first choice, while giving the beast to the Temple, which will then sell it to someone else at value, is conceived as an alternative. The reason why redemption is preferable in the case of the firstling is evident upon examining other laws concerning firstlings, in which it is presumed that the firstling will be redeemed and remain in its owner's possession. Thus, here too that procedure is preferred and leads to the same result.[26]

Josephus (*Ant.* 4.70-71) states that the redemption price of the firstling of unclean animals is one-and-a-half shekels. Even according to rabbinic *halakhah*, the redemption of a firstling ass may be effected with something other than a lamb, although the lamb is preferred. *B. Bek.* 11a explicitly states, 'Resh Laqish said: If one has a firstling of an ass and no lamb with which to redeem it, he may redeem it for something of equivalent value'. This coincides with Philo's statement (*Spec. Leg.* 1.135) that the firstling of any unclean animal may be redeemed by paying its value.

Even the sum specified by Josephus ($1\frac{1}{2}$ shekels) is repeated by R. Tarfon (*b. Bek.* 11a);[27] compare also the wording of the baraita in *b. Bek.* 10b: '"You shall redeem" implies with a thing of whatever value', and R. Gershom's comment, *ad loc.*, that one may redeem an ass even with a lamb valued at no more than one *zuz*[28] (and see also his further remarks in the same discussion, at 11a).

To summarize: the laws concerning the firstling offer several answers as to how to deal with the firstling of unclean animals. According to the ancient sources—Exodus 13 and 34—the firstling of an ass is to be redeemed with a lamb. But in those laws which initially[29] applied to a

---

26. Concerning Lev. 27.26-27, see J. Milgrom, *Cult and Conscience*, pp. 44-55, especially pp. 49, 50, 53. Milgrom also compares the laws concerning the firstling of unclean animals (v. 27) and the unclean animal (vv. 11-13). I find that we agree in most conclusions.

27. See also Albeck, *Mishnah: Seder Qodashim, Introduction to Masekhet Bekhorot*, pp. 153-54 n. 3.

28. *Ibid.*

29. This description of the law (Num. 18) resembles the alternative possibility which I mentioned above, §1.

broader definition of the firstling (see above), the rule was altered to include redemption through payment of the value of an ass or one of the other kinds of unclean animals. This coincides with the rule in Numbers 18 (and Neh. 10) which extends the priestly portions.

The ancient law that speaks of the redemption of an ass with a lamb may be regarded as implying a purely symbolic act. This is clearly defined in the rabbis' statement, '"Thou shalt redeem" implies with a thing of whatever value', or 'The Torah did not intend by the law of redemption with a lamb to make it difficult for one, but on the contrary, to make it easier for one' (*b. Bek.* 11a). Thus, the rule in Numbers 18 and its parallels is to impose the letter of the law on the owner by demanding that one redeem the beast at full value, and not merely, as it was in the past, by making a symbolic payment (i.e. a lamb).

As for Leviticus 27, one way of understanding it is that it prescribes the same law as Numbers 18, but it may also be that it demands even more (see the second possibility, above).

3. *The Problem of Double Formulation in the Law of the Firstling of the Ass*

The third problem involved in the firstling of unclean animals is that of the dual formulation found in the law of the firstling ass in Exodus 13 and 34. Alongside the order concerning the redemption of the ass with a lamb, it is written, 'Or if you will not redeem it, you shall break its neck' (cf. Exod. 34.20). This alternative procedure, seemingly left to the owner's discretion,[30] is strange,[31] and one may inquire as to the actual situation underlying these rules.[32]

The rabbis interpreted the two procedures mentioned in the law as two alternatives, albeit redemption is clearly viewed by them as the preferred option. Only when there is no possibility of redeeming the animal does one who breaks the ass's neck also fulfil the demands of the

---

30. This is also Gray's opinion (*Sacrifice in the Old Testament*, p. 24).

31. The possibility of alternatives in a law is very rare. Cf. the law concerning the tithe (Deut. 14.22-27). On the entire subject of double laws, see above, Chapter 1, §2.iv.

32. According to the second explanation given above concerning Lev. 27.27, even there a choice is given between two actions: if the owners of a firstling unclean animal wishes, they may redeem it (as in Num. 18:15); or if they wish, they may consecrate it with an additional sanctification (see above, n. 24, for explanations and bibliography).

law: 'The commandment of redeeming takes precedence over the commandment of breaking its neck, as it is written: "Or if you will not
redeem it, you shall break its neck"' (*m. Bek.* 1.7).

On the other hand, one could say that these reflect two stages of
development of the law. It may be that the people refrained from
redeeming their firstling asses: knowing that an ass could not be offered
as a sacrifice, they thought they could profit by not redeeming it with a
sheep. Later on, the legislator[33] closed this loophole in the law by
ordering that those who did not redeem should forfeit the full value of
the ass[34] by being required to break its neck.[35] This alternative was even

---

33. The system of two stages of a law is openly expressed in the Hittite laws.
These laws contain such formulae as: 'Until now they used to pay *x*...but now they
pay *y*', etc. Cf. the concluding section of Chapter 1, 'Double Laws in the Bible'.

34. Cf. the language used in *b. Bek.* 10b: 'He [the Israelite] caused the priest
monetary loss [by not redeeming it with a sheep]; therefore he shall lose his money',
regarding the greater loss imposed upon the owner when the ass is beheaded.

35. According to the explanation brought above, the breaking of the ass's neck is
a sanction against one who did not fulfil the law of redemption. Kaufmann (*History*, I,
p. 146) sees it as a kind of substitution for the burning of the animal, thus 'giving'
the beast to God. Some scholars, on the other hand, explain the beheading as a kind
of ritual. Robertson Smith sees in it echos of an old taboo (*The Religion of the
Semites*, pp. 463-65; Campbell Thompson, *Semitic Magic*, p. 234). For material on
the Arabs' avoidance of beheading asses, preferring instead to release them altogether,
see Robertson Smith, *Religion*, p. 450. On the libel that Jews offered sacrifices to
asses, see below, n. 40. On the text of the LXX to Exod. 13.13, see below, 'Summary',
and n. 40.

The absence of beheading in later sources (Lev. 27; Num. 18) is explained by
Robertson Smith (*Religion*, pp. 463-65) and Elliger (*Leviticus*, pp. 390-91) as a
change of the ancient law from breaking its neck to redemption (cf. above, n. 24). On
beheading as a pagan cultic act, see Isa. 66.3, which A. Kahana (*Commentary on
Exodus*) connects with Exod. 13.13. On beheading as a sacrifice, see A. Rofé, 'The
Breaking of the Heifer's Neck', p. 127, and the bibliography there. Some scholars
attempt to connect the graves of asses from the Hyksos period in Tel-Agul with the
beheading of firstling asses, but there is no real connection between these phenomena.
At most, we may conclude from these caves that the ass was a cultic object in the Near
East (S. Bodenheimer, *Fauna in the Biblical Lands*, I, p. 286; Bilik-Beinart, 'Ass').

One must be careful with parallels, e.g. the Ugaritic document UT, no. 62 (AB I
28): *ṭbḥ šb'im ḥmrm*, which means, according to Gordon, 'she will slaughter seventy
asses'. But since prior to this verse mention is made of seventy oxen, seventy sheep,
seventy mountain goats, etc., it may be that the correct reconstruction is *yḥmrm*
(roebucks) rather than *ḥmrm* (asses). The description of this text in Bilik-
Beinart, 'Ass', as 'a sacrificial offering of she-asses' seems exaggerated. Compare

worse in terms of the owners, owing to the high value of the ass.[36] Note the Talmudic saying concerning these matters: 'The Torah did not intend by the law of redemption with a lamb to make it difficult for one, but on the contrary, to make it easier for one' (*b. Bek.* 11a).

The above solution concerning the two stages could also be explained in terms of some other historical or ideological matter, but even then my proposal[37] of two stages would still be valid.

4. *Conclusion*

From the above analysis, it will be seen that the beheading of the ass cannot be explained as the vestige of some ancient ritual, as may be seen in the arrangement of the details of the law. Beheading is mentioned in the second half of the verse, as a secondary option, and is hence executed only if the usual redemption with a lamb has not been carried out. Had beheading been the survival of an ancient taboo, as some scholars think, it is logical that it should have appeared in the first half of the law, which would then have read: 'And the firstling of an ass you shall behead; and if you do not do so, you shall redeem it with a lamb'. The rabbinic dicta, based upon the actual arrangement of the two parts of the law, is apt: 'The commandment of redeeming it takes precedence over the commandment of breaking its neck' (*m. Bek.* 1.7).

Y. Leibovitz, 'The Cult of the Ass', p. 131. Even the idiom conventionally used in Near Eastern treaties, *ana ḥa-a-rim qatalim* (*ARM* 2.37.6) *ḥa-ra-am qutul* (*Syria* 19, 109, p. 23), that is, 'killing an ass', has no connection with the beheading of firstlings of asses, but is rather concerned with noting a ceremony for making a covenant. Thus Nielsen, 'Ox and Ass in the Old Testament', pp. 270-71, who rejected any connection between the above idiom and the cult.

36. According to Gray, *Sacrifice*, p. 35, the lamb brought to redeem the ass is eaten by the owner in a sacred meal. According to this interpretation, the owner's loss in the case of the beheading is even greater than that estimated above, as the owner derives benefit from the sacred meal, while one gains no benefit from the beheading. But I do not believe that Gray's interpretation of the lamb's fate is correct. Analysis of the law of the firstling of a clean animal in Exod. 13 indicates that it was either offered as a sacrifice or given as a gift to the priests; the law treats the redemptive lamb in the same manner as the firstling of a clean animal.

37. This solution is similar to that of the law concerning the owner of a goring ox: 'the ox shall be stoned, and its owner also shall be put to death' (Exod. 21.29). But v. 30 contains another possibility: 'If a ransom is laid on him, then he shall give [it] for the redemption of his life'. This may be seen as a later stage of the law, whereby the death penalty was replaced by the payment of ransom. See above, Chapter 1, §2.ii.

The Septuagint reads here ἐὰν δὲ μὴ ἀλλάξῃς λυτρώσῃ αὐτό, that is, 'and if you do not exchange it, you must redeem it'. That is, the two alternative options are redemption with a lamb or redemption by money. Some say that the LXX reflects a variant text in the Hebrew, such as ואם לא תפדה וערכתו ('or if you will not redeem it, you shall valuate it'), reading וערכתו[38] ('you shall valuate it') instead of וערפתו[39] ('you shall break its neck'). But it does not seem to me that the Septuagint here reflects any original text. Perhaps its reading had some polemical point related to the reality of life in Egypt, where the Jews were accused by Gentiles of sacrificing to asses.[40]

38. See, among others, Kahana, *Commentary on Exodus*, p. 42.

39. In 1858, the Karaite Mordecai Sultansky suggested reading Exod. 13.13 (without any connection to the LXX), 'And if you do not redeem it, you shall pay its value' (וערכתו instead of וערפתו). He arrived at this suggestion after comparing Exod. 13.13 with Lev. 27.27 (*Teitiv Da'at*, p. 116); cf. A. Geiger, in Steinschneider's *Hebraische Bibliographie* 4 (1861), p. 62.

40. Philo and Josephus, as mentioned above, do not mention the possibility of beheading—according to Albeck, because of the LXX. He believes that the LXX itself failed to mention the beheading of the ass in order not to offer support for the libel used by the enemies of the Jews against them, that they offered sacrifices to asses (Albeck, *Mishnah: Qodashim*, p. 153 n. 1).

Chapter 9

PROBLEMS CONCERNING THE FIRST-BORN OF HUMAN BEINGS

1. *Introduction*

The laws concerning the consecration of the first-born state that the first-born of human beings must be given to God (or other similar wordings). The question, of course, concerns what is meant by this demand.

According to one opinion, these laws originally alluded to the sacrifice of the human first-born, in the literal sense. Such a view, however, is utterly unacceptable, whether in terms of the meaning of the language used in these laws or on the basis of logic—one simply cannot imagine the existence at any time of a cultured human society which regularly killed its first-born.[1]

But neither can one accept the view that the redemption mentioned further on in this law ('Every first-born of man among your sons you shall redeem') is itself identical to the consecration required by this same law ('All that opens the womb is mine'). This is so for two reasons:

a. An analysis of the structure of the law reveals[2] that the 'general clause' was the earliest component of the laws of first-born, which at a certain stage existed independently.[3] Only at a later stage were specific clauses added to it, stating that the first-born of human beings are to be redeemed.

b. The essential meaning of redemption is the abrogation of the consecration to God. This being so, the exegetical option of equating consecration with the act of redemption makes no sense, since redemption is in fact the negation of this consecration.

---

1.   The problem of the offering of human first-born as sacrifices is discussed in my unpublished doctoral dissertation, 'The First-Born in Israel', pp. 134-48.

2.   See above, Chapter 6, §§1, 4.

3.   Chapter 6, §4.

It follows that these laws reflect two stages in the destiny of the first-born: the latter requires the redemption of the first-born, while the former requires consecration to God. The meaning of this consecration shall be discussed further on in this chapter.

But even if we could clearly determine the meaning of the consecration thus mandated, there remains another biblical source—Numbers 3—which would require a further solution. We shall attempt to understand how this source fits in with the other laws of the human first-born.

Hence, the order of our discussion in this chapter shall be the following: first, an explanation of the various types of law regarding the human first-born; thereafter, questions pertaining to the phrase 'all that opens the womb' and the sex of the first-born, and an examination of the meaning of the wordings used to express consecration, with the aim of determining the nature of the divine command in the laws of the human first-born. After discussing these preliminary issues, we will be able to elucidate the history of the laws of first-born, and to trace the place of Numbers 3 within the overall framework of the chapters discussed.[4]

2. *The Various Types of Laws concerning Human First-born*

The laws concerning the human first-born occupy a fixed place among the laws of consecration of the first-born, appearing in nearly all of them. The sole exception is Deut. 15.19-23, which only speaks of the firstling of clean animals. This is explained by the particular subject of this text, which addresses itself to the arrangements for sacrificing the firstlings of clean animals 'at the place which the LORD shall choose'.

The question of the destiny of the human first-born is depicted in a number of ways:

a. The first group of texts includes Exod. 13.2, which calls upon one to consecrate to God the first-born of human beings (and animals), without any mention of redemption. One should note that among the other laws, the 'general law'—such as Exod. 13.2—only appears as an introduction, being followed by clauses detailing each of the 'kinds' of firstling;[5] in the case of the first-born of human beings, it states there that he ought to be redeemed (see below, b).

---

4. Lev. 27.26-27 does not fall under the rubric of independent laws of the first-born. See above, Chapter 8.

5. See above, Chapter 6, Table and §5.

The passage in Exod. 22.28-29,[6] using various phrases regarding the first-born that are indicative of it being a gift to God, likewise belongs to this group. There also appear there phrases identifying the lot of the firstling animals with that of the first-born of human beings: 'The first-born of your sons you shall give to me. You shall do likewise with your oxen and with your sheep'.

b. In the second group, Scripture speaks of the redemption of the first-born, but does not specify the method of redemption (Exod. 13.13; 34.20).

c. The third group includes the law in Num. 18.15, which speaks of the redemption of human first-born, while v. 16 explains the method of its redemption: 'And their redemption price (at a month old you shall redeem them)...five shekels in silver'.[7]

Neh. 10.36-37 contains an instruction 'to bring to the house of our God...the first-born of our sons and of our cattle, as it is written in the law'. This seems to relate to the law in Numbers 18 regarding the redemption of the first-born of human beings,[8] but explicitly adds that on the occasion of the ceremony the first-born of human beings is to be taken to the house of the Lord.

One may infer from various writings that the bringing of the first-born to the Temple for purposes of the ceremony of redemption was a regular practice. Thus, Lk. 2.23 notes that the infant Jesus was brought to a ceremony at the Temple in Jerusalem.[9] However, the practice of bringing the child to the Temple was not accepted by the rabbis in the later halakhah: 'Just as one is allowed to give the first-born of man to

6. On the difficulties concerning the interpretation of this verse, see F. Blome, *Die Opfermaterie*, p. 388-92, and his summary of scholarly opinion concerning the subject. See also Mader, *Die Menschenopfer*, pp. 122-23, 125-26.

7. The redemption of first-born Israelites for five shekels also appears in Num. 3.47, which will be discussed further on.

8. One may not assume that the demand to bring them to the house of the Lord at such a late stage during the period of the Return involved any intention other than redemption. See A. Ehrlich, *The Literal Sense of the Bible*, p. 428, in his comment on this verse.

9. G. Allon believes that Philo's remarks (*Spec. Leg.* 1.152) concerning the bringing of gifts to the Temple reflect an ancient law. Among other proofs that it was customary to redeem the first-born in Jerusalem, he cites Lk. 2.23 in support of Philo's conjecture (*Studies*, I, pp. 83-86). Compare *Cant. R.* 7.2: 'When a first-born son is born to one of you...when you go up on the pilgrimage festivals, he is brought up...to appear before Me'.

the priest at any place one chooses, so is it with the firstling of animals...' (*Sifre, Koraḥ*, to Num. 18.15; *Mek., Bo'* to Exod. 13.2; *Yal. Shim'oni* 1.755).[10]

3. *The Question of That Which 'Opens the Womb' in Human First-Born*

The law of the sanctity of the first-born is concerned with the first-born of human beings and of animals. While it is self-evident in the case of firstling animals that one is speaking of that which 'opens the womb', since there is no possibility of a paternal firstling, in the case of human beings one must examine the exact wording used by the various laws with respect to this question.

Indeed, the very expression פטר רחם, which appears in most of these laws, indicates that even in the case of humans one is speaking of the first-born of the mother. But even in those cases in which Scripture does not use the phrase פטר רחם regarding the human first-born, one may reach the same conclusion on the basis of various proofs.

Thus, for example, 'Every first-born of man among your sons' in Exod. 13.13 refers to the first-born of the mother, because it appears as a detailing item following the opening formula, 'all that first opens the womb'. Again, one may infer that one is speaking of that which opens the womb also with regard to human beings through analogy to the law of firstling animals which appears next to it.

Consequently, one must reject the exegesis[11] that the phrase, 'The first-born of your sons you shall give to me' (Exod. 22.28-29) refers to the first-born of the father. Such an approach is based upon the view that the word בכור signifies the paternal first-born, and that according to this verse only one of the maternal first-born ('that opened the womb') from any one father (among his various wives) is to be given to God. All this is based upon the fact that the term 'the first-born of your sons' (בכור בניך—i.e. in the masculine) is used, rather than 'that which opens the womb'. One may argue against this approach as follows:

---

10. See Kaufmann, *History*, IV, p. 335.
11. J. Hempel, 'Das Ethos des Alte Testament', 312.

a. בכור is used in the Bible to refer to the maternal first-born as well.[12]
b. The use of the term בכור with regard to animals, as in Num. 18.15 and Deut. 15.19, among other places, counters the above view, since among animals one always necessarily follows the mother.[13]

4. *On the Question of the Sex of the Human First-Born*

In a number of passages, it is explicitly stated that the requirements apply only to a male first-born. Thus, for example, the chapter concerning the redemption of the first-born by the Levites contains a clear instruction to count every male first-born for purposes of their redemption (Num. 3.40, 42). Indeed, from this issue itself one may conclude that one is speaking of the male first-born, as the census of the Levites for purposes of that self-same redemption counted every male among the Levites above the age of one month (3.15). The analogy between the Levites and the first-born is facilitated by the fact that the language of substitution is used there explicitly. Thus, for example, 'I have taken the Levites...instead of every first-born that opens the womb...The Levites shall be mine, for all the first-born are mine...'

On the other hand, the question of the sex of the first-born[14] of human beings is not mentioned in the laws[15] of the first-born. Hence,

---

12. On this problem, see Brin, 'The First-Born of the Mother and the First-Born of the Father', pp. 33-38.

13. On the phrase *peter rehem* generally, see Brin, 'First-Born', pp. 35-36. Cf. there on the relationship between the terms בכור and פטר רחם and the approach of the sages to the problem of a child who was born following a Caeserean section or other unusual conditions of delivery.

14. The term *bekor* as such gives no indication of the sex of the child, because this term may be understood as referring to the type in general. According to Pedersen, *Israel*, III-IV, p. 698, we learn from this that it refers to both male and female first-born. By contrast, the rabbis' perception is that the phrases 'every first-born of man among your sons' (Exod. 13.13) or 'the first-born of your sons' (Exod. 22.28) indicate 'your son and not your daughters' (*b. Qid.* 29a; cf. Pedersen, *ibid.*). However, this is not a conclusive proof, since the term 'your sons' (בניך) in these idioms means descendants. Thus, this phrase is inadequate evidence of the sex of the first-born mentioned in these passages.

15. With the exception of the LXX to Exod. 13.12, which reads 'males' in a verse referring to the first-born of human beings and beasts. Perhaps this comes about through the connection between v. 12a and 12b, which in fact speaks about the firstlings of clean animals. That is, according to LXX all of v. 12 refers to the firstling

the answer to this question must be determined through various parallels:

a. The material mentioned above, namely, the substitution of the first-born for the Levites;

b. Further proof that one is speaking of a male first-born follows from the subject of the cost of the redemption. Num. 18.16 states that each first-born is to be redeemed for five shekels. This corresponds to the valuation of a male child between the ages of one month and five years (Lev. 27.6), rather than that of a female child (which is three shekels alone; see Lev. 27.6).[16]

c. A third proof is derived from examination of the laws of the first-born in their totality, that is, by drawing an analogy from that which is stated regarding firstling animals to the first-born of humans. It is explicitly stated in a number of sources that the firstlings of clean animals must be male; see Exod. 13.12, 'All the firstlings of your cattle that are males shall be the LORD's'; 13.15, 'Therefore I sacrifice to the LORD all the males that first open the womb; and Exod. 34.19, 'all your male cattle', and so on.

The drawing of an analogy from the verses that explicitly stipulate the sex of the firstling to those which do not make a clear statement on this matter is typical of the reasoning of the rabbinic sages, who utilized here the rule, 'a general rule which requires specification'. For example, from Deut. 15.19, which explicitly mentions 'All the firstling males...', they inferred that Exod. 13.2 likewise refers to males (*b. Bek.* 19a; *Tanḥ., Bo'*, 11; *Yal. Shim'oni* 1.214).[17]

The basic law in Exod. 13.2, which does not specifically mention that one is speaking of a male first-born, is interpreted in Lk. 2.23 on the basis of this same approach, where this law is cited[18] as follows: 'As it is written in the law of the LORD, "Every male that opens the womb shall be called holy to the LORD"'. That is to say, according to the sources that interpret this detail, Exod. 13.2 is also understood as specifically requiring a male first-born. By this method, the rabbis specifically

animal. For a similar understanding of this verse, see above, Chapter 6, §2, and the notes there.

16. This argument is invoked by Gray, *Numbers*, p. 230.

17. However, this analogy is not drawn in the case under discussion with regard to the first-born of human beings, but only regarding a firstling clean animal.

18. That Lk. 2.7 does in fact relate to Exod. 13.2 was observed by Michaelis, πρωτότοκος, p. 877.

inferred that there are two conditions that must be fulfilled regarding the first-born: (1) that it be that which opens the womb, that is, the first-born of its mother; (2) that it be a male—to exclude the case of a male that was born following a female (*b. Bek.* 19a).[19]

5. *Towards an Understanding the Meaning of the Languages of Consecration of the First-Born*

i. *Introduction*

Five different kinds of wording are used in the laws of the first-born and in other related passages (Num. 3.11-13; 8.16-19), whether regarding human beings or beasts: 'sanctify to the LORD', 'given to the LORD', 'pass over to the LORD', 'it is the LORD's' (etc.)—on the one hand; and the phrase 'you shall redeem' (and its like), on the other.

Three of these phrases are verbal, indicating what is to be done with the first-born, while one, 'it is the LORD's', is a statement of the status of the first-born in relation to God. The fifth phrase, 'you shall redeem', constitutes the opposite pole to the first four phrases.

ii. *'Given to the LORD'*

The phrase 'given to the LORD' (נתן לה׳) appears in the law of the first-born in Exod. 22.28-29, where it states, 'The first-born of your sons you shall give to me. You shall do likewise with your oxen...you shall give it to me.'

Examination of the phrase 'give to...'[20] reveals that it is concerned with transfer from one person's domain to that of another; thus, 'give to the LORD' connotes transferral to the domain of the Divine. For this reason, we find such languages as 'give to the LORD' or 'gift' when speaking of holy gifts, and the like. This is the case regarding the half shekel (Exod. 30.12-13), while in the law of first-fruits we find a double use of the phrase 'give to': 'The first ripe fruits of all that is in their land, which they give [RSV: bring] to the LORD, shall be yours [i.e. the priests'; lit. "is given to you"]' (Num. 18.12). Thus, this verse depicts the transfer of the first-fruits from God to the priests. Note also the use of the nominal form (Deut. 16.17) in the expression, 'each man

---

19. It seems to me that the literal meaning of this is that the child who is born first to its mother is considered a פטר רחם by law, even if its birth was preceded by other (unnatural) births which did not result in viable offspring.

20. See Exod. 30.12, 13; Num. 15.4; 18.12; Deut. 18.4; etc.

according to the gifts of his hand',[21] and in Exod. 28.38, 'the gifts of their holy things'.[22]

We should take special note of a particular use of the term of giving to the LORD: in Hannah's words to Samuel, it states, 'I will give him to the LORD all the days of his life' (1 Sam. 1.11). By the very use of the idiom 'all the days of his life', and on the basis of Samuel's biography, it is clear that one is speaking here specifically of holy service.[23]

One should also note the fact that the idiom 'and I will give him to the LORD' is exchanged during the course of the narrative for the phrase 'I have lent him to the LORD' (השאלתיהו לה); as long as he lives, he is lent to the LORD' (1 Sam 1.28). Compare also 2.20, 'for the loan which she lent to the LORD'.

The use of 'give to the LORD' in the sense of holy service likewise appears in the chapter concerning the outstanding servants in the Temple of the LORD, the Levites,[24] who are described as 'a gift given to the LORD' (Num. 18.6). Elsewhere, we read 'for they are given to Him' (Num. 8.16); and 'their brothers the Levites I have given to all the service of the sanctuary of the house of God'[25] (1 Chron. 6.33).[26]

21. On the phrase ... נתן ל. ('gave to') as motivating the obligation to give to the holy realm, see O. Eissfeldt, *Erstlinge und Zehnten*, p. 6.

22. On Ezek. 20.25-26, 'and I defiled them them through their very gifts', and v. 31, 'when you offer your gifts and sacrifice your sons by fire' (cf. Ezek. 16.21, 36). I discussed the connection of these passages to the problem of the first-born in my dissertation, 'The First-Born in Israel', pp. 138-41.

23. One should note that Mic. 6.7, 'Shall I give my first-born for my transgression', is not related to this issue at all, because this verse does not speak of 'giving to the LORD', but only makes regular use of the verb נתן.

24. In Num. 18.7, the phrase מתנה ('gift') is used in relation to the service of the priests, and this in an unusual way. Compare Speiser's discussion of this verse ('Sanctification Which was not Recognized'), where he explains that the meaning of מתנה is הקדשה (i.e. consecration). Cf. Zimmerli, 'Erstgeborne', p. 461; Fishbane, *Biblical Interpretation*, pp. 186-87.

25. The Levites and the first-born are likewise associated through use of the idiom 'and they [the Levites] shall be mine' in Num. 3.12 (and in 3.45; 8.14). See below, §5, concerning the use of the phrase, 'it is the LORD's' (להי הוא).

26. Note that one of these groups, the lowest among the servants of the temple, was called the *Netinim*. See M. Haran, 'Netinim', p. 985, and the suggestions there concerning the connection to the use of the verb נתן regarding the Levites.

On the connection between the *netinim* and the *širkutu*, which was a religious order dedicated to the service of various gods, see Speiser, 'Sanctification', p. 505. The name of the order of *širkutu* is derived, like that of the *netinim*, from a root whose

In brief, the phrase 'given to the LORD' may serve in a variety of meanings and variants. However, the common denominator is their general and unelaborated meaning. For this reason, the phrase, 'the first-born of your sons you shall give to me' must be understood in terms of an unqualified transferral to the divine realm.[27] Thus, one need not necessarily infer from the case of Samuel or that of the Levites that 'give to the LORD' necessarily implies divine service.

iii. *'Set Apart to the LORD'*

The sense of being 'given to the LORD' clearly fits the specific linguistic use, 'to set apart to the LORD' (העבר לה'). In the general introduction pertaining to the first-born of both human beings and beasts in Exod. 13.12a,[28] we read, 'you shall set apart to the LORD all that first opens the womb'. It should be noted that this verse is a stylistic variant of its parallel in Exod. 34.19,[29] 'All that opens the womb is mine'. Hence, the phrase 'set apart to the LORD' is equivalent to '[set apart] to Me' (i.e. the LORD).

The use of 'set aside to...' appears elsewhere in the Bible, where its general sense is also that of transfer from one domain to another. Thus, in Num. 27.7: 'surely give to them [the daughters of Zelophehad] an inheritance...and pass the inheritance of their fathers to them'. Or in v. 8, 'and you shall pass over their inheritance to his daughter'. Again, in Est. 8.2, 'And the king removed his ring, which had passed over from Haman, and gave it to Mordecai'.[30]

iv. *'Consecrate to the LORD'*

The third usage, 'consecrate to the LORD' (קדש לה'), in the *pi'el* or *hif'il* construction, is similar to the two previous ones. This idiom appears in the *hif'il* construction in Num. 3.13: 'for all the first-born are mine...I consecrated for my own all the first-born...they shall be mine'

---

sense is presenting or consecrating to God, like נתן.

27. On the fact that the idiom נתן לה' is not unequivocal in meaning, and that we must rely upon the context and other sources in order to understand its nature, see Blome, *Die Opfermaterie*, p. 391 n. 20.

28. On the nature of Exod. 13.12 in general, see above, Chapter 6.§2.

29. On the relationship between these two laws, see above, Chapter 6.§2.

30. On the relationship of the idiom העבר לה' (here translated 'to set apart to the LORD') to the chapters on the Molekh, see Brin, 'The First-Born in Israel', in the appendix on the problem of sacrificing human first-born, pp. 142-48.

(and compare 8.17). The phrase 'consecrate to the LORD' (or: 'to me') is explicated twice in the body of the verse: 'for all the first-born are mine...they shall be mine'. The same is true of Deut. 15.19: 'All the firstling males...you shall consecrate to the LORD your God'. Thereafter are mentioned the concrete acts through which is expressed their consecration to God, that is, their belonging to the Divine.

The verb קדש, as used in the *hif'il* form, has a number of meanings; among others, 'consecrate to me', signifying transfer to the realm of the Temple and the *heqdesh*, that is, the making of a given object into holy property (see Exod. 28.38; Lev. 22.2; 27.14, 15, 16, and many other places in that chapter). This usage is presumably the most suitable for those verses appearing in the chapter of the first-born, since the results of the consecration are articulated, as mentioned, by the phrase 'they shall be mine'.

But it is worth noting that the term הקדש ל... is also used in the sense of 'to set aside', as in Jer. 12.3: 'and set them apart to the day of slaughter'.

The idiom קדש לה' also appears in the *pi'el* form in Exod. 13.2: 'Consecrate to me all the first-born; whatever is the first to open the womb'. The term קדש לה' is also clearly explicated in this verse, which opens with the instruction, קדש לי ('consecrate to me') and concludes with לי הוא ('...is mine').[31] We therefore find that both idioms—in the *hif'il* and in *pi'el*—are interpreted by the verse in the same manner:[32] as a statement that one is to transfer the first-born to the ownership of God.

Philo likewise interprets the idiom 'consecrate to the LORD' as implying that the first-born are the property of God (*Rer. Div. Her.* §§117-19).

In addition to these meanings, the *pi'el* form of קדש carries the sense of acquiring sanctity. This interpretation may also follow from the use of the verb in *hif'il*, but not in as characteristic a way (and see further below).

It follows that, in addition to the sense of belonging to God which

31. The view that קדש לה' implies that the first-born are the property of God was derived in *Midrash Ḥadash* on the Torah by comparison of קדש לה' with לי הוא; See M.M. Kasher, *Torah Shelemah*, XII, p. 89. W.W. Baudissin, *Studien*, p. 63, likewise arrives at the same interpretation through comparison of קדש לה to נתן לה.

32. On the relationship of the *hif'il* and *pi'el* forms of the verb קדש, see Gesenius–Buhl, *Handwörterbuch*, *s.v.* קדש.

follows from all three phrases discussed thus far ('given to God', 'passed over to God', 'consecrate to God'), this last usage carries an additional meaning, that of the sanctity of the first-born, that is, that those first-born who are set apart to God are in fact holy. This interpretation is confirmed by an explanation found in the law of the first-born in Num. 18.17, stating that one may not redeem the firstlings of clean animals because 'they are holy'. It is interesting that to 'consecrate to the LORD' is also interpreted in this way. This may be seen, among other sources, from Lev. 27.14: 'when a man dedicates his house to be holy to the LORD...' The house that has been sanctified becomes part of the holy property (*heqdesh*), and as such is 'holy to the LORD'. One may again see here the connection between the *pi'el* and *hif'il* forms of the root קדש.

The law of the first-born in Exod. 13.2 is interpreted in a similar manner in Lk. 2.23, where it states,[33] 'Every male that opens the womb shall be called holy to the LORD'.[34]

There are some exegetes who interpret the imperative 'Consecrate to me' (Exod. 13.2) in the sense that one shall declare the first-born to be holy (Ibn Ezra; S.D. Luzzatto; Ehrlich).[35] However, it does not make sense that this interpretation is the straightforward, literal meaning, as I have demonstrated above.

In brief, it seems to me that the understanding of the consecration of the first-born goes hand in hand with the instruction to transfer it to the realm of the holy.

v. *'It is the LORD's'*

The fourth expression reiterates the same meaning: the determination that the first-born belongs to God. The language used in this case is

33. See A. Plummer, *Luke*, pp. 64-65. He believes that the quotation there is an (inexact) conflation of Exod. 13.2 and v. 12.

34. The sanctity of the first-born is also expressed in *Jub.* 2.19-20, and in the Aramaic Targum to 1 Chron. 5.1-2, in which the transfer of the birth-right from Reuben to Joseph (and to Judah) is defined in terms of the cancellation of his advantages—first and foremost the negation of his holiness as the first-born: אפסותיה קדושתיה.

On the sanctity of the first-born among other peoples and its manner of expression, see D. Jacobson, *The Social Background of the Old Testament*, pp. 96, 160; R.H. Lowie, *Social Organization*, p. 150.

35. Ehrlich cites as a parallel the phrase, וטמא הכהן (Lev. 13.22-23, etc.), whose meaning is to declare impurity, or to declare him to be impure.

לה' הוא or לי הוא or לי ('it is the LORD's' or 'it is mine'). This is the clearest of the four formulations with regard to the significance in question.[36] The relationship of this idiom to the others may be seen from the fact that it appears in these same laws as a complement or parallel description to the demand stated in other language. For example, in Exod. 13.2: 'Consecrate to me...is mine'. The same proximity may also be seen in the law in Lev. 27.26, which states that one may not sanctify the first-born through a special consecration, as in any event 'it is the LORD's'.

In brief, analysis of these four idioms reveals that they all tend toward the same basic meaning: namely, the statement in principle that all kinds of first-born belong to God. The practical significance of this fact of belonging to God changes for each type of first-born. Thus, for example, there are clear indications that the firstling of a clean animal was sacrificed as a burnt-offering, as in Exod. 13.15: 'Therefore I sacrifice to the LORD all the males that first open the womb'. Num. 18.17-18 and Deut. 15.19-23 likewise contain explicit statements concerning the arrangements for the sacrifice.

The firstlings of the unclean animal—or the first-born of an ass—were presumably transferred to sacred ownership,[37] until their law was altered so as to require redemption with a lamb (see Chapter 8 above).

The laws of the first-born contain some explicit remarks regarding the redemption of the first-born of humans. As I have already conjectured,[38] logic suggests that the stage of redemption must have been preceded by some other stage, since we cannot assume that the requirement of consecration as such was expressed by the negation of this sanctification.

It is therefore reasonable to assume that the principle of the first-born belonging to the realm of the holy was expressed in the case of human first-born by a certain relationship of the first-born to the realm of the Divine, namely, the Temple (see below on the nature of this relation). As a result, the clause concerning redemption is the result of a later stage, in which they already wished to undo that relationship.

36. See GKC §129a.
37. See on this Chapter 8, above.
38. See above, at the beginning of the present chapter.

6. *Toward an Explanation of the History of the Laws of the Human First-born*

All of the various laws of the first-born begin with the assumption that all 'firsts' of the fruit of the womb, of both human beings and beasts, are to be given to God. I have already explained that the practical meaning of this assumption varied with regard to each particular kind of first-born. We shall now turn our attention to the significance of this assumption regarding the first-born of human beings.

It would seem that even the first-born of human beings were understood as belonging to God. This belonging found its expression in the various appearances of the 'general law'[39] (Exod. 13.2; 12a; 34.19; Num. 18.15), as well as in the law in Exod. 22.28-29, all of which state that one is to transfer the first-born of human beings to the domain of God.

This requirement may perhaps be explained as a kind of statement concerning their attachment to the realm of the holy as a kind of auxiliary force for the conducting of cultic activity, or at times even in tasks of priesthood *per se* or the like[40] (but see below for a more precise formulation of this subject). Compare the related phrases, 'I will give him to the LORD' (1 Sam. 1.11), and the like, in the chapter concerning the 'loaning' of Samuel to the temple at Shiloh.

Let us now examine how the laws of the human first-born were carried out in practice. The first-born had always been understood as responsible for conducting the family cult in memory of the familial ancestors, and other similar functions. It is therefore reasonable to assume that, during that stage that preceded the establishment of the tribe of Levi as the priestly tribe, they would be seen as most suitable to serve in the holy.

39. On this term and its significance, see above, Chapter 6.

40. On sanctification to God in the sense of service in temples, see J. Henninger, 'Menschenopfer', p. 770. He even observes there, pp. 790-792, that consecration to the Godhead in the sense of becoming servants to God exists among the Arabs. For such an exegesis of Exod. 22.28-29 (among other exegetical possibilities), see Mader, *Die Menschenopfer*, pp. 122-26. Against that, see Campbell Thompson, *Semitic Magic*, p. 234. On the priesthood of the first-born in Israel, see also Blome, *Die Opfermaterie*, p. 390, and the bibliography there. On the priesthood of the firstborn in various tribes in modern times, see Lowie, *Primitive Society*, 238; *idem*, *Social Organization*, 150.

However, it is difficult to assume a situation within the social framework of Israel during the biblical period in which all of the first-born functioned as priests, that is, that the first-born of each family was taken to serve in the public cult. Moreover, since the law of the first-born applies to those that open the womb, it would be incumbent upon the Israelite man to give over to the public realm all of the first-borns of his wives. The concrete fulfilment of such an interpretation of the law would have been difficult within the reality of ancient Israel, whether from the social and economic viewpoint or in terms of the history of the cult and the manner of its development in Israel during the ancient period.

But to this one must add that, notwithstanding the numerous biblical passages concerned with the cult and its description, we have not found even one explicit verse from which one may clearly infer that the first-born ministered in the holy service (but see further below concerning the problem of Num. 3).

It therefore seems to me that, while in fact some of the first-born did serve in the cult,[41] the requirement that all of the first-born be transferred to the divine realm remained a theoretical law that was not carried out in fact. This stage is reflected in the 'general law', as well as in Exod. 22.28-29.

Over the course of time, with the establishment of an organized cult run by special professionals,[42] it was seen fit to completely forego the use of some of the first-born, as well as those remnants of the law

---

41. Gray, *Numbers*, p. 26, invokes various arguments against such an interpretation. Among his arguments are these: (1) that Samuel served as the result of a special oath of his mother, despite the fact that he was the first-born, and therefore needed, in any event to serve by law; (2) Micah appointed 'one of his sons' (Judg. 17.5) to be a priest for him, and it does not speak there specifically of the first-born.

As for the matter of Samuel, one may argue that the story is intended to note the childbirth by a barren woman, for which reason the mother was prepared to forego her first son so that he might be given to the holy service, if only she might be redeemed from her barrenness. Since this was the main point of the story, the author unwittingly ignored the explicit law requiring that Samuel be turned over to the realm of the holy, even without any need for an oath. One may also imagine that the law of first-born was not observed in practice in the area of Elkanah's residence, or put forward some similar argument.

Regarding the house of Micah, the entire story is built around the intention to criticize Micah and his temple. Evidently, even the fact that he 'installed one of his sons' adds to this negative characterization.

42. See below concerning Num. 3.

whereby the first-born were consecrated to the holy, which, as stated above, was not carried out in the case of most of the first-born owing to force of circumstance. At this stage, clauses concerning redemption were added to most of the laws of the first-born: 'Every first-born of man among your sons you shall redeem' (Exod. 13.12), in effect nullifying the sanctity of the first-born.[43] These clauses were not added to the law in Exod. 13.2, nor to that in Exod. 22.28-29.

The clause regarding the redemption of the firstling ass also originates from this stage. At this stage, the identity of the status of human first-born and of firstling asses is expressed in several ways:

a. In those laws in which the first-born of human beings and of beasts are mentioned, the firstlings of unclean animals[44] and the first-born of man always appear together.[45]

b. The use of the verb פדה is common to both kinds of first-born. See, for example, Num. 18.15, 'Nevertheless the first-born of man you shall redeem, and the firstling of unclean beasts you shall redeem'.[46] On the

---

43. The law of dedication in Lev. 27 teaches the connection between the consecration of an object or animal and the nullification of this sanctity through means of payment. For example, the dedication of a house or of a field to the LORD leads to its description as 'holy to the LORD' (Lev. 27.14), but further on it states, 'and if he who dedicates it wishes to redeem his house...it shall be his'. Hence, despite their description as 'holy' they are susceptible of redemption. See also Zimmerli, 'Erstgeborene', pp. 462-63.

44. On the relationship between the laws mentioning 'that which opens the womb' and those which interpret it as the firstling of unclean animals, see above, Chapter 8. Here there may arise the question of the relationship between the extension of the applicability of the law (so as to encompass all firstlings of unclean animals) and the question of redemption, whose meaning is the abrogation of its sanctity, the two tendencies being contradictory.

The answer to this contradiction may be that the tendency to extend its applicability applied before, or together with, the matter of the redemption (for example, that it existed among those circles according to whose approach the law applies *ab initio* to all firstlings of unclean animals).

But it may also be that, from the time that the redemption of the firstling ass was seen as a kind of priestly gift, the extension of the law was automatically seen as reflecting a strictly priestly interest, without any contradiction between the tendencies of the two stages. See on this above, Chapter 6, §5.

45. On the proximity of the laws of the first-born of humans and the firstlings of unclean animals, see above, Chapter 6, §5.

46. The rabbinic sages observed the similarity between the two types of first-born mentioned above—see *Num. R.* 4.8; *b. Bek.* 4a, cf. 4b; 12b; and compare *Yal. Shim.*

other hand, the difference between their destiny and that of the firstlings of clean animals is clearly accentuated: 'But the firstling of a cow, or the firstling of a sheep, or the firstling of a goat, you shall not redeem; they are holy' (v. 17). That is, one may not redeem them because they remain within the realm of their original sanctity, unlike the first-born of human beings and the firsting of unclean animals, whose holiness has been abnegated.[47]

At this stage—that is, once the clauses of redemption had already been included in the laws—the method of redemption of the firstling ass is stated explicitly: 'Every firstling of an ass you shall redeem with a lamb' (Exod. 13.13; 34.20).[48] Regarding the first-born of human beings we find in those same laws the unelaborated phrase, 'you shall redeem'. One may conclude from the proximity of this verse to the law of the firstling ass that the human first-born is not redeemed with a lamb. This being so, we may assume that the redemption of the human first-born was performed with any object or any sum that their fathers might bring as a gift to the sanctuary, provided that it was reasonable.[49] As against this, some scholars thought that the term 'you shall redeem' implied that a substitute animal sacrifice was required in exchange for the person.[50]

689; also 755. One should note that the sum total of the comparisons brought in these places have no real connection to the matter discussed here. Among other subjects, they discuss there the obligation of the Levite to bring a first-born animal to the holy place, but add that he is exempt from bringing a firstling ass or the first-born of human beings, 'and from the firstling ass, because it is made analogous to the first-born of humans'. See Raba's argument, 'Scripture said, "you shall surely redeem"—I compared it for purposes of redemption, and not for any other matter' (*b. Bek.* 12b), and other similar things; cf. *t. Bek.* 1.2.

47. The means of drawing a connection in Neh. 10.37 are even more striking. It states there, 'the first-born of our sons and of our cattle' (i.e. impure animals; see above, Chapter 8) against 'the firstlings of our herds and of our flock', which are mentioned separately (see *ibid.*).

48. On the question of the beheading of the firstling ass, see Chapter 8, §3.

49. One may perhaps compare this with the *baraita* that interprets (regarding the firstling ass): 'You shall redeem—redeem for any amount' (*b. Bek.* 10b).

50. A. Alt, 'Zur Talionsformel'; Jacobson, *The Social Background*, p. 304; N.H. Tur-Sinai, *Language and Book*, I, pp. 121-22 (he learns this, among other things, from an expression such as מלך אמר in the Phoenician inscriptions, which denotes a substitute offering of a sheep for מלך אדם, which in his opinion refers to human sacrifice). Cf. Loewenstamm, 'The Investiture of Levi'.

For a reconstruction of the tradition of substituting a firstling animal for a first-born human, see Campbell Thompson, *Semitic Magic*, p. 220. Cf. his p. 234, where in

However, there is no proof of the correctness of this interpretation. As for Genesis 22 (the binding of Isaac), which is generally speaking cited as a proof, this has nothing to do with the subject, since it does not relate at all to the question of the first-born, and even the word 'first-born' does not appear there at all. The essential point of this text is to tell the story of how Abraham stood up to the test imposed by God. As for earlier tendencies, assuming the author of this text was at all aware of such, on the basis of the condition of the present material it is impossible to make any conjecture.

I thus interpret the phrase 'you shall redeem' as indicating one among a variety of different ways of redemption that were, as mentioned, available to the father. It is therefore possible that there were those in the community who were accustomed to bring a sacrificial lamb as a substitute for the redeemed first-born human. But this was only one of the options practiced at this stage of the observance of the law.[51]

The next stage in the history of the laws of the human first-born is that represented by the law in Numbers 18.[52] Here, the subject of the redemption of the first-born human already acquires a clear and fixed formulation:[53] 'And their redemption price (at a month old you shall redeem them) you shall fix at five shekels in silver' (Num. 18.16).[54] This

his view the sheep is consumed in a shared ceremonial meal, as a vestige of the custom of cannibals (*sic*), who used to do so with human first-born in the more distant past.

51. Bäntsch, *Exodus*, p. 113, and Driver, *Exodus*, on Exod. 13.13, believe that the unelaborated use of the phrase 'you shall redeem' indicates that the redemption price originally varied according to the status of the father and other circumstances. See also below, n. 54.

52. On the one hand, this confirms our conclusion as to Num. 18 being the latest of the laws of first-born. On the other hand, one may advocate the solution that I proposed regarding the question of firstlings of unclean animals, namely, that Num. 18 reflects an independent temple tradition (and see Chapter 7 in the summary, and Chapter 8, §1) regarding the manner of redemption of first-born humans, whereas the earlier sources speak of 'you shall redeem' without elaboration (see above on the meaning of this phrase).

Deut. 15 is silent concerning the matter of first-born of humans, because it has nothing to add here; but compare Eissfeldt, *Molk als Opferbegriff*, p. 56, who interprets this silence differently. A summary of the laws of the first-born is found in Zimmerli, 'Erstgeborene', pp. 468-69; cf. Fishbane, *Biblical Interpretation*, p. 182.

53. Regarding the firstling of unclean animals, the phrase 'redeem' is used here without elaboration. See Chapter 8 n. 19.

54. Philo explains the question of redemption for five shekels as a fixed and

is the same as the value of a male child between one month and five years of age, according to the chapter of valuations (Lev. 27.6).[55]

7. The Relationship between the Laws of First-Born and the Law of Valuations (Leviticus 27)

An interesting parallel to the final stages of the laws of the first-born (see above) appears in the law of sacred dedication in Leviticus 27. This law deals with the consecration of free-will offerings and pledges freely given by those who offer them, rather than with obligatory sacred-offerings. The parallelism between the two may be observed in two matters:

a. The law itself, which is close or similar (in the two chapters);

b. Indications of the existence of two stages in each of the two systems of laws mentioned. These stages are: i. the stage of dedication; ii. the stage of redemption (*ge'ulah* or *pidyon*).

a. One who dedicates an unclean animal may change his mind, and redeem it from the domain of the holy by means of a payment in the amount cited in the verse. Various other kinds of property which were dedicated to God (a field, homestead, house, etc.) are likewise subject to redemption[56]—Lev. 27.11-25. That is, both stages, dedication and redemption, are possible. In the case of the law of the firstling of an unclean animal, only the stage of redemption exists, because one is obligated to redeem it,[57] while in the case of sacred things both options are stated.

b. Lev. 27.9-10 states that the practical significance of the dedication to the Lord of a clean animal is that said animal belongs to the realm of

uniform way for all, which does not take into consideration the economic situation of the father of the first-born (*Spec. Leg.* 1.137-140).

55. On the question of bringing the first-born up to the Temple city for the ceremony of their redemption, see above, §2 of the present chapter.

56. It states that when the field of inheritance is released in the jubilee—if it has not been redeemed before hand by its owners—it remains 'holy into the Lord'; this expression is explicitly interpreted as meaning 'the priest shall be in possession of it' (Lev. 27.21; and compare the subject of the firstling of a clean animal, Num. 18.17-18). That is, it is redemption that nullifies the sanctity of holy things.

57. Thus, according to the reading of all the laws of firstlings of unclean animals, but in part of them there is added the phrase, 'or if you will not redeem it you shall break its neck'. See on this Chapter 8, §§2–3.

the holy, and may not be redeemed for any sum whatsoever. The meaning of such dedication is presumably the offering of that animal as a sacrifice to God. 'If it is an animal such as men offer as an offering to the LORD, all of such that any man gives to the LORD is holy. He shall not substitute anything for it or exchange it...it shall be holy' (Lev. 27.9-10).

Thus, in the case of a clean animal the stage of dedication appears in a clear formula, while the stage of redemption is expressed in terms of a prohibition: 'He shall not substitute anything for it or exchange it, a good for a bad, or a bad for a good' (v. 10). Note also the interesting parallel in the law of the firstling of a clean animal: 'But the firstling of a cow, or the firstling of a sheep, or the firstling of a goat, you shall not redeem; they are holy. You shall sprinkle their blood upon the altar...' (Num. 18.17).

c. In the law of dedication of a person, it states, 'When a man makes a special vow of persons to the LORD at your valuation, then your valuation of a male...' (Lev. 27.2-3). We therefore find that, when one dedicates a person, what one is dedicating in practice is his or her fixed valuation by age and sex, which are recorded in detail in the accompanying verses (27.1-8).

Here, only the stage of redemption is mentioned clearly, while that of dedication is not mentioned at all. However, it seems reasonable to assume, on the basis of analogy with the two previous cases mentioned there—a clean animal; an unclean animal (as well as house, field, etc.)—as well as the inner logic of the entire chapter of sanctifications, that regarding human beings there was a stage that preceded the dedication of a person's valuation, namely, the consecration of the person to the holy.

This act of consecration evidently provided an auxiliary force of people who served in the sanctuary.[58] This seems to have been the background of the chapter of valuations of those who consecrate human beings. Evidently, there occurred here the same process that I believe to have occurred regarding the first-born of humans, namely, that over the course of time, with the establishment of an organized cult with professionals set aside for that purpose, lay people ceased to be consecrated for

58. On this aspect of the background of the chapter, see Noth, *Leviticus*, on Lev. 27.2-8, pp. 204-205; and compare Elliger, *Leviticus*, pp. 386-87. We learn that human beings were dedicated to the service of the temples from the story of Hannah and Samuel.

this task (see above in the previous discussion). As a vestige of the earlier practice, some individuals performed the pious act of voluntarily giving the valuation of a person to the treasury of the holy domain.

8. *Numbers 3 and its Relation to the Laws of First-Born*

Chapter 3 of the book of Numbers presents a unique picture of the issue of the first-born, the main bulk of the chapter containing an account of the initial dedication of the Levites as servants of the priesthood. This matter is discussed in various sections of the chapter, in only part of which do the first-born also enter into the picture.

Analysis of Numbers 3 reveals certain difficulties concerning its composition, the relationship among the various forms of redemption of the first-born raised therein, and the problem of the firstlings of animals. In the following discussion, I shall only relate to that material which is pertinent to the question of the first-born. Those sections dealing with the consecration of the Levites, their tasks, their numbers, and so on, will only be discussed insofar as needed for the completeness of our primary discussion regarding the firstborn.

i. *Composition of Numbers 3*

Num. 3.5-10 relates how the Levites were placed before Aaron so as to become servants of the priests. Verses 11-13 speak of the act of substitution whereby God adopted for himself the Levites instead of the first-born.[59] The third passage, vv. 14-39, is concerned with the details of the clans of the Levites, the description of their specific functions, and the number of the Levites in toto (based upon their division by families).

The fourth passage, vv. 40-51, returns to the matter of the first-born, including instructions about the census of the first-born and their

---

59. Based upon the difference between the two passages, Gray states (*Numbers*, p. 26) that the two of them are not by the same author. He also finds difficulty in the attribution of each one of them to a different layer of P. According to von Rad, *Die Priesterschrift*, pp. 91-93, these passages are duplicates. Whereas according to one the Levites belong to Aaron and his sons, according to the second they belong to God. It follows from this that they reflect two different viewpoints regarding the origins of the tribe of Levi as a tribe ministering in the holy service. According to his approach, vv. 11-13 preceded vv. 5-10 (pp. 89-91). According to A.H.J. Gunneweg, vv. 5-10 is the earlier passage (*Leviten und Priester*, p. 149). Likewise Loewenstamm, 'The Investiture of Levi', p. 162; and compare Noth, *Numbers*, pp. 33-34. On the composition of this source, see Zimmerli, 'Erstgeborene', pp. 468-69.

substition by the Levites. Together with this, there appear instructions for the redemption of the remaining first-born Israelites at five shekels per head.

It seems quite clear that vv. 11-13 is directly related to vv. 40-51, because the general definition in the former passage of the Levites as a substitute for the first-born is only interpreted in the latter (vv. 40-51) by means of practical instructions as to how to affect these substitutions.[60] One should note that the substitutions required by vv. 11-13 seem different, on the face of it, from those described in vv. 40-51. Verses 11-13 speak about the substitution of all of the Levites for all of the first-born (without an exact count), as against vv. 40-51, which provides an exact reckoning. However, a comparison between v. 12, 'Behold, I have taken the Levites from among the people of Israel instead of every first-born that opens the womb among the people of Israel. The Levites shall be mine', and v. 41, 'And you shall take the Levites for me—I am the LORD—instead of all the first-born among the people of Israel' (cf. v. 45), reveals that the collective substitution is no more than a general description of that which is brought about through the individual substitution, which utilizes the very same expressions. This being so, one cannot distinguish between vv. 11-13 and vv. 40-51 in terms of the principle of substitution, the latter passage being the practical detailing of the former.[61]

The basic idea of vv. 40-51 is the exchange of 22,000 Levites for a like number of first-born, the remainder of the first-born—273 in number[62]—being redeemed at five shekels per head. It follows that the

60. According to Noth's approach (*Numeri*, pp. 38-39), vv. 40-51 is secondary in relation to vv. 11-13 (and ipso facto with respect to vv. 14-39, which serves as its basis); and cf. Zimmerli, 'Erstgeborene', p. 467; cf. below.

61. S.H. Hooke, 'The Theory and Practice of Substitution', pp. 11-12. According to Hooke, the entire tribe of Levi served as a collective substitute for the first-born. This substitution is conceived in concrete, materialistic terms, to the extent that an exact accounting is rendered of the remaining first-born, who are redeemed for money, as above. From his formulation of the subject, it would seem that he believes the two passages to constitute one sequence.

62. There is an inexact element in the given formula, in that the sum of the numbers of the various Levitic clans yields a greater figure than that given in the summation of the number of members of the tribe. Even the sages were already troubled by this; see the traditional commentaries to the verse. Cf. G. Ben-Ami Zarfati, 'Number', p. 180. According to his approach, in all those places in the Bible in which calculations seem incorrect, this is to be attributed, not to arithmetical error,

calculations in the unit in vv. 40-51 are based upon the total number of Levites as brought in vv. 14-39.[63] It is therefore possible that the present text of Numbers 3 represents the merger of two separate, originally independent units:

a. The division into the clans of the Levites, as well as the recording of their functions regarding the service of the Temple and its vessels, together with their enumeration by families. This fits well with the unit in vv. 5-10, giving the general instruction concerning the status of the Levites.

b. The passage in vv. 11-13 and its continuation in vv. 40-51 bring no new details as to the numbering of the Levites or the details of their function, but is constructed, as mentioned, upon the numerical basis appearing in vv. 14-39.

Thus, while vv. 5-10 and 14-39 can stand on their own, the same is not true with regard to vv. 11-13 or 40-51, which depend upon the previous passages.

This may be seen clearly from the two different subjects that appear in the chapter: (a) the service of the Levites, their numbers, and the detailing of their tasks; (b) the relationship between the Levites and the first-born. The former relates to a description of the nature of the tribe of Levi; the latter takes the approach of narrating the history of the cultic servants (see more on this below).

We must now ask how the author of Numbers 3 arrived at this theory of the substitution of the Levites for the first-born. It would appear that those phrases which speak of the consecration of the first-born—'given to the LORD', 'he is the LORD's', 'sanctify to the LORD'—were understood by him as a demand for transferring the first-born to the divine realm, in the sense that the first-born were intended to be servants of the cult. It follows that the main idea in the story of the exchange of the first-born for the Levites is rooted in the relationship between the two basic levels found in Numbers 3, which we have reconstructed above. We have already seen that the counting of the Levites

but to inexact transmission of the text.

63. Num. 3.14-39 as a unit deals indepedently with the description of the tasks of the Levites and the recording of their numbers. Von Rad, *Die Priesterscrift*, pp. 92-93, argues that, despite the antiquity of this section (in relation to vv. 11-13), it was influenced by the latter. A sign of this is that, despite the fact that the chapter speaks about the Levites and their service—that is, it assumes that they are adults—their census is taken from the age of one month and up, i.e., including minors.

and their assignment to tasks as servants of the cult constitutes the primary unit. Related to this, there arose a question pertaining to the history of the servants of the cult: if the Levites were first consecrated to this task only now, how did the cult function prior to the establishment of the tribe of Levi and the the house of Aaron? The answer given by Num. 3.11-13, 40-51 is: the first-born originally served as priests (on the realistic value of this testimony in Num. 3, see below).

It follows that the author of this chapter knew, on the one hand, the laws of the first-born, including the unelaborated clause concerning their redemption (Exod. 13.13; 34.20), that is, without any knowledge of the manner of that redemption.[64] On the other hand, he knew of the law of

64. Bäntsch describes Num. 3.11-13 as an independent exegetical tradition ignoring the law of redemption of humans (*Numeri*, p. 457). Compare Noth, *Numeri*, pp. 33-34, who contends that, according to the approach of the author of this passage (3.11-13), redemption by substitution of an animal for the human first-born is superfluous. Loewenstamm ('The Investiture of Levi') is more explicit. According to him, Num. 3.11-13 is a late attempt to nullify the laws of the first-born, connected with the shock undergone by the people at the time of the Destruction, which led them to take exception to laws reminiscent of Molech worship. A vestige of this negation survives, in his opinion, in Num. 8.16-19. But over the course of time, the law was renewed (Num. 18.15-17), following ancient tradition and under pressure of the financial needs of the priesthood.

In support of this theory, he cites Num. 18.6, 'And behold, I have taken your brethren the Levites from among the people of Israel; they are a gift to you, given to the LORD, to do the service of the tent of meeting'. This passage mentions the investiture of the Levites, but does not connect it with their exchange for the first-born. The law of the first-born is repeated again in v. 15, so that it is no longer possible to even mention the negation of the law. (Compare also *Num. R.* 3.5: 'As it says, "Behold, I have taken the Levites from among the people of Israel instead of every first-born..."' [Num. 3.12]. I might infer that from that day hence the first-born will not be holy; Scripture says, "they shall be mine" [*ibid.*, v. 13]—this indicates that they require redemption'.)

On the other hand, one should note that Num. 3.9, which is considered by Loewenstamm to be earlier than vv. 11-13, as well as Num. 8.19, also make use of language of the Levites being given to the priests, without mentioning the exchange of the first-born. Furthermore, Num. 3.9, 8.19 and 18.6 all speak of the relation of the Levites to the priests. Thus, it speaks there of the Levites as being given to the priests from among the Israelites, without referring to the task of the first-born. This is proven by Num. 8.19, since 8.16 mentions the exchange of the first-born by the Levites from the view-point of God ('for they are wholly given...instead of all that open the womb', etc.), whereas 8.19, which speaks of the matter from the view-point of the priests, states, 'And I have given the Levites as a gift to Aaron and his sons

redemption detailed in Numbers 18. It therefore occurred to him that one might also see the Levites, who were also seen as being given to God (or to Aaron the priest—'And you shall give the Levites to Aaron...they are wholly given to him', Num. 3.9; 'and I have given...as a gift to Aaron and his sons', 8.19; 'they are a gift to you, given to the Lord', 18.6) as constituting the 'redemption' offered in exchange for the first-born, who until then had been 'given to the Lord'.

Hence, the author of Numbers 3 conceived the exchange of the Levites for the first-born: 'for mine is every first-born' (v. 13) against 'instead of every first-born...the Levites shall be mine' (v. 12). 'And they [the Levites] are mine' (v. 13), as against 'for mine is every first-born...they shall be mine' (3.13; cf. 3.41; 8.16-18).[65] The 22,000 first-born who were redeemed in this one-time manner[66] are designated by the author as 'those redeemed of the Levites' (v. 49).[67]

Against the detailed law of redemption found in Numbers 18, there appears an additional detail concerning those first-born who remained over and above the Levites, and who for this reason needed to be redeemed at five shekels per head. Thus, the two types of redemption that appear in the laws of the first-born are both represented in this story.[68]

---

from among the people of Israel'. There is no point here in mentioning the exchange of the first-born. Cf. Gray, *Numbers*, p. 221.

Moreover, the claim that Num. 3.11-13 may be considered as nullifying the laws of the first-born ignores the fact that already in the early laws there appears a clause concerning the redemption of human first-born. This being so, the uniqueness of Num. 3 lies in its noting the method of redemption, and not in the actual fact of redemption.

65. Num. 8.16-18 relies upon 3.11-13. See Snaith, *Leviticus and Numbers*, p. 216. Cf. Noth, *Numbers*, pp. 62-63.

66. See R. Obadiah Sforno's interpretation of Num. 8.18: '"And I have taken the Levites"—only in that same generation'. Cf. n. 68 below.

67. This phrase also appears in the Samaritan (and cf. LXX and the Old Latin) to Num. 3.12, as an addition. Following the words 'of the children of Israel' it states there, 'their redeemed shall be'.

68. According to L. Elliot-Binns, *Numbers*, p. 15, the two forms of redemption mentioned in the chapter may be combined by explaining that the Levites were taken in exchange for all those first-born who were alive at the time, while the redemption with money was addressed to those who would be born later on.

If the conclusion reached above concerning the relation between the collective redemption (vv. 11-13) and the individual redemption (vv. 40-51) is not correct, then these must be read as distinct chapters. That is, the stage of the redemption of the 273 additional first-born was secondary, added at a later stage in an attempt to harmonize

One should note that Num. 3.40-51 relies entirely upon Num. 18.15-16, since the sum of the redemption money per individual is five shekels. But while in Num. 18.16 the sum is suitable for a male child from one month to five years of age, as in the law of valuations in Lev. 27.6 (cf. Num. 18.16, which speaks of 'their redemption price; at a month old you shall redeem them'), this is not the case according to Num. 3.40-51, which speaks of the 273 remaining ones, not all of whom are subject to this specific 'tax', since one is speaking here of the remainders of the first-born of Israel during the generation of the wilderness, which included adults. One can only explain this discrepancy on the basis of the fact that the section was based upon the law of redemption in Num. 18.15-16, while ignoring of the unique situation of Numbers 3.

To summarize the matter: Numbers 3 is not to be considered as a law *per se*, since it does not contain any instructions for future generations. Rather, it is a theoretical presentation, taking the form of a story about the one-time act of exchange of the Levites for the first-born during the generation of the desert. The purpose of this presentation is, as I said, to

the systems of law involving unelaborated redemption—such as in Exod. 13.13—which are interpreted in Numbers 3 as referring to redemption by the Levites, with the demand for redemption by five shekels (Num. 18).

According to Loewenstamm ('Investiture'), a later stage from Num. 18 penetrated into vv. 40-51. This stage was expressed in the story of the remainders, whose purpose is to allude to the doubt that exists regarding any particular first-born as to whether he was in fact redeemed by the Levite; therefore, he needs to be redeemed for five shekels. That is, according to his approach, the two forms of redemption found in this chapter reflect two stages. The earlier one, whose tendency is to nullify the laws of the first-born (see above, n. 64), speaks of giving the first-born to God, whereas the latter tendency—the story of the remainders—attempts to 'bring in' to the earlier story the tendency of the latter stage (namely, the renewal of the laws of first-born). Cf. what I have written in n. 64 against this tendency.

To this, I should add the folowing:

a. If the penetration of this last stage is to be understood as a revival of laws of the first-born that had been negated, why didn't these later elements regarding the firstling of animals penetrate, which according to the explanation even negated these laws of the first-born?

b. Loewenstamm's explanation concerning the tendency of these additions is difficult, since they are stated within the framework of a story, and not that of a law. This being so, one might enquire which first-born in any generation began to feel these doubts, given that the story by its very nature speaks of a clearly defined generation—the generation of the desert—whereas against that there appear explicit laws concerning the first-born.

provide an answer to the question: who served in the cult prior to the Levites. It therefore should be seen as no more than a narrative attempt to solve the problem of the relationship between the Levites and the first-born. For this reason, it is irrelevant to challenge the author of the chapter with such arguments as: if all of the first-born were redeemed by the Levites, why did a law remain in force requiring the redemption of the first-born in Israel by paying his value to the priest? The author of this chapter did not address his attention to such issues at all.

However, one may not infer from this text that, according to its author, all of the first-born in fact served in actual cultic capacities or in various subsidiary tasks in the various temples; nor may one infer that all of the first-born were replaced by the Levites through a one-time act. That is, there is nothing in Numbers 3 to refute the above interpretation concerning the practical significance of the languages of dedication used in the laws of the first-born. Similarly, one may not assume that the author had a tradition concerning the service of all of the first-born in the holy.

On the other hand, the rabbis did assume that the Levites replaced the first-born as those who served in the holy place. Presumably, this conjecture was based upon a logical consideration: just as the Levites who came 'instead of every first-born...' (Num. 3.11) were servants in the holy place, so were the first-born.[69] However, it would seem that this

69. See on this *m. Zeb.* 14.4; *Gen. R.* 63.13; and cf. *j. Meg.* 1.13, concerning those first-born who served and were proud, etc., and were the first to sin in the matter of the calf.

However, any comparison between the service of the Levites and that of the first-born is not identical, because the rabbis assume the service of the first-born in all cultic functions, and not only in positions of service. Their conjecture concerning the extent of the service of the first-born thus necessarily follows from the period in which they locate the service of the first-born in the holy: 'Before the Sanctuary was constructed, high places were permitted and the service was with the first-born' (*m. Zeb.* 14.4). This is stated in greater detail in *Gen. R.* 84.8: 'At the beginning the first-born served, until the tribe of Levi arose' (the concept of 'the tribe of Levi' applies to all parts of the tribe, including the priests).

Under the influence of the rabbis, we have also found this outlook concerning the service of the first-born in the Aramaic targumim. Thus, for example, in *Targ. Onq.* to Exod. 24.5, concerning the young men among the Israelites who offered burnt-offerings and sacrifices at the covenant ceremony on Sinai, the Targum translates 'the young men of the people of Israel' as 'the chosen ones of the Israelites' (and a further expansion is found in *Targ. Ps.-J. ad loc.*, as is his way). The midrash in *Num. R.* 4.5-6 (and cf. 6.2) relates to this passage in Exod. 24, designating the young

was not the historical picture. See also above (§6) on the arguments against the reconstruction of a reality of regular cultic service of all the first-born.

ii. *The Problem of Firstling Animals in Numbers 3*

The unique nature of Numbers 3 is indicated by an additional element, namely, the subject of firstling animals. In Num. 3.11-13, we find a formula which ties together the consecration of the first-born of human beings and beasts in Israel with the plague of the first-born in Egypt (Num. 3.13; 8.17). But while the opening sentence (v. 11-12) speaks of the exchange of the Levites 'instead of every first-born that opens the womb among the people of Israel', presumably referring to the first-born of humans alone, the subject of firstling animals appears as an argument for the sanctity of the firstlings, as in the following verse, 'for all the first-born are mine; on the day that I slew...I consecrated for my own all the first-born...both of man and of beast' (v. 13). But further on, it does state that the animals of the Levites shall redeem the firstling animals of the Israelites (Num. 3.41, 45). The uniqueness of this story is thus expressed in a number of matters:

a. Unlike all other chapters of laws of first-born in the Torah, in which the subject of the firstling of animals occupies a separate and independent status, one feels here that the reference to firstling animals is done as an aside.

b. Unlike the laws of firstling animals, which draw a distinction between the firstlings of clean animals and those of unclean animals,[70] here it speaks of animals indiscriminately.

c. Unlike the exact instructions concerning the census of human first-borns and its exact details for purpose of their exchange for Levites, there is no instruction here concerning the counting of the firstlings of

men of Israel as 'the chosen ones among the first-born' (הבחורין שבבכורות; the subject of the midrash there is the service of the first-born in the holy place).

According to the approach of *Num. R.* 4, the first-born were already priests from primaeval times, beginning with Adam, who was 'the first-born of the world'.

Among the other privileges of the first-born, there is also mentioned the right of priesthood (and see *Targ. Onq.* and *Targ. Ps.-J.* to Gen. 49.3; and cf. *Yal. Shim.* 1.157, etc.).

70. With the exception of the appearances of the 'general rule' (see above, Chapter 6), in which there is likewise no separation relating to the different kinds of animals.

animals. Even the instruction that the animals of the Levites should redeem the firstlings of the animals of the Israelites is given in a general way, compared with the details of the census and the subject of the remainders of the human first-born.[71]

It is possible to resolve these and other difficulties in a number of ways. For example, the sages suggested that one is speaking here of the firstlings of asses, and that one sheep of a Levite redeemed several firstling asses of the Israelites (*b. Bek.* 4b; cf. Rashi to Num. 3.45). This interpretation is clearly based upon the fact of the redemption, mentioned here regarding animals. It is mentioned elsewhere that the firstling ass is redeemed with a sheep, while the firstlings of clean animals may not be redeemed altogether (Num. 18.17), since they are ultimately meant to be offered as sacrifices, thus the animals mentioned in the present chapter were identified as firstling asses. But since one may assume that the number of firstling asses in Israel was greater than the number of sheep of the Levites, they assumed (as opposed to the regular law) that a sheep of a Levite redeemed a number of firstling asses of Israelites.[72] However, this solution was not based upon the literal meaning of the verse, but was intended to harmonize the text of Numbers 3 with the other laws of the first-born, without noticing the uniqueness of Numbers 3 by comparison with the laws of first-born among human beings and beasts.

One may assume that this passage did not intend to deal with the subject of firstling animals at all, but rather with the first-born of human beings and their replacement by the Levites (as I proposed above). The mention of firstling animals appears by association with the general statement in v. 13 concerning the consecration of the first-born of human beings and beasts in connection with the plague of first-born, which originally (in v. 12) speaks only of the redemption of the first-born of humans. There may also have operated here an analogy in principle: just as the Levites redeem the first-born, so do the animals of the Levites redeem the firstlings of animals. That is, there is a mechanical

---

71. Nor is it even mentioned in the passage that the redemption of animals was in fact carried out, as opposed to what is explicitly stated concerning the execution of the redemption of first-born humans in vv. 49-51.

72. The rabbis inferred this matter from a homiletic nicety in the formulation of Num. 3.45: 'and the cattle (בהמת; according to the rabbis: singular) of the Levites instead of *their* cattle (בהמתם; according to the rabbis: plural)—*b. Bek.* 4b; and cf. *Yal. Shim.* 1.689.

copying to the realm of firstling animals of the solution regarding the first-born of human beings, even though the former did not really require a solution of this type at all. In fact, the laws of firstling animals do not raise problems similar to those involved in the first-born of humans.

This approach is totally different to everything known to us about the firstling of animals in other laws.[73] However, the problems confronted by the author of this chapter regarding human first-born were entirely different from those regarding firstling animals (for which reason his solution seems quite artificial).

Support for this interpretation, namely, that in practice this is not an independent discussion of the firstlings of animals, may perhaps be found in the fact that the parallel section, Num. 8.16-18, mentions the exchange of the first-born Israelites by the Levites, without mentioning the subject of firstling animals at all (see especially v. 18).[74]

73. According to Noth, *Numeri*, pp. 38-39, the reference to the animals of the Levites is theoretical, and appears to be an artificial addition within the framework of the chapter. Moreover, since the firstling of the clean animal is always sacrificed, there is no room at all for the substitution mentioned in Num. 3.

74. According to another proposed solution, the reading of v. 41 ought to be corrected (based upon one of the exegetical options in v. 45). This verse states: 'and the cattle of the Levites instead of their cattle'. According to the proposed interpretation, the possessive pronoun in 'their cattle' refers back to the first-born mentioned at the beginning of the verse. This being the case, this refers to the substitution of the animals belonging to the first-born Israelites by the animals of the Levites. Hence, one ought to read verse 41 as: 'and the cattle of the Levites instead of cattle of the first-born of the people of Israel'. According to this reading, this chapter does not speak at all of the firstlings of cattle. See Gray, *Numbers*, on the verses in question, and cf. Eliot-Binns, *Numbers*, p. 20. She believes that the text of 3.41 is corrupted, but does not propose any alternative reading. However, these suggestions have no basis, in that they introduce here an element of the animals belonging to the first-born, of which the text knows nothing. Why should the animals belonging to the first-born specifically have some value (of sanctity), and not other kinds of property belonging to them? On the other hand, the ordinary interpretation does have certain support in the fact that the firstling animals have a certain element of sanctity, as we know from the overall picture of the laws of the first-born.

Chapter 10

THE LAWS OF INHERITANCE OF THE FIRST-BORN

1. *The First-Born's Portion in the Family Inheritance*

i. *Terms Used for the First-Born's Share of the Inheritance*

It follows from the biblical law in Deut. 21.15-17 that the first-born son enjoyed an extra share in the inheritance, over and above that received by the other brothers. In other places in the Near East, it was also customary that the first-born received an additional portion, albeit the extent of this extra portion differed from place to place. We shall compare below biblical and external sources pertaining to this matter.

The principle of granting the first-born an extra portion in the family inheritance is reflected in a number of fixed linguistic expressions which serve to express the additional privilege due to the first-born. In the Bible, we find the term משפט הבכורה ('the right of the firstborn', Deut. 21.17) used to refer to the extra portion, or the word בכורה ('birthright'), as in the story of the sale of the birthright by Esau to Jacob: 'first [lit.: "today"] sell me your birthright' (Gen. 25.31).[1]

In the rabbinic lexicon, the phrases חלק בכורה ('the portion of the first-born', *b. B. Bat.* 126b; 142b; 159a; etc.), or the term בכורתו ('his birthright', as in the sentence 'and he takes his birthright', *b. B. Bat.* 138b) are used regarding this matter.

In Akkadian literature, one finds the fixed term *elâtu* (in Sumerian SIB.TA), meaning: the extra portion which the first-born receives in inheritance. See, for example, Document *OECT* 8 16.2, concerning a certain person who received a house as a regular part of his inheritance, plus another property as his additional portion (*elâtu*).[2]

---

1.   I. Mendleshon sees the word שכם (Gen. 48.22) as bearing a similar meaning, that is, an (extra) portion of the inheritance that was given to Joseph ('On the Preferential Status of the Eldest-Son', p. 39 n. 9). But it does not seem to me that this is a fixed term, but merely a picturesque figure of speech.

2.   For the different combinations of *elâtu*, see J. Klíma, *Untersuchungen zum*

ii. *The Size of the First-Born's Share in the Inheritance*
Wherever it was customary to give the first-born an additional share of the inheritance, it bore a fixed relation to the share of the other heirs, albeit each place had its own particular custom concerning the actual definition of this relation.

The fixed size of the first-born's share may be proven on the basis of a number of documents:

1. Certain documents state that the brothers are to divide the estate equally among themselves after the first-born receives his portion.[3] It is clear from this that one is speaking of a fixed portion, since, had that general definition been a mere suggestion, without a fixed definition of the size of this portion, this would be likely to cause conflicts and bedlam.[4]

2. Other documents speak of the participation of the sons in paying off the debts of their father or other family expenses according to their share in the inheritance.[5] Compare *b. B. Bat.* 124a, 'If there was a note of indebtedness against them [i.e. the brothers], the first-born gives [i.e. participates in paying the debt] a double portion', proportionate to his additional share in the estate (see on this below).

3. Section 5 of the Hermopolis codex from Egypt (3rd cent. BCE) states that the portion of the first-born is to be 'the customary portion'.[6] This language clearly indicates the fixed nature of the share of the first-born.

---

altbabylonischen Erbrecht, p. 22 n. 1. And see also *CAD*, A, p. 78, *s.v.* elâtu; and cf. in F.R. Kraus, 'Erbrechtliche Terminologie', pp. 55-56. On *da-dirig* as a term used to describe the extra portion in Ur of the early Babylonian period, see Kraus, 'Neue Rechtsurkunden', p. 126; cf. A. Poebel, *Babylonian Legal and Business Documents*, p. 26.

3. See, for example, M. Schorr, *Urkunden*, Text §20, ll. 7-9, pp. 38-39, and Text §6, ll. 10-15; and cf. Poebel, *Documents*, p. 36.

4. See Poebel, *Documents*, pp. 26, 36.

5. *VAS* 4 39.3 (accdg. to *CAD, s.v.* 'zittu', p. 141). On various shared expenses which so-and-so paid his brother the first-born in proportion to their shares in the inheritance, see: *Dar* 379.63 (accdg. to *CAD, ibid.*); *VAS* 15 40.37. Cf. the document from Nippur published by R.T. O'Callaghan, 'A New Inheritance Contract from Nippur', pp. 137-38, 141, concerning brothers who share the expense entailed in paying off their father's debt in a manner relative to the size of their inheritance (apart from the youngest, who because of his single status is freed of this), ll. Rv 9-11.

6. G. Mattha, 'Rights and Duties of the Eldest Son', p. 115.

Examination of various documents from the ancient Near East reveals the existence of differences between one place and another regarding the share of the first-born. The most widespread approach was one that set aside two portions of the inheritance for the first-born, albeit there were also other systems. We shall now examine the various sources in a systematic manner, according to the size of the portion given to the first-born.

iii. *The Approach of* שנים פי *(the 'Double Portion')*
Biblical law defines the portion of the first-born with the words, 'but he shall acknowledge the first-born...by giving him שנים פי of all that he has' (Deut. 21.17). It seems to me that the idiom שנים פי may be interpreted in the sense of two portions of his property (see below). Indeed, according to the documents from Nuzi, Assyrian law, documents from Middle Assyria, and other sources, the first-born is to enjoy a double share of the inheritance, that is, the portion he receives is equivalent to that of two of the 'ordinary' brothers (Heb. פשוטים, a term used in the Talmud to designate ordinary sons; see *b. B. Bat.* 13a, etc.)

Thus, the formula for calculating the size of the portions is as follows: if the total number of sons is n, an ordinary son receives $\frac{1}{n+1}$ and the first-born $\frac{2}{n+1}$.

In one document from Nuzi it states:[7] *mār bīti rabû 2 qātā i-laq-qé-ma*; that is, 'so and so [is] the first-born and he shall receive two portions'.

According to Assyrian law (Tablet B, clause 1),[8] the first-born receives two portions, but there is a difference in the manner of carrying out this division, depending upon the nature of the inheritance: in uncultivated land, the first-born takes two portions to begin with, whereas in cultivated land, he first receives one portion, while his second portion is distributed by lot[9] together with those of his brothers (but a

---

7. C.J. Gadd, 'Tablets from Kirkuk', pp. 92-93 (Doc. No. 6). Cf. Doc. No. 5, ll. 14-15; P. Koschaker, 'Fratriarchat, Hausgemeinschaft und Mutterrecht', pp. 34-35, 42; *idem*, 'Drei Rechtsurkunden aus Arrapa', p. 192; M. David, *Die Adoption*, p. 59. On a similar formula in an adoption contract from Middle Assyria, see *VAT* 8947 KAJ I 1.

8. See Driver–Miles, *The Assyrian Laws*, on this clause; cf. E. Szlechter, 'Chronique, Droits Cuneiformes', pp. 144-45; G. Cardascia, *Les lois Assyriennes*, pp. 261-64.

9. Division by lot was so common in Mesopotamia that the formulae *isqa nadû*

document from middle Assyria[10] speaks of a double portion without elaborating).

The double portion of the first-born was also customary in other parts of Mesopotamia: in Larsa,[11] Mari[12] and elsewhere.[13]

In the Bible, the subject of the portion of the first-born only appears in passing, in the law in Deut. 21.15-17. During the course of a discussion of the son of a beloved wife and that of a hated wife, it states that the first-born is to be given 'שְׁנַיִם פִּי of all that he has'. The phrase פִּי שְׁנַיִם also appears in the Bible in Zech. 13.8: 'In the whole land, says the LORD, פִּי שְׁנַיִם shall be cut off and perish, and one third shall be left alive'.[14] According to the verse in Zechariah, the idiom פִּי שְׁנַיִם would seem to mean two-thirds; indeed, there are even those scholars who attempted to

---

and *isqa iddû*, literally, the throwing of lots, came to mean a portion of the inheritance. The same was true of the word *isqa* used by itself. See Klíma, *Untersuchungen*, p. 34. The connection between the lot and the family inheritance is likewise expressed in the biblical phrase, 'you will have none to cast the portion by lot' (חֶבֶל בְּגוֹרָל, Mic. 2.5) or in Sir. 14.15, 'Wilt thou not leave thy wealth to another, and thy labour to them that cast the lot'.

10. E.F. Weidner, 'Eine Erbteilung in mittelassyrischer Zeit' (and see the analysis there of two documents pertaining to this subject); and cf. *idem*, 'Das Alter der mittelassyrischen Gesetztexte', p. 54.

11. L. Matous, 'Les contracts de partage de Larsa', pp. 154, 159-162, Text No. TCLx155, ll. 6-7; Kraus, 'Von altmesopotamischen Erbrecht', p. 12 (and the bibliography there); Mendleshon, 'On the Preferential Status', p. 39; and cf. G. Boyer, *Textes juridiques*, pp. 181-82, but it may be that this approach was not practiced on a regular basis in Larsa.

12. See the adoption contract in Boyer, Text no. 1, who interprets the phrase *ši-it-ti-in i-li-qí-(ma)* in the document as referring to the two portions that are due to the first-born. Cf. *ibid.*, pp. 181-82, and cf. Mendleshon, 'On the Preferential Status'. According to H.W.F. Saggs, Review of *Akkadisches Handwörterbuch*, by W. von Soden, pp. 413-14, this document ought to be identified with the declaration demanded by the law in the code of Hammurabi, §170, concerning the sons of the hand-maiden; that is, in the document in question the one adopted is recognized as a son. However, it does not seem to me that there is any connection between the two subjects. In any event, the portion of the first-born here is double. Noth interprets the extra portion in this document differently; on that, see below, n. 15.

13. Kraus, 'Von altmesopotamischen Erbrecht', p. 12 (and bibliography); cf. Klíma, *Untersuchungen*, p. 22 n. 2 (on the double portion in Israel and the Near East, and the bibliography there). Cf. *CAD*, XXI, *s.v.* 'zittu', p. 139 (right column). According to T. Ashkenazi, *The Beduins*, p. 114, the first-born among the Beduins receives double, and the others only one portion; but cf. below, n. 34.

14. Cf. 2 Kgs 2.9, and compare below.

242 *Studies in Biblical Law*

interpret the use of this idiom in Deuteronomy 21 in a similar light, claiming on its basis that the first-born in Israel enjoyed two-thirds of all of his father's property (while all the other brothers had to divide the remaining third among themselves).[15] However, the Akkadian parallels mentioned above clearly indicate that the intent of the law is that the portion of the first-born is to be equal to two portions of the inheritance. This interpretation, that he received two portions, is that of the sages (*b. B. Bat.* 118b-119a; 122b-123a),[16] and earlier that of the LXX,[17] Philo (*Spec. Leg.* 2.130) and Josephus[18] (*Ant.* 4.249).[19]

15. H.N. Granqvist, *Birth and Childhood among the Arabs*, pp. 38, 212; D. Jacobson, *The Social Background*, p. 96; and cf. B.A. Zarfati, 'Number', pp. 172, 180-181. Zarfati notes that this is proven by examination of the formulation of numbers in biblical Hebrew (but he admits that this may also be interpreted in the sense of two portions—on the basis of practice both in the ancient Near East and of the Talmud). It is interpreted likewise by E.A. Speiser, 'Of Shoes and Shekels', p. 19 n. 4. M. Noth, *Die Ursprunge des alten Israel*, pp. 19-20, interprets פי שנים as meaning two-thirds, and thinks that the language of the extra portion in the adoption document from Mari should be interpreted in like fashion. It is surprising that he did not mention on this occasion the arguments mitigating against his approach from the Nuzi documents and from the laws of Assyria, and elsewhere. Cf. n. 12, above.

16. On the Talmudic halakah relating to the inheritance of the first-born, see Gulak, *Foundations of Hebrew Law*, III, pp. 84-85.

17. As also *Targ. Onq.* and others.

18. Likewise in both classical and more recent exegesis: Rashi, Ibn Ezra, and others. Cf. G.A. Smith, *Deuteronomy, ad loc.*; D.Z. Hoffmann, *Das Buch Deuteronomium, ad loc.*; A. Wolff, *Das judische Erbrecht*, p. 43; Mendleshon, 'On the Preferential Status', p. 39; and others. Cf. Boyer, *Textes juridiques*, pp. 181-82.

19. N.H. Snaith, *Leviticus and Numbers*, pp. 309-10, interprets the ten portions granted the daughters of Zelophehad on the west of the Jordan (Josh. 17.3-6) as the portion of the first-born: five (daughters) multiplied by two (= 10). However, such an approach is inconsistent with ordinary calculations of inheritance, nor is there any question of birthright involved here. The principle of a 'collective' birthright (five daughters who together constitute one first-born for purposes of the 'double portion') is totally unknown in any system of birthright known from Israel or the Near East generally. On the sages' calculations concerning the ten districts taken by the daughters of Zelophahad, including the portion that Zelophehad said he took as the first-born of Hefer, see *b. B. Bat.* 118b, and Rashbam's comment *ad loc.*, and cf. his comment to 116b. On the other hand, I believe that it is possible to interpret the division of courses in 1 Chron. 23 (16 lots to Eleazar and 8 to Itamar) as clearly related to inheritance arrangements, since Eleazar assumed the place of Nadab the first-born and his second Abinadab, so that the double portion of the first-born in the 24 priestly courses may have been transferred to his account; that is, he was given 16,

One should note that regarding both scriptural passages (Deut. 21 and Zech. 13) one may draw a distinction between the interpretation of the term פי שנים in principle and its specific meaning in the use in question. By chance, in each of the two verses one is speaking of two 'figures': in Deuteronomy 21 it is the son of the beloved wife and the son of the one who is disliked, whereas in Zechariah 13 it is two groups of people: those who shall in the future be destroyed ('פי שנים shall be cut off and perish') and the others who will be saved ('and one third shall be left alive'). Since the meaning of פי שנים is two portions[20] (i.e. portions of the whole), the mathematical result of the cases described in both passages is in fact that the first component in each pair is in fact two-thirds of the whole.[21] That is, the specific arithmetical meaning of the description in Deuteronomy 21 was what led to the mistaken impression that the portion of the first-born in Israel generally speaking is two thirds.[22]

A certain allusion to the law of the double portion due to the first-born may also be found in the words of Elisha to Elijah (2 Kgs 2.9): 'let me inherit a double share (פי שנים) of your spirit', that is, would that I

---

while his 'younger' brother was given 8. Perhaps the statement made regarding Hannah, who received מנה אחת אפים (1 Sam. 1.5) was a compensation for her barrenness and for not having given Elkanah a first-born son, but because of her love she enjoyed the portion of the beloved 'first-born' (but cf. F. Rundgren, 'Parallelen zu Akk. *šinēpūm*', p. 30, who interprets this verse as a double portion, invoking a parallel from the Syrian, חד תרין being used in the same sense).

20. פי appears in biblical Hebrew and in parallel Semitic languages in the sense of a portion; see Rundgren, 'Parallelen', pp. 29-30. However, פים (*pîm*, as in 1 Sam. 13.21) is derived from another root. See Speiser, 'Of Shoes and Shekels', pp. 18-19 (and the bibliography there), on its use in the sense of 2/3.

21. In Akkadian, *šinēpūm* means 2/3 (and see in detail in Rundgren, 'Parallelen'). Cf. A. Goetze, 'Numbers Idioms', p. 202, and from there the Ugaritic *šnpt*, borrowed from the Akkadian in the same sense. See C.H. Gordon, 'New Data on Ugaritic Numerals' (on פים, see the previous note). But despite this interpretation of the Akkadian formation, Loewenstamm (*The Fathers and the Judges*, p. 364 n. 40) has commented on the dual meaning of the Hebrew פי שנים: (1) double; (2) two-thirds. Cf. Rundgren, 'Parallelen'. However, if the interpretation which I cited above is correct, then the sense of 2/3 for the Hebrew פי שנים is to be seen as a specific interpretation of the general meaning: namely, two portions. Thus, we do not have here two independent usages.

22. Thus the opinion of L.R. Fischer, 'An Amarna Age Prodigal', pp. 116-17, namely, that the interpretation of פי שנים in the sense of double is secondary to its meaning as 2/3, does not stand the test of probability.

were to be considered as your first-born heir[23] (in the metaphorical sense). One cannot assume that Elisha sought a precisely defined share of Elisha's spirit in the mathematical sense.

The use of the idiom פי שנים also appears in post-biblical Hebrew. Thus, for example, in Sir. 12.4-5, 'No (return of) kindness (cometh) to him that giveth satisfaction to the ungodly; nor hath he done any benevolence. Twofold (פי שנים) evil shalt thou obtain for all the good thou shalt have brought him'. That is, those who comfort evil-doers will receive two 'portions' of evil, corresponding to the 'portion' of good that they have done to the evil-doer. The same is true of Sir. 18.32, 'Delight not thyself in overmuch luxury, for double is the poverty thereof'. That is to say, the illicit pleasure causes a 'portion' of poverty double to that of the pleasure itself (cf. various commentaries, *ad loc.*).

The definition of פי שנים in Deuteronomy 21 (like the wording from Nuzi, 'he shall take two portions'; see above) relates to the share of the first-born[24] as one unit, that is, his regular share plus his extra portion. On the other hand, there are other texts that maintain a sharp distinction between the two portions of the first-born[25] (i.e. the standard and the extra).[26]

---

23. Compare Driver, *Deuteronomy*, p. 246; and Noth, *Die Ursprünge*, pp. 19-20 (and cf. R. David Kimhi [Radak] in his commentary *ad loc.* in the name of his father; likewise R. Levi Gersonides [Ralbag] and others; but Rashi evidently interpreted פי שנים in the sense of double). Therefore, perhaps the use of the title 'father' in the words of Elisha to Elijah are appropriate, 'My father, my father! the chariots of Israel and its horsemen' (2 Kgs 2.12). According to Speiser, 'Of Shoes and Shekels', p. 19, the narratives of Elisha and Zech. 14 were influenced by its interpretation as two-thirds in Deut. 21. See also E. Cecil, *Primogeniture*, p. 1.

24. We learn from the Talmud (*b. B. Bat.* 13a) that division according to order of birth may also hold true in relation to a servant or impure animal, in which case the benefit from their labour is divided in such a way that the first-born son receives 'a double portion' in relation to that of an ordinary brother.

25. Klíma, *Untersuchungen*, p. 29, notes that there is a difference in relation to the size of the portion of the first-born depending upon different methods of calculation. That is, the size of the portions may be affected by whether the two portions of the first-born were given together or separately. On the matter of the division of the inheritance, see the mathematical literature that exists regarding this matter: S. Gandz, 'The Algebra of Inheritance'; Neugebauer–Sachs, *Mathematical Cuneiform Texts*, pp. 52-53, 99-101 (and the bibliography there).

26. It is worth comparing this subject with the division described in *Jub.* 36, according to which there are enumerated in detail the various kinds of property that Isaac bequeathed to his sons. The only expression that indicates the relationship of

We may also learn that there were fixed practices regarding the means of giving the extra portion from *b. B. Bat.* 12b, 124a, where it states that it was customary to give the first-born his two portions of land from the estate adjacent to one another, that is, that the inheritance of the first-born was not to be physically divided.

iv *Other Approaches regarding the Extra Share*
a. In other sources,[27] the extra portion is calculated in a different manner from that described in the previous section. Hunter[28] found that in texts from Nippur one is speaking of a extra ten percent.[29] His calculations are confirmed by the description found in another document, published by O'Callaghan[30] (which in his opinion is also from Nippur, even though

---

the various parts to one another in terms of size is the statement of Isaac that he wishes the greater portion among them 'to the first-born' (*Jub.* 36.13). *Jub.* 8 depicts the distribution of the portions among the three sons of Noah. Even though the preferential portion due to the first-born is not stated there explicitly, one may reach the conclusion that the description of the inheritance of Shem—the first-born— includes various benefits that were given him by virtue of his birthright: (1) his inheritance is described first (and is presumably the best); (2) in the summary of the section in v. 30, it states concerning the inheritance of Ham and Japheth: 'But it is cold, and the land of Ham is hot, and the land of Shem is neither hot nor cold, but it is of blended hot and cold'; (3) the fact that the Garden of Eden is included in his portion, and that perhaps because of this he was the only one to receive the wondrous *Book of Medicines* (10.14)—all these are part of his first-born portion. 'And he gave all the books that he had written to Shem, his eldest son; for he loved him very much above all his sons.'

27. It is interesting to note that in China (at a much later period) the extra share given the first-born varies between an additional one percent to as much as a double portion, in the various districts of the state. See on this in M.H. van der Valk, 'The Law of Succession', pp. 98-99.

28. G.R. Hunter, *Sumerian Contracts*, pp. 29-30 n. 2; and also Kraus, 'Von altmesopotamischen Erbrecht', p. 12.

29. On the system whereby the first-born receives a bonus of 10%, see *Hindu Laws*, p. 103 (I did not read this source), quoted by Driver–Miles, *Assyrian Laws*, pp. 296-97. As against this, the laws of Manu speak of an added portion of 1/20 given the first-born (but cf. §117, there). For a comparison to the Roman practice, see Driver–Miles, *ibid.*

30. O'Callaghan, 'A New Inheritance Contract', pp. 135-38. The generalization made by E.F. Weidner, 'Eine Erbteilung', p. 121, would seem to indicate that he does not agree with this theory concerning the size of the portion in Nippur, or that he was not familiar with those views.

the name of the place is not mentioned there).[31]

b. It would appear from some Near Eastern texts that the first-born receives half of the property as his share of the inheritance, as in the documents from Nippur,[32] which state that the first-born received a portion equal to that taken by the four other brothers. However, owing to the sparcity of documentation it is not clear whether this form of division constituted a fixed approach.[33]

The inheritance of half of the property by the first-born appears in the modern period among half-Beduin tribes in the north of Israel, the remaining brothers dividing the other half.[34]

c. According to the Hermopolis Codex from Egypt[35] (§8), the property is divided among all the brothers as follows: the first-born receives twice as much as an ordinary son, while the latter receives twice as much as a daughter.[36] The wording in §5 referring to the 'customary

31. See his proofs for the identification of the place, 'A New Inheritance Contract', pp. 135-38.

32. See Poebel, *Babylonian Documents*, p. 26, and the references there to additional documents. Poebel notes, however, that it is difficult to reach a clear conclusion because of the poor condition of the texts.

33. In documents from the neo-Babylonian period and later (see *Dar* 379.52 and 59), it appears that the first-born enjoyed half of the inheritance. This is stated explicitly in *Dar* 379.27: 'The oldest brother shall take this as his portion in the inheritance, equal to half of all the inheritance' (according to *CAD*, 'zittu', p. 141). On the other hand, it is not clear how many brothers are referred to here; perhaps there were three, so that even according to the approach of a 'double portion' half of the inheritance was due to the first-born; see the summary in *CAD*, *s.v.* 'zittu', p. 148. There the matter is formulated in a general way, stating that in this period the first-born enjoys a half, and his two (sic!) brothers share the other half. If the intention there is that only the three oldest brothers inherit at all, then the portion of the first-born is in fact half. On the matter of the three eldest brothers, see also *CAD*, *s.v.* 'aplu', p. 176. On the approach of inheritance of half within the framework of the history of research in the laws of inheritance, cf. O'Callaghan, 'A New Inheritance Contract', pp. 139-40.

34. J. Henninger, *Die Familie*, pp. 122-24. This is in contrast to real Beduins, who do not show any preference to the first-born. See *idem*, 'Zum Erstgeborenrecht', pp. 167-68.

35. On this codex, see above, n. 6; and cf. Pestman, *Laws of Succession*, p. 65. On the state of publication of this codex, see Pestman, p. 65 n. 1.

36. Pestman, *Laws of Succession*, p. 66. Mattha interprets the codex of Hermopolis as speaking of three portions for the first-born, two for the regular sons, and one portion for the daughter ('Rights and Duties', p 116). On the portion of the first-born in Egypt during the Ptolemaic period, see also E. Lüddeckens,

portion' indicates that this was a fixed system. According to the codex, the first-born likewise received the shares in the estate of those brothers who predeceased their father,[37] or who died subsequent to the division without leaving offspring.

d. The extra share of the first-born is known from other sources as well, but on the basis of the documentation it is difficult to determine the size of the portion in each case.[38]

e. In some documents, the extra portion of the first-born is described by identifying that object which serves as the special (extra) portion of the first-born, rather than by comparing the size of his portion to the relative size of the 'ordinary' portions. Sometimes the special portion of the first-born included the household idols. Various other objects related to the cult of the dead of the family or to various other family rituals also fall to the portion of the first-born.[39] We likewise hear from various sources of the granting of a family office or titles being given to the first-born.[40]

Ägyptische Eheverträge, p. 333 n. 1.

According to E.R. Goodenough, *Jurisprudence of the Jewish Courts*, pp. 56-57, the portion of the first-born was double the portion of the 'regular' son in Ptolemaic Egypt. See also Colson (ed.), *Philo*, VII, pp. 626-27. An Egyptian text from 1200 BCE states that the first-born received a special portion as his extra share for the birthright, but it does not state the extent of this portion (Pestman, *Laws of Succession*, p. 66). The Egyptian saying (from the sixth dynasty) about giving to the great one according to his greatness and the young one according to his youth is an indication of the existence of an extra portion, but there is no exact statement of its size. See Seidl, 'Vom Erbrecht der alten Agypter', pp. 271-72.

37. Unlike the customary practice in Israelite law. In *b. B. Bat.* 142b, we read that the first-born does not have any preferential right over the inheritance of his brother who has died (after the death of his father); regarding these portions, all the brothers share equally. See also R. Saadyah Gaon, *Sefer Yerushot*, pp. 16-17. The same is true of Nippur. Hunter, *Sumerian Contracts*, pp. 29-33 n. 2, states that the right to an extra portion does not apply to the inheritance of the brothers who died. See also Koschaker, Review of *Sumerian Contracts*, by G.R. Hunter, p. 342.

38. Klíma argues that several different sizes for the extra portion of the first-born may appear in one document, depending upon the various types of inheritance. See his book, *Untersuchungen*, p. 31. For further examples, see Brin, 'Two Problems in the Laws of Inheritance', pp. 238-42.

39. Thus, regarding various different countries, see McCulloch, 'First-Born', p. 33; Pestman, *Laws of Succession*, p. 66; Mattha, 'Rights and Duties', pp. 115-16.

40. On the connection between the inheritance of the father's office and the status of first-born, see C.H.W. Johns, *Babylonian and Assyrian Laws*, p. 162. In his

2. *Other Customs of Inheritance*

We have thus far discussed those systems of inheritance whereby the
first-born enjoyed a preferred portion in the family inheritance, the
difference among the systems lying in the amount of the preference and
its form. We shall now examine other forms, which differ in principle
from those described previously. It may be that, through comparison to
these forms, we will be able to find some explanation for the origins of
the system of preference of the first-born in the family inheritance.

As we have seen above, the biblical material is very scanty regardng
this subject. We must therefore take note of every slight allusion that is
discovered. In my opinion, such a thing is to be found in Gen. 25.5,
'Abraham gave all he had to Isaac', while he only left gifts to the rest of
his sons (25.6): 'But to the sons of his concubines Abraham gave gifts,
and while he was still living he sent them away from his son Isaac'.[41]

This story has an extremely archaic flavour, and even seems to carry
a unique stamp because of the nature of the heros and the period. It
nevertheless seems to reflect certain actual practices of inheritance, to be
interpreted in the following manner:

It may be that during this period the law of the first-born as practiced
in Israel according to the description in Deut. 21.15-17 was not yet
known. Instead, this story reflects a custom whereby the father gave all
of his property to the first-born,[42] while the others received gifts and the
like.[43]

opinion, the very fact of giving the property is clearly connected with the holding of
the office. Thus, the inheritance of office is directly connected with the inheritance of
property.

On the inheritance of family titles and offices by the first-born in China, see van der
Valk, 'The Law of Succession', pp. 88-89. On family offices as the inheritance of the
first-born in various societies, see Cecil, *Primogeniture*, p. 9.

41. The testimony of Scripture on the order of the birth-right in the household of
Abraham (Gen. 25.5-6) in relation to Ishmael and the sons of the concubines is
discussed in Brin, 'The First-Born in Israel', *passim*.

42. T.E. McComisky, 'The Status of the Secondary Wife', p. 73, sees Gen. 25.5
as concerned with a gift of an extra portion to the first-born, in comparison with the
other brothers. That is, he does not see this as a vestige of some special practice of
total inheritance by the first-born. Likewise, R. Yaron, *Gifts in Contemplation of
Death*, pp. 4-5, does not see this as a total inheritance because, since the sons of the
concubines enjoyed gifts (which were admittedly smaller than a standard portion),
Isaac remained to enjoy alone all that was left.

Such a reality, according to which the first-born received all of the property[44] by virtue of being heir to leadership of the family as the replacement of the father, is no longer alluded to in biblical writing. It seems highly doubtful whether a conclusion of this type may be derived from such verses as Gen. 27.29, 'Be lord over your brothers, and may your mother's sons bow down to you',[45] since that verse is not at all concerned with the question of inheritance, and therefore does not deal with the size of the portions of the family inheritance. The main interest of this verse is rather in the description of power relationships and questions of political superiority or inferiority.

Further material concerning the form of inheritance may be found if we turn to an examination of the structure of biblical society, in all that

43. An interesting parallel to this chapter is found below, §3. Yaron asks whether Abraham violated the laws of inheritance in disinheriting the children of the concubines (*Gifts*, pp. 4-5). Z. Falk answers this in the negative ('Testate Succession', pp. 72-73), because this narrative comes to speak about the power of the father to do with the inheritance as he wishes. Elsewhere, Falk sees in the story of the giving of gifts to the children of the concubines and their dismissal (as well as the story of the adoption of Ephraim and Manasseh) an attempt to restrict the authority of the father regarding inheritance arrangements (*Hebrew Law*, pp. 166-67).

44. A. Eberharter, *Ehe und Familienrecht*, p. 180, believes that formerly the first-born in Israel inherited all of the property, but does not mention any proofs for the existence of such a stage in the history of the laws of inheritance. See also Falk, *Hebrew Law*, pp. 165-66, and compare *idem*, 'Endogamy in Israel', pp. 31-32.

45. As against Eberhardt, *Ehe und Familienrecht*, pp. 78-79. He also thinks that Isaac's words to Esau, 'Behold, I have made him your lord' (Gen. 27.37), support his view. On the possibility of the existence of a stage prior to Deut. 21, in which all of the property is inherited by the first-born, see also J. Mittelmann, *Der altisraelitsche Levirat*, p. 8 n. 1, and O'Callahan, 'Historical Parallels', p. 401. In a different direction, see the remarks of Nahmanides, who wishes to conclude from the dispute over the birthright between Esau and Jacob that the rule of the 'double portion' presumably did not hold at that time. The birthright fulfilled a function only regarding the inheritance of the status of the father and his authority, although the first-born may also have received slightly more than an ordinary brother in terms of property. On the possibility that the practice of a 'double portion' was not observed prior to Deut. 21, see the commentary of S.D. Luzzatto (Shadal) on Gen. 48.5, and the exegetical distinction drawn from the verse 'Ephraim and Manasseh shall be mine, as Reuben and Simeon are' (Gen. 48.5). If the rule of the double portion were observed, it should have read, according to Luzzatto, 'like Reuben' (alone!), or 'like Simeon and Levi'. Against this, one should note that what is written in Gen. 48.5 is not at all connected to matters of inheritance; as a result, it is impossible to infer anything from it vis-à-vis how the law of the first-born was practiced at that time.

pertains to the form of family life within the framework of the nuclear family. I refer to the possibility of continuity of shared family life even after the death of the father. Agrarian societies by nature require that one not divide the inheritance, for by so doing the strength of the family is progressively weakened. The reality implied by the situation described in Deut. 25.5, 'If brothers dwell together...' is one of a family whose inheritance is not divided. Even though the status of the first-born is not mentioned in this context, it seems reasonable to assume that he was the head of the group.[46]

Within the framework of such a family structure, the first-born was responsible for the support of dependent members of the family (his mother,[47] his unmarried sisters, etc.).[48] He was also the one to decide in matters concerning common property. According to this approach, the first-born held all of the family property, not as actual owner, but as the 'temporary' holder so long as the inheritance was not divided.

Such a social reality, in which the inheritance was not divided and business dealings were handled in common, is implied by several descriptions in the Talmud. Thus, for example, various Talmudic *sugyot* mention the 'partner brothers'. *M. B. Bat.* 9.4 states, 'Brothers who were partners, one of whom was drafted [to work] as an artisan [for the

46. See F. Buhl, *Die Socialen Verhältnisse*, p. 55 n. 2; B. Stade, *Geschichte des Volkes Israel*, I, p. 392. According to Cross, *The Hebrew Family*, pp. 191-93, it was impossible to divide the inheritance during the period of the wanderings, for which reason the first-born handled all of the property. This was not the case during the period of settlement, when there already existed a division of property. However, his remarks do not go beyond the realm of unproved speculation. Moreover, this does not make sense from a sociological viewpoint, because it was precisely during the period of wanderings that people were open to accept changes on the tribal level, more so than during a period of consolidation, in which the family inheritance constituted a single unit of power, so that there is a tendency against the division of inheritances, as explained above in the body of the chapter.

47. There is proof from Egypt concerning the responsibility of the first-born for his mother; for example, in various documents one sees the veto right of both—the first-born and the mother—over the property brought into the marriage by the mother. This is as protection against arbitrary actions by the father regarding this property. See Pestman, *Marriage and Matronial Property*, p. 40.

48. See Neufeld, *Ancient Hebrew Marriage Laws*, p. 263. It is surprising that none of the sources noted there addresses itself to the matter under discussion. Cf. Smith, 'Inheritance', p. 307, who invokes the opinion that the extra portion as such, according to Deut. 21.15-17, came about because of the first-born's responsibility for the widow and her dependents. Cf. Goodenough, *Jewish Jurisprudence*, pp. 56-57.

king], [the profit or loss] goes to the middle [i.e. the common pot]...
Brothers, some of whom sent groom's gifts...when the groom's gifts
were returned, it returned to the middle'. The significant point here is
that it speaks of a family business conducted in common, so that both
profits and losses are applied to the common treasury ('in the middle').
We likewise find the term 'property of the house' הבית הפוסה, used in the
Talmud, *b. B. Bat.* 137b, indicating a shared treasury: 'The brothers
who bought an *etrog* from the property of the house'. Compare also the
term 'blessing of the house' (ברכת הבית), which similarly indicates shared
ownership (*b. B. Bat.* 144b). We also find various instructions concerning their common expenses, such as, 'The brothers may say to him,
"If you are with us, you have support, and if you are not with us, you
do not have support"' (*ibid.*). Again, see *b. B. Bat.* 126b, regarding the
legal nature of the activities of the first-born relating to the property of
an ordinary brother, whether they take effect or not.

Perhaps the words of one of the multitude to Jesus, 'Teacher, bid my
brother divide the inheritance with me' (Lk. 12.13-14),[49] are to be
interpreted as reflecting a situation of an undivided inheritance, initially
through an agreement not to divide it, and over the course of time
through its dominance by the first-born.[50]

3. *The Father's Authority in Relation to Various Laws of Inheritance*

The law in Deut. 21.15-17 is opposed to the possibility that the father
will prefer the son of his beloved wife, who is not a first-born, over the
first-born, who is the son of the hated wife. It would seem to follow
from what is stated there that this was a polemic against known
practices in the society. According to these customs, the father acted
against the laws of inheritance, which required that he prefer the first-
born, in that he preferred other sons over the first-born. The tendency
of this law was to limit the ability of the father to engage in manipula-
tions intended to get around the accepted order. I have already
explained[51] that the instruction not to deviate from the law stems from
the understanding in Israel of the birthright as having a sacred character.

---

49. See W.F. Arndt, *Luke*, p. 315.
50. On extra-biblical material concerning methods of calculation of the inheritance
of the first-born, see Brin, 'The First-Born in Israel', pp. 249-60.
51. See below, in section 4 of this chapter.

Examination of biblical sources reveals[52] that the preference of another son over the first-born did occur in reality, and that the preferred son enjoyed the privileges of the first-born, although not the actual title.

The wording of the law in Deuteronomy 21 suggests that one must take note here of the relationship between inheritance based upon law and inheritance based upon the testament of the father. The present law does not deal at all with the question of discrimination or removal of an 'ordinary' son from the inheritance (nor does any other biblical text deal with this).[53] Its main concern is to protect the right of the first-born to a 'double portion'. We thus find that the first-born enjoys the 'double portion' in the case of intestate inheritance; the same is true with regard to the time of executing the will.

The distinction between inheritance based upon law and inheritance based upon testament is felt particularly strongly in rabbinic law. In a case where there is no will, one follows the straightforward law. Where there is a will, the sages nevertheless saw themselves as subject to the prohibitions of the Torah, and limited the father's right to deviate from the law when making up his will—specifically with regard to the rights of the first-born (and not of any other son).

Hence, we find in the Mishnah, *m. B. Bat.* 8.5, 'One who says, "Such and such a person, who is my first-born son, shall not receive a double portion"...did not say anything, for he has made a condition against that stipulated in the Torah'. Note the Talmudic discussion in *b. B. Bat.* 130a-b, allowing the father room to maneuver in his considerations regarding the inheritance of all of the sons, with the exception of the inheritance of the first-born.[54]

Nevertheless, the father was left an opening by which to deviate from the ancient law prohibiting one to give preference to one who is not a first-born, by giving him the option to distribute various gifts of his own

52. *Ibid.*

53. Yaron, *Gifts*, p. 10, infers from Deut. 21 that the father is not allowed to deviate from the arrangements regarding the distribution of the inheritance to all of his sons, not just in relation to the first-born.

54. There is a dispute among halakhic authorities as to whether a will which deviates from the law regarding the first-born is totally invalid, or only partly abnegated—that is, only regarding that which pertains to the first-born—the other sections of the will remaining valid as written. See Gulak, *Foundations of Hebrew Law*, III, pp. 73-75, and cf. Yaron, *Gifts*, pp. 37ff.

free will, even if these are not in accordance with the order of birth. However, care was taken that the father not use terminology of inheritance, for if he did his act was null and void.[55] We may learn the extent to which the sages saw themselves as formally bound by the law of preference of the first-born from the discussion in *b. B. Bat.* 138a: 'One who was dying and said, "Give two hundred zuz to so-and-so my first-born son, as is fitting him", he takes them, and also takes the birth-portion'. That is to say, the extra portion (birthright) is not subject to alteration within the context of inheritance. Therefore, the father's words are interpreted as an additional gift.[56]

Let us now turn to ancient Near Eastern material. In many places in the Near East, a fixed law existed concerning the manner of preference of the first-born.[57] But here, too, the father had a certain right to maneuver in this matter; indeed, the limitation placed upon the father by biblical law—in Deuteronomy 21—is not found in the ancient Near Eastern material.[58]

---

55. See Gulak, *Foundations*, pp. 73-75, and cf. *m. Bek.* 8.5: 'One who wrote all of his property to others and abandoned his sons—that which he did is valid, but the spirit of the sages is not happy with him'. And cf. *ibid.*, 'If he gave more to one son and less to another, and made the first-born equal to them—his words are valid'. But: 'If he said: "as their inheritance"—he has done nothing..."as a gift"—his words are valid'. We find that, from now on, the entire matter of the prohibition against negating the privileges of the first-born bears a strictly formal character. Yaron, *Gifts*, p. 37, cites *t. B. Bat.* 7.12: 'One who says, "My sons shall divide my property equally", and there was a first-born among them: if they received the property during the lifetime of their father, he does not take a double portion, but if not, he takes a double portion'. This source is not insistent upon the use of the term gift; however, what is said there is not accepted as binding halakhah. Cf. Yaron, *ibid.*

56. See Yaron, *Gifts*, pp. 45, 233. But note further the continuation of the Talmud's remarks there ('if he said, "with his first-born"...') for the possibility of a different formulation by which the first-born is allowed to choose between taking an extra portion and gifts. Compare *t. B. Bat.* 7.12 (in a somewhat different formulation): 'And he has the advantageous position. If he wished, he took them; if he wished, he took twice'. And see Yaron, *Gifts*, pp. 37ff.

57. See above, §1.

58. Falk compares Deut. 21 with Hammurabi, §§168-69, which speaks of the impossibility of depriving a son his inheritance unless he has committed various transgression, *Hebrew Law*, p. 40. As for the limitations upon the right of the father to dispossess the first-born, this is to be seen, according to him, as reflecting the influence of the late transition from a tribal way of life—in which the power of the father was greater—to a more centralized system, in which the father must bring the

In a document from Nuzi, HSS XIX.23,[59] lines 4-5, the father states: *ina mi-it-[ḫa]ri-iš i-zu[-uz-zu]/ina ŠÀ^{bi}-šu-nu GAL^{bi} yānu*. That is, they, the sons, will divide equally, there will not be among them a firstborn. In other words, none of them will enjoy the preferred portion due to the first-born (in Nuzi this portion was equal to two normal portions, as in biblical society). We thus find here an explicit order not to prefer the first-born.

Similarly, in Document HSS XIX.17, lines 12-14, concerning lands, buildings, and the like, which are to be given to three sons, we read that 'among my sons there is not one who is the first-born' (*ina [ša-š]u-nu ša mārīya rabî yānu*). That is, the three sons will inherit equally in the various kinds of inheritance, none of them receiving the extra portion befitting the first-born. (One can also see here the father's authority to decide according to his will, in that further on in the same document it states that even if ten more sons will be born, these will not inherit at all). In another document, HSS XIX.37, the same person appoints so-and-so among his sons as first-born, who thereby receives a double portion.[60] Thus, despite the fact that the system of preference of the first-born was generally speaking practiced,[61] it was subject to change at the will of the father.

A similar situation is described in the Hermopolis Codex from Egypt, where the preference of the first-born was also practiced. However, it states in the codex that the father is free to order at will that the youngest son receive all of the property, or to make any other decision that he wishes.[62] By the same measure, the codex recognizes the possibility that the father may transfer all of his property to the first-born, and not only the special portion. This again reflects the father's authority to determine inheritance arrangements, thereby deviating from

matter to the judicial institutions if he wises to behave contrary to a particular law. See Falk, *Hebrew Law*, pp. 165-66; *idem*, 'Testate Succession', pp. 72-73.

59. Speiser, 'A Significant New Will from Nuzi', pp. 66, 70.

60. See Speiser, 'A Significant New Will from Nuzi', pp. 66, 70, who emphasizes the father's authority in Hurrian society to decide about the inheritance as he wishes.

61. See M. David, 'Ein beitrag zum mittelassyrischen Erbrecht', pp. 79-81. David thinks that one must be careful in drawing comparisons between the law in Deut. 21.15-17 and Assyrian laws, despite the fact that both of them speak about the double portion due to the first-born. This, because Deut. 21 does not allow the father to write a will prefering one of his sons over the first-born, unlike the case in Assyrian law. See on this matter Yaron, Review of *Les lois assyriennes*, by G. Cardascia.

62. Mattha, 'Right and Duties', p. 114.

fixed practice with regard to the portion of the first-born.

It is perhaps also possible to learn of the father's authority to act as he sees fit in matters of inheritance from the Egyptian myth of the goddess Geb. The goddess Geb divided Egypt equally between Hur the first-born and Setti, but afterwards regretted this and gave everything to Hur the first-born[63] (it makes no difference that one is speaking here of a goddess, and not of a father in the literal sense). One again sees the father's authority to act as he sees fit in an Egyptian marriage contract from the third century, which states at the outset who will be the first-born and how much he will inherit.[64]

A document from Ugarit[65] may serve as a good example of the father's authority to act as he chooses in matters of inheritance. In this case, a certain person allows his wife to decide who will inherit and who will be disinherited, on the basis of the sons' behavior in relation to their mother. One should note that in this document two of the sons are mentioned by title: *aḫu rabû* (i.e. the first-born brother) and *aḫu ṣeḫru* (the youngest). We find that, despite one of the sons being the first-born, he does not automatically gain any preferential status by virtue his birthright. The father (or whoever acts through authority emanating from him—in this case the mother) is able to deprive him of any portion whatsoever in the inheritance.

The same point of view is found in an Egyptian text from the time of Amnamahet III, which states that the woman is to determine who is the heir.[66] Similarly, Hammurabi's code, §150, leaves an option for the mother to grant preference in inheritance to the son whom she loves. In Akkadian texts from Elam,[67] we find complete disinheritance in a case where the son failed properly to respect the mother.

---

63. Wilson, *ANET*[2], p. 4.

64. These contracts are discussed in G. Brin, 'The First-Born of the Mother and First-Born of the Father', pp. 48-50, and cf. Section 4 of the present chapter. See also Luddeckens, *Ägyptische Eheverträge*, pp. 277-79, 333. The important clause in these contracts, also for our purposes, is that which says, 'My first-born son, your first-born son, is the master of all that belongs to me and of all my property which I may acquire'—that is, all of the property was promised to the first-born. However, other clauses in parallel contracts acknowledge the possibility that the other brothers will also inherit in addition to the first-born.

65. F. Thureau-Dangin, 'Trois contrats de Ras Shamra', pp. 249-51, RS 8.145; and see Rainey, *Social Structure in Ugarit*, p. 98.

66. Pestman, *Marriage and Matrimonial Property*, p. 121.

67. Klíma, 'Untersuchungen zum elamischen Erbrecht', p. 52.

Studies in Biblical Law

We have thus far spoken of sources in which the preference of the first-born was the customary practice,[68] and have noted the extent of the father's power to act in a manner that is different from the law and from the customary preference of the first-born. The next example reflects a different direction. The laws of Hammurabi grant no preference to the first-born; however, §165 speaks of the father's power to grant an extra portion (above the standard portion) to any one of his sons whom he happens to like.[69] This again brings out the power of the father to deviate from the usual norm (in this case, to depart from the norm of equality in the distribution of inheritance).

There has been much deliberation among scholars as to which son is spoken of here. There are those who interpreted the law as if it were intended to favour the first-born.[70] As opposed to the 'automatic' preference existing in various sources (see above), in the Laws of Hammurabi this took the form of a gift, dependent upon the will of the

68. Apart from the mention of Hammurabi, §150; and cf. below on the laws of Hammurabi.

69. And perhaps one may see in the formulation of Deut. 21.15-17 a polemic against clauses of this type (Hammurabi §165), and not a polemic against the preference of the younger brother in the stories of the patriarchs, as the motivation of this law is usually interpreted. What leads me to this conjecture is the use of the terms 'beloved' and 'disliked', including the possibility that the father is liable to alter the order of primogeniture based on his love of the mother. Hammurabi §165 explicitly speaks of departure from the rule found in his own laws of inheritance, namely, the inheritance of equal shares by all the sons. According to this clause, it is possible that the father may give a gift to his beloved son, in addition to the normal portion of that same son. Cf. the remarks of David, 'Ein Beitrag'.

70. Kraus, quoted in David ('Ein Beitrag'), p. 12, and cf. p. 22. Against this, see B. Landsberger, 'Kritische Bemerkungen', pp. 32-33. That one is speaking here of the first-born has been remarked both by T.J. Meek, *ANET*, p. 173, and Miller (in Driver, below). However, Driver–Miles, *The Babylonian Laws*, I, p. 345-47; II, pp. 233-35, noted that the term *aplu* does not serve to describe the first-born, and that Hammurabi himself uses another term in the prologue and epilogue to his laws when he is speaking literally of the first-born. Why then does he suddenly here (in §165) make use of a different term? Moreover, the absence of the term *elâtu* (an extra portion—of the first-born) in the code of Hammurabi is further proof against the view that one is speaking here of a first-born. Even I. Mendelsohn ('On the Preferential Status', p. 40 n. 14) interprets this clause as speaking of an ordinary son; generally speaking, he sees §§150, 165, 170 as a vestige of the period during which the first-born enjoyed a preferred portion. *CAD*, *s.v.* 'aplu', p. 175, also interprets this as speaking of an ordinary son; and so Henninger, 'Zum Erstgeborenrecht', pp. 170-77.

father.[71] But examination of this text and its terminology reveals that it refers to all of the sons, and not specifically to the first-born. It follows from this that, notwithstanding the fact that the Code of Hammurabi speaks of equality among the sons,[72] it is possible to deviate from this through a decision of the father.[73]

4. *Deviations from the Order of First-Born in the Bible*

The unique status of the first-born granted him hegemony over his family, and under normal circumstances he became the head of the family upon his father's death; he himself passed on his leadership of the family to his first-born son, and so on. However, sometimes circumstances brought it about that the leadership of the family could not pass on to the first-born son, so that the continued leadership of the family was transferred to another branch, thereby interrupting the geneological continuity of the family in the 'line of the first-born'.

The law in Deut. 21.15-17 opposes granting preference to one who is not the first-born above the first-born by reason of the father's love of this child's mother.[74] This polemic is presumably directed against cases that occurred in reality, in which one who was not a first-born was preferred above one who was.

71. Klíma, *Untersuchungen*, pp. 10-12; cf. the sources for the decision of the father to remove them from their inheritance, *CAD*, *s.v.* 'aplu', p. 177.

72. Hammurabi §166 speaks of the extra portion given the youngest for his marriage expenses. Cf. Klíma, *Untersuchungen*, p. 13. In one document, we find an instruction concerning the giving of a preferential portion to the daughter, who was consecrated to be a sacred prostitute (Grant, Smith College, No. 260:6, according to *CAD*). In the laws of Lipit-Ishtar, which likewise do not mention the preference of the first-born, there appears in §32 (which is truncated) a mention of the possibility that the expenses of marriage may be given to the first-born by his father. See Korošec, 'Keilschriftrecht', p. 77.

73. The question of the father's authority to act even against conventional practice and law is discussed extensively in Brin, 'The Transfer of Hegemony', pp. 47-55. Cf. also §4, in the continuation of this chapter.

74. I discuss the problem of determining the first-born of the father in the event of multiple marriage with women of different statuses in Brin, 'First-born of the Mother and First-born of the Father', pp. 31-50. From what I explained there, it follows that the case in which the first-born of the principal wife is recognized as the first-Born of the father, even though the first-Born of the servant woman was born before him, is not to be seen as a deviation from the rule in Deut. 21. See on this J.D. Michaelis, *Commentaries*, I, p. 448.

In the formulation in Deuteronomy 21, the noun and the verb are both derived from the same root: '...the first-born (הבכור)...he (the father) can not prefer (לבכר)'. The meaning of this verb is 'to prefer',[75] that is, to grant those benefits due to the first-born.[76]

I shall now cite some other biblical passages which illustrate that the law in Deut. 21.15-17 is indeed directed towards cases in which the first-born was removed from his birth-right for various reasons. It may even be that the displacing of the first-born was a customary practice in certain circles.

a. In 2 Chron. 11.22, it states, 'and Rehoboam appointed Abijah the son of Maacah as chief prince among his brothers'. From what is stated there, it would seem that Abijah was the first-born of Rehobom's second or third wife, so that it is clear that he was not the first-born of his father. Nevertheless, Rehoboam appointed him as chief, that is, gave him a status of hegemony, with the explicit intention 'to make him king' (11.22). He did this because of his love of Abijah's mother: 'he loved Maachah above all his wives and concubines', as stated there explicitly (v. 21).

b. Similarly, in the case of Hosah of the sons of Merari (1 Chron. 26.10-11), it is said, 'And Hosah...had sons: Shimri the chief (הראש), for though he was not the first-born, his father made him chief; Hilkiah the second, Tebaliah the third...'

The phrase 'his father made him chief (לראש)' clearly refers here to the appointment of one who was not a first-born ('though he was not the first-born') to the office of chief,[77] while generally speaking 'chief' and 'first-born' apply to the same figure. Thus, the intention of this sentence is to designate Shimri as chief (ראש, i.e. appointed) and not as 'natural' first-born (בכור). This verse hence teaches us something of the power that the father had to appoint one of his other sons as heir in place of the first-born.

---

75. Even in the epic of *Krt* in the Ugarit writings (UT III 128, l. 16), we have found use made of בכר in the identical sense. In this place, the god says *ṣgrthn 'abkrn* ('I shall prefer the younger'), that is, it speaks of the transfer of the birthright to the younger. But one might infer from this text that without the interference of the father (or of God), in a natural sense, the hegemony would go to the first-born.

76. A. Hockel, *Christus der Erstgeborene*, interprets the word לבכר in this verse in the sense of: 'to make [him] a first-born'.

77. On the rarity of this case, see Michaelis, *Commentaries*, I, p. 449.

c. There are other cases of transfer of hegemony found in the Bible: the story of Esau and Jacob; that of Reuben, Judah and Joseph; and the incident of Ephraim and Manasseh. These, however, will not be discussed in the present work.[78]

It is nevertheless possible to learn from these and other cases that even a first-born who has been removed from his task as head of his brethren is still called the first-born (בכור); that is, the natural first-born retains the title of first-born even in those cases where the title has been emptied of its contents, following the transfer of the privileges of the birthright to another. We infer this from those passages which were cited above, to which we shall now return.

We have seen that Abijah was promoted to 'chief prince among his brothers' even though he was not explicitly called 'first-born'.[79] The case of Hosah and his son Shimri likewise teaches that hegemony and the title of 'first-born' are not necessarily identical. The verse reads, 'Shimri the chief, for though he was not the first-born, his father made him chief'. The comment, 'though he was not the first-born',[80] indicates the need felt by the author of these lines to explain the reason for Shimri being made chief, even though this was not the usual practice.

Nevertheless, this comment is not sufficiently clear, since it does not clearly explain to whom it refers. On the one hand, it may have been intended as general information, stating that there was no first-born in this particular family for whatever reason, such as that there was a daughter who was the first-born, or that the natural first-born had died,

---

78. See Brin, 'The First-Born in Israel', pp. 199-226; now in expanded form in my *Issues in the Bible*.

79. Compare the account of the coronation of Jehoram, which is formulated along lines similar to those in the story of the coronation of Abijah, albeit in one detail the two titles differ. Concerning Jehoram, it says, 'but he gave the kingdom to Jehoram, because he was the first-born (2 Chron. 21.3), unlike the case of Abijah, of whom it says, 'And he appointed Abijah...as chief prince...for he intended to make him king' (2 Chron. 11.22), and all this because he was the chief (ראש, appointed), and not the natural first-born (בכור).

80. The formula given, 'because he was not the first-born', may be parallel to what is stated in two documents from Nuzi, cited above, §3 ('there will not be among them a first-born'; HSS XIX.23 1. 5-6; HSS XIX 17.12); cf. Speiser, 'A Significant New Will', pp. 66, 70, and cf. below. But it seems to me that the situation does not correspond to that cited regarding the case of Hosah and Shimri, in that the Nuzi documents speak of the extra portion of the first-born without any argument in principle 'that he was not a first-born', such as that implied in the verse about Hosah.

or had been deposed, or the like.[81] On the other hand, the comment may refer to Shimri, who is the last person mentioned prior to the appearance of the word 'first-born' in the verse. According to Rothstein,[82] the verse ought to be read, 'for he was not the first-born' (כי לא היה הבכור).[83]

If one accepts this reading, it becomes clear that there are no longer two exegetical possibilities, but only one, namely, that it refers to Shimri alone. But even without this gloss, this interpretation is preferable for syntactical reasons: the pronouns that follow the phrase 'for he was not the first-born' all refer to Shimri: 'he made him', 'his father', and so on. In general, the entire verse (26.10) speaks only of Shimri,[84] so that presumably the phrase in question also deals with him.

It seems reasonable to assume that the choice of Shimri for the position of chief was connected with arrangements of the birthright. Even before he was appointed chief, Shimri was second to the first-born, being perhaps the first-born of another wife of Hosah or the like. Once he was appointed chief of the brothers, he was called 'chief' (ראש; 'Shimri the chief'...'his father made him chief') and not 'first-born', as we have seen above. But it is clear that these speculations are uncertain, and it is possible to suggest others as well.

The distinction between the rights of the first-born and the title of first-born is also found among the sages. In fact, we find a definition of it in principle in a haggadic midrash to *Ki Teze* (Deut. 21.17):[85] 'Even though it says, "I have given to you one portion above your brothers"

---

81. That the first-born of Hosah died without leaving any sons (compare the formula of the Peshitta to this verse), has been suggested by J. Keil (*Chronicles*, p. 275) and approximately thus also by Rothstein–Hänel (*Kommentar*, p. 466). Others see the case in question as involving the actual removal from the primogeniture of the predecessor of Shimri and the appointment of Shimri in his place. See O'Callahan, 'Historical Parallels', p. 401; Bennett, *s.v.* 'Heir'.

82. *Kommentar*, p. 466.

83. This suggestion is likewise accepted by Begrich (= BH³).

84. One should note that the interpretation of the verse in question by the LXX is confused. Instead of the personal name Shimri, they read φυλάσσοντες—that is, a general noun, 'body guards' (as if the Hebrew were שומרי and not שמרי); for this reason, in LXX^AB there is added the phrase τῆς διαιρέσεως τῆς δευτέρας, that is, that the sons of Hosah were the body guards of the second watch. This is presumably the reason why the words 'Hilkiah the second' are omitted in LXX^B to v. 11.

85. According to Kasher, *Torah Shelemah*, VIII, p. 1769.

[Gen. 48.22][86]...Joseph was not called the first-born of Jacob, but rather Reuben, "for he shall acknowledge the first-born, the son of the disliked"'. Compare the penetrating remarks of R. Samuel b. Meir (commentary to *b. B. Bat.* 123a), on the verse, 'he is not enrolled in the geneology according to the birthright' (1 Chron. 5.1): 'The birthright was not given to him [Joseph] that he might be called the first-born, for Reuben is eternally called the first-born of Israel; but rather that he might take two portions as the first-born'.[87]

From the overall context of these things, there become clear the power of the father to determine who is to be the first-born, to remove him, to appoint another son in his place,[88] and the like.[89] It is therefore interesting that, in total opposition to this, examination of the appropriate cases within biblical literature reveals that there is not even a single case in which one who received the status of hegemony also acquired the privilege of being designated as first-born. That is, the transferral of the privileges of the first-born to another son, which we have seen to be possible (even in Israel), did not entail a corresponding transfer of the title of first-born. The latter remains in the hands of the one who had previously held it, even if in reality he was no longer the one wielding hegemony over the family. This statement is not an *argumentum ex silentio*, but may be proven in practice from the cases that have been brought in Scripture.

86. That is, that he transferred to him the privileges of the first-born, such as a preferred portion in the inheritance, and so on.

87. Benno Jacob thinks that the entire matter depends upon the distinction between the terms בכור and בכורה (i.e. 'first-born' and 'birthright'). Whereas the former is never transferred, the latter—the right of primogeniture—is subject to transfer (*Der Erste Buch der Tora*, pp. 575-76). However, it seems to me that in practice we do not have here a distinction in terminology, but a substantive distinction: the title is not transferred, but the privileges are subject to transfer.

88. See McComisky, 'The Status of the Secondary Wife', p. 70. In his opinion, it would seem that Jacob was appointed as *māru rabû* (i.e. first-born) in the house of Laban. But these things do not seem correct to me.

89. Albeit this paternal privilege was limited in some ways; for example, in the case of Ammishtamaru king of Ugarit, who on the one hand needed to commit him-self to coronate the first-born of his divorced wife, but on the other hand was allowed by the Hittite king not to appoint him under certain conditions (see RS 17.159, PRU IV, p. 126; and RS 17.348, PRU IV, p. 128; and compare A. Rainey, *Social Structure in Ugarit*, pp. 23, 41-42, 46-47, 125). On the question of the restriction of the father's right to maneuver regarding matters of the first-born and the inheritance with regard to princes, see W. Otto, *PW*, Sup. II, col. 135.

One may explain the difference between the practice regarding the first-born in Israel and that in Mesopotamia and Egypt as stemming from a different conception of the institution of the birthright.[90] By its origins, the birthright in Israel was an institution of a religious nature. The first-born was seen as holy to God, and a divine aura rested upon the first-born in general.[91] As a result, it was inconceivable that a status of this sort, which was conveyed as the result of a natural fact, should be transformed into an acquired status. It would appear that this view persisted, even though over the course of time the outlook regarding the sanctity of the first-born changed, and even became completely obscured. Here, the biblical solution emerged: it is impossible for an outsider to enjoy the title of first-born,[92] even one to whom the privileges of the birthright have been transferred from the natural first-born.

On the other hand, we learn from the Mesopotamian documents (and others)[93] that in the ancient Near East the birthright primarily bore an

90. As I demonstrate at length in Brin, 'The Transfer of Hegemony'; cf. §3 of the present chapter.

91. See above, in Chapter 6 of this book.

92. 1 Chron. 9.31, which mentions the first-born status of Mattithiah, as follows, 'And Mattithiah, one of the Levites, (he is) the first-born of Shallum the Korahite...', is unusual among the biblical verses that define any first-born. The formula הוא הבכור ('he is the first-born') creates the impression of a polemic with some tradition or other, according to which someone else was the first-born in the family. Indeed, in 1 Chron. 26.1-2, Zechariah is described as the first-born of Meshelemiah of the Korahites. If Shallum the Korahite and Meshelemiah of the Korahites are the same person, then there is a problem regarding the name of the first-born. One may explain this discrepancy as stemming from different traditions that were current concerning the name of the first-born in this family, or one may be speaking of different first-borns at different times (J. Liver, *History of the Priests and Levites*, p. 112). In my opinion, it seems that we have here a struggle surrounding the appointment of the first-born of the father. According to one testimony, Zechariah was declared first-born (26.2; 9.21), while another tradition, which knew the earlier tradition, disagreed and asserted polemically, 'And Mattithiah...is the first-born of Shallum the Korahite...' (9.31). In any event, I do not see this as reflecting the removal of the first-born and the appointment of another in his place, who bore the title of first-born. On the relationship of the names Shallum and Meshelemiah, see J. Liver, 'Meshelemiah', p. 567. Cf. on this question Rothstein, *Kommentar*, p. 178; Myers, *Chronicles*, p. 72. On the suggestion that one see Shallum and Meshelemiah as two brothers, see Curtis, *s.v.* 'Geneology', col. 124.

93. One is speaking here of different types of documents, including the Wisdom

economic character,[94] that it was seen as the social status of the one who was the chief among his brothers, and who was destined to fill the place of the father after his death. According to this view, the birthright is not conceived as stemming from a special divine relation, nor have we found that the firstborn are considered to be holy. As a result, the father's room to manipulate and to make changes in the order of hegemony were far greater than in Israel.

composition, *Ludlul bēl nēmeqi*, which deals in principle with problems of the first-born. Cf. W.G. Lambert, *Babylonian Wisdom Literature*, pp. 84-87.

94. The functions fulfilled by the first-born in the home cult do not contradict what I have said about the status of the first-born in the Near East. The connection to the home cult is derived among other things from an etymological analysis of the Sumerian term IBILA and by other proofs. See, for example, F.R. Kraus, 'Erbrechtliche Terminologie', pp. 35ff. (and the bibliography there). It seems to me that the cult of the fathers of the family is a stage in making the first-born the head of the family. See R.E. Bradbury on the nature of the burial ceremony among the tribes of Eḍo (in southern Nigeria) and other tribes, where the ceremony serves as a transition to the official appointment of the first-born as the head of the clan ('Fathers, Elders and Ghosts', pp. 134-35).

Chapter 11

THE FIRST-BORN AND THE INHERITANCE OF THE MONARCHY

1. *Introduction*

A unique variety of inheritance is that entailed in the inheritance of
monarchy. In the present chapter, we shall examine the status of the
first-born of the king with the aim of arriving at some understanding of
his rights to his father's throne. Towards this end, we shall examine the
manner in which the monarchy was passed on in Israel and in other
kingdoms of the ancient Near East.

The unique facet of the inheritance of the monarchy lies in the fact
that only one son can inherit it,[1] because the maintenance of proper
order in the kingdom requires that the throne not be divided among a
number of sons.

The king's main legacy is the rulership of the kingdom, all of his
wealth and property stemming directly from this position as ruler.
Indeed, a central question to be asked is that of the relationship between
the inheritance of the throne and that of the royal property. Even
though there is no extant material on this question, it seems reasonable
to assume that ascent to the royal throne brought with it the riches of
the kingdom and its property. Consequently, the brothers of the heir
needed to suffice with personal gifts rather than with clearly defined
portions of their father's property[2] (see further below on the question of
Jehoshaphat).

1. On this system of inheritance, see above, Chapter 10, §2.
2. On the relationship between inheritance of the throne and inheritance of
property, see Cecil, *Primogeniture*, pp. 78-79. On total inheritance by one son and its
resemblance to inheritance of the throne, and its relation to partial inheritance (that is,
in which each son receives some portion), see E. Seidl, 'Vom Erbrecht der alten
Ägypter', p. 272.

2. *On the Manner of Inheriting Rule*

In those biblical passages dealing with the enthroning of one of the kings of Judah, we repeatedly find the stereotypical formula, 'and so-and-so slept with his fathers...and so-and-so his son reigned in his stead'[3] (e.g. 2 Kgs 14.31; 15.8, 24, etc.), indicating that the usual method of crowning a new king was for the son to ascend to the throne upon the death of his father.

In one case, this stereotypic formula is absent because the king in question died childless: 'And (Ahaziah) died, as was the word of God...and Jehoram reigned in his stead[4]...for he had no son' (2 Kgs 1.17). In the case of a disorganized monarchy, in which there was outbreak of rebellion and the murder of the ruler, as happened many times in the kingdom of Israel, this formula is missing. In its stead we find: 'and so-and-so...struck him down, and slew him, and reigned in his stead' (2 Kgs 15.10, 14, 30, etc.).

The procedure for passing on the kingdom is also discussed in Sir. 45.25 (Greek version): 'Also his covenant with David, the son of Jesse....The inheritance of the king is his son's alone', that is, the kingship is continued from father to son.[5]

Scripture testifies that this method of inheriting the throne was also customary in Ammon (2 Sam. 10.1), in Aram (2 Kgs 13.24) and in Assyria (2 Kgs 19.37). Indeed, from direct evidence from the countries of the ancient Near East we also learn that this was a regular system for inheriting the kingship. Moreover, in the Assyrian king lists, which depict many generations of royal succession, the system used is likewise that of father, son, grandson, and so on.[6] So much so, that one may

---

3. K. Galling, *Die israelitische Staatsverfassung*, pp. 18ff.; A. Poebel, 'The Assyrian King-List', p. 271 n. 59, noted that, according to the book of Kings, the sequence of inheritance from father to son continued through twelve generations.

4. In the Vulgate, in the Peshitta, and in Lucianus, there is added here the word: 'his brothers'. And indeed, Jehoram and Ahaziah were brothers, the sons of Jehoshaphat.

5. There are some who conclude here from comparison with the Syriac—'the inheritance of the king alone he inherited'—that the original reading was evidently נחלת מלך לבנו לבדו ('the inheritance of a king is for his son alone'). That is, while the priesthood was the inheritance of all the sons, the throne could be inherited by only one son. See B.Z. Segal, *Ben-Sira*, p. 316.

6. Poebel, 'Assyrian King-List', pp. 247-90, 481-86, especially pp. 268, 282,

assume that this fixed order led to the tendency of scribes and chroniclers to introduce alterations within the king lists so that every king within a legal dynasty would be considered the son of the king who preceded him.[7]

The same holds true for the founders of new dynasties, who presented themselves as the sons[8] of kings of the previous dynasty.[9]

481 and n. 211, etc.; and see also *ibid.*, II, pp. 56-60. One can see from the summarizing table (II, pp. 85-87) that 95% of the lists are composed according to the principle of father–son–grandson, etc. Similarly, in Jacobsen, *Sumerian King-List*, *passim*. On the principles of composition of the lists of kings, see A. Malamat, 'King-Lists', pp. 9-15. On the succession of sons in Ugarit, see M. Tsevat, 'Marriage and Monarchical Legitimacy', p. 239. On the inheritance of rulership in the ancient Near East, cf. Liver, 'Kingship', cols. 1049-95.

7.   Yeivin, *Studies in Jewish History*, p. 238 n. 15.

8.   H. Frankfort, *Kingship and the Gods*, p. 312 n. 1.

9.   The question of the inheritance of the monarchy in Edom during the ancient period is extremely complex. A series of kings who reigned one after another appears in Gen. 36. Based upon their names and the names of their fathers, as well as the formula, '*X* died, and *Y* reigned in his stead' (Gen. 36.33, 34, 35, 36, 37, etc.), it is clear that this does not reflect a system of throne passed down from father to son. Galling, *Die israelitische Staatsverfassung*, p. 22, conjectures that there was an element of choice before the enthroning of each one of these rulers. Cf. S. Loewenstamm, 'Edom', pp. 102-103.

W.F. Albright, *Archaeology and the Religion of Israel*, p. 206, attempted to solve this dilemma by suggesting that the continuity was via the offspring of the women; however, there is no proof of this. For critique of a view similar to this, see Loewenstamm, 'Edom'. However, this passage may reflect a social picture of special systems of family relationship, somewhere between patrilineality and matrilineality. But, as we have noted, we do not have sufficient material to determine this with certainty. Cf. S.A. Fox, *Kinship and Marriage*, *passim*.

In Elam there was another system of inehriting the throne, namely, a kind of levirate marriage in which, upon the death of the king, his brother would marry his widow and become king; cf. W. Hint, *Das Reich Elam*, p. 76; P. Koschaker, 'Fratriarchat', pp. 53-54.

D.O. Edzard has attempted to relate the system of inheritance of the throne in ancient Mesopotamia as a whole to questions of the patriarchate and the inheritance of the brothers, but he does not bring any proof for the accuracy of his conjecture ('Sumerer und Semiten', p. 255). Further opposed to his view is the clear approach according to which the Assyrian kings lists are arranged—namely, as mentioned, on the basis of father, son, etc.

3. *Evidence for the Reign of the First-Born in Israel*

Since the usual system of obtaining the throne within Israel was that of inherited kingship, we must examine the identity of those sons who inherited the royal throne. The arrangements for inheriting the throne seem to have been the same as other arrangements of familial inheritance, even though it is clear, as I noted above, that, owing to considerations of harmonious government and civil administration, only one son could inherit ruler's throne. Just as the first-born assumed his father's place in matters of familial office and titles,[10] one may assume that the first-born of the king ascended the throne in his father's place.

The assumption that the first-born prince was to reign in place of his father is confirmed by two kinds of proofs: (1) the evidence of narratives and other accounts concerning the enthroning of the first-born[11] (albeit there is also direct evidence for cases in which those who were not the first-born were crowned; see on this below); (2) evidence to the fact that in principle the first-born ought to rule.

We shall now examine several such passages, primarily those of the second type:

1. In 2 Kgs 3.27 it is stated that the king of Moab offered up as a sacrifice upon the wall 'his eldest son[12] who was to reign in his stead'. We find here that the ordinary definition of the first-born of the king is as the one who is to reign following the death of his father.

2. One may derive the same conclusion from Saul's remarks against the friendship of his son Jonathan with David. Saul argues to Jonathan that, upon David's ascent to rule, Jonathan will be displaced from the

10. On this matter, see above, Chapter 10, §1, but there is no proof of this matter from Israelite material.

11. Against this, W. Caspari, *Tronbesteigungen und Tronfolge*, pp. 247-48, thinks that only six among the kings were first-born (see there, pp. 244-47, on the question of inheritance of the throne). This is in contrast to the view of Driver–Miles, *The Babylonian Laws*, I, p. 332, that in the Bible the crown ordinarily passes to the first-born, but that at times the youngest may reign because of his mother. Cecil, *Primogeniture*, p. 80, noted that the Israelites are unusual regarding matters of kingship, in that among them the first-born reigns (her proof is from 2 Chron. 21.3), unlike other peoples. However, she does not bring any proof for the correctness of her view.

12. It makes no difference whether one is speaking of the son of the king of Edom or the like; and see on this the commentaries.

throne (1 Sam. 20.31), 'for as long as the son of Jesse lives upon the earth, neither you nor your kingdom shall be established'. Given that Jonathan was Saul's first-born son,[13] the anticipation that he would eventually reign was extremely likely.

3. In the Septuagint's formulation of Prov. 31.2, it states, 'What, my son? What, Lemuel, my first-born (πρωτογενές)? Let me say to you...'. As Lemuel is described in the previous verse (31.1) as king (and possibly as the king of Massa), we may conclude that Lemuel became king by virtue of being first-born.

4. In the enumeration of those struck during the plague of the first-born, it states, 'the Lord smote all the first-born...from the first-born of Pharaoh who sat on his throne...' (Exod. 12.29). According to one possible understanding, the subordinate clause 'who sat on his throne' refers to Pharaoh's son, meaning: even the first-born of the king, who now sits upon the throne, was struck by the plague.

Alternatively, this clause may refer to the conjunctive, 'from the first-born (i.e. Pharaoh)', referring to the first-born of Pharaoh who shall in the future be enthroned instead of his father. Compare *Targum Onqelos*: 'from the first-born of Pharoah who shall in the future sit upon the royal throne' מבוכרא דפרעה העתיד למיתב על כרסי מלכותיה *Targum Pseudo-Jonathan* and other ancient and modern exegetes read likewise.[14] In his commentary, Cassuto offers two interpretations to this verse, both of which refer to the first-born: (1) he who is to sit upon the royal throne; (2) he who sits upon the prince's throne.

5. The best proof for the crowning of the first-born is to be found in the passage concerning Jehoshaphat, 'but he gave the kingdom to Jehoram, because he was the first-born' (2 Chron. 21.3), while his brother was dismissed with 'great gifts, of silver, gold, and valuable possessions, together with with fortified cities in Judah' (*ibid.*).

The motive clause cited in this verse, 'for he was the first-born', is of greater value as evidence than the previous ones, such as 'who was to reign in his stead' (2 Kgs 3.27) or 'who sat on his throne' (Exod. 12.29). In our case, in 2 Chronicles 21, we are given a statement in principle

---

13. Liver, 'Jonathan', pp. 533-35. On the birthright of Jonathan and his being the heir apparent, see Feigin, *From the Secrets of the Past*, pp. 71-72. I would prove the fact of Jonathan being the first-born from his appearing first (without exception) in the various places where the geneology of the house of Saul is mentioned (1 Sam. 14.49; 1 Chron. 8.33; 9.39).

14. See Liver, 'Kingship', p. 1095, who interpreted it thus.

that it is the nature of the first-born of kings to take their fathers' place upon the throne.[15]

The motive clause in this verse, 'for he was the first-born', was interpreted by the sages as clearly indicating that the first-born has the right to reign, and that every deviation from this rule—in which one who is not a first-born is anointed to rule—evokes against itself the verse 'for he is the first-born' and the question: 'shall the younger reign before the older?' (compare, e.g., *b. Hor.* 11b concerning Jehoahaz son of Josiah, who reigned before his older brother Jehoiakim). Another formulation of this idea (*b. Ker.* 5b) appears in the phrase 'and who places the younger before the elder?'. In *Num. R.* 6.2 there are explicit remarks to this effect, directly formulated: that the Holy One blessed be He conveyed honour upon the first-born, who are deserving of the kingship.[16]

Against this, modern scholarship interprets the testimony of Jehoshaphat and Jehoram as indicating that the system of reign of the first-born only became customary from that time on, but that this had not been the case during the period preceding the Jehoshaphat's reign. Yeivin, for example, presents this argument,[17] inferring this from the very fact that the motive phrase 'for he was the first-born' is found only here.[18]

---

15. H. Hempel, 'Das Ethos des Alte Testament', p. 201, thinks that the Semitic peoples were not particularly strict about arrangements of birthright, except in the case of royal succession. However, this generalization is opposed to everything we know about the significant status of the first-born, which is expressed in various ways.

16. Compare also *Targ. Ps.-J.* to Gen. 49.3, where the phrase יתר עז ('pre-eminent in power') is interpreted as referring to the kingship. This was meant to be Reuben's inheritance by virtue of his birthright, but because he was denied the privileges of the birthright it passed on to Judah. Cf. the Aramaic Targum to 1 Chron. 5.1-2, and compare *Yal. Shim.* I.157: '"pre-eminent in power"—this refers to the kingdom'.

17. Yeivin, 'David', table on p. 640; *idem, Studies*, p. 204.

18. Without any connection to the status of the motive clause, there are those who argue for the lateness of the method of inheritance of the kingdom by the first-born. Caspari, *Tronbesteigungen*, p. 248, argues that this approach was not followed in olden times, and that only upon the development of the kingship did there begin to be fixed rules regarding the rule of the first-born. He also observes the multifarious activities of the first-born princes as commanders of cities and in other tasks, from which it follows that there was originally no perceived necessity that they must specifically be the heirs to rule. A similar thesis appears in Szikszai, 'King', p. 12.

To this, one may answer that: (1) analysis of the sources reveals that the enthroning of the first-born was customary in Judah consistently.[19] If a younger son ruled, this was seen as an exception, which Scripture sees fit to comment upon (see below for a discussion of this matter). (2) Examination of all of the appearances in the Bible[20] of the motive clause 'for he is the first-born' indicates that its function is to describe any subject connected with the first-born and his established rights, and that this sentence is not intended to express any change in the rights and status of the first-born.

Something else that may be learned from the incident of Jehoshaphat concerns the relationship between inheritance of the throne and that of royal property. From an analysis of what is stated in 2 Chronicles 21, one clearly sees that, in contrast with Jehoram's inheritance of the rulership, the other brothers were dismissed with gifts alone. It follows from this that one is not speaking here of a division of the estate in the usual, accepted sense. Instead, the son who inherited rule simultaneously inherited all of the king's property. The matter of gifts was a kind of farewell blessing, rather than a calculated share based exactly upon the number of brothers and with the ratio of a 'double portion' for the first-born.[21] For a similar situation, see below on Abijam's inheritance of the

On the late date of the testimony in 2 Chron. 21.3, see also MacNeile, 'First-Born'. Bennett, 'Heir', sees 2 Chron. 21.3 as the first evidence in principle for the succession to reign of the first-born.

19. From the absence of any hint of a dispute among the sons concerning the inheritance of the throne, Feigin infers that the right of the first-born to the crown was already inviolable. Such a thing would only be possible if the first-born regularly came in place of the father. But it seems to him that the appointment of the first-born as heir apparent already took place during the father's lifetime (*From the Secrets of the Past*, p. 71). According to H. Tadmor, 'Jehoram', p. 539, Jehoram's becoming king was not an innovation. The story of his being named king during his father's lifetime was intended to prevent disputes on the part of his brothers, who hated him because of his marriage to Athaliah—yet nevertheless there were rebellions against him.

On the fixing of the reign of the first-born, see also E. Neufeld, *Ancient Hebrew Marriage Laws*, p. 264, and A. Malamat, cited in Talmon, 'History of the *Am Ha-Aretz*', p. 49.

20. I discuss this issue in my dissertation; see Brin, 'The First-Born in Israel', pp. 177-79.

21. Yaron, *Gifts*, pp. 4-5, thinks otherwise. He argues that, since the inheri-tance of the throne is involved here, one is automatically speaking of a single heir. See

throne of Rehoboam, at which time his brothers received generous gifts of provisions and the like.

There is, to my mind, an interesting parallel to the incident of Jehoshaphat and Jehoram in Gen. 25.5-6: 'Abraham gave all he had to Isaac. But to the sons of his concubines Abraham gave gifts, and while he was still living he sent them away from his son Isaac'. I observed earlier[22] that Gen. 25.5-6 reflects an ancient norm of inheritance, whereby the first-born inherits all of the property (while the other brothers were dismissed with gifts). The inheritance of the throne is likewise inherited exclusively by the first-born (!); here too—in the case of Jehoshaphat—it is mentioned that the others were dismissed with gifts alone.

Examination of the principles of inheritance of the kingship during the Second Temple period reveals that then, too, the birthright was seen as a binding principle with regard to the kingship. In Josephus's *War* 1.70-71, it is stated that Aristobulus, the first-born son of John Hyrcanus, ruled after him. In *War* 1.85, Alexandrus ascended to the throne after the death of his father because 'he was deserving of the office according to his years (and the qualities of his soul)', that is, by virtue of being the first-born.

We similarly find that the kingship was given to Hyrcanus because he was the first-born (*Ant.* 14.17-18; *War* 1.120-22). Even after he was denied his portion and the throne was transferred to his brother Aristobolus, it states that according to his measure and under the law of the first-born, Hyrcanus was deserving of the throne (*War* 1.131-1.32; cf. *ibid.*, 124-25, 'on the rulership due to him according to the rule of the first-born'). Note also Hyrcanus's complaint regarding this matter (*Ant.* 14.42): 'even though he was the first-born, the kingship was taken from him' (compare *War* 1.109, that Hyrcanus 'was the first-born [and was appointed] high priest, for to him was the rule of the first-born' and his mother was herself the queen).

Similarly, during the Herodian dynasty there is mentioned the consideration in principle which requires the inheritance of the throne 'by necessity' (*Ant.* 16.79; 16.92), namely, the choice of the first-born. In *War* 1.447-48, Antipater is chosen heir to the throne 'according to his

above, Chapter 10, §2 n. 41, concerning Gen. 25 and the problem of the gifts given to the sons of the concubines.

22. Above, Chapter 10, §2.

age' (and see 1.459-60, on Antipater's birthright).[23]

For other cases involving deviations from the right of the first-born during the Second Temple period, see the discussion below.

4. *Proofs from Near Eastern Sources for the Enthronement of the First-Born*

Since the method of passing on kingship in the Near East was one of inheritance from father to son, as we have seen above, it seems reasonable to assume that there too—as in Israel—the first-born inherited the throne.[24] This point may be inferred from evidence concerning the actual practice of crowning the first-born.[25] Thus, for example, Nebuchadnezzar, whose name indicates that he was the first-born (I refer to the component of *Kudurru* in his name).[26] Note his remarks, '*jāti DUMU-UŠ-šu rēštā narām libbišu*' (*VAB* 4.122 v 4),[27] that is, 'I am his first-born [literally, his chief heir, i.e., of Nabopolassar], the beloved of his heart'.

But it is also significant that those kings who were not the first-born presented themselves as first-born, with the aim of legitimizing their rule. For example, Merodach-baladan, whose name is written in Akkadian *Marduk(a)pl(a) iddin(a)*, meaning, 'the god Marduk has given an heir, a first-born'. In one inscription he actually designates himself as the first-born of the king of Babylon, although this is not the case.[28] To the same

---

23. A. Schalit, *King Herod*, p. 291, sees the reason given for the ascent of Antipater—his being first-born—as a tactic used by Herod towards the religious leaders. This reason reappears in the provocative speech by Eurycles (*War* 1.517-518); cf. Schalit, *King Herod*, p. 303-305.

24. On the use of the identical principle in the enthroning of kings in Israel and among the peoples of the Near East, see Galling, *Die israelitische Staatsverfassung*, III-IV, p. 22.

25. According to Kraus, 'Erbrechtliche Terminologie', p. 26, the term *aplu* used for a prince, the heir apparent, is to be understood in the sense of: he who comes after the head of the family, the king, as heir to the throne. In practice, this is Kraus's interpretation of the term as used regarding all the first-born (of course, without the reference to the crown), and not only a first-born prince. On *aplu* as a term for the first-born who is heir to the kingdom, cf. *ibid.*, p. 45.

26. Ef'al, 'Nebuchadnezzar', p. 737.

27. According to *CAD*, 'aplu', p. 175.

28. Artzi, 'Merodach-baladan', pp. 445-46.

end, Burnaburiash III[29] King of Babylon represents himself as the first-born son of Kadashman-Enlil I.[30]

5. *Exceptions to the Rule of Enthronement of the First-Born*

Examination of the exceptions to this rule in the Bible, in which one who was not the first-born was crowned king, may again be indicative of the general rule of the crowning the first-born—in this case, by means of the difficulties and justifications that the one crowning a non-first-born needs to provide. As in the case of the law of general inheritance, from these cases too one may infer the degree of authority of the father to act contrary to accepted law concerning the enthroning of the first-born (see above, Chapter 10, §3).

1. *The Davidic dynasty*[31]

In 1 Kgs 1.5, Adonijah undertakes various different acts in order to be made king: 'I will be king'. His behavior as an heir apparent, with chariot and horsemen,[32] is likewise part of his program (as was done by Absalom, 2 Sam. 15.1-6).

The unusual detail, 'and he was born next after Absalom' (1 Kgs 1.6), is brought here to indicate[33] Adonijah's status within the framework of David's family. The sense of this sentence is that Adonijah was at the time the eldest of David's living sons and was therefore deserving to be

---

29. K.A. Kitchen, *Suppiluliumas*, p. 10 n. 5.

30. On the enthronement of the first-born in Egypt, see Frankfort, *Kingship and the Gods*, pp. 101-102; for example, Senusert, the first-born of Amenemhet I, who ruled instead of his father. Cf. Galling, *Staatsverfassung*, pp. 21-22. On the system of inheritance by the first-born in the land of the Hittites, see R. de Vaux, *Ancient Israel*, p. 10. In his opinion, this was not the situation in the Aramaic kingdoms. On the situation in Ugarit regarding this point, see A. Van Selms, *Marriage and Family Life*, pp. 140-43.

31. Caspari, *Tronbesteigung*, p. 244, believes that the history of the Davidic dynasty specifically indicates that there was no set arrangement for the crowning of kings.

32. On the Ugaritic concept, 'officers of the heir apparent', see Rainey, *Social Structure*, pp. 46-47, 74.

33. See the discussion in my article, Brin, 'The First-Born of the Mother and the First-Born of the Father', pp. 40-41.

made king,[34] since all his predecessors had died.[35]

Another element that confirms this interpretation appears further along in the narrative, when Adonijah's seeks to take Abishag as a wife. In his outraged reply, Solomon makes some explicit comments about Adonijah's right to the throne (1 Kgs 2.22): 'Ask for him the kingdom also, for he is my elder brother'.[36] We find here an explicit statement that the older brother deserves to inherit the throne of his father. That this is not merely an internal matter of the royal family, but that this arrangement was known by all, is implied by Adonijah's words to Bathsheba: 'You know that the kingdom was mine [i.e. that I deserved to be king][37] and that all Israel fully expected me to reign' (1 Kgs 2.15). That is, the people themselves knew the arrangement whereby the first-born (or eldest living son) is to reign,[38] and that this order of birthright may only be altered through God's intervention: 'however the kingdom was turned about and become my brother's, for it was his from the LORD' (2.15).[39] In a practical sense, this is expressed

34. Liver, 'Davidic Dynasty', pp. 52-53; Feigin, *From the Secrets of the Past*, pp. 70-72.

35. On the death of Kaleb (i.e. Daniel, in 1 Chron. 3), who is mentioned as second to Amnon in 2 Sam. 3.3, see the haggadic account in *b. Šab.* 55b; *b. B. Bat.* 17a; etc. On this figure, see also *b. Ber.* 4a, and compare A. Steinsaltz, 'Kaleb son of David'. Modern scholars also accepted as correct the view regarding his death. See Yeivin, *Studies*, p. 196 n. 76; H.W. Hertzberg, *Samuel*, p. 207.

36. Feigin, *From the Secrets of the Past*, pp. 70-72, suggests that the phrase 'and he was born after Absalom' (1 Kgs 1.6) was intended to explain Adonijah's right to be king. One may infer from the words of Solomon to Bathsheba that he in fact knew that Adonijah deserved the kingship.

37. Josephus, *Ant.* 7.345, quotes Adonijah's words to his friends (before the rebellion), and among other things raises there the argument that he deserves the kingship 'by law'.

38. De Vaux, *Ancient Israel*, p. 101; Liver, 'Kingship', p. 1095.

39. On the element of divine choice in the enthronement of Solomon, see 1 Chron. 28.5-6. After speaking of the choice of David per se, the verse states, 'And of all my sons—for the LORD has given me many sons—he has chosen Solomon my son to sit upon the throne of the kingdom of the Lord over Israel. He said to me, "it is Solomon your son...for I have chosen him to be my son, and I will be his father"'. Cf. 29.1: 'Solomon my son, whom alone God has chosen'. Likewise, in 2 Chron. 1.8-9, they speak about the divine choice of Solomon. It may also be that the statement in 1 Chron. 29.24, 'All the leaders and the mighty men, and also all the sons of King David pledged their allegiance to King Solomon', is meant to indicate the agreement with the rule of Solomon on the part of all the rivals to the birthright

in the father's authority to alter the usual arrangement.[40] I have already observed elsewhere[41] that, in the case of deviation from the order of birth for various reasons, it was usual to formulate matters in such a way as to claim them as the result of a divine decision. This is perhaps based upon the perception of the hoary antiquity of the arrangements of birthright, including the inheritance of the throne by the first-born; so much so, that only a decision by God is able to change it.

2. *Abiam (or Abijah) son of Rehoboam.* Abiam reigned 'in his [father's] stead', and was the first-born of Maacah, the second (or third) wife[42] of Rehoboam (2 Chron. 11.18-20); Abiam was thus the first-born of his mother, but not of his father.[43] Because he was only 'partially' first-born, his father, Rehoboam, took steps so that he would be considered deserving to inherit the throne—all this because of his great love for Maacah, Abiam's mother. This is stated explicitly in Scripture:

post factum, after he had been chosen by God. Through this choice, his kingship was given legitimacy. On the divine intervention expressed in the use of the verb סבב, see Abramski, 'The Rebellion of Jeroboam', p. 50. On divine choice of kings in the Near East, see Frankfort, *Kingship and the Gods*, p. 312, and cf. Liver, 'Kingship,' pp. 1095-96. On the other hand, in the case where one who was not the first-born was crowned king, the sages used the formula, 'He was the substitute of his father' (*b. Ket.* 103b).

40. Compare Liver, 'The Davidic Dynasty', pp. 52-53; 'Kingship', pp. 1095-96. Cf. Szikszai, 'King', p. 12, who contends that, in the case of Adonijah and Solomon, there was a conflict between the right of the first-born to reign and that of the father to choose his successor. According to I. Mendelshon, 'On Marriage in Alalakh', p. 357, Solomon's ascent is to be seen as a matter of transferring the rights of the first-born to the younger son. According to E. Day, 'Was the Hebrew Monarchy Limited?', p. 101, the Israelite monarchy was chosen, and there does not seem to be any proof of an obligation to enthrone the first-born, invoking as proof the case of Absalom and Adonijah. Cf. Caspari, *Thronbesteigung*, p. 244, on the choice of the king, and p. 247, on the fact that there was no natural right to the crown, but only what determined as the royal command.

41. See Brin, 'The First-Born in Israel', p. 225.

42. See Yeivin, 'David', in the geneological table following p. 640 n. 10, where he holds that she was his second wife. The author of the Aramiac Targum and the traditional Hebrew exegetes saw her as the third wife. N. Aloni, 'Abihail', p. 24, proposes a correction of the text with the intent of seeing Mahlath and Abihail as one woman and her father.

43. On these concepts, see the discussion in Brin, 'The First-Born of the Mother and the First-Born of the Father'.

'Rehoboam loved Maacah the daughter of Absalom above all his wives and concubines, for he took eighteen wives and sixty concubines' (v. 21). We thus a clear case here of the 'son of the beloved [wife]' (to quote the law in Deut. 21.15-17). The verse goes on to tell us that Abiam was specifically made chief (נגיד) among his brothers to prepare the way for his crowning as king: 'and he appointed Abijah...as chief prince (ראש) among his brothers, [LXX: for he intended, ὅτι βασιλεῦσαι διενοεῖτο αὐτόν] to make him king. And he dealt wisely, and distributed some of his sons...'

His choice as 'chief' (ראש) and as 'chief (נגיד) among his brothers' is intended to place him above his brothers. He does not serve in these functions by natural right, as he is not the first-born.

A comparison of those passages which speak of Abiam, on the one hand, and of Jehoram, on the other, may be useful in illustrating the difference between a natural first-born and an appointed chief (ראש):

2 Chron. 11.22-23: 'And he appointed Abijah...as chief prince (ראש) among his brothers, for he intended to make him king. And he dealt wisely, and built and broke through more than his sons...through all the...fortified cities; and he gave them abundant provisions'.

2 Chron. 21.3: 'Their father gave them great gifts...together with fortified cities in Judah; but he gave the kingdom to Jehoram, because he was the first-born'.

One should note the appearance in both of these passages of the same motifs: the multiplicity of sons; the fact that the father gave numerous gifts (or the like) to his other sons, apart from the chief; and the mention of 'fortified cities' in connection with the sons. It is therefore particularly interesting to observe a certain inconsistency that is revealed through this comparison. I refer to the absence of a parallel to the motive clause, '(but the kingship he gave to Jehoram) for he was the first-born'. The reason for this absence, alongside the other details that are parallel in the two cases, only becomes clear if we assume that Abiam was indeed not recognized as the first-born, so that the verse was unable to define the giving of the kingship into his hands with the reason that he was the first-born (for other details see above, Section 3 of this chapter, concerning Jehoshaphat and Jehoram).

3. *Ahaziah*. In 2 Chron. 22.1 it states, 'And [they] made Ahaziah his youngest son king in his stead; for the band of men...had slain all the older sons...' (and cf. there 21.17). The function of the motive clause,

'for...had slain all the older sons...', is to explain how it came about that the youngest of the sons came to reign. The explanation is that none of his elder brothers was alive at that time.[44]

4. *The Line of Josiah.* We know of unusual cases of kingship arrangements from the dynasty of Josiah, in which the first-born did not reign.[45] In this case, the exception to the system was created by the fact that there was not a natural succession to the throne, but that rather the עם הארץ intervened in order to crown the person they wanted to be king (2 Kgs 23.30). Thereafter the king of Egypt crowned Jehoiakim (23.34). Further on in the account, there were additional departures from the accepted order. The sages already pondered the inconsistencies between the list of the sons of Josiah in 1 Chron. 3.15 and the story of the enthronement in the book of Kings, in an attempt to harmonize the two. To this end, they even coined the term 'first-born for kingship' to defend the use of the title 'first-born' with regard to Johanan in 1 Chron. 3.15, which did not fit their calculations. Having identified Johanan with Jehoahaz, they saw him as the first king among the sons of Josiah; that is, he was the first-born (i.e. first) for kingship, but not literally the first-born.[46]

44. Liver, 'Davidic Dynasty', p. 52 n. 14.

45. On the death of Josiah's first-born Johanan according to 1 Chron. 3.15, see E.L. Curtis, 'Geneology', according to whom he fell together with his father at Megiddo. In any event, it is a fact that the continuation of his genealogy (details of his descendants and the like) does not appear in the list of descendants of Josiah in 1 Chron. 3.

46. For a detailed discussion of the list of the sons of Josiah in 1 Chron. 3, see Liver, 'Davidic Dynasty', pp. 4-6. Liver believes (p. 5) that the order of birth of Josiah's sons in this list is confused by comparison to the narrative in 2 Kgs 23.31, 36, which mentions their age upon assuming the throne. See *b. Hor.* 11b; *b Ker.* 5b; *j. Soṭ.* Ch. 8 (22c), and Ibn Ezra on 1 Chron. 3.15: 'Johanan was the first-born, but he did not attain the kingship'. Liver suggests that one see the words, 'the first-born', 'the second', etc. in the list as a secondary element added by the editor. Indeed, in some secondary manuscripts of the LXX, the list is brought without identification by number. For further opinions on the genealogical list of the sons of Josiah in 1 Chron. 3, see Yeivin, *Studies*, pp. 289-90 and n. 169, and there also on the switching of the names Jehoahaz and Johanan (it should be noted that in Lucianus' reading to 1 Chron. 3 the name Jehoahaz is substituted for Johanan). In practice, an attempt is made here to provide a solution based upon the same difficulties that were noted by the exegetes at a later period. In *b. Hor.* 11b, the difficulty of the numerical identifications in the list of sons of Josiah (which are not consistent with the order in which

Let us now examine the exceptions to the rule of accession of the first-born during the Second Temple period:

We already saw above that the consideration of order of birth remained the determinitive factor during the Second Temple period, even though examination reveals that other elements sometimes brought about exceptions to the reign of the first-born. One must remember that Herod's decisions regarding the heirs to his throne changed a number of times during his lifetime. The considerations that he raised were: (1) birth position; (2) the pedigree of the mother of the potential heir. For this reason, he initially preferred the sons of Mariamne the Hasmonean (*War* 1.431-34; 435-37),[47] notwithstanding the fact that they were not the first-born. He thereafter changed his mind, elevating the first-born of his first wife, Doris (*War* 1.444-48), once he no longer approved of the sons of Mariamne. Herod's considerations relating to the degree of admiration which one son or another held towards him are likewise mentioned; nevertheless, the formal reason given is the order of birth (and indeed, Antipater the first-born of Doris was Herod's first-born). In *War* 1.457-60, we find a combination of heirs to his throne: Antipater the first-born of Doris and the sons of Mariamne the Hasmonean, 'the one according to his age (that is, the consideration of birthright), and the others according to their pedigree'. Herod himself appeals to the people to show respect to his sons, each one 'according to the number of his years'. He will thereby not detract from the honour due to the brother who was oldest in years.

The consideration of the family pedigree of the princes' mother is

these sons reigned) is overcome by following simultaneously two parallel systems of exegesis, for example, 'the third [in order of] birth, the fourth to reign', etc. Of course, one cannot accept this solution, which bears an explicitly homiletical character, since one may not assume that the author would use different criteria within the same list without explicitly stating so.

47. It is interesting not only that Mariamne's pedigree is included among the considerations of Herod, but also that he married her after he had become king, whereas he married Doris, his first wife, when he was still a commoner. That is, not only was the status of the woman determinative of her son's status, but also the king's own status at the time of his marriage to her. It is interesting to compare this to a parallel phenomenon in the Nupe tribe of northern Nigeria, in which the king chooses as heir to the throne only that son who was born after he became king, rather than his first-born or some other son (the same is true in some other tribes). See J. Goody, *Succession to High Office*, p. 33; on the fact that this principle is followed consistently in South African tribes, see M. Glukman, *Politics, Law and Ritual*, p. 139.

likewise implied by the provocation of Eurycles: he argues (to the sons of Mariamne) that the first-born of Doris ought to be displaced because he is 'the son of a commoner woman' (*War* 1.517-18).[48] He further argues on behalf of the sons of Mariamne for 'the righteous hopes of Alexandrus and Aristobulus for the kingship, being sons of the daughter of kings' (*War* 1.624-25).[49]

Again, Herod commands that upon the death of Antipater he should not be succeeded by his own son, but by Herod's own son (*War* 1.573). See also *War* 1.587-88, on Antipater' complaint that his hope to inherit the kingdom to his sons after him was stolen from him by his father.

In *War* 1.664, a new will of Herod is published, which goes back to the order of birth, in that it designates the eldest of his living sons πρεσβύτατον[50]—Archelaus—as heir to throne. It is interesting that Archelaus's enemies argue to the people that it would be more fitting to depart from the arrangements of inheritance by departing from the birthright, and choose instead other rulers, more deserving of the throne (*War* 2.90-92).

It is also interesting to take note of the matter, mentioned in *Ant.* 16.92 and especially in 16.129, in which Herod was given special permission by the emperor to apply his own judgment in the choice of an heir to his throne (this after he had been disappointed by the sons of Mariamne), and not to subject to 'necessity' (that is, not to follow the regular rule of inheritance). This would imply that there was a certain limitation placed upon the right of the father arbitrarily to depart from arrangements of birthright in terms of the inheritance of the throne. Only confirmation by the emperor could give legitimacy to such deviations.

According to Otto,[51] the reason for these restrictions upon the father's right to choose was because the sons of Mariamne were princes, while regarding commoners the decision remained in the hands of the father.

---

48. Simultaneously, Eurycles tells Antipater, the son of Doris, that he (Antipater) deserves to inherit the throne because he is the first-born (*War* 1.519-520).

49. On Herod's relationship with another woman and the influence of that relationship regarding his son, see *War* 1.599-600, on Mariamne, daughter of the high priest.

50. See Schalit, *Herod the King*, p. 320, who sees in this a return to the predominance of the birthright.

51. W. Otto, 'Herodes', col. 135; cf. Schalit, *Herod*, p. 290.

A parallel to this need for supernal confirmation of the deviations by the father-king from accepted arrangements of birthright appears when one is speaking of the displacement of the first-born from inheriting the throne. Thus, Ammishtamaru king of Ugarit receives permission from Tudkhaliyas IV king of the Hittites not to name his first-born as heir to the throne, provided that the son in question goes after his divorced mother (RS 17.159, *PRU*, IV, p. 126).

In another document (RS 17.348, *PRU*, IV, p. 128),[52] we find explicit permission to name a different heir to the throne (although one cannot assume that this matter involves the fulfilment of the condition mentioned in the previous document, since in this case the permission to alter the arrangements of the first-born under the conditions in question had already been stated). It seems to me that one is speaking here of another condition, or of permission as above, but without stipulating any condition that the son follows his mother.

And in fact, Ammishtamaru was succeeded by Ibiranu, who was Ammishtamaru's son from another wife, and therefore not the first-born of the king. We find that here, too, the enthronement of one who was not the first-born depended upon the approval of some supreme authority.[53]

In Ugarit, one also finds fragment UT 49 I 16-18 concerning Baal's agreement that the goddess Asherah would determine which of the sons would be king.[54] This may reflect the possibility that someone besides the first-born might ascend to the throne, owing to various motivations of the father or the mother (if the decision was in their hands).

We likewise learn from Mesopotamia that an ordinary son may reign in stead of the first-born, in accordance with the personal decision of the regnant king. Thus Esarhadon became king, despite being the youngest of the sons,[55] owing to the influence upon the king of his mother.[56]

52. There is some question as to whether the divorce of the king's wife and the incident of the 'daughter of the noblewoman' mentioned in another document refer to the same situation. The description I have brought in the body of this chapter is based upon the assumption that the two are identical (see below).

53. See Rainey, *Social Structure*, pp. 23, 41-42, 46-47, 125 (and the works there).

54. See C.H. Gordon, *Ugaritic Textbook*, *ad loc.*; and Van Selms, *Marriage and Family Life in Ugarit*, p. 139.

55. S. Smith, *CAH*, III, 69, 79. On his struggle with his elder brothers, see Ef'al, 'Sannaherib', col. 1065.

56. See J. Guttman, 'Esarhadon', p. 484.

From the case of the inheritance of the throne of Esarhadon, we learn of the father's power to determine the heir to rule. He appointed his youngest son, Ashurbanipal, to rule over Assyria, which was the main part of his legacy, being the center of the empire; his oldest son,[57] Shamash-shum-ukin, was named ruler of Babylon alone. Interestingly, because of his youth, Ashurbanipal had initially been intended only for a priestly office. Nevertheless, we find Ashurbanipal declaring that he was the first-born of the dynasty, and that the gods had destined him from the womb to be king.[58] Note that, despite the fact that he was designated by his father to be heir to the throne, he sought ways to legitimize his rule by asserting his alleged birthright, as well as claiming divine election. This is identical to the approach in the above-cited words of Adonijah, 'for from God it was to him' (1 Kgs 2.15). Divine intervention provides the justification to depart from the normal order.[59]

The crowning of a younger son because of the father's desire to make him the first-born also appears in Document TCL 6.4 (according to *CAD*, XVI, p. 182), where it states that the king of a strange land sent his first-born into exile, and raised up the youngest in his place.

In another text, YOS 10.31 II 4 (cited in *CAD* A II, p. 175), we find that the heir to the throne is determined by lot. According to this statement, if certain signs appear on the lot, the first-born will reign: *aplum rabûm kussām iṣabbat*. If, however, certain other signs appear, the youngest will reign instead (*aplum ṣeḥrum*).

---

57. It would seem that the true first-born had already died before this. See M. Streck, *Asurbanipal*, pp. 185, 249-50. On the reign of Asurbanipal and his brothers and the preference shown to the younger Asurbanipal, see Smith, *CAH*, pp. 85-86. The same subject was published in Letter §129 in the collection by B. Parpola, *Letters from Assyrian Scholars*, pp. 102-105.

58. See Parpola, *Letters*, §132, pp. 106-107, stating that the gods Ashur and Shamash had determined him as heir because of his mother's loyalty to them.

See also Speiser, *Dawn of Civilization*, p. 141; Smith, *CAH*, pp. 85-87; Liver, 'Kingdom', col. 1095; and cf. S. Mowinckel, *He That Cometh*, pp. 34ff.

59. Even regarding El's declaration, *ṣġrthn 'abkrn*, that is, 'I shall prefer the younger', in *KRT* III.16, one should note the divine decision concerning the ascent of the younger to the throne of rulership.

In the various chapters of this book, I have gathered studies of selected topics in biblical law, classified under two headings. In the first part, I selectively discussed certain fundamental matters in biblical law. Thus, for example, the topic of 'double laws' was discussed at length. In this discussion, I defined the problem and exemplified the appearance of this phenomenon in a long series of laws. I concluded that, despite the fact that one is superficially speaking of one phenomenon, this heading in fact includes different derivatives of laws from the biblical period.

By tracing the totality of laws discussed in this chapter, one learns of an extremely important line in the framework of the laws, in that it exposes to us the methods of development of laws during the biblical period. The process of tracing the development of double laws is likely to enrich our knowledge of the restraints under which the legislators stood and the social and legal problems they confronted during biblical times. The solution that they used bears a 'literary' character in that it pertains to the form of the law, that is, the existence of an additional option for fulfilling the obligations within the law. It is not my intention here to state that the phenomenon of development of biblical laws found its expression in this way alone; nevertheless, it is worth emphasizing the relative richness of the methods that found expression in this technique.

Another aspect of the subject of development of laws is treated in Chapter 4, 'The Uses of אֹו ["or"] in Legal Texts'. It became clear that, by tracing the use of the term 'or', one could uncover, among other things, one of the forms of expression of development of the laws in the biblical period. Alongside this, other functions of the use of 'or' in various laws became clear.

In Part I, in Chapters 1–5, I discussed certain fundamental phenomena in biblical law. In this framework, I clarified one of the practices of biblical legislators relating to the mentioning of punishments in the laws. A certain aspect of the mentioning of sanctions in certain biblical laws followed from this discussion. It would appear that in certain kinds of laws the legislator saw fit to include a sanction against one who refused to fulfil its stipulations. In the discussion (Chapter 2), I clarified the nature of those laws in which alone this special component of sanctions is found.

As I discussed the manifold aspect of biblical law in this portion of the book, with an emphasis upon the subject of development of the laws, I saw fit to carry the discussion of the development of the subject beyond the parameters of the Bible. Hence, in Chapter 5 I examined 'Biblical Laws in the Dead Sea Scrolls' with regard to three laws, as these find expression in the writings of the Judaean Desert sect.

It became clear to us from these discussions that the development of biblical law did not cease with the period of the Bible, but continued during the following period. In the three discussions within this chapter, additional phenomena became clear, namely, that the authors of the scrolls concealed its unique pattern of development behind a veil of pseudo-biblical composition. Thus, despite the fact that the laws have a different character and ideology than their biblical source, and at times are even of an explicitly sectarian type, for a variety of reasons the sectarian authors refused to present their teaching as such, because they wished to claim their presentation of the law as like its basic source from the time of Moses. Thus, regarding this subject they saw fit to emphasize the fact that they had preserved the most ancient material, thereby representing the demand to preserve the correct, original form of the laws, and that they were not revolutionists who, so to speak, come to alter that which is ancient and sanctified.

In Part II I concentrated upon one subject: the legal aspects of the subject of first-born and firstlings. In this way, I was able on the one hand to exemplify my basic understanding of biblical law as it appeared in the first part of the book and in accordance with my views in other writings; on the other hand, this discussion also complements my examination of the institution of the first-born, as published in various sources.

In this discussion, spread over six chapters, it was possible for me to present the laws of the first-born from the point of view of literary composition, as an introduction to the focused discussion upon a series of topics relating to the first-born of human beings and beasts. The implication of the sanctity of the first-born in Israelite law upon the system of demands in various areas of the first-born became clear. The institution of the first-born also bears social and legal implications, and I therefore concluded my examination with those aspects. As mentioned, I dealt here with the 'civil' aspects of the birthright, thereby complementing the analysis of the sanctity of the first-born. We thus have before us a complete monograph on the legal status of the first-born, both with regard to that which relates to its understanding as holy and with regard to the unique rights of inheritance pertinent to it. This picture combines with my studies concerning the other components of the subject of the first-born, which have been gathered in my book, *Issues in the Bible and in the Dead Sea Scrolls*.

BIBLIOGRAPHY

Abramski, S., 'The Rebellion of Jeroboam and the Background to "Ephraim Has Removed itself from Judah"' [Heb.], *Beth Miqra* 18-19 (1964), pp. 46-56.

Aharon ben Elijah the Karaite, כתר תורה (Gozlawa: Firkovitz, 1866).

Albeck, H. (ed.), ששה סדרי משנה [Six Orders of Mishnah] (6 vols.; Jerusalem: Devir, 1959).

Albright, W.F., *Archaeology and the Religion of Israel* (Baltimore: Johns Hopkins University Press, 1942).

Allegro, J.M., *Qumran Cave 4* (DJD, V; Oxford: Clarendon Press, 1968).

Allon, G., מחקרים בתולדות ישראל, I (Studies in Jewish History; Tel-Aviv: ha-Kibbutz ha-Me'uhad, 1957).

Aloni, N., 'אביהיל' [Heb.], *EncBib*, I, pp. 24-25.

Alt, A., 'Zur Talionsformel', *ZAW* 52 (1934), pp. 303-305.

—'Zu hit'ammer', *VT* 2 (1952), pp. 153-59.

—'Die Ursprünge des israelitischen Rechts', *Kleine Schriften*, I (Munich: C.H. Beck, 1953), pp. 278-332.

Arndt, W.F., *The Gospel according to Luke* (Bible Commentary; St Louis, MO: Concordia Publishing House, 1956).

Artsi, P., 'מרודך בלאדן' [Heb.], *EncBib*, V, pp. 445-49.

—'Translation: Document No. 17 from the Mari Documents, Vol. 14 (ARM xiv, 17)' [Heb.], *Shenaton le-Miqra ule-mizrah ha-qadum* 4 (1980), pp. 270-72.

Ashkenazi, T., הבדואים [The Beduins] (Jerusalem: Reuven Mass, 1957).

Bäntsch, B., *Exodus, Leviticus, Numeri* (GHAT [=HKAT]; Göttingen: Vandenhoeck & Ruprecht, 1903).

Baillet, M., J.T. Milik and R. de Vaux, *Les Petites Grottes de Qumran: Discoveries in the Judaean Desert of Jordan*, III (DJD, 3; Oxford: Clarendon Press, 1962).

—*Qumran Grotte 4* (DJD, 7; Oxford: Clarendon Press, 1982).

Barthélemy, D., and J.T. Milik, *Discoveries in the Judaean Desert*, I (DJD, 1; Oxford: Clarendon Press, 1955).

Batten, L.W., *Esra and Nehemiah* (ICC; Edinburgh: T. & T. Clark, 1913).

Baudissin, W.W., *Studien zur semitisch Religionsgeschichte*, II (Leipzig: F.W. Grunow, 1876).

Beer, G., *Exodus* (HAT; Tübingen: J.C.B. Mohr, 1939).

Beilik, E., and M. Beinart, 'חמור' ['Ass'], *EncBib*, III, cols. 166-71.

Ben-Ami Zarfati, G., 'מספר' ['Number'], *EncBib*, V, cols. 170-85.

Ben-Shammai, N.H., and D. Noy, 'בכור' ['First Born'], *EncHeb*, VIII, cols. 691-95.

Bennett, W.H., 'Heir', *DOB*, II, pp. 341-42.

Bertholet, A., *Leviticus* (KHAT; Tübingen: J.C.B. Mohr, 1901).

Blome, F., *Die Opfermaterie in Babylonien und Israel* (Sacra scriptura antiquitatibus orientalibus, 4; Rome, 1934).

Bodenheimer, S., החי בארצות המקרא [Fauna in the Biblical Lands], I (Jerusalem: Mosad Bialik, 1950).

Boyer, G., *Textes juridiques* (ARM, 8; Paris: Imprimerie Nationale, 1958).

Bradbury, R.E., 'Fathers, Elders and Ghosts in Edo Religion', in M. Banton (ed.), *Anthropological Approaches to the Study of Religion* (London: Tavistock Publications, 1966), pp. 127-53.

Brin, G., 'The First-Born in Israel during the Biblical Period' [Heb.] (Doctoral Dissertation, Tel Aviv University, 1971).

—עיונים בספר יחזקאל [Studies in the Book of Ezekiel] (Tel-Aviv: ha-Kibbutz ha-Meuhad, 1975).

—'Two Problems in the Laws of Inheritance during the Biblical Period—A Comparative Study' [Heb.], *Dinei Yisra'el* 6 (1975), pp. 231-49.

—'The Transfer of Family Hegemony and the Problem of the Title *Bekor*' [Heb.], *ha-Zevi Yisrael; Sefer le-zekher Braude* (Tel Aviv: Mifalim Universitai'im, 1976), pp. 47-55.

—'Linguistic Remarks concerning the Temple Scroll' [Heb.], *Leshonenu* 43 (1979), pp. 20-28.

—'The Bible as Reflected in the Temple Scroll', *Shenaton le-Miqra ule-mizraḥ ha-qadum* 4 (1980), pp. 182-224.

—'The Formulae "From...and Onward/Upward" in the Bible', *JBL* 99 (1980), pp. 161-71.

—'The First-Born of the Mother and the First-Born of the Father in Scripture' [Heb.], *Sefer Ben Zion Luria* (Jerusalem: Kiryat Sefer, 1980), pp. 31-50.

—הנביא במאבקיו [The Prophet in his Struggles] (Tel Aviv: Mifalim Universitai'im, 1983).

—'Concerning some Uses of the Bible in the Temple Scroll', *RQ* 48 (1987), pp. 519-28.

—'Working Methods of Bible Translators and their Relevance in Establishing the Text' [Heb.], *Tarbiz* 57 (1988), pp. 445-49.

—'The Biblical Prophecy in the Dead Sea Scroll' [Heb.], in *Sha'arei Talmon, Studies in the Bible, Qumran, and the Ancient Near East Presented to Shemaryahu Talmon* (Winona Lake, IN: Eisenbrauns, 1992), pp. 101-12.

Brin, G., and Y. Hoffman, 'The Usage of Chiasmus in the Bible' [Heb.], *M. Zeidel Jubilee Volume* (Jerusalem: Kiryat Sefer, 1962), pp. 280-89.

Buhl, F., *Die socialen Verhältnisse des Israeliten* (Berlin: Reuther & Reichard, 1899).

Caloz, M., 'Exode XIII, 3-16, et son rapport au Deutéronome', *RB* 75 (1968), pp. 5-62.

Campbell Thompson, R., *Semitic Magic* (New York: Ktav, 1971).

Cardascia, G., *Les lois Assyriennes* (Littératures anciennes du Proche-Orient, 2; Paris: Editions du Cerf, 1969).

Caspari, W., *Tronbesteigungen und Tronfolge der israelitischen Könige* (Altorientalische Texte und Untersuchungen, I.3; Leiden: Brill, 1917).

Cassuto, U., 'The Second Chapter of Hosea' [Heb.], in *Sefer Zikaron le-Shmuel A. Posnanski* (Warsaw: Great Synagogue Committee, 1927), pp. 115-35.

—פירוש לסי שמות [Commentary to Exodus] (Jerusalem: Magnes, 1959).

Cecil, E., *Primogeniture* (London: J. Murray, 1895).

Charles, R.H., *Apocrypha and Pseudepigrapha of the Old Testament* (Oxford: Clarendon Press, 1913).

Chernovitz, H. (Rav Tsair), תולדות ההלכה (New York: Vaad haYovel, 1935–1950).

Childs, B.S., *The Book of Exodus* (OTL; Philadelphia: Westminster Press, 1974).

Cole, L.J., 'Sex Ratio', *Encyclopedia Britannica* (1964 edn), XX, pp. 419-22.

Cross, E.B., *The Hebrew Family* (Chicago: Chicago University Press, 1927).

Curtis, E.L., 'Genealogy', *DOB*, II, pp. 121-37.

Daube, D., *Studies in Biblical Law* (Cambridge: Cambridge University Press, 1947).

David, M., *Die Adoption in altbabylonischen Recht* (Leipzig: Th. Weicher, 1927).

—'The Codex Hammurabi and its Relation to the Provisions of the Law of Exodus', *OTS* 7 (1950), pp. 149-78.

—'Hit'āmēr' (Deut. xxi 14; xxiv 7)', *VT* 1 (1951), pp. 219-21.

—'Ein Beitrag zum mittelassyrischen Erbrecht', M. David (ed.), *Essays*, pp. 78-81.

David, M. (ed.), *Essays on Oriental Laws of Succession* (Studia et Documenta ad Iura Orientis Antiqui Pertenentia, 9; Leiden: Brill, 1969).

Day, E., 'Was the Hebrew Monarchy Limited?', *AJSL* 40 (1929), pp. 98-110.

Dillmann, A., *Die Bücher Numeri Deuteronomium und Joshua* (Kurzgefasstes exegetisches Handbuch zum Alten Testament, 13; Leipzig: S. Hirzel, 1886).

DJD I. See Barthélemy, D., and J.T. Milik.

DJD III. See Baillet, M.

DJD V. See Allegro, J.M.

DJD VII. See Baillet, M., J.T. Milik and R. de Vaux.

Driver, G.R., and J.C. Miles, *The Assyrian Laws* (Oxford: Clarendon Press, 1935).

—*The Babylonian Laws* (2 vols.; Oxford: Clarendon Press, 1952).

Driver, S.R., *Deuteronomy* (ICC; Edinburgh: T. & T. Clark, 3rd edn, 1902).

—*Exodus* (CB; Cambridge: Cambridge University Press, 1911).

Eberharter, A., *Ehe und Familienrecht der Hebräer* (Münster: Aschendorff, 1914).

Edzard, D.O., 'Sumerer und Semiten in der frühen Geschichte Mesopotamiens', *Geneva* 8 (1960), pp. 241-58.

Ef'al, I., 'נבוכדנאצר' ['Nebuchadnezzar'] *EncBib*, V, cols. 733-38.

Ehrlich, A., *Randglossen zur hebräischen Bibel*, II (Leipzig: J.C. Hinrichs, 1909).

—מקרא כפשוטו [The Literal Sense of the Bible] (Berlin: Poppelauer, 1919–1921).

Eichrodt, W., *Theologie in d. A.T.* (Stuttgart: E. Klotz, 7th edn, 1962–1964).

Eisenman, R.E. and J.M. Robinson, *A Facsimile Edition of the Dead Sea Scrolls* (Washington, DC: Biblical Archaeology Society, 1991).

Eisenman, R.E. and M. Wise, *The Dead Sea Scrolls Uncovered* (Shaftesbury: Element, 1992), pp. 200-205.

Eissfeldt, O., *Erstlinge und Zehnten in Altes Testament* (BZAW, 22; Berlin: Töpelmann, 1917).

—*Molk als Opferbegriff im Punischen und Hebräischen und das Ende des Gottes Molch* (Halle a/S: M.N. Niemeyer, 1935).

Elliger, K., *Leviticus* (HAT; Tübingen: J.C.B. Mohr, 1966).

Elliot-Binns, L., *Numbers* (WC; London: Methuen, 1927).

Engert, T., *Ehe und Familienrecht der Hebräer* (Studien zur alttestamentlichen Einleitung und Geschichte, 3; München: Lentner, 1905).

Fabry, H.J., 'דל', *TDOT*, III, pp. 208-30.

Falk, Z.W., 'Testate Succession in Jewish Law', *JJS* 12 (1961), pp. 66-77.

—'Endogamy in Israel' [Heb.], *Tarbiz* 32 (1963), pp. 19-34.

—*Hebrew Law in Biblical Times* (Jerusalem: Wahrmann Books, 1964).

Feigin, S., מסתרי העבר [From the Secrets of the Past] (New York: Sefarim, 1943).

Finkelstein, J., *The Ox that Gored* (Transactions of the American Philosophical Society, LXXI, Pt. 2; Philadelphia: University of Pennsylvania, 1981).

Fishbane, M., *Biblical Interpretation in Ancient Israel* (Oxford: Clarendon Press, 1985).

Fisher, L.R., 'An Amarna Age Prodigal', *JSS* 3 (1958), pp. 113-22.

Flusser, D., 'Sanctus und Gloria', in O. Betz *et alii* (eds.), *Abraham unser Vater, Festschrift O. Michel* (Leiden: Brill, 1963), pp. 142ff.

Fox, R., *Kinship and Marriage* (Middlesex: Pelican Books, 1967).

Frankfort, H., *Kingship and the Gods* (Chicago: University of Chicago Press, 1948).

Frazer, J.G., *The Golden Bough* (London: Macmillan,1922–1925).

Fustel de Coulanges, N.D., *The Ancient City* (New York: Doubleday, 1956).

Gadd, C.J., 'Tablets from Kirkuk', *RA* 23 (1926), pp. 49-141.

Galling, K., *Die israelitische Staatsverfassung in ihrer vorderasiatischen Umwelt* (AO, 28, Heft 3-4; Leipzig: J.C. Hinrichs, 1929).

Gamoran, M., 'The Biblical Law against Loans on Interest', *JNES* 30 (1971), pp. 127-34.

Gandz, S., 'The Algebra of Inheritance', *Osiris* 5 (1938), pp. 319-91.

Gaster, T.H., 'The Service of the Sanctuary, a Study in Hebrew Survivals', in *Mélanges Syriens Offerts a M. Rene Dussaud* (Librairie orientaliste; Paris: P. Geuthner, 1939), II, pp. 577-82.

Geiger, A., in M. Steinschneider, *Hebraische Bibliographie*, IV (Berlin: A. Asher, 1861), pp. 61-62.

Gemser, B., 'The Importance of the Motive Clause in the Old Testament Law', in G.W. Anderson, *et al.* (eds.), *Congress Volume, Copenhagen 1953* (VTSup, 1; Leiden: Brill, 1953), pp. 50-66 (= *Adhuc Loquitur* [Leiden: Brill, 1968], pp. 96-115).

—and F. Buhl, *Hebräisches und aramäisches Handwörterbuch über das Alte Testament* (Berlin: Springer Verlag, 1915–1917).

Gluckman, M., *Politics, Law and Ritual in Tribal Society* (Oxford: Blackwell, 1965).

Goetze, A., 'Numbers Idioms in Old Babylonian', *JNES* 5 (1946), pp. 185-202.

Goodenough, E.R., *The Jurisprudence of the Jewish Courts in Egypt as described by Philo* (Reprint: Amsterdam: Philo Press, 1968).

Goody, J., *Succession to High Office* (Cambridge: Cambridge University Press, 1966).

Gordon, C.H., *Ugaritic Textbook* (Rome: Pontifical Biblical Institute, 1965).

—'New Data on Ugaritic Numeral', *Festschrift J. Bakoš* (Slovenskey akadémie vred, 1; Bratislava: Vydovatel stvo, 1965).

Granqvist, H.N., *Birth and Childhood among the Arabs* (Helsingfors: Soderstrom, 1947).

Gray, G.B., *Numbers* (ICC; Edinburgh: T. & T. Clark, 1903).

—*Sacrifice in the Old Testament* (Oxford: Clarendon Press, 1925).

Gray, J., 'Cultic Affinities between Israel and Ras Shamra', *ZAW* 62 (1950), pp. 207-20.

Greenberg, M., 'Some Postulates of Biblical Criminal Law', *Y. Kaufmann Jubilee Volume* (Jerusalem: Magnes, 1960), pp. 5-28.

—'Ideal and Reality in Law and Prophets', in E.B. Firmage, B.G. Weiss and J.W. Welch (eds.), *Religion and Law* (Winona Lake, IN: Eisenbrauns, 1990), pp. 120-25.

Grintz, Y.M., 'בכור' ['First-Born'], *EncHeb*, VIII, cols. 695-97.

Gulak, A., תורת המשפחה והירושה .III יסודי המשפט העברי [Elements of Hebrew Law. III. Family and Inheritance Law] (Berlin: Devir, 1967).

Gunneweg, A.H.J., *Leviten und Priester* (Göttingen: Vandenhoeck & Ruprecht, 1965).

Guthe, H., 'Das Passahfest nach Dtn. 16', in *Festschrift Baudissin* (BZAW, 33; Berlin: Töpelmann, 1918), pp. 217-32.

Guttman, Y., 'אסרחדון' ['Assarhadon'], *EncBib*, I, cols. 484-86.

Haran, M., 'כהונה, מתנות כהונה' [Priesthood, Priestly Gifts], *EncBib*, IV, cols. 39-45.

—'נתינים' [Nethinim], *EncBib*, V, cols. 983-86.

Hartom, A.S., 'בכור' ['First-Born'], *EncBib*, II, cols. 123-26.

Heinemann, J., התפלה בתקופת התנאים והאמוראים—טיבה ודפוסיה [Prayer in the Period of the Tannaim and Amoraim—Its Nature and Forms] (Jerusalem: Magnes, 1966). [English: *Prayer in the Talmud* (Studia Judaica, 9; New York: W. de Gruyter, 1977)].

Heinisch, P., *Leviticus* (Die Heilige Schrift; Bonn: Hanstein, 1935).

Hempel, J., 'Eine Vortrag zum Erstgebursopfer', *ZAW* 54 (1936), pp. 311-13.

—Das Ethos des Alte Testament (BZAW, 67; Berlin: Töpelmann, 2nd edn, 1964 [1938]).

Henninger, J., 'Die Familie bei die heutigen Beduinen Arabiens und seiner Randgebiete', *Internationales Archiv fur Ethnographie* 42 (1943), pp. 1-188.

—'Menschenopfer bei den Arabern', *Anthropos* 53 (1958), pp. 721-805.

—'Zum Erstgeborenrecht bei den Semiten', in *Festschrift W. Caskel* (Leiden: Brill, 1968), pp. 162-83.

Hertzberg, H.W., *Samuel* (ATD; Göttingen: Vandenhoeck & Ruprecht, 1960 [ET: *Samuel* (OTL; London: SCM Press, 1964)]).

Hinz, W., *Das Reich Elam* (Urban-Bücher, 82; Stuttgart: Kohlhammer, 1964).

Hockel, A., *Christus der Erstgeborene* (Düsseldorff: Patmos, 1965).

Hoffmann, D.Z., *Das Buch Leviticus* (Berlin: M. Poppelauer, 1905).

—Das Buch Deuteronomium (Berlin: M. Poppelauer, 1913).

—פירוש לס' דברים [Commentary to Deuteronomy] (2 vols.; Tel-Aviv: Nezah, 1960–1961).

Holzinger, H., *Exodus* (KHAT; Tübingen: J.C.B. Mohr, 1900).

Hooke, S.H., 'The Theory and Practice of Substitution', *VT* 2 (1952), pp. 2-17.

Horst, F., *Gottes Recht* (TBü, 12; München: Chr. Kaiser, 1961).

Hunter, G.R., *Sumerian Contracts from Nippur* (Oxford Editions of Cuneiform Texts, 8; London: Oxford University Press, 1930).

Hurvitz, A., בין לשן ללשון—לתולדוה לשן המקרא בימי בית שני [The Transitional Period in Biblical Hebrew] (Jerusalem: Mosad Bialik, 1972).

Jackson, J.B., 'Reflections on Biblical Criminal Law', *JJS* 24 (1973), pp. 8-38 (reprinted in his *Essays*).

—Essays in Jewish and Comparative History (Leiden: Brill, 1975).

Jacob, B., *Das Erste Buch der Tora* (Berlin: Schocken Books, 1934).

Jacobsen, T., *The Sumerian King List* (Chicago: Chicago University Press, 1939).

Jacobson, D., *The Social Background of the Old Testament* (Cincinnati: Hebrew Union College Press, 1942).

Johns, C.H.W., *Babylonian and Assyrian Laws, Contracts and Letters* (Library of Ancient Inscriptions, 6; Edinburgh: T. & T. Clark, 1904).

Josephus, Flavius, קדמוניות היהודים [Jewish Antiquities] (trans. and ed. A. Schalit; Jerusalem: Mosad Bialik, 1955).

Kahana, A., פירוש לספר שמות [Commentary on Exodus] (Kiev: Kahana, 1913).

Kalish, M.M., *Leviticus* (London: Longmans, Green, Reader & Dyer, 1872).

Kasher, M.M., תורה שלמה [Torah Shelemah] (43 vols.; Jerusalem: Bet Torah Shelemah, 1927–1992).

Kaufmann, Y., תולדות האמונה בישראל [A History of Israelite Religion] (4 vols.; Tel-Aviv: Devir, 1952–1955).

Keil, J., and E. Delitzsch, *Chronicles* (Commentary on the Old Testament; Grand Rapids: Eerdmans, 1952–1967).

Kitchen, K.A., *Suppiluliuma and the Amarna Pharaohs* (Liverpool: Liverpool University Press, 1962).

Klíma, J., *Untersuchungen zum altbabylonischen Erbrecht* (Prag: Orientalisches Institut, 1940).

—'Untersuchungen zum elamischen Erbrecht', *ArOr* 28 (1960), pp. 5-54.

Knobel, A., *Die Bücher Numeri, Deuteronomium und Joshua* (KHAT; Leipzig: S. Hirzel, 1861).

Knohl, I., 'The Sabbath and the Festivals in the Priestly Code and in the Laws of the Holiness School' [Heb.], *Shenaton le-Ḥeqer ha-Miqra veha-Mizrah ha-Qadum* 7-8 (1983–1984), pp. 109-46.

Korošec, V., 'Keilschriftrecht', in B. Spuler (ed.), *Orientalisches Recht* (Handbuch der Orientalistik, Abt. 1, Er. 3; Leiden: Brill, 1964), pp. 49-219.

Koschaker, P., Review of *Sumerian Contracts from Nippur*, by G.R. Hunter, *OLZ* 34 (1931), pp. 341-43.

—'Fratriarchat, Hausgemeinschaft und Mutterrecht in Keilschriftrechten', *ZA* 7/41 (1933), pp. 1-89.

—'Drei Rechtsurkunden aus Arrapa', *ZA* 14/48 (1944), pp. 161-221.

Kraus, F.R., 'Neue Rechtsurkunden der altbabylonischen Zeit', *WO* 2/1 (1955), pp. 120-36.

—'Erbrechtliche Terminologie im alten Mesopotamien', in M. David (ed.), *Essays*, pp. 18-57.

—'Von altmesopotamischen Erbrecht: Ein Vortrag', in M. David (ed.), *Essays*, pp. 1-17.

Lambert, W.G., *Babylonian Wisdom Literature* (Oxford: Clarendon Press, 2nd edn, 1960).

Landsberger, B., 'Kritische Bemerkungen', in M. David (ed.), *Essays*, pp. 30-35.

Leibovitz, Y., 'The Cult of the Ass in Antiquity' [Heb.], *Yedi'ot* 18 (1954), pp. 129-34.

Levine, B.A. (ed.), ספר ויקרא [Leviticus] (Olam Hatanakh; Ramat Gan: Revivim, 1987).

—*Leviticus* (The JPS Torah Commentary; Philadelphia: Jewish Publication Society, 1989).

Liver, J., תולדות בית דוד [History of the Davidic Dynasty] (Jerusalem: Magnes, 1959).

—פרקים בתולדות הכהונה והלוייה [Chapters in the History of the Priests and the Levites] (Jerusalem: Magnes, 1968).

—'יהונתן' ['Jonathan'], *EncBib*, III, cols. 533-35.

—'מלוכה' ['Kingship'], *EncBib*, IV, cols. 1080-1112.

—'משלמיהו' ['Meshelemiah'], *EncBib*, V, cols. 567-68.

Loewenstamm, S.E., מסורת יציאת מצרים בהשתלשלותה [The Development of the Tradition of the Exodus] (Jerusalem: Magnes, 1965).

—'Law' [Heb.], in B. Mazar (ed.), האבות והשופטים [The Fathers and the Judges: History of the Israelite People], II (Tel-Aviv: Masada, 1967), pp. 272-89.

—'The Investiture of Levi' [Heb.], *Eretz Israel* 10 [Zalman Shazar Volume, ed. B.Z. Luria] (1971), pp. 169-72.

—*Comparative Studies in Biblical and Ancient Oriental Literature* (Neukirchen–Vluyn: Neukirchener Verlag, 1980).

—'מלכי אדום, אדום' ['Edom; Kings of Edom'], *EncBib*, I, cols. 102-103.

—'משפט המקרא, משפט' ['Law; Biblical Law'], *EncBib*, V, cols. 614-37.

—'שור נגח' ['The Goring Ox'], *EncBib*, cols. 604.

Lowie, R.H., *Primitive Society* (London: Routledge, 1921).

—Social Organization (London: Routledge & Kegan Paul, 1961 [1950]).

Lüddeckens, E., *Ägyptische Eheverträge* (Wiesbaden: Harrassowitz, 1960).

Luzzatto, S.D., פירוש לתורה [Commentary on the Torah] (Tel Aviv: Devir, 1966).

MacNeile, A.H., *Exodus* (WC; London: Methuen, 1931).

—'First-Born', *DOB* (ed. J. Hastings, 3rd edn, 1914, in one volume), pp. 263-64.

Mader, A.E., *Die Menschenopfer der alten Hebräer* (Freiburg im Breisgau: Herder, 1909).

Maine, H.J.S., *Ancient Law* (London: Oxford University Press, 1931).

Malamat, A., 'King Lists of the Old Babylonian Period and Biblical Geneology' [Heb.], *Yedi'ot* 31 (1967), pp. 9-28.

Malbim, M.L., אילת השחר (Bucharest, 1860) [included also in the introduction to his exegesis of the Book of Leviticus, *Ha-Torah veha-Mizvah*; see below].

—התורה והמצוה [*A Commentary on the Books of the Pentateuch*; Miqra'ot Gedolot, Lublin Edition] (Jerusalem: Pardes, 1956).

Matous, L., 'Les contracts de partage de Larsa provenant des archives d'Iddin-Ammurum', *ArOr* 17/2 (1949), pp. 142-73.

Mattha, G., 'Rights and Duties of the Eldest Son according to the Native Egyptian Laws of Succession of the Third Century B.C.', *Bulletin of the Faculty of Arts, Cairo University* 12 (1958), pp. 113-18.

Mays, A.D.H., *Deuteronomy* (NCBC; London: Marshall, Morgan & Scott, 1981).

McComisky, T.E., 'The Status of the Secondary Wife' (Dissertation; Ann Arbor, MI: University Microfilms International, 1965).

McCulloch, J.A., 'First-Born' (Introduction and Primitive), *ERE*, VI, pp. 31-34.

McKeating, H., 'The Development of the Law on Homicide in Ancient Israel', *VT* 25 (1975), pp. 46-68.

Mekilta. מכילתא דרבי ישמעאל (ed. H.S. Horowitz and A. Rabin; Jerusalem, 1960).

Mendelssohn, M., פירוש לספר ויקרא [Commentary on Exodus] (Bi'ur Series; Fuerth: Anton Schmidt, 1824).

Mendleshon, I., 'On Marriage in Alalakh', in J.L. Blau (ed.), *Essays on Jewish Life and Thought; Baron S.W. Jubilee Volume* (New York: Columbia University Press, 1959), pp. 351-57.

—'On the Preferential Status of the Eldest Son', *BASOR* 156 (1959), pp. 38-40.

Micaelis, J.D., *Commentaries on the Laws of Moses*, I (London: F.C. & J. Rivington, 1814).

Michaelis, W., 'πρωτότοκος, πρωτοτοκεῖα', *ThWNT*, VI, pp. 872-83.

Milgrom, J., *Cult and Conscience* (Leiden: Brill, 1976).

—*Numbers* (JPS Torah Commentary; Philadelphia: Jewish Publication Society, 1992).

Mittelmann, J., *Der altisraelitische Levirat: Eine rechthistorische Studie* (Leiden: Ginsberg, 1934).

Morgenstern, J., 'The Oldest Document of the Hexateuch', *HUCA* 4 (1927), pp. 1-138.

—*Rites of Birth, Marriage, Death, and Kindred Occasions among the Semites* (Chicago: Hebrew Union College, 1966).

Mowinckel, S., *He that Cometh* (Oxford: Blackwell, 1959).

Mulder, M.J., 'Die Partikel *'im*: Syntax and Meaning', *Oudtestamentische Studien* 18 (1973), pp. 15-48.

Myers, J.M., *Chronicles* (AB; Garden City, NY: Doubleday, 1965).

Neufeld, E., *Ancient Hebrew Marriage Laws* (London: Longmans, Green, 1944).

—*The Hittite Laws* (London: Luzac, 1951).

—'The Prohibition against Loans in Ancient Hebrew Laws', *HUCA* 26 (1955), pp. 355-412.

Neugebauer, O., and A. Sachs, *Mathematical Cuneiform Texts* (New Haven: American Oriental Society–American Schools of Oriental Research, 1945).

Newsom, C., *Songs of the Sabbath Sacrifice: A Critical Edition* (Atlanta, GA: Scholars Press, 1985).

Nielsen, E., 'Ox and Ass in the OT', in F. Huidberg (ed.), *Festschrift J. Pedersen* (Hauniae: E. Munksgaard, 1953), pp. 263-74.

Noth, M., *Überlieferungsgeschichte des Pentateuch* (Stuttgart: Kohlhammer, 1948).

—*Die Ursprunge des alten Israel im Lichte neuer Quellen* (Köln: Westdeutscher Verlag, 1961).

—*Exodus* (OTL; London: SCM Press, 1962).

—*Leviticus* (ATD; Göttingen: Vandenhoeck & Ruprecht, 1962 [ET: OTL; London: SCM Press, 1977]).

—*Numeri* (ATD; Göttingen: Vandenhoeck & Ruprecht, 1966).

O'Callaghan, R.T., 'Historical Parallels to Patriarchal Social Custom', *CBQ* 6 (1944), pp. 391-405.

—'A New Inheritance Contract from Nippur', *JCS* 8 (1954), pp. 137-41.

Otto, W., 'Herodes', *PW* supp., II, cols. 1-200.

Parpola, S., *Letters from Assyrian Scholars to the Kings Esarhaddon and Assurbanipal* (AOAT, 5; Neukirchen: Kerelaer, Butzon & Bereker, 1970).

Paul, S.M., *Studies in the Book of the Covenant* (VTSup, 18; Leiden: Brill, 1970).

Pedersen, J., *Israel*, III-IV (London: Oxford University Press, 1954).

Pestman, P.W., *Marriage and Matrimonial Property in Ancient Egypt* (Leiden: Brill, 1961).

—'The Law of Succession in Ancient Egypt', in M. David (ed.), *Essays*, pp. 58-77.

Phillips, A., *Deuteronomy* (NCB; Cambridge: Cambridge University Press, 1973).

—'Another Look at Murder', *JJS* 28 (1977), pp. 105-26.

—'The Laws of Slavery', *JSOT* 30 (1984), pp. 51-66.

Philo (ed. F.H. Colson and G.H. Whitaker; 10 vols.; LCL; London: 1956–1962); Marcus, R., Supplementary vols. I-II (London: W. Heinemann, 1953).

Plummer, A., *Luke* (ICC; Edinburgh: T. &T. Clark, 5th edn, 1922).

Poebel, A., *Babylonian Legal and Business Documents* (Philadelphia: University of Pennsylvania Press, 1909).

—'The Assyrian King-List from Khorsabad', *JNES* 1 (1942), pp. 247-306; 460-92; *JNES* 2 (1943), pp. 56-90.

Porter, J.R., *Leviticus* (NCB; Cambridge: Cambridge University Press, 1976).

Qimron, E., 'אל in our Early Sources' [Heb.], *Sefer ha-Yovel le-Ze'ev ben-Hayyim* (Jerusalem: Magnes, 1983), pp. 473-82.

—*The Hebrew of the Dead Sea Scrolls* (Harvard Semitic Studies, 29; Atlanta, GA: Scholars Press, 1986).

Rad, G. von, *Die Priesterschrift im Hexateuch: Literarisch untersucht und theologisch gewertet* (Stuttgart: Kohlhammer, 1934).

—*Studies in Deuteronomy* (SBT, 9; London: SCM, 1961).

—*Old Testament Theology*, II (Edinburgh: Oliver, 1965).

—*Deuteronomy* (OTL; London: SCM Press, 1966).

Rainey, A., המבנה החברתי באוגרית [The Social Structure in Ugarit] (Jerusalem: Mosad Bialik, 1967).

Ringgren, H., *Sacrifice in the Bible* (London: Lutterworth, 1962).

Robertson Smith, W., *The Religion of the Semites* (New York: Meridian, 1956).

Rofé (Roifer), A., 'The Breaking of the Heifer's Neck' [Heb.], *Tarbiz* 31 (1962), pp. 119-43.

—מבוא לספר דברים—חלק ראשון ופרקי המשך [Introduction to Deuteronomy] (Jerusalem: Academon, 1988).

Rothstein, J.W., and J. Hänel, *Kommentar zum erster Buch der Chronik* (KAT; Leipzig: A. Deichertsche Verlagsbuchhandlung, 1927).

Rudolph, W., *Esra und Nehemia* (HAT; Tubingen: J.C.B. Mohr, 1949).

Rundgren, F., 'Parallelen zu Akk. šinepum = 2/3', *JCS* 9 (1955), pp. 29-30.

Saadiah Gaon, ספר ירושות (Paris: A. Lero, 1897).

Saggs, H.W.F., Review of *Akkadisches Handwörterbuch*, by W. von Soden, *JSS* 5 (1960), pp. 410-17.

Salonen, A., *Die Möbel des alten Mesopotamien* (Helsinki: Suomalainen Tiedeakatemia, 1963).

Schalit, A., הורדוס המלך [King Herod] (Jerusalem: Mosad Bialik, 1960).

Schiffman, L.H., *The Halakhah at Qumran* (Leiden: Brill, 1975).

—'The Sacrificial System of the Temple Scroll and the Book of Jubilees', in *SBLSP* (Atlanta, GA: Society of Biblical Literature, 1985), pp. 224-25.

Schorr, M., *Urkunden des altbabylonischen Zivil und Prozessrechts* (Leipzig: J.C. Hinrichs, 1913).

Seeligmann, I.L., 'Loan, Guarantorship and Interest in Biblical Law' [Heb.], *Meḥqarim ba-Miqra uva-Mizraḥ ha-Qadmon* (FS Loewenstamm; Jerusalem: A. Rubenstein, 1978), pp. 183-205.

Seidl, E., 'Vom Erbrecht der alten Ägypter', *ZDMG* 107 (1957), pp. 270-81.

Smith, G.A., *Deuteronomy* (CB; Cambridge: Cambridge University Press, 1918).

Smith, H.P., 'Inheritance', *ERE*, VII, pp. 306-308.

Smith, S., *CAH*, III (Cambridge: Cambridge University Press, 1954).

Snaith, N.H., *Leviticus and Numbers* (Century Bible; London: Nelson, 1967).

Sonsino, R., *Motive Clause in Hebrew Bible* (Ann Arbor, MI: University Microfilms International, 1980).

Speiser, E.A., 'Of Shoes and Shekels', *BASOR* 77 (1940), pp. 15-20.

—'A Significant New Will from Nuzi', *JCS* 17 (1963), pp. 65-71.

—'Sanctification Which was not Recognized' [Heb.], *'Oz le-David* (FS D. Ben-Gurion; Jerusalem: Kiryat Sefer, 1964), pp. 503-507.

—בשחר הציוויליזציה [At the Dawn of Civilization], III, 'The Historical Tradition' (History of the Jewish People, 1; Tel Aviv: Masada, 1966), pp. 122-42.

Stade, B., *Geschichte des Volkes Israels*, I (Berlin: G. Grote, 1887).

—*Biblische Theologie des Alten Testaments*, I (Tübingen: J.C.B. Mohr, 1905).

Stamm, J.J., *Erlösen und Vergeben im Alten Testament; Eine begriffsgeschichtliche Untersuchung* (Bern: Francke, 1940).

Stegemann, H., 'The Origin of the Temple Scroll' (VTSup, 40; Leiden: Brill, 1988), pp. 235-56.

Steinsaltz, A., 'Caleb son of David in Rabbinic Midrash' [Heb.], *Sinai* 62 (1968), pp. 89-90.

Steuernagel, C., *Deuteronomuim und Josua* (HKAT; Göttingen: Vandenhoeck & Ruprecht, 1900).

Streck, M., *Assurbanipal und die letzten assyrischen Könige* (Leipzig: J.C. Hinrichs, 1916).

Strugnell, J., 'Moses-Pseudepigrapha at Qumran: 4Q375, 4Q376, and Similar Works', in L.H. Schiffman (ed.), *Archaeology and History in the Dead Sea Scrolls: Yadin's Memorial Volume* (JSPSup, 8; Sheffield: JSOT Press, 1990), pp. 221-56.

Sultansky, M., ספר חיטיב דעת (Eupatoria: Firkovitz, 1858).

Sussman, Y., 'The History of the Halakhah and the Dead Sea Scrolls—Preliminary Observations on *Miqṣat Ma'aseh ha-Torah* (4QMMT)' [Heb.], *Tarbiz* 59 (1990), pp. 11-76.

Szikszai, S., 'King', *IDB*, III, cols. 11-17.

Szlechter, E., 'Chronique, Droits Cuneiformes', *RHD* 42 (1964), pp. 139-47.

Tadmor, H., יהורם ['Jehoram'], *EncBib*, III, cols. 539-41.

Talmon, S., 'The History of the *"Am Ha-aretz"* in the Judaean Kingdom' [Heb.], *Beth Miqra* 31 (1967), pp. 27-55.

—'Fragments of Scrolls from Masada' [Heb.], *Eretz Israel* [Sefer Yigael Yadin] 20 (1989), pp. 278-86.

Thompson, R.J., *Penitence and Sacrifice in Early Israel outside the Levitical Law* (Leiden: Brill, 1963).

Thomsen, P., 'Esel', *Eberts Reallexikon der Vorgeschichte*, III, pp. 122-23.

Thureau-Dangin, F., 'Trois Contracts de Ras Shamra', *Syria* 18 (1937), pp. 245-55.

Tov, E., *Dead Sea Scrolls on Microfiche* (Leiden: Brill, 1993).

Tur-Sinai, N.H., הלשון והספר; [Vol. I] הלשון [*Language and Book*. I. *Language*] (Jerusalem: Mosad Bialik, 19572).

Tsevat, M., 'Marriage and Monarchical Legitimacy in Ugarit and Israel', *JSS* 3 (1958), pp. 237-43.

Valk, M.H. van der, 'The Law of Succession in Chinese Law', in M. David (ed.), *Essays*, pp. 93-127.

Van Selms, A., *Marriage and Family Life in Ugaritic Literature* (Pretoria Oriental Series, 1; London: Luzac, 1954).

VanderKam, J., 'Zadok and the SPR HTWRA HHTUM in Dam. Doc. v, 2-5', *RQ* 11 (1982–1984), pp. 561-70.

—*The Book of Jubilees* (Leuven: Peeters, 1989).

—'The Temple Scroll and the Book of Jubilees', in E. Brooke (ed.), *Temple Scroll Studies* (JSPSup, 7; Sheffield: JSOT Press, 1989), pp. 211-36.

Vaux, R. de, *Ancient Israel* (London: Darton, Longman & Todd, 1961).

Volz, P., Die biblischen Altertümer (Stuttgart: Calwer Verlag, 2nd edn, 1926).

Wacholder, B.Z., *The Dawn of Qumran* (Cincinnati: Hebrew Union College, 1983).

Weidner, E.F., 'Das Alter der mittelassyrischen Gesetztexte', *AfO* 12 (1937), pp. 46-54.

—'Eine Erbteilung in mittelassyrischer Zeit', *AfO* 20 (1963), pp. 121-24.

Weinfeld, M., 'Deuteronomy—The Present State of Inquiry', *JBL* 86 (1967), pp. 249-62.

—*Deuteronomy and Deuteronomic School* (Oxford: Clarendon Press, 1972).

Weiss, A.H., דור דור ודורשיו [Each Generation and its Exegetes], III (Vilna: Goldenberg, 1904).

Wellhausen, J., *Prolegomena zur Geschichte Israel* (Berlin: G. Reimer, 5th edn, 1899).

Westbrook, R., *Studies in Biblical and Cuneiform Law* (Paris: J. Gabalda, 1988).

Wolff, A., *Das jüdische Erbrecht* (Berlin: H. Itzkowski, 1888).

Yadin, Y., מגילת המקדש [The Temple Scroll] (3 vols.; Jerusalem: Israel Exploration Society, 1977 [English: 3 vols.; Jerusalem: 1983]).

Yaron, R., *Gifts in Contemplation of Death in Jewish and Roman Law* (Oxford: Clarendon Press, 1960).

—*The Laws of Eshnunna* (Jerusalem: Magnes, 1969).

—Review of *Les lois assyriennes*, by G. Cardascia, *Bib* 51 (1970), pp. 549-57.

Yeivin, S., מחקרים בתולדות ישראל וארצו [Studies in Israel and its Land] (Tel-Aviv: M. Newman, 1960).

—'דוד' ['David'], *EncBib*, II, cols. 629-45.

Zer-Kavod, M., פירוש לעזרא ונחמיה [Commentary on Ezra and Nehemiah] (Jerusalem: Reuven Mass, 1949).

Zulueta, F. de, *The Institutes of Gaius*, I (Oxford: Clarendon Press, 1946–1953).

Zimmerli, W., 'Erstgeborene und Leviten: Ein Beitrag zur exilisch-nachexilischen Theologie', in H. Goedicke (ed.), *Near Eastern Studies in Honor of W.F. Albright* (Baltimore, MD: Johns Hopkins University Press, 1971), pp. 459-69.

INDEXES

INDEX OF REFERENCES

BIBLE

PHILO

JOSEPHUS

NEAR EASTERN TEXTS

INDEX OF AUTHORS

JOURNAL FOR THE STUDY OF THE OLD TESTAMENT

Supplement Series